THE PREDICTION OF PERFORMANCE
IN CLINICAL PSYCHOLOGY

by

E. Lowell Kelly
University of Michigan

and

Donald W. Fiske
University of Chicago

GREENWOOD PRESS, PUBLISHERS
NEW YORK

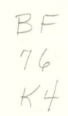

Copyright © 1951 by the University of Michigan Press

First Greenwood Reprinting 1969

SBN 8371-2383-6

PRINTED IN UNITED STATES OF AMERICA

CONTRIBUTORS TO THE PROJECT

I.   Consultants on Experimental Design and Planning

Hedda Bolgar   Donald G. Marquis
Urie Bronfenbrenner   Dorothy P. Marquis
Raymond Cattell   James G. Miller
Lee J. Cronbach   George A. Satter
Fred E. Fiedler   David Shakow
Howard F. Hunt   David Rapaport
Max L. Hutt   William Soskin
Donald MacKinnon   Ruth Tolman

II. Persons Who Served on the Professional and Technical Staff
     (*Indicates persons with major or continuing staff responsibilities)

*Ruth Bishop   Kenneth Isaacs
*Richard Boynton   Elton McNeil
 Rae Carlson   *Hobart Osburn
 Haskell Coplin   Alzire Block Segal
 Sarah Counts   Saul Siegal
 Charles A. Dailey   James A. Simkin
 Kenneth Davidson   Audrey Snyder
*Fred E. Fiedler   *Ernest C. Tupes
 Barbara Fiske   *Steven G. Vandenberg
 Arthur Hartman   *Fae Kaufman Weiss
 Ralph Heine   Benjamin White
 Gerald Hover   Kate Wolfson

III. Persons Serving as Members of One or More Assessment Staffs

Legend:

A = FAC 1946   D = Ann Arbor 1947
B = Farmingdale 1946   E = Wellesley 1948
C = Asilomar 1947   F = Ann Arbor Reassessment

Donald R. Adams	D	Leon Cohen	F
Mrs. Alvarez-Tostado	C	William Console	B
Marvin Aronson	F	Roberta Crutcher	C
Robert P. Barrell	D	Charles Dailey	F
Joseph Bennett	F	John Darley	C
Nathan Berlow	F	Andrew Dibner	F
Robert D. Boyd	D, E	John Dollard	A
Marvin Brandwein	F	Albert Eglash	F
Urie Bronfenbrenner	A, B, C, D	Martha C. Ericson Dale	D, E
John Brownfain	F	John Fearing	D
George Calden	F	Harold A. Feldman	D
Dwight Chapman, Jr.	B, E	Kenneth Fisher	B, E
Sidney Cleveland	F	Donald W. Fiske	A, B, C, D, E
Hubert S. Coffey	C, E	Frank M. Fletcher	A

Glenn Garman	F	Woodrow Morris	A
Stanley Goldstein	F	Theodore M. Newcomb	A
Louis Granich	D	Hobart Osburn	F
Eugenia Hanfman	B, E	Z. A. Piotrowski	B
Robert E. Harris	C	David Rapaport	A, B
Ross Harrison	D	Egan Ringwall	D, E
Molly Harrower	B	Julian B. Rotter	A
Karl F. Heiser	D, E	Henry A. Samuels	D, E
Josephine R. Hilgard	C	George A. Satter	C, E
William F. Holmes	A	Earl Saxe	B
James Q. Holsopple	B, D, E	Stanley Schneider	F
Harold Housman	F	Richard Sears	A
Gerald Hover	F	Stanley Segal	F
Wilfred Hulse	B, D, E	David Shapiro	F
Howard F. Hunt	D, E	Albert Shire	F
Max L. Hutt	A, B, C, D	Cora Shoecraft	A
Virginia Ives	C	Herbert Silverman	F
E. Lowell Kelly	A, B, C, D, E	James Simkin	F
George A. Kelley	A, E	Robert Sinnett	F
Bruno Klopfer	C	Audrey Snyder	F
Morris Krugman	B	William F. Soskin	A, B, C, D, E
Julian J. Lasky	D, E	Morris Stein	B
Donald W. Lauer	A	Bernard Stotsky	F
Henry Luidens	A	Milton Theaman	D, E
Jean Macfarlane	C	Burton D. Thuma	E
Barbara MacKenzie	D	Ruth S. Tolman	B, C
Donald W. MacKinnon	A, B	G. F. Train	B
Edward Malcom	F	Frances Triggs	B
Donald G. Marquis	A, B	Frieda Tryon	C
Dorothy P. Marquis	A, B, C, D	Robert C. Tryon	C
E. Mason Mathews	D, E	Edmund Walker	A
Elton McNeil	F	Edward L. Walker	E
Florence R. Miale	D, E	Gertha Williams	D
James G. Miller	A, B, C	William Winter	F
E. Ohmer Milton	D, E	Herbert J. Zucker	D, E
Clellen L. Morgan	D		

iv

PREFACE

This volume is the report of a five-year research program directed at the evaluation of techniques for the selection of professional personnel. More specifically, the project was concerned with the selection of graduate students for training in a four-year doctoral program in clinical psychology. It is believed, however, that both the methods of investigation and the resulting findings will be of interest to those concerned with the selection of other groups of professional students. And, although the primary object of the project was that of evaluating selection procedures, we believe that many of the findings will also be of interest to psychologists not immediately concerned with the problems of selection.

This project differs from previous studies of its kind in several ways:

1. Scope. Thanks to the continued financial support of the project by the Veterans Administration, it was possible to carry out a series of interrelated investigations of greater scope than any previously attempted. "Scope" here refers both to an almost total sampling of training institutions and to the evaluation of an unusually large number of different predictive devices and criterion measures.

2. Emphasis on Criteria of Professional Competence. In part because clinical psychology is still a developing profession it was possible for us to ask, "What specific professional functions does a clinical psychologist carry out and how can we measure his competence in these functions?" We know of no other professional group which has thus far made a comparable attempt to develop objective measures of professional skills. Minimal professional competence is usually assumed on the basis of such a priori criteria as completion of professional training, passing a certifying or licensing examination, or continued successful practice. In this study approximately half of our research efforts were devoted to the evaluation of the professional competences of clinical psychologists. While we are keenly aware of the fact that our battery of criterion measures has many inadequacies, we hope that our explorations in this area will at least indicate the problems involved and suggest some approaches to their solution.

3. Comparison of Clinical and Objective Approaches to Prediction. Most of the work on the selection of non-professional personnel has relied heavily on objective measures of aptitude, whereas currently used selection programs for professional personnel place more emphasis on impressions which the candidate and his record make on a human judge, who attempts to integrate these impressions into a global judgment about the candidate. In this project we incorporated both approaches in a aparallel design and have, we believe, the most definitive findings available concerning the relative merits of these two contrasting approaches to personnel selection.

Although the results relative to the selection of clinical psychologists are believed to be of some importance, they may ultimately be of less significance than other findings herein reported. This was not only a study of the selection of students for clinical psychology; it was also an evaluation of the predictive value--for one situation--of a number of the more widely used diagnostic techniques of clinical psychology, including the clinician as a diagnostic instrument. In still another sense, it surveys the training program for and the present practices of clinical psychology. We believe that certain of our findings have potential relevance to the future planning and administration of graduate training programs while other findings point to needed research on the efficacy of current practices. Finally, we believe that some of the methods which were developed within the project may prove useful to other investigators in the design of a wide range of researches in clinical psychology.

While certain of our findings cast doubt on the validity of some widely used techniques in clinical psychology, we would emphasize the fact that our findings are based on a fairly homogeneous group of subjects. Such findings do, however, suggest the desirability of other checks on these techniques in other situations. In this respect, we believe that clinical psychologists occupy a unique position: trained both as scientists and as practitioners, they are equipped with research techniques which permit them to evaluate their professional procedures and even the validity of themselves as an integral part of those procedures. Only thus can clinical psychology be certain that it is best serving society by utilizing primarily those techniques which have demonstrated validity and reasonable efficiency in contributing to a specific service function. Unfortunately, clinical psychologists in the past have often been asked to assume service responsibilities for which they had not been adequately trained and for which no techniques had been specifically validated. Confronted with this situation, they have sometimes tended to use techniques which "looked as if they ought to work." The question, "How well do they work for the job?" is one to which definitive answers, although difficult to obtain, are possible. All too often, however, we seem to be satisfied with an impression that "they work well." For example, our findings with respect to the contribution of the interview suggest that the user's confidence in a technique is an extremely fallible index of its actual validity in a specific situation.

The most widespread and cogent criticism elicited by earlier reports of this project were directed at our extensive use of ratings as a means of recording and evaluating clinical judgments. It was suggested that the lack of validity of certain clinical procedures in this situation had resulted from our requirement that all clinical judgments be translated into ratings that in this process much of the richness of the clinical approach had been lost. Because of the very real possibility that this was the case, we undertook a fairly elaborate comparison of the relative accuracy with which trainees at the time of assessment and again four years later, could be matched (a) by clinicians on the basis of qualitative descriptions, and (b) by statistical matching of profiles of ratings. Matching, the only technique available for estimating the validity of qualitative evaluations, was not practical in the major analyses because of the cost of qualified judges in the number required. We believe the results of the comparative study of qualitative vs. rating profile matching (reported in Chapter D I) will support the essential correctness of our original decision to utilize ratings as a means of recording clinical judgments. The methodology of this particular experiment would also appear to have considerable utility in a variety of researches on clinical problems.

Obviously neither time nor funds have permitted anything approaching a complete analysis of all of the data collected during the past five years. In our analyses, priority was given to questions most relevant to the primary objectives of the project. This means that a great many other potentially interesting but less immediate problems have not been attacked even though our data are pertinent to them. Even so, it has not been possible to report the results of all analyses of data undertaken. Decisions as to what analyses to include and exclude have been based on the general policy of making the report as meaningful as possible with a minimum of distracting details. We have, therefore, selected what we consider to be the most essential data for tabular presentation and discussion. Any scientific colleague who wishes to secure the more detailed results of our specific analyses for further study or to carry out additional analyses of our basic data is welcome to the use of our research files either in person or on payment of the actual costs of making the data available to him.

We have not attempted to integrate into the report the detailed findings of the ten doctoral dissertations based entirely or in part on the project's data, but abstracts of each of them are included in Appendix IV. Neither have we undertaken to discuss the implications of our findings with respect to problems of training students or to problems of clinical practice. These and related topics will be treated in separate publications.

This report has been organized in five parts: Part A, The Problem, is devoted to a general presentation of the problem and the groups studied; Part B, Predictor Measures, describes each of the large number of predictor measures and the relationships among them; Part C, Criterion Measures, presents the rationale for and the techniques used in collecting a wide array of criterion data; Part D, Validational Analyses, is devoted to an analysis of the validities of each of the predictors for appropriate criterion measures; and Part E contains a brief summary and discussion of the findings. As a guide to the reader, each chapter is introduced by a statement outlining its content. Finally, we have included in the Appendices certain materials and tables which the interested reader may wish to study in more detail.

Although we have assumed the primary responsibilities for this project from its inception to the writing of this report, it is obvious that we are deeply indebted to a great many other persons without whose continued cooperation a project of this magnitude would have been impossible. Those who have been most closely associated with the project as staff members and consultants have been named on pages iii and iv. Whenever possible we have tried also to identify individuals responsible for specific contributions to the project but in many instances this was not possible. Much of the constructive thinking occurred in group discussions involving many staff members and the origin of some of the ideas was never recorded.

We are especially indebted to a group of colleagues who read a draft copy of this report and offered many constructive criticisms, most of which were incorporated in the final copy. This group includes: Gerald Blum, Lorraine Bouthilet, John Butler, Lee Cronbach, Fred Fiedler, Robert Holt, Howard Hunt, Max Hutt, Daniel Miller, James Miller, George Satter, David Shakow, and Ruth Tolman.

In addition to collaborators listed on the preceding pages there have been hundreds of others: the directors of clinical training and clinical staff members of the cooperating universities; the chief and staff psychologists of all VA training installations; and last but not least the hundreds of VA trainees who served as subjects in this research. To each of these go our sincere thanks for their contributions to the project.

We are appreciative of the broad conception of government-financed research embodied in the contract between the Veterans Administration and the University of Michigan. In no small part, this resulted from the wisdom of General Paul R. Hawley, Dr. Daniel Blain and Dr. James G. Miller of the Veterans Administration. Dr. Miller served as "Scientific Officer" for the contract during the first two years of the project; since 1948 he has been one of our most helpful consultants. We also much appreciate the continued interest in and active support of the project by Dr. Harold M. Hildreth who succeeded Dr. Miller as Chief, Clinical Psychology Section, Neuropsychiatry Division, Department of Medicine and Surgery, Veterans Administration.

We also profited from the frequent exchange of research ideas and interim findings between this project and the companion study on procedures for the selection of psychiatrists. This study, also sponsored by the Veterans Administration, was carried on during the same period by investigators at the Menninger Foundation.

The University of Michigan and the University of Chicago, which held a subcontract for work on the development of criterion measures, have both contributed facilities in excess of the contract overhead costs received. We are especially grateful to the School of Public Health (University of Michigan) for the use of its tabulating equipment and to Mr. John Freysinger of that organization for his aassistance in making efficient use of this equipment.

Among the other unnamed contributors to the project are a number of clerical and statistical assistants whose careful computations and recomputations give us confidence in the probable correctness of most of the thousands of figures which we report. Finally, although never formally a member of the project staff, Mrs. Caroline Weichlein is primarily responsible for the preparation of the successive manuscripts of this report, including the preparation of the copy for litho-printing.

E. Lowell Kelly
Donald W. Fiske

Ann Arbor, Michigan
September, 1951

TABLE OF CONTENTS

Chapter   Page

A-I   AN OVERVIEW OF THE PROJECT   1

         Introduction   1
         Salient Characteristics of the Project   2
             Practical Applicability of Findings
             Contributions of a More General Nature
         The Operating Philosophy of the Project   2
             Group Planning and Execution
             Eclectic Approach to the Predictor Problem
             Experimental Approaches to the Criterion Problem

A-II   SEQUENTIAL PHASES OF THE RESEARCH   5

         The First Year, 1946-47   5
         The Second Year, 1947-48   7
             1947 Ann Arbor Summer Assessment Program
             Analysis of Data
             Testing Program for Applicants for Training
             Collection of Criterion Data
         The Third Year, 1948-49   9
             The Wellesley Assessment Program
             Development of Criterion Measures
         The Fourth Year, 1949-50   11
             Analyses of Criterion Data
             Development of New Criterion Measures
             Reassessment of 1947 Cases
         The Fifth Year, 1950-51   12

A III   THE SUBJECTS AND THEIR TRAINING   13

         Subjects   13
             Range of Talent
         Variations in Training   21
             Formal Instruction
             Field Experience
             Prevailing Trainee Attitudes
             Personal Therapy of Trainees
         Inter-Institutional Differences   28
         Miller Analogies Scores   28
         Content Examination   28
         Differences in Clinical Experience   30
             The Interest Pattern of Clinical Psychologists as Compared
             with Those of Psychiatrists and Other Physicians

B I   PREDICTORS   36

         The Choice of Predictor Measures   36
         University Predictors   36
             For the 1946 Group
             For the 1947 Group

Objective Measures   37
Clinical Measures--The Assessment Programs   39
    The 1947 Ann Arbor Assessment Program
    The 1948 Wellesley Abbreviated Assessment Program
    The 1949 Reassessment

B II   ANALYSES OF PREDICTION MEASURES   54

University Predictions   54
The Assessment Ratings   54
    Factor Analysis
    Interjudge Reliability of Assessment Ratings
    Correlations between Ratings at Different Stages
    Agreement between 1947 and 1948 Predictions on Reassessed Cases
    Individual Differences between Staff Members in Their Correlations
    with Final Pooled Ratings
    The Liking Variable
    Frames of Reference for Ratings
    Intercorrelations between Assessment Ratings and Scores
    on Objective Tests
    Correlations between Ratings on Scale A and Guilford-Martin Scores

C I   THE CRITERION PROBLEM   71

Definitions   71
The Background   71
An Analysis of the Criterion Problem   72
    First-Order vs. Second-Order Criteria
    The Selection of Criteria
    Specific vs. General Measures

C II   CONVENTIONAL CRITERIA OF PROFESSIONAL SUCCESS   76

The Content Examination   77
Subjective Evaluations as Criteria   79
    Ratings
Factor Analysis of the Composite Criterion Ratings   84

C III   THE MEASUREMENT OF DIAGNOSTIC COMPETENCE   88

An Approach to the Problem   88
    A Definition of Diagnostic Competence
    Requirements for a Test of Ability to Predict Behavior
    Prediction and Postdiction
    Statistical and "Cultural" Chance
Developmental Work on the Diagnostic Prediction Test   93
    Predictions without Face-to-Face Interaction
Measures of Diagnostic Competence Used as Criteria   95
    The Final Form of the Diagnostic Prediction Test
    Correlation of Scores on Diagnostic Prediction Test
    with Rated Diagnostic Competence

C IV   THE MEASUREMENT OF THERAPEUTIC COMPETENCE   99

    An Approach to the Problem   99
        Identification of Competence
        Requirements for Measures of Therapeutic Competence
        A Rationale for the Indirect Measurement of Therapeutic Competence
    Experimental Approaches to Measuring Therapeutic Competence   102
        Experimental Measures Based on the "Ideal" Therapeutic Relationship
        The Therapist's Understanding of His Patient as a Determinant of
        the Relationship
        Expressed Feelings as a Measure of the Relationship
        Measures of Therapist's Feeling Reactions toward His Patients
        Recordings of Therapy
    Measures of Therapeutic Competence Used in Subsequent Validational
    Analyses   110
        Intercorrelations between Measures of Therapeutic Competence

C V   THE MEASUREMENT OF RESEARCH COMPETENCE   114

    Some Studies of Research Competence   114
    A Rationale and a Procedure for the Evaluation of a Research Product   115
        Criteria of Research Activity and Productivity
    Rated Research Competence   120

C VI   THE EVALUATION OF OTHER PROFESSIONAL QUALIFICATIONS   121

    Competence as a Supervisor   121
    Professional Inter-Personal Relations   121
    Integrity of Personal and Professional Behavior   122

D I   THE PREDICTION PROBLEM   123

    Components in the Prediction Problem   123
    A Psychometric Analysis of the Validational Problem   127
    Agreement between Sets of Personality Ratings Made Three Years Apart   130
    A Comparison of Qualitative and Quantitative Matching   135
        Case Materials and Design Used in Matching Study
        The Objective Matching of Profiles of Ratings

D II   THE VALIDITY OF UNIVERSITY PREDICTIONS   141

D III   THE VALIDITIES OF OBJECTIVE TESTS   144

    The Problem of Identifying Significant Validities   144
    Tests of Intellectual Abilities   145
    Personality Tests   147
    Interest Tests   148

D IV   THE VALIDITIES OF ASSESSMENT RATINGS   160

    The Validity of the 1947 Final Pooled Predictions of Overall Suitability
    for Clinical Psychology   160
    The Validities of the 1947 Final Pooled Predictions on Other Scale C
    Variables   162
        Validities of Predictions on Specific Clinical Variables
        Validities of Predictions on Other Variables

The Effect of Personal Therapy upon Validities of 1947 Final Pooled Predictions   165

Assessment Predictions of Criterion Competences Based on Limited Materials   166

The Validities of Assessment Ratings as a Function of the Role of the Assessor and the Material Available to Him   167
    Sequence I
    Predictions Based on Specific Procedures
    The Validities of Assessment Ratings Made without Personal Interaction

The Prediction of Criterion Ratings from Descriptive and Evaluative Ratings   175

Clinical Pooling of Ratings as Compared with Arithmetical Pooling and with Individual Ratings

D V   THE PREDICTION OF SPECIFIC CRITERION SKILLS   179

    The Prediction of Academic Achievement   179
    The Prediction of Research Competence   181
    Measures of Research Activity   181
    The Prediction of Therapeutic Competence   181
    The Prediction of Diagnostic Competence   182
    Interrelation of Assessment Predictions and Criterion Measures of Diagnostic and Therapeutic Competence   184
    The Prediction of Personal and Professional Integrity   185
    The Prediction of General Clinical Competence   186
    Personality Variables Associated with Clinical Skills   188
    The Prediction of Dichotomous Criteria   190

E I   SUMMARY AND DISCUSSION   193

    Summary and Major Findings   193
        Method
        Major Findings
        The Need for Follow-Up Studies
        More General Outcomes
    Discussion   198
        Implications of Findings for the Selection of Students
        Validity of a Technique as Related to Confidence of the User
    Improving the Accuracy of Prediction   199
    Interrelatedness of the Problems Investigated   199
    Special Problems in Clinical Prediction   200

LIST OF APPENDICES   205

BIBLIOGRAPHY   303

INDEX OF NAMES   307

INDEX   308

LIST OF TABLES

Table   Page

A II-1   Multiple Applications for VA Training Program (Spring, 1948)   10

A III-1   Comparison of Test Scores for VA Clinical and Non-Clinical Graduate Students in Psychology   15

A III-2   Comparison between the 1947 Assessment Group and the 1948 Assessment Group on Selected Objective Tests   22

A III-3   Amount of Classroom Instruction in Major Categories Reported by Students in the VA Training Program   23

A III-4   Number of Patients in Each of Several Categories Tested, as Reported by Students in the VA Training Program   24

A III-5   Research Activities Reported by Students in the VA Training Program   25

A III-6   Trainee Evaluations of the Quality of Their Training in Diagnosis, Therapy and Research   27

A III-7   Trainee Preferences for Selected Psychological Activities   27

A III-8   Distribution of Raw Scores on Miller Analogies Test of 1947 and 1948 Assessed P-1 Applicants by Accepting Universities   29

A III-9   Distributions by Universities of Scores on Content Examination   31

A III-10 Distributions by Universities Showing Amount of Trainees' Experience with Patients   32

B I-1   Objective Test Scores Utilized as Predictors   38

B I-2   Final Overall Ratings (A42) of P-1 Applicants Assessed at Wellesley (Summer, 1948)   52

B II-1   Predictions by University Departments: Their Reliability and Their Correlation with Assessment Ratings (Summer, 1947)   55

B II-2   Correlations between Final Pooled Ratings and Ratings Made at Preceding Stages in 1947 Ann Arbor Assessment Program   64

B II-3   Correlations between Objective Test Scores and Final Rating on Overall Suitability (A42)   70

C II-1   Intercorrelations of Subscores on Content Examination   78

C II-2   Estimated Intra-Source Reliabilities of 1951 Criterion Ratings   83

C II-3   Intercorrelations of Composite Criterion Ratings   85

C II-4   Rotated Factor Loadings of Criterion Ratings   86

C III-1   Reliability Coefficients for the Diagnostic Prediction Test   96

C IV-1   Intercorrelations between Measures of Therapeutic Competence   112

C V-1   Obtained Scale Values for Various Types of Research Contributions   117

C V-2   Measures of Research Activity   119

D I-1a   Correlations of Colleague Ratings on Scale A with Ratings from Various Assessment Sources, and Reliabilities of 1947 Assessment Ratings   132

D I-1b   Correlations of 1950 Colleague Ratings on Scale B with Two Assessment Ratings on the Same Variable   133

D I-2   Comparison of Correlations between 1947 Final Pooled Assessment Ratings and 1950 Colleague Ratings for Trainees with or without Intervening Personal Therapy   136

D II-1   Correlations between Predictions by University Staff Members (1947) and Criterion Ratings (1950)   142

D III-1   Correlations between Scores on Tests of Intellectual Ability and Criterion Measures   146

D III-2   Correlations between Scores on Guilford-Martin Battery and Criterion Measures   147

xiii

D III-3   Correlations between Scores on the Minnesota Multiphasic Inventory and Criterion Measures   149

D III-4   Correlations between Criterion Measures and Groups I, II, and V Scores of the Strong Vocational Interest Blanks, 1947 Group   150

D III-5   Correlations between Criterion Measures and Groups VIII, IX, X and IV Scores of the Strong Vocational Interest Blank, 1947 Group   152

D III-6   Correlations between Criterion Measures and Miscellaneous Scores of the Strong Vocational Interest Blank, 1947 Group   153

D III-7   Correlations between Criterion Measures and Scores on the Kuder Preference Record, 1947 Group   155

D III-8   Correlations between Criterion Measures and Scores on the Allport-Vernon Study of Values, 1947 Group   156

D III-9   Summary Showing the Three Objective Test Scores Yielding the Highest Correlations with 13 Criterion Measures, 1947 Group   158

D III-10   Comparable Validity Coefficients for 1947 and 1948 Groups for Best Test Predictors of 13 Criterion Measures   159

D IV-1   Correlations between 1947 Assessment Final Pooled Predictions and Criterion Measures   161

D IV-2   Comparison of Validity Coefficients for 1947 Trainees with or without Intervening Personal Therapy   166

D IV-3a   Validities of Assessment Ratings Based on Sequential Appraisals of Cumulative Data   168

D IV-3b   Validities of Assessment Ratings Based on Sequential Appraisals of Cumulative Data and Validities of Ratings Based on Specific Procedures   169

D IV-4   Comparison of the Validities of Predictions Based on Four Projective Tests   172

D IV-5   Comparison of Correlations between Criterion Measures and Corresponding Assessment Ratings (1947, 1948, and 1949)   174

D IV-6   Final Pooled Scale A and B Ratings vs. Selected 1950 Criterion Ratings   176

D V-1   Correlation of Assessment Prediction and Criterion Measures of Therapeutic Competence   182

D V-2   Intercorrelations of Assessment Predictions and Criterion Measures of Diagnosis and Therapy   185

D V-3   Best Predictors of Criterion Ratings of General Clinical Competence   187

D V-4   Correlations of 1950 Colleague Ratings on Scale A and B Variables with Selected 1950 Criterion Ratings   189

D V-5   Bi-Serial Correlations for Final Pooled Assessment Predictions and Selected Test Scores against Dichotomous Criterion Groups   191

LIST OF FIGURES

Figure   Page

A III-1   Graphs Showing Distribution of Strong Interest Scores of 63 Young
           Physicians, 118 Residents in Psychiatry and 129 VA Clinical Psychol-
           ogy Trainees When Scored on (a) Production Manager Key and (b)
           Certified Public Accountant Key   34
B II-1   Mean Ratings Assigned by Raters in Different Roles   68
C II-1   Graphical Representation of Factor Loadings of Criterion Ratings   87
C IV-1   Diagram Illustrating Various Measures of Assumed Similarity
           Derived from Forced Choice Descriptive Tests (2 alternatives)   108
D I-1   Components in the Validation of Assessment Procedures   124
D I-2   Illustration of Design for Matching Study Showing Nine of the 380 Triads   137
E I-1   Diagram Illustrating Relationships between Variables Involved in Mul-
           tiple Prediction   201

CHAPTER A-I

AN OVERVIEW OF THE PROJECT

As indicated by the title, this chapter is designed to give the reader a broad perspective of this five-year research project: its origins; its purposes, and its general methodology.

Introduction

During the Spring of 1946, the Veterans Administration completed its plans for training large
numbers of clinical psychologists in the graduate departments of psychology of many universities. Anticipating the probability that the number of applicants each year would exceed the number of training positions available, the Veterans Administration decided also to institute a program of research designed to make possible a more effective selection of trainees than might
otherwise occur. Because individual university departments were to retain local autonomy with
respect to both the training curriculum and the selection of students, it seemed appropriate that
this research program should be a cooperative endeavor among training institutions rather than
a Central Office project. Early in the summer of 1946, the University of Michigan was approached as to its willingness to accept the responsibility for the direction and coordination of such a
research program. After considerable discussion, a research contract was arranged which provided:

1. That the project be carried out on a purely experimental basis, pointed toward the development of techniques for possible future use in the selection of candidates, but with no
   selection of students studied on the basis of techniques being evaluated.

2. That the project be established on a sufficiently broad and long term basis to permit:

   a. The experimental study of the validity of all potentially predictive devices including
      not only conventionally used objective tests but also clinical judgments based on a wide
      variety of materials such as projective test protocols, autobiographical materials,
      interviews, psychodrama, and other situation tests.

   b. The development of criterion techniques and the accrual of meaningful measures, not
      only of success in completing training but also of the actual performance of profession-
      al duties.

3. That the project be regarded as a cooperative enterprise among the training institutions
   which, in return for assistance in the collection of data, would be provided with the resulting research findings for such use as each institution wished to make of them in the selection of future students.

4. That all data collected on individual students in the experimental program be classified as
   confidential, to be retained in the research files at the University of Michigan and not to
   be released to the Veterans Administration, to the individual student, or to his university
   without his written consent.

The above conditions were agreed upon and a research contract between the Veterans
Administration Central Office and the University of Michigan was signed in September, 1946.

1

The actual research program was begun the same month and was carried on continuously for five years in accordance with the original schedule.

Salient Characteristics of the Project

Practical Applicability of Findings

The most immediate practical objective was, of course, the identification of measures which would predict success in subsequent training and performance in clinical psychology. The VA wanted to make available to the cooperating universities in the VA training program in clinical psychology information as to the predictive value of various selection techniques. Presumably the findings applicable to the selection of VA trainees would, for the most part, also hold for the selection of non-VA clinical graduate students. Beyond that point the specific findings on the validity of specific techniques could not be generalized. However, certain tentative generalizations on these data might be made with regard to the selection of non-clinical graduate students in psychology. Furthermore, this selection project was a case study in professional selection. Most of the problems involved in the selection of candidates for the profession of clinical psychology would also be met in selection for any professional training or professional activity.

Contributions of a More General Nature

In spite of the practical aspects of the research, the project staff has never felt that the sole contribution (or perhaps even the major contribution) of the project to psychology would be the findings pertaining to selection. For this reason we attempted to maintain a broad perspective throughout the planning and administration of the research project. For example, we used a wide variety of diverse psychological tests with sizeable if not fully heterogeneous samples. For many of these psychological techniques we can provide data relevant to their validity for selection purposes; data which may hold implications for the validity of these procedures when they are used for other purposes. Furthermore, a number of new tests and measuring instruments were developed as part of the project's operations. It is hoped that these methods, the principles involved in their construction and development, and data on their relationship with other variables will prove useful to future investigators.

In addition to these more concrete contributions to psychological measurement, we feel that this research has made some contribution to the theory and practice of psychological inference. How does a clinician make correct inferences about another person? What factors contribute to his relative success or failure in attempting to make accurate psychological judgments? While our investigations did not provide definitive answers to these questions, many of our findings appear to have considerable relevance to such questions

The Operating Philosophy of the Project

Group Planning and Execution

This was a cooperative group project in many different ways. It involved the evaluation of applicants and students of about 40 departments of psychology, each of which has cooperated repeatedly in supplying essential data. Approximately 75 psychologists and several psychiatrists drawn from a dozen different universities and from other professional activities have served on the staff of the project sometime during the five-year period. The staff clinical psychologists of every VA training installation have been called upon repeatedly to supply crucial data. The successful completion of the project depended on the wholehearted cooperation of all of these groups.

Perhaps equally important is the fact that the detailed planning and actual conduct of the research was essentially a group endeavor. Each major phase of the project was discussed at
length with local psychology staff members and such visitors as could be prevailed upon to help.
This meant that many points of view and even divergent philosophies were considered in formulating the eventual experimental design.

Eclectic Approach to the Predictor Problem

From the outset, the planning group agreed on the desirability of trying out every promising
technique and procedure: objective, projective, subjective, clinical and quantitative. It was
further agreed that, within the limits of feasibility, the research design should provide for determining the independent validity of each technique or group of techniques. Where this was not
feasible, because of research costs, it was agreed that each technique would be evaluated in terms
of its incremental contribution to a battery of procedures arranged in order of their availability
and cost to an employing institution. Thus, since it is unlikely that applicants will be interviewed
by a person who has not reviewed the applicant's credential file, the design did not provide for
determining the value of the interview alone, but rather its value in improving the prediction made
by the same staff member on the basis of the credential file alone.

Another characteristic of the project was the parallel use of clinical and quantitative methods.
Most previous work on personnel selection has relied primarily on objective tests and empirically derived scoring or weighting procedures. To a large extent, however, this work has dealt
with the selection of skilled or semi-skilled employees. Because of the unique problems involved in the selection of professional personnel and because of the marked confidence in less
objective clinical methods by those who have used them in the evaluation of personality (Cf. OSS
Assessment Staff, 1948), it was decided that both approaches would be used in this study.

Although the writers' previous experiences in selection research led them to anticipate more
economical and probably more accurate prediction from objective procedures, a very high proportion of the research effort expended on the collection of predictive data was devoted to qualitative materials. However, in order that conclusions arrived at from the analysis of qualitative
materials could be subjected to statistical analyses, staff members were asked to express their
interpretations of the qualitative data in quantitative form, i.e., in ratings. Correlation and
many other rigorous techniques are available for analyzing numerical scores, whereas few procedures are available for dealing with qualitative descriptions. More important is a consideration of the project's objectives: our immediate goal was the prediction of each trainee's relative
standing on several variables corresponding to his future performance as a clinician. If one
grants the desirability of predicting future performance in each of a series of professional activities, then it seems reasonable to have definitive predictions made on the same variables.

Explicitly or implicitly, many clinical psychologists hold that the diagnostician's primary job
is the formulation of an idiographic description of the individual patient, which is in turn used as
a basis for decisions about the management of the case. Although it is freely admitted that such
ideographic descriptions may well serve as a means toward making better predictions about the
patient, it would seem that all too often the means becomes confused with the ends and the diagnostician is satisfied with the case description. In our assessment programs, individual staff
members were urged to use such personality theory or theories as they found most acceptable
and were permitted to formulate the dynamics of their cases in any manner they wished. However, we could think of no way in which the relative correctness of different personality formulations for the same subject could be evaluated directly. We decided therefore to require the staff
members to take the next step and make definite predictions about the future performance of each
trainee. As will be found in our later treatment of the measurement of diagnostic competence, we

believe that the same logic applies to the diagnosis of clinical patients.

Experimental Approaches to the Criterion Problem

Because of the relative youth and continuing development of the profession of clinical psychology, we were confronted with the awkward fact that there were no generally accepted criteria of success in the profession. In most research on selection, the sponsor designates the criterion or criteria against which predictors are to be validated. In this project, we were in the position of having to define success in clinical psychology and confronted with the necessity of developing new criterion measures. Just as we tried out a diverse assortment of possible predictive procedures, we have used a variety of criterion measures of clinical competence. Because no generally acceptable criterion of competence in clinical psychology was available, we developed measures representing several possible types of criteria. We are admittedly not satisfied with our work on the criterion problem. It is an exceedingly difficult problem on which little previous research has been done. For this very reason, however, we feel that our developmental work in this area is one of the project's most important contributions.

CHAPTER A-II

SEQUENTIAL PHASES OF THE RESEARCH

Because these investigations extended over a period of five years and involved the study of several different groups of subjects with somewhat different procedures, this chapter attempts to round out the overall perspective by providing a description of the sequential phases of the project. Although these details of sequence are not necessary to an understanding of the chapters which follow, it is believed that they may help the reader by identifying the sources of data to be reported, by providing a frame of reference for the later analysis of the data, and by indicating the reasons for the several aspects of the research plan.

The first year of the project was devoted largely to refinements of the original experimental design growing out of experiences with three "pilot" assessment programs. In addition, however, data were collected which made possible: (a) a comparison of clinical and non-clinical graduate students in psychology, and (b) an evaluation of the validity of the selection procedures currently used by departments of psychology.

During the second year, our major efforts were expended in an assessment program carried out during the summer of 1947. This involved the intensive study of 137 trainees from 30 universities. The remainder of the year was devoted to a preliminary analysis of the resulting data, to the collection of preliminary criterion measures, and to obtaining a series of measures on applicants to the VA program for the following year.

The third year involved a major experiment with an "abbreviated" assessment program at Wellesley, the collection of a second set of criterion measures, and considerable exploratory work on the development of criterion measures.

The fourth year of the project was devoted largely to an intensive attack on the development and refinement of criterion measures, but also included a "reassessment" of the 1947 subjects on the basis of materials collected in 1947, but without face-to-face contact.

Major activities of the fifth year were: the administration of an extensive battery of criterion measures to all subjects previously studied, a full scale analysis of all data, and the preparation of this technical report.

The First Year, 1946-47

During 1946-47, there were 228 VA Clinical Psychology trainees in 22 different universities. Our plans called for:

a. Obtaining predictions by staff members from each department concerning the probable future success in training of each of its entering trainees. It seemed desirable to ascertain the validity of such estimates as a base line against which the relative merits of other predictive techniques could be compared.

b. Evaluating as many of these trainees as possible in three "pilot" assessment programs.

5

The term "assessment" throughout this report is used to refer to the evaluation of the personality and the prediction of the future professional success of subjects studied over an extended period, with a variety of techniques, by a team of staff members who eventually pool their individual clinical judgments to arrive at a final evaluation and prediction of future performance. These programs were planned not only to collect predictive materials on the trainees but also to enable us to try out a wide variety of procedures and to perfect the details of a large scale assessment program to be carried out in the summer of 1947.

c. Administering a comprehensive objective test battery to all VA trainees and to a comparison group of non-clinical graduate students in psychology. This was to be done in order to discover what differences, if any, existed between clinical and non-clinical graduate students in psychology.

d. Initiating and maintaining a continuing program for the collection of several varieties of criterion data:

1. Withdrawals and failures in the program and reasons for each.
2. Ratings by academic departments on training progress.
3. Ratings by training supervisors on clinical competence.

e. Administering the Strong Vocational Interest Blank to all full-time VA Clinical Psychologists in order to develop a new ad hoc scoring key which should be more appropriate for use in the project than any other available keys.

The above plans were carried through. Previous planning made it possible to carry out the first pilot assessment program at the University of Michigan Fresh Air Camp (FAC) within two weeks after the research contract was signed. In the course of a seven-day program, 20 staff members (both psychologists and psychiatrists) evaluated 23 University of Michigan students, of whom 18 were VA trainees. This program was a hurried and exhausting one for both staff and students. We tried to utilize too many techniques; the schedule was long and stressful. But we did learn a great deal about how to conduct (and how not to conduct) the next assessment program, which was carried out at Farmingdale, Long Island, during the Christmas Holidays. Again a staff of some 20 psychologists and psychiatrists (approximately one half of whom had served in the FAC program) carried out a modified one-week assessment program. The subjects were 24 VA trainees from four universities in the New York area. Although this program ran much more smoothly than the FAC one, it was obvious that at least one more exploratory or pilot program was desirable before freezing the design for use in the extensive assessment program planned for the summer of 1947.

Accordingly the staff spent many hours reviewing the data and experience growing out of the two previous programs and planned a detailed revised schedule for a third pilot assessment to be held on the West Coast immediately after the close of the second semester. This program was carried out at Asilomar, California, between June 12 and 18, 1947. Here a comparable staff (including persons with both FAC and Farmingdale experience) assessed 24 VA trainees from three West Coast universities. Thanks to lessons learned at FAC and Farmingdale and to careful planning, the staff agreed that with relatively few changes in the design, we were ready to undertake the extensive program planned for the summer of 1947. The major change was increasing the program from seven to nine days for each class of 24 students.

In all, 68 trainees at all training levels from eight universities had been assessed during 1946-47. Because all three assessment programs in the first year were experimental in nature, it does not seem advisable to include here the details of materials, tests, procedures, and rating scales employed in each. Those which were judged to be useful and feasible were retained in the design for the 1947 program and will be described later.

The Second Year, 1947-48

1947 Ann Arbor Summer Assessment Program

As has been indicated above, much of the work of the first year was pointed toward the development of a promising assessment program which would permit the uniform evaluation of all P-1 trainees accepted for the program for the Fall of 1947. By this time, 35 different universities were participating in the VA training program. Each was asked to urge its accepted trainees to come to Ann Arbor for a nine-day assessment program before entering the program the following fall. It was agreed that the research project would pay the trainees' travel expenses and provide board and room during the assessment period. Under these conditions, the project assessed 137 beginning (P-1) trainees from 30 different universities. Each came to Ann Arbor between June 21 and August 27. (We had planned six successive classes of 24 each. Actually 140 different people were assessed; this included three non-VA trainees who were introduced to maintain balanced student teams.)

This large-scale program in the summer of 1947 provided for the collection of the most important predictive data of the entire project. A description of the procedures and the major analyses of these data are presented in later sections of this report.

Analysis of Data

During the winter of 1947-48, most of our efforts were devoted to analyses of the data collected during the previous summer. This mass of data included 65 objective test scores and 25 sets of ratings on each of 42 traits for each of the subjects assessed--in addition to non-quantified material such as an autobiography, character sketches, and protocols of the several projective tests.

Testing Program for Applicants for Training

In the course of the analysis of the Summer 1947 data, we became increasingly concerned with the desirability of carrying through a subsequent assessment program to determine how well the more promising techniques would function in an actual selection situation. In all of our previous programs, the students had already been accepted for training and had submitted to assessment with the understanding that the results of assessment would in no way influence their status as students or employees of the VA. In other words, they were simply participating in a research project. Even under these conditions, our observations and data indicated that many students had attempted to portray themselves in the most favorable light. A few, however, had been overly frank and appeared to make little effort to cover their personal liabilities.

Since any practical applications of our findings would involve assessment under conditions which would incline the applicant to put his best foot forward, it was felt necessary to assess a new group of P-1 applicants before the universities had acted on applications for admission. Ideally, we should have preferred to have processed all applicants through the same program as had been used in the Summer of 1947.

For several reasons, this was impossible. Most cooperating departments wanted to act on applications and notify applicants before the end of the second semester, yet it did not seem appropriate to ask applicants to miss a week of the last semester of their senior year in college. Moreover, although the number of probable applicants was unknown, it was obvious that it would total several times the number assessed during the previous summer. Most important, our available research funds would not begin to cover the cost of such a large-scale assessment. Furthermore, it did not appear justifiable to expend research funds for the assessment of applicants who would not be accepted and on whom no subsequent criterion data would become available. Finally, even if sufficient funds had been available, we could not have assembled the staff necessary to carry out the program during the academic year.

Under these circumstances, two alternatives were considered:

a. Postponing this crucial test of assessment in an actual selection situation until the spring vacation week in 1949.

b. Undertaking a greatly modified program of assessment, one which would not involve bringing applicants and staff together.

This decision was a most difficult one. Postponement of the assessment would mean delaying our eventual findings by at least one more year. On the other hand, the idea of assessing applicants without even an interview was most disconcerting to staff members who felt that such face-to-face contacts with the subject constituted the most important aspect of the entire assessment program.

The issue was eventually decided in favor of the immediate, modified program. Two factors were primarily responsible for this decision.

a. Preliminary analyses of the 1947 data (to be reported in Chapter B-II) suggested that clinical judgments based on materials available without a face-to-face contact correlated reasonably well with final judgments based on all assessment procedures; furthermore, it appeared that staff members tended to make better clinical use of case materials if they knew they would never see the subject than if they expected to interview him and see him in situations later.

b. The cost of the more elaborate assessment (1947 style) had been so great as to preclude the probability of its practical application by most cooperating universities. (The actual cost per person assessed in 1947 had been approximately $275 per candidate. Assessment programs utilizing selected validated procedures would, of course, cost less.) It seemed desirable therefore to determine the maximum validity that could be expected of an assessment program based only on such materials as could be obtained directly from the student and from a test battery administered in geographically distributed testing centers.

Accordingly, plans were made for the administration of a battery of tests to applicants and securing other materials from all first year applicants seeking admission to the training program in the Spring of 1948. Each university department was asked to cooperate by advising applicants that their applications would not be acted upon until after these procedures had been completed at one of the testing centers and a report had been received from this project. Actually only the Miller Analogies Test score and the Strong Vocational Interest Profile were reported to the university departments for such use as they wished to make of them in the actual selection of students. All other test data and materials from the applicants were retained by the project for research use only.

In all, 30 universities agreed to cooperate in this procedure. Several were just beginning their VA training programs and did not have their application procedures fully organized. Two universities had already selected their trainees at the time the request was made. One university department refused to cooperate in this phase of the project on the grounds that it was unfair to applicants to imply that all of the procedures were to be used in their selection when actually some of the tests were being given for research purposes only.

During the spring of 1948, 545 applicants to 30 different universities were tested in 32 testing centers. The cost of test administration was borne by the project but students went to the testing centers at their own expense. For the first time, we had some indication of the amount of overlap in the applications made to the cooperating universities. According to our records, 263 applicants applied to only one institution, the other 282 applied to two or more. The actual distribution of the multiple applications is shown in Table A II-1.

Actually 117 of the total of 545 applicants were eventually admitted as P-1 (first year) trainees at one of the training institutions. Thirteen more were admitted as P-2 (second year) trainees and four as P-3 (third year) trainees.

The materials and test data collected in the Spring 1948 testing program served as the basis for the final assessment program carried out at Wellesley College in August, 1948.

Collection of Criterion Data

Throughout 1947-48, the project continued to collect data on separations from the program, as well as performance ratings on trainees from university departments.

In addition, we began a series of intensive discussions concerning the development of suitable criterion measures of professional competence in clinical psychology. Ideally, of course, these measures should have been developed during the early part of our program and the collection of predictive data undertaken only after adequate criterion measures were available. However, because the relatively long training program necessitated a period of several years between the collection of prediction data and the availability of minimal criteria data, we had decided to reverse this procedure.

The Third Year, 1948-49

The Wellesley Assessment Program

During the summer of 1948, our staff assembled and prepared the test data collected in the spring for use by an assessment staff in August, 1948. Because of the proximity to Boston and the following meetings of the American Psychological Association, it was decided to hold this program on the Wellesley College campus. Here, between August 18 and September 3, a staff of 24 persons, all with experience in one or more of the previous assessment programs, carried on an assessment without actually seeing the candidate whom they were assessing. Without interviews or situation tests, it was possible to complete the evaluation of 143 candidates within a two week period. Thus the investment of staff time was roughly one fourth to one fifth that of the program during the summer of 1947.

Development of Criterion Measures

In addition to the continuing analyses of data and the routine collection of training progress data, a major activity of the project for the remainder of 1948-49 was the development and field-testing of criterion measures of clinical competence. A working agreement was reached with the American Board of Examiners in Professional Psychology to cooperate in arriving at necessary decisions concerning the content and methods to be sampled by these measures of clinical competence. The development of these procedures was the responsibility of a staff unit located at the University of Chicago. With the assistance of the American Board of Examiners and a series of

TABLE A II-1

MULTIPLE APPLICATIONS FOR VA TRAINING PROGRAM
(Spring, 1948)

Number of Institutions applied to:	Frequency	Number of Trainees Accepted**		% of Applicants Accepted
		P-1	P-2 or P-3	
1	263	38	11	19
2	80	21		26
3	55	15	1	29
4	33	10		30
5	36	9	2	31
6	19	6	1	37
7	16	4	1	31
8	12	4		(33)*
9	9	3	1	(44)*
10	6	2		(33)*
11	2			
12	5	1		(20)*
13	2	1		(50)*
14	2	2		(100)*
15	1			
16				
17				
18	1			
19				
20				
21	1	1		(100)*
22	1			
23				
24	1			
Total	545	117	17	24.6

Total number of different applications: 1595
Total number of different institutions: 30

*These values are based on small frequencies.

**P-1, P-2, and P-3 refer to the first, second and third year levels respectively in the training program.

consultants appointed by them* this unit developed preliminary forms of content examinations in clinical psychology and in several areas of general psychology. Preliminary drafts of an examination in experimental methods and statistics were administered to all available P-2 and P-3 trainees throughout the country in the spring of 1949.

During 1948-49 considerable effort was devoted to a general analysis of the criterion problem and to the formulation of plans for the development of other measures of clinical competence. Many alternatives were suggested, explored carefully, and then discarded for theoretical reasons or for reasons of impracticability (Cf. Appendix II G).

In the late spring of 1949, criterion ratings were collected from the university and the installation supervisors of the VA trainees and, for the first time, from the trainees themselves. The criterion ratings collected in previous years had indicated some of the problems involved. The primary difficulty resided in the fact that the many raters were located in 30 universities and 40 installations, each with its local frame of reference. In an attempt to provide a common frame of reference we asked that trainees be ranked with respect to several clinical skills. A rating was requested on "Overall Clinical Competence." We also attempted to obtain from each rater a rough indication of his impression concerning the calibre of the students rated by him as compared to the total national population of VA trainees.

The Fourth Year, 1949-50

Analyses of Criterion Data

Item analyses of the two content examinations were made using total score on each section as the criterion. The two scores from the content examination were also intercorrelated with available criterion ratings. The statistical analyses of the ratings included estimations of their reliabilities, a study of their intercorrelations, and factor analyses of the ratings from each of the three sources. We concluded that the criterion rating scales previously used were only barely satisfactory for our purposes. While the interjudge reliability was reasonably high, the judges did not differentiate sufficiently among the separate scales. It was obvious that an improved rating scale was needed.

Development of New Criterion Measures

Throughout the year the University of Chicago staff unit explored the possibility of developing work sample measures of clinical competence. Of the various techniques developed and field-tested, most were found inadequate or unsatisfactory for nation-wide administration. Detailed accounts of these preliminary investigations are given in later sections of this report.

Reassessment of 1947 Assessment Cases

During the spring of 1949, plans were made for the reassessment of the trainees originally evaluated in 1947. We wished to compare the accuracy of the predictions made by advanced trainees with the accuracy of those made by the more experienced clinicians who had served as staff members in previous assessment programs. We also wanted to determine how the validity of pooled judgments on paper-and-pencil materials (such as those used in the 1948 Wellesley program) would compare with the validities of judgments based on all kinds of data (as in the 1947

---

*This research project and the American Board of Examiners are deeply indebted to the following consultants who devoted their time and energy to the very demanding and tedious task of writing, editing, and revising the multiple choice items: Roger Bellows, Frank Fletcher, Thomas Richards, Dewey Stuit, and William Hunt.

program). Finally, the accuracy with which an assessor-trainee predicted later criterion measures promised to provide a highly satisfactory criterion measure of that trainee's diagnostic competence.

The 1949 reassessment program was divided into two parts. In the first part, 24 VA trainees in their first, second, or third year of the training program at the University of Michigan served as the assessment staff. They reassessed 100 cases from the 1947 assessment program. (All identifying data were removed from the assessment materials and no trainees whom the assessors might know personally were included in the group.) Ratings were based on the credential file, objective test scores, projective tests, and the autobiography and biographical inventory--all materials collected in the 1947 program.

The second part of this 1949 reassessment program was a more intensive study of the ratings based on projective protocols. Four trainees experienced in the Rorschach, Sentence-Completion, TAT, and Bender-Gestalt tests, examined all of the projective protocols of 20 1947 cases. Each rater made ratings on the basis of each protocol separately; e.g., he did not know which Rorschach belonged with which TAT protocol. From these ratings it was possible to determine the intra-judge agreement of ratings based on the same projective techniques and, finally, a second estimate of the relative validity of each type of rating against criterion measures.

The Fifth Year, 1950-51

The summer of 1950 was largely devoted to making final field tests of various work sample criterion measures. A much improved type of criterion rating scale was conceived and developed and plans were made for the collection of final criterion data. Between November and December an extensive bettery of criterion measures was administered to all available subjects studied by the project. Objective content examinations were administered at each installation. Ratings were again made by installation supervisors, by university supervisors, and by colleagues. With the cooperation of the installation staff members, work sample materials were also collected. These included predictions of checklist responses of patients referred for diagnosis, similar predictions for patients treated in therapy, progress notes on ten therapy interviews, and actual recordings of therapy interviews conducted by VA trainees. In addition, each trainee reported, in a Training Experience Inventory, the kind and quality of his graduate training and the extent of his experiences in diagnosis, therapy, and research (Cf. Appendix II D).

It was, of course, impossible to collect all types of criterion measures on all VA trainees: some trainees were not doing any therapy (or had never done any therapy), some trainees were devoting almost full time to their dissertations and were not even doing diagnostic work at the time. Fortunately it was possible to collect such materials from a sufficiently large number of trainees to utilize these data in subsequent validational studies. No attempt was made to collect work sample data on trainees who had left the program for any reason. However, university supervisors were asked to rate such people whenever they had sufficient basis to do so.

The rest of the final year was devoted to the task of processing these criterion measures and to a definitive analysis of all data. First the criterion measures themselves were analyzed to determine their reliability and their intercorrelations with each other. Then representative measures were used in the validational analyses. Simultaneously with the analysis of the criterion data, work was begun on the preparation of this final technical report.

CHAPTER A III

THE SUBJECTS AND THEIR TRAINING

The subjects studied in this selection research were young men from all parts of the country who had been accepted by the participating universities as VA trainees in Clinical Psychology. Under such conditions it was natural to suspect a wide variety of background factors as well as considerable differences in ability and personality traits. At the inception of this project there was little systematic information regarding the characteristics of persons attracted to clinical psychology, although in some quarters there was considerable speculation about the matter. In view of this situation a number of questions present themselves which are relevant to the interpretation of the validational data as well as to general conceptions about the field of clinical psychology. In the first part of this chapter a comparison is made between VA clinical and non-clinical graduate students in psychology and between graduate students in psychology and the available norms. This comparison will be made with respect to possible group differences and to the very important question of range of talent among the subjects studied by this project.

The second part of this chapter is concerned with one of the most vexing problems encountered by this project: the lack of uniformity among training universities and VA installations. This project has been conducted on a nation-wide basis. The 700 subjects were students in some 40 universities and had their field training in at least 50 different VA installations. These conditions lead to two sources of variability in the criterion measures which may have a potentially depressing effect on the obtained validity coefficients of all predictors. The first source of variability is the difference in training and orientation to which the trainees have been exposed during the interim period between the collection of predictive data and the final criterion evaluations. The second source of variability, closely related to the first, is the variability among training institutions with respect to the calibre of trainees at each institution and hence differences in frame of reference from one institution to another. When ratings are basic criterion data as is the case for this project, a common frame of reference among the persons providing the criterion ratings is, of course, highly desirable. Data relevant to these problems are presented in the second part of the chapter under "Variations in Training."

This chapter also includes a brief section summarizing the results of a study of the similarities and differences of the interest patterns of young physicians, psychiatrists, and clinical psychologists. The interest patterns of psychiatrists and clinical psychologists are remarkably similar, and both differ markedly from those of young physicians.

Subjects

Group Differences

In order to obtain normative and at least some potentially predictive data on all students in the VA program during its first year, cooperating departments were asked to administer a battery of objective tests to all VA trainees, during the academic year 1946-47. At that time there was considerable difference of opinion as to whether graduate students being attracted to the VA program differed from other graduate students in psychology. In order to obtain objective evidence on this point, cooperating departments were asked to administer the same battery of tests to a comparison group composed of an equal number of graduate but non-clinical students, matched in terms of previous amount of graduate work completed, who the department believed would continue to the Ph. D. degree. Approximately 160 graduate students in each category were tested.

The test battery used included:

1. The Miller Analogies Test (Form G)
2. The Primary Mental Abilities Tests
3. The Allport-Vernon Study of Values
4. The Minnesota Multiphasic Personality Inventory
5. The Guilford-Martin Battery of Personality Inventories
6. The Strong Vocational Interest Blank
7. The Kuder Preference Record

Distribution of scores on these tests for the clinical and non-clinical group are shown in Table A III-1.

The first and most striking impression on looking at these results is the high degree of similarity in the distribution of scores for both groups. With respect to intellectual ability, the distributions of Miller Analogies scores are almost identical; on only two of the six PMA scores is the difference between means statistically significant and even here, the absolute difference is small--favoring the clinical group on Number Factor scores and the non-clinical group on the Space Factor scores.

On the non-intellectual tests there are more statistically significant differences, but even here one is more impressed with the overlap of the distributions than with the differences. Thus, only one of the six scores on the A-V Study of Values shows a significant difference: the clinical group tends to score slightly higher on the scale of Social Values.

The two personality inventories yielded 23 different scores. Twelve of these yield critical ratios significant at the 5% level, but again none of the differences are large. Most of the statistically significant differences show a slight tendency for VA clinical trainees to score toward the "better adjusted" end of the continuum (the Pd scale excepted!) but before rushing to any conclusions, an important factor must be considered. Clinical students as a group are likely to be more sophisticated with respect to paper and pencil inventories than are their non-clinical peers. They perhaps also felt more ego-involved in the testing program because of its sponsorship by the VA. Assuming that the testing situation was one which tended to encourage the subject to try to make favorable scores, the clinical students were at an advantage. This is suggested by the fact that the VA clinical group scored significantly higher on the K (Suppressor) variable of the Multiphasic Inventory.

Looking next at the distributions of scores on the Strong Vocational Interest Blank, we again note a surprising degree of overlap of the two distributions on all variables. Critical ratios were not computed for the differences on specific scales, but inspection reveals a tendency for the VA trainees to score higher than non-clinical students on the following scales: Personnel Manager, Y-Secretary, Sales Manager, Life Insurance Salesman and Lawyer. They tend to score lower on:

15

TABLE A III-1

COMPARISON OF TEST SCORES FOR VA CLINICAL AND NON-CLINICAL GRADUATE STUDENTS IN PSYCHOLOGY*

MILLER ANALOGIES, PMA, AND ALLPORT-VERNON SCORES

		01-10	11-20	21-30	31-40	41-50	51-60	61-70	71-80	81-90	91-100	Critical Ratio VA-Non VA
ANALOGIES (Miller-Form G)							vvvvvv	vvvvvV	vvvvv			
							nnnnnn	nnnnnnN	nnnnnn			
Thurstone PMA	NUMBER									vvvvvvvvvVv		2.50
										nnnnnnnnNnn		
	VERBAL								vvVv			
									nnNn			
	SPACE					vvvvvvvvvvvvVvvvvvvvvv						-2.99
						nnnnnnnnnnnnnNnnnnnnnnn						
	WORD FLUENCY							vvvvvvvvvvvvvvVvvvvvvv				
								nnnnnnnnnnnnnnnNnnnnnn				
	REASONING							vvvvvvvvvVvvvvv				
								nnnnnnnnnnNnnnnn				
	MEMORY						vvvvvvvvvvVvvvvvvvv					
							nnnnnnnnnNnnnnnnnnnn					
Allport-Vernon	THEORETICAL									vvVvv		
										nnNnn		
	ECONOMIC		vvvvvvvvvVvvvvvvvvvvv									
			nnnnnnnnnNnnnnnnnnnnn									
	AESTHETIC				vvvvvvvvvvvvvvvvvvvvvvVvvvvvvvvvvvv							
					nnnnnnnnnnnnnnnnnnnnNnnnnnnnnnn							
	SOCIAL							vvvvvvvVvvvvvvv				4.08
								nnnnnnNnnnnnnnnnn				
	POLITICAL		vvvvvvvvvVvvvvvvvvvv									
			nnnnnnnNnnnnnnnnnnn									
	RELIGIOUS	vvvvvvvvvVvvvvvvvvvvvv										
		nnnnnNnnnnnnnnnnnnnnnnnnn										

*The interval from Q_1 to Q_3 is indicated by v and n for VA and non-clinical groups respectively. V and N indicate the two medians.

TABLE A III-1 (cont.)

GUILFORD MARTIN BATTERY OF PERSONALITY INVENTORIES

Percentiles of General Norms

	01-10	11-20	21-30	31-40	41-50	51-60	61-70	71-80	81-90	90-100	Critical Ratio VA-Non VA
S (Social Extraversion)						vvvvv	vvvvv	vvvvV	vvvvvv	vv	
						nnnnnn	nnnnN	nnnnnn	n		
T (Thinking Extraversion)				vvvvv	vvvvv	vvvvV	vvvvv	vvvvv			2.24
				nnnnn	nnnnnn	Nnnnn	nnnnn	n			
D (Freedom from Depression)								vvvvvv	Vvv		3.92
								nnnnnn	nnNnn	n	
C (Freedom from Cycloid Tendencies)									vvVvv		4.93
									nnnnnn	nnnnnnNn	
R (Rhathymia-Lack of Control)				vvvvvv	Vvvvvv	vvvv					
				nnnnnnN	nnnnnn	nnnnn					
G (General Activity)	vvvvvv	vvvVv	vvvvvv								-2.89
	nnnnnn	nnnnN	nnnnnn	nnnnnn	n						
A (Ascendance)					vvvvvv	vvvvvv	vvVvv	vvvvvv			
					nnnnnn	nnnnnn	nNnnnn	nnnnnnn			
M (Masculinity)								vvvvvv	Vvvvv		*
								nnnnnn	nnnnnNnnnn	n	
I (Lack of Inferiority Feelings)						nnnnnn	vvvvvv	Vvvvvv	vv		2.55
						nnnnnn	nnnnnn	Nnnnn	nnnnnn		
N (Lack of Nervousness)						nnnnn	vvvvvv	Vvvvv	vv		4.56
						nnnnn	nnnnnn	nnnnNnnnnnn			
O (Objectivity)								vvvvv	vvvvvVvv		2.53
								nnnnnn	nnnnnNnnn	n	
Ag (Agreeableness)						vvvvv	vvvvvv	Vvvvv	vvvvv		
						nnnnnn	nnnnnn	Nnnnnn	nnnn		
Co (Cooperativeness)								vvvvvvvv	Vvvvv	vvvv	3.28
								nnnnnnnn	nnNnnn		

*The non-clinical non-VA group contained more women than the VA group. There is no significant difference between the means of the two groups on Masculinity so ~ ~~ omitted from the non-clinical group.

TABLE A III-1 (cont.)

MINNESOTA MULTIPHASIC PERSONALITY INVENTORY

Percentile of General Norms

	01-10	11-20	21-30	31-40	41-50	51-60	61-70	71-80	81-90	91-100	Critical Ratio VA-Non VA
T Score*	01-36	37-41	42-44	45-47	48-49	50-52	53-55	56-58	59-63	64-Up	
Hs (Hypochond-riasis)		vvVvvvvvvvvvv nnnNnnnnnnn									-2.89
D (Depression)				vvvvvvvvvvVvvvvvvvvvv nnnnnnnnnnnNnnnnnnn							
Hy (Hysteria)						vvvvvvvvvVvvvvvvv nnnNnnnnnnnnn					
Pd (Psychopathic Deviate)			vvvvvvvVvvvvvvvvvvvv nnnnnnnNnnnnnnnnnnn								2.03
Mf (Femininity Interest Pattern)								vvvvvvvvvvvvVvvvv nnnnnnnNnn		**
Pa (Paranoia)				vvvvvvvvVvvvvvvvvv nnnnnnnnnnnnnNnnnnnnn							
Pt (Psychasthenia)	vvvvVvvvvv nnnnNnnnnnn										-2.74
Sc (Schizophrenia)		vvvvvVvvvvvv nnnnNnnnnn									
Ma (Hypomania)			vvvvvvvvvvvvvvVvvvvvvv nnnnnnnnnnNnnnnnnnnnn								
K (Suppressor)										vvvVvv nnNnnnnnnn	3.45

*T Score = a Standard Score with a mean of 50 and a S.D. of 10.

**The non-clinical group contained more women than the VA group. There is no significant difference between the means of the two groups on Masculinity when the women are omitted from the non-clinical group.

TABLE A III-1 (cont.)

STRONG VOCATIONAL INTEREST BLANK

		C	C+	B-	B	B+	A	Critical Ratio VA-Non VA
Group I	Artist	vvvvvvvvvvvVvvvvvvvvvv nnnnnnnnnnnnnnNnnnnnnnnnnn						
	Psychologist				vvvvvvvvvvvVvvvvvvvvv nnnnnnnnnnNnnnnnn			
	Architect	vvvvvvvvvvvvVvvvvvvvvvvv nnnnnnnnnnnnnnnnNnnnnnnnnnnn						
	Physician			vvvvvvvvvVvvvvvvvvvvvvvv nnnnnnnnnnnNnnnnnnnnnnnnnnnn				
	Dentist	vvVvvvvvvv nnnnnNnnnnnnnnnnnnnn						
II	Engineer	vvvvvvvvvVvvvvvvvvvvvv nnnnnnnnnnNnnnnnnnnnnnnnn						
	Chemist			vvvvvvvvvvvVvvvvvvvvvvvvvvvvv nnnnnnnnnnnnnnnnNnnnnnnnnnnn				
III	Production Manager	vvvvvvvvvvVvvvvvvvv nnnnnnnnnnnnnNnnnnnnnnnn						
IV	Carpenter	vvVvvvv nnnNnnnnn						
	Math-Science Teacher			vvvvvvvvvvvvvvVvvvvvvv nnnnnnnnnnnnnnnnnnNnnnnnnnnn				
	Policeman	vvvvvVvvvvvvvvvv nnnnnNnnnnnnnnnn						
	Forest Service	vvvvvvvVvvvvvvvvvvvv nnnnnnNnnnnnnnnnnnn						
V	Personnel Manager				nnnnnnnnnnnnnnnnnnnNnnnnnn	vvvVvvvvv		
	YMCA Secretary	vvvvvvvvvvvvvVvvvvvvvvvvvvvv nnnnnnnNnnnnnnnnnnnnnnnnn						
VI	Musician			vvvvvvvvvvvvvvvvvvvVvvvvvv nnnnnnnnnnnnnnnnnnnNnnnnn				

(Continued on next page)

TABLE A III-1 (cont.)

STRONG VOCATIONAL INTEREST BLANK
(cont.)

		C	C+	B-	B	B+	A	Critical Ratio VA-Non VA
Group VIII	Accountant	vvvVvvvvvvvv nnNnnnnnnnnnnnnn						
	Office Worker		vvvvvVvvvvvvvvvvv nnnnNnnnnnnnnnnnnn					
	Purchasing Agent	vvvVvvvv nnnNnnnnnn						
IX	Sales Manager		vvvvvvvvvvvvvvVvvvvvvvv nnnnnnnnnNnnnnnnnnnn					
	Life Insurance Salesman			vvvvvvvvvvvvVvvvvvvvvvvv nnnnnnnnnnnNnnnnnnnnn				
X	Lawyer				vvvvvvvvvvvVvvvvvvvv nnnnnnnnnnNnnnnnnnnnnnn			
	Author Journalist				vvvvvvvvvvVvvvvvvvv nnnnnnnnnnNnnnnnnnnn			
	Group I					vvvVvvvvv nnnnnnnnnnnnnnnnnnNnnnn		- 2.44
	Group II				vvvvvvvvVvvvvvvvvvvvvvvvvvv nnnnnnnnnnnnnnnnnnnnNnnnnnnn			- 2.78
	Group V					vvvvvVvvvv nnnnnnnnnnnnnnnnnnNnnnn		5.36
	Group VIII	vvVvvvvvvvv nnnnNnnnnnn						
	Group IX			vvvvvvvvVvvvvvvvvvvvvv nnnnnnnNnnnnnnnnnnnn				2.58
	Group X				vvvvvvvVvvvv nnnnnnnnnNnnnnn			
	Occupational Level						vvVvv nnNnn	
	Masculinity Femininity				vvvvvvvvvvvvvvvvvvVvvvvvvvv nnnnnnnnnnnnnnnnNnnnnnnnnn			*

*The non-clinical non-VA group contained more women than the VA group. There is no significant difference between the means of the two groups on Masculinity scores when the women are omitted from the non-clinical group.

Artist, Psychologist, Architect, Physician, Dentist, Engineer, Chemist and Musician. (Note that the VA trainees score significantly higher on Groups V and IX scores and significantly lower on Groups I and II scores.) In general, the clinical group appears to show an interest pattern more like men in the professions which involve contact with people, social welfare and persuasive activities. The non-clinical group tends to show interests more like professional groups concerned with things and ideas rather than people. Since the original Strong Psychologist Key was based on the responses of a group containing almost no clinical psychologists, the above noted difference on the Psychologist Key is not at all surprising.

Although these differences in Strong scores are in the direction which might have been expected, the large overlap in the distribution is even more impressive. Perhaps, the differences between clinical and non-clinical psychologists is not as real as some had feared--and others had hoped!

Both VA clinical and non-clinical students as a group tend to differ markedly from the normative groups. The total group is intellectually superior even when compared with graduate students in other fields. On the A-V Scale, it tends to score relatively high on Theoretical, Aesthetic, and Social Values and low on Economic, Political, and Religious Values. On the basis of the Guilford-Martin scores, we may say that graduate students in psychology (as compared with the normative groups) are much more socially extraverted, much freer from depressive and cycloid tendencies, slightly more compulsive, much less physically active, more ascendant and more masculine. They are also much less subject to inferiority feelings, admit to far fewer nervous habits, and are more objective, agreeable and cooperative.

From the Minnesota Multiphasic scores, we get a picture of a group which deviates from the normative population in being less hypochondriacal, slightly more subject to depression, considerably more hysterical, extremely feminine, much less psychasthenic and less schizoid. But we must also add--a group far more able and inclined to put its best foot forward as indicated by the extremely high K scores! This tendency certainly accounts for at least part of the generally superior adjustment reflected in the scores just summarized.

It will be noted that both groups score as "free from depression" on the G-M Inventory but slightly "subject to depression" on the Minnesota test. Whether this reflects a difference in the normative groups for the two scales or the fact that these tests are not measuring the same thing is not known at present. Even more dramatic is the finding that the group scores very "masculine" on the G-M Inventory but extremely "feminine" on the MMPI.

Range of Talent

The two experimental groups on which the majority of the validational analyses are based were made up of 128 cases assesssed in the summer of 1947 and 99 cases who were studied in the summer of 1948. (The nine female VA trainees assessed in 1947 were omitted from validational analyses in order to make the group homogeneous with respect to sex.)

The 1947 Assessment Group

The 1947 assessment group was made up of first year students who had been accepted by the universities of their choice prior to their participation in the assessment program. In making the selections the universities followed their usual procedures for selecting graduate students. In general these selections were made on the basis of the student's credential file, letters of recommendation and perhaps an interview. In rare cases objective test scores were used. These trainees were brought together in the summer of 1947; by that time they had already been informed of their selection by the admitting university.

The first question to be asked about the 1947 assessment group is whether or not they were less variable with respect to certain objective test scores than the general run of graduate students in psychology.

A comparison between the 1947 assessment group and a comparison group consisting of non-clinical students in psychology shows some differences in terms of the variability of the two groups. The differences which were found correspond closely to the general differences between VA trainees and non-clinical students reported above. In general the 1947 clinical group was less variable in two respects: they tended to be more homogeneous with respect to their interest in helping people and in their lack of interest in the physical sciences. This is reflected in significant differences in the variances between the two samples on Strong Group II and V scores and on Kuder Social Service scores. The 1947 group was also somewhat more homogeneous in their tendency to score favorably on personality variables susceptible to facading ("faking good"). The variances were significantly different for several of the Guilford-Martin variables which were related to neurotic tendencies. There were no significant differences between the variabilities of scores on tests of intellectual ability. In fact, the two groups appear to be quite similar with respect to their variability on most objective test scores.

The 1948 Assessment Group

As has already been noted, the 1948 assessment group was not brought together physically for an assessment program. Instead, test data, biographical materials, etc. were secured from them by mail, and these materials were evaluated by the assessment staff without the actual presence of the candidates. At the time these data were collected, the students had not been selected by the parent university; consequently, in contrast to the 1947 group, the data for the 1948 assessment were collected under "selection conditions." This project reported back to the parent university the candidates' scores on the Miller Analogies Test and on the various Strong Keys including the VA Clinical Psychologist Key. Presumably these test scores were used by some of the parent universities in selecting the 1948 trainees. In the case of the Miller Analogies Test the effects of such selection are clearly evident. As shown in Table A III-2, the 1947 and 1948 groups are significantly different with respect to both means and variances of Miller scores, the 1948 group having a higher mean and smaller variance. In the case of the Strong Vocational Interest Blank, the two scores most likely to have been used in selection are the Strong Psychologist Key and the VA Clinical Psychologist Key. As may be seen from Table A III-2, the differences between the groups with respect to these two variables are not significant. Therefore, we may conclude that the principal dimension on which the 1948 group was selected as compared with the 1947 group was intellectual ability. Since the intellectual component constitutes one of the major predictable aspects of the criterion data, we may expect generally lower validity coefficients for the more homogeneous 1948 group than for the 1947 group.

Variations in Training

Along with the collection of criterion measures in 1950, the trainees were asked to fill out a "Training Experience Inventory" (see Appendix II D). This was a structured questionnaire concerning the amount and kinds of experience to which trainees had been exposed during the period of training in the VA clinical psychology program. These data give us some idea about the variability of training experienced by subjects in the interim between the collection of prediction measures and the collection of final criteria. It may be said at the outset that the trainees studied by this project have been exposed to widely varying opportunities for learning as well as to qualitative differences in the types of clinical materials which have been emphasized at the various

TABLE A III 2

COMPARISON BETWEEN THE 1947 ASSESSMENT GROUP
AND THE 1948 ASSESSMENT GROUP ON
SELECTED OBJECTIVE TESTS

	Miller Analogies	Strong Psychologist	Strong VA Clinical Psychologist
Critical Ratio Between Means	3. 76**	1.08	.69
F Test Between Variances	1.65*	1.36	1.41

**Significant at the 1 percent level, 1948 group mean higher.

*Significant at the 5 percent level, 1948 group less variable.

training institutions.

The Training Experience Inventory sought to cover four aspects of the relevant experiences of the trainees: (a) Formal Instruction, (b) Field Experience, (c) Prevailing Trainee Attitudes, (d) Personal Therapy Experience of Trainees. The data for each category will be analyzed in terms of the gross variability within the groups and with reference to possible differences between the 1947 and 1948 assessment groups. In all comparisons of the 1947 and 1948 groups, it must be remembered that at the time the form was completed the 1948 group had had only 2 1/2 years of formal training as compared with 3 1/2 years for the 1947 group.

Formal Instruction

The trainees were asked to indicate the number of semester hours of instruction they had received in the following subjects, (a_1) Objective Tests, (a_2) Projective Tests , (b) Research Methods (including statistics), and (c) Psychotherapy. Summaries of the resulting data are shown in Table A III-3. As can be seen, there is less variability among the trainees with respect to classroom instruction in research methods and projective techniques than for objective tests and psychotherapy. Note that about 20 percent of the trainees report no formal instruction in objective tests, and 10 to 15 percent report no formal instruction in psychotherapy. On the other hand, almost all of the trainees reported some instruction in projective tests and research methods.

There are no appreciable differences in the reports of the 1947 and 1948 groups with the exception of psychotherapy: the 1948 group reports less formal instruction in psychotherapy than the 1947 group. Presumably didactic instruction in psychotherapy tends to come later in the curricula than instruction in diagnosis and research.

TABLE A III-3

AMOUNT OF CLASSROOM INSTRUCTION IN MAJOR CATEGORIES
REPORTED BY STUDENTS IN THE VA TRAINING PROGRAM
(N=71 for 1947 group; N= 76 for 1948 group)

Number of Semester Hours of Instruction	Projective Tests Group 47 %	Projective Tests Group 48 %	Objective Tests Group 47 %	Objective Tests Group 48 %	Number of Semester Hours of Instruction	Research Methods Group 47 %	Research Methods Group 48 %	Psychotherapy Group 47 %	Psychotherapy Group 48 %
6+	34	25	24	18	6+	69	68	35	20
4-6	52	54	30	38	5-6	13	16	28	14
1-3	13	20	24	21	3-4	13	14	18	37
0	1	1	21	22	1-2	3	1	7	12
					0	3	1	11	16

Field Experience

Diagnosis

The trainees were asked to indicate the approximate number of patients they had studied utilizing diagnostic procedures. The results, broken down into broad categories of patients, are shown in Table A III-4. In general trainees reported more diagnostic experience with adult male neurotics and psychotics than with children and females. This findings reflects the fact that the trainees have had most of their field experience in VA installations.

In terms of diagnostic experience there is a clear difference between the 1947 and 1948 assessment groups, the 1948 group having tested fewer patients than the 1947 group. Again this is not surprising since the 1948 group has had one year less experience than the 1947 group. The median for the 1947 group is approximately 130 patients. The variability in the amount of experience with patients in both groups is great: the range extending from less than 50 to more than 350 patients.

Trainees also reported the approximate number and type of diagnostic instruments utilized. Projective tests were found to be much more frequently administered than tests in any other category--half of the 1947 group report that they have interpreted more than 300 projective tests, while more than half of the group report giving less than 21 objective tests. The rank order of the various diagnostic instruments as determined by the frequency with which the trainees report utilizing them is, 1. Projective Tests, 2. Wechsler-Bellevue, 3. Diagnostic Interview, 4. Objective Tests of Interest and Personality.

TABLE A III-4

NUMBER OF PATIENTS IN EACH OF SEVERAL CATEGORIES TESTED, AS REPORTED BY STUDENTS IN THE VA TRAINING PROGRAM

(N = 71 for 1947 group; N = 76 for 1948 group)

Neurotic No. Tested	Group 47 %	48 %	Psychotic No. Tested	Group 47 %	48 %	Child No. Tested	Group 47 %	48 %	Total Female No. Tested	Group 47 %	48 %	Total Male and Female No. Tested	Group 47 %	48 %
281+	4		176+	1		141+	3		71+	3		351+	15	1
241-280	1		151-175		1	121-140	1		61-70			301-350	7	4
201-240			126-150	8	1	101-120			51-60			251-300	14	5
161-200	4		101-125	3	3	81-100	1		41-50	1	3	201-250	10	8
121-160	7	4	76-100	13	3	61-80		1	31-40	3	1	151-200	17	18
81-120	13	8	51-75	17	9	41-60	7	4	21-30	6	5	101-150	23	28
41-80	30	24	26-50	38	43	21-40	20	9	11-20	23	12	51-100	13	26
1-40	39	64	1-25	20	39	1-20	30	54	1-10	52	55	1-50	1	9
0	1		0			0	38	32	0	13	24	0		

Psychotherapy

The majority of trainees reported having treated from 1 to 15 patients in psychotherapy. Almost all of the 1947 group reported some therapeutic experience, and the differences between the 1947 and 1948 groups are not as large in this respect as in the case of diagnostic experience. This finding may reflect an increasing emphasis on psychotherapy in the training installations.

Research

The trainees were asked to submit abstracts of their doctoral dissertations or, failing that, to indicate the approximate stage of completion of their doctoral problem. They also indicated research papers which had been published or submitted for publication, research presented to psychological societies, and any unpublished research studies that they had carried out since entering the VA training program. Table A III-5 shows the distributions of these data for the two groups. As expected, the 1947 group was much further along with their dissertations than the 1948 group. However, for published research and total number of research titles reported, the differences between the two groups are not nearly so large. In fact, for the total number of research titles reported, there is practically no difference between the 1947 and 1948 groups. This finding may reflect an increasing emphasis on research in the training universities or it is possible that the 1948 group was more carefully selected in terms of research interests. The former interpretation appears to be more probable since, as mentioned earlier, there is also evidence for increasing emphasis on psychotherapy. These findings suggest that there is an increasing tendency to emphasize the therapeutic and research functions of the VA trainees and to give less attention to purely diagnostic functions.

TABLE A III-5

RESEARCH ACTIVITIES REPORTED BY STUDENTS IN
THE VA TRAINING PROGRAM

(N = 71 for 1947 group; N = 76 for 1948 group)

Progress on Dissertation	Group 47 %	Group 48 %	Articles Published No.	Group 47 %	Group 48 %	Papers Presented to Psychological Societies No.	Group 47 %	Group 48 %	Total Titles Reported No.	Group 47 %	Group 48 %
No title	34	78	0	80	87	0	99	99	0	23	14
Title Only	14	9	1	11	9	1	1	1	1	24	33
Design	28	8	2	4	4	2			2	27	17
Data	18	4	3	3		3			3	10	17
Interpretation			4	1		4			4	4	4
Completed	4	1	5			5			5	6	9
Published	1		6			6			6	7	5

About 20 percent of the 1947 group as against 13 percent of the 1948 group have published research or submitted a paper for publication. On the other hand, about 80 percent of both groups report at least one research title. Only one person in each group reported having presented a research paper at a meeting of a psychological association.

Prevailing Trainee Attitudes

Trainees were asked to estimate the quality of their training in the areas of diagnosis, therapy, and research. The resulting findings are summarized in Table A III-6. As can be seen from the table, trainees were relatively more satisfied with the quality of their training in diagnosis and less satisfied with the quality of their training in psychotherapy; estimated quality of research training falls between the estimates for diagnosis and therapy.

Trainees were also asked to rank the following activities: administration, diagnosis, research, teaching, and psychotherapy, with respect to their preferences to engage in them. Preferences for diagnosis, research, and therapy are summarized in Table A III-7. Perhaps the most interesting aspect of this table is that the 1948 group is more favorable toward research and therapy and less favorable toward diagnosis than the 1947 group.

Personal Therapy of Trainees

In view of the observation that some VA trainees have entered personal therapy during their period of training, it seemed desirable to ascertain the incidence of this practice and the reasons for it. We therefore included several questions in the Training Experience Inventory which concerned personal therapy. The findings may be summarized briefly. Thirty-one percent of the 1947 group and 37 percent of the 1948 reported some personal therapy. Of those who have had therapy, the majority of both groups report that their motivation for entering therapy was primarily because of personal difficulties rather than to improve clinical skill. Seventy-three percent of the 1947 group and 93 percent of the 1948 group report better social adjustment as a result of therapy, and about 85 percent of both groups felt that therapy improved their clinical skill. In terms of their approach to clinical research, about 30 percent of both groups who had had therapy reported that as a result of therapy they became less quantitatively minded; only 6 percent indicated that personal therapy had made them more quantitatively minded.

In summary, our analyses of data from the Training Experience Inventory indicate considerable variability among the trainees with respect to the amount of exposure to various psychological techniques. Data not summarized here reflect similar variation in trainees' orientation towards the field of clinical psychology. In view of these differences, the problem of differing frames of references among the criterion raters is a serious one. We must assume that considerable error variance has been introduced into the criterion ratings as a result of varying conceptions of the role and function of the clinical psychologist among those supervisory clinicians who provided the criterion evaluations. Also insofar as the criterion ratings reflect clinical competences which are primarily the result of training, the criterion ratings will reflect variability in training as well as aptitude for profiting from training.

However, there appears to be a core of consistency in the training programs which could be characterized as a fairly uniform emphasis on projective techniques and research methodology in the universities and a large amount of diagnostic experience with adult male neurotics and psychotics in the VA installations.

There appears also to be a trend in the VA clinical psychology program towards greater emphasis on research. It may be that these two rather diverse trends reflect the different emphases

TABLE A III-6

TRAINEE EVALUATIONS OF THE QUALITY OF THEIR TRAINING
IN DIAGNOSIS, THERAPY, AND RESEARCH

(N = 70 for 1947 group; N = 75 for 1948 group)

	Diagnosis		Psychotherapy		Research	
	Group		Group		Group	
Evaluation of	47	48	47	48	47	48
Training	%	%	%	%	%	%
Excellent	15	16	7	16	15	16
Good	65	59	36	24	41	36
Adequate	15	21	28	24	30	39
Inadequate	4	4	28	35	14	9

TABLE A III-7

TRAINEE PREFERENCES FOR SELECTED
PSYCHOLOGICAL ACTIVITIES

(N = 68 for 1947 group; N = 70 for 1948 group)

	Diagnosis		Psychotherapy		Research		Teaching		Administration	
	Group		Group		Group		Group		Group	
Rank	47	48	47	48	47	48	47	48	47	48
Order	%	%	%	%	%	%	%	%	%	%
1	21	14	35	49	25	29	15	7	7	4
2	31	34	26	27	15	20	16	18	7	3
3	25	13	19	13	18	30	25	28	16	14
4	15	26	15	7	19	17	25	39	25	9
5	9	13	4	4	24	4	19	7	44	70

by the universities and the training installations. Judging from the Boulder Report on Training in Clinical Psychology (1950), it may be assumed that the universities are tending to emphasize the research function of the clinical psychologists. On the other hand a greater opportunity to engage in psychotherapy may be available in the training installations.

Inter-Institutional Differences

It has already been noted that VA trainees in clinical psychology show (a) a wide range of individual differences on objective test scores and (b) a similarly wide range with respect to the amount and kind of experience to which they have been exposed during their training period. It is now of interest to inquire if such variability is characteristic of the trainees accepted by a single university or whether a given university tends to select students who as a group differ from those selected by other universities. We shall also inquire whether the trainees in different institutions differ systematically with respect to amount and kind of training received. Obviously, significant differences among training institutions with respect to training standards will tend to lower the obtained validity of all predictions. Also such differences imply some dissimilarities among the frames of reference of the supervisors who provided the criterion ratings.

Unfortunately, because of the relatively small number of candidates assessed as compared with the relatively large number of training institutions represented, the average number of assessed candidates per university is small. For this reason only a limited analysis of inter-university differences has been attempted.

Miller Analogies Scores

The distribution of Miller scores, by quarters, for the trainees accepted by each of the 35 cooperating institutions is presented in Table A III-8. That the variation from institution to institution is greater than could have resulted by chance as indicated by is Epsilon squared value of .13. (For N = 230 and K = 35, a value of .093 is significant at the 1% level). No attempt was made to determine the significance of the deviation of any mean for an individual row, but the following marked deviations appear striking:

   a.   7 of 9 trainees at B are in the upper half of the distribution.

   b.   6 of 7 trainees at K are in the upper half of the distribution.

   c.   11 of 14 trainees at DD are in the upper half of the distribution.

By contrast, note that:

   a.   11 of 15 trainees at F are in the lower half of the distribution.

   b.   5 of 6 trainees at J are in the lower half of the distribution.

   c.   all of the trainees at M are in the lower half and 8 of the 11 are in the lowest quarter!

Note that this table includes 1948 trainees, for whom Miller scores were available to selecting institutions. A similar analysis based only on 1947 trainees revealed even more striking inter-university variability. For example, one trainee was accepted with a Miller score of 29 which is only four points above a chance score; as of September, 1950 this student was still in the program.

Content Examination

The Content Examination, an objective test of achievement in the fields of clinical and general

TABLE A III-8

DISTRIBUTION OF RAW SCORES ON MILLER ANALOGIES
TEST OF 1947 AND 1948 ASSESSED P-1 APPLICANTS
BY ACCEPTING UNIVERSITIES

University	Lower Quarter 65 and below	66-72	73-80	Upper Quarter 81 and over	N
A		1	1	1	3
B	1	1	5	2	9
C	1	1	3		5
D	1	4	11	7	23
E	1	1	1	2	5
F	5	6	1	3	15
G	1		1		2
H	1				1
I				1	1
J	4	1	1		6
K	1		2	4	7
L	2	3	1	3	9
M	8	3			11
N		2	2		4
O	1	4	1	1	7
P		1	1	2	4
Q	1	2			3
R	1		1	1	3
S	2			4	6
T	2	2	2	4	10
U	2			1	3
V	4	2	2		8
W		2		4	6
X		2		1	3
Y		1	3	1	5
Z	2	2	1		5
AA		4	1	1	6
BB	3	2	4	1	10
CC	2		2	3	7
DD	3		4	7	14
EE	1	4			5
FF	3	3	2	1	9
GG		1	1	1	3
HH	4	1	2	1	8
II	1	1		2	4
Total	58	57	56	59	230

psychology, was administered to the trainees in the fall of 1950. This test, designed to evaluate the extent of the trainees' factual knowledge about the field of psychology, was given in two sections: (a) Clinical and (b) General Psychology. Separate distributions were made for each university on the two sections. The distributions are shown in Table A III-9.

The Epsilon squared value for the clinical section was .11 and for the general section .13. Both of these values are significant at the 5% level, indicating that there is significant variation among universities with respect to the factual knowledge of their students. However, as noted above, these results must be evaluated with consideration for the small number of cases for each university. In general, the differences are of approximately the same magnitude as was found for the Miller Analogies scores.

Differences in Clinical Experience

In addition to the study of the variability among trainees separate distributions were tabulated for each university on 6 of the more objective variables in the Training Experience Inventory. These variables are: (a) Number of Adult Neurotics Tested, (b) Number of Adult Psychotics Tested, (c) Number of Children Tested, (d) Number of Females Tested, (e) Total Number of Subjects Tested, and (f) Number of Patients Treated in Psychotherapy. The resulting distributions are presented in Table A III-10. The significance of the variations among institutions was tested by Epsilon squared and values significant at the 1% level were found for all variables except for (b) Number of Adult Psychotics Tested.

In summary these results show that there is significant variation among universities with respect to the calibre of student selected as well as significant variation among universities in the achievement as measured by the Content Examination. Universities also differ significantly with respect to the amount and kind of clinical experience obtained by their students.

These differences serve to point up the wide range of variability from institution to institution on almost any variable that is relevant to the selection and training of students in clinical psychology. The problem of differing standards and frames of reference among the institutions participating in this study is indeed a vexing one. The results just reported show that our concern over institutional differences was not unfounded, and that such variability must be kept in mind in interpreting the validational data.

While the fact that this research has been conducted on a nationwide basis increased the difficulties in measuring clinical performance, this same feature results in more generality of the resulting findings than if our efforts had been confined to a single institution or training installation. This generality has been achieved at the expense of ideal measurement conditions, but the results appear to have fully justified such a procedure. The findings may be interpreted with confidence that they are not a function of a local bias with respect to conceptions of the role of clinical psychologists. Thus, the obtained correlations between predictors and criteria may be assumed to be representative of the nationwide conditions prevailing at the time the data were collected.

The Interest Pattern of Clinical Psychologists as Compared with Those of Psychiatrists and other Physicians

Because of the overlapping of certain professional functions of clinical psychologists and psychiatrists, we felt it desirable to compare groups of trainees in each of these fields. The Menninger Foundation Project on the Selection of VA Psychiatric Residents supplied us with the Strong Vocational Interest Scores of 119 psychiatric residents evaluated by that project. Fortunately, we were

TABLE A III-9

DISTRIBUTIONS BY UNIVERSITIES OF SCORES
ON CONTENT EXAMINATION

Univ.	Clinical Section 155 or below	156-163	164-171	172-179	180 or above	Total	General Section 141 or below	142-151	152-161	162-171	172 or above	Total
A			1	2		3			3			3
B	1	2	2	1		6	2	1	1		2	6
C			1	1		2			1	1		2
D		1	5	4	5	15		3	5	3	4	15
E	1	1	3	2		7		2		3	2	7
F	4	1	2	3	2	12	5	2	2	2	1	12
G	1				1	2		1		1		2
J	2	1				3	1	1	1			3
K	1	1	1		2	5	1		1	1	2	5
L	1	2	1	1		5	1		2	2		5
M	4		2			6	2	1	3			6
N			2		1	3	1		1		1	3
O		2	2	1	1	6			3	2	1	6
T	1	2	4	2		9		1	3	5		9
U		2	1			3			2	1		3
V	2	2	1	1		6	1	2	2	1		6
W				2		2					2	2
X		1	1	1		3	1		1		1	3
Y				2	1	3				1	2	3
Z		4		1		5	2	1	2			5
AA			2	1	1	4				2	2	4
BB	2	1		1		4		1	2	1		4
CC	3		4		1	8	4	1	1	2		8
DD	2	1	2	4	6	15	2	2	5	1	5	15
EE	1	1	1			3	1	1	1			3
GG		1	1			2			1		1	2
HH	1	2			1	4	2		1		1	4
II	1		1	1		3	1	1		1		3
JJ		1		1		2	1	1				2
Total	28	29	40	32	22	151	28	22	44	30	27	151

TABLE A III-10

DISTRIBUTIONS BY UNIVERSITIES SHOWING AMOUNT
OF TRAINEES' EXPERIENCE WITH PATIENTS

Univ.	No. of Adult Neurotics Tested					No. of Adult Psychotics Tested					No. of Children Tested				
	40 or below	41-80	81-120	121 or above	Total	25 or below	26-50	51-75	76 or above	Total	0	1-20	21-40	41 or above	Total
B	2	3		1	6	0	3	1	2	6	2	4			6
C		2	1		3		3			3	1	1	1		3
D	8	3	1		12	5	4		3	12	1	8	3		12
E		4	2	1	7	2	4		1	7	5	1	1		7
F		1		7	8	2	3	1	2	8	5	3			8
G	1				1			1		1				1	1
H			1		1		1			1	1				1
I	2				2		2			2		2			2
J		1	1	1	3		1		2	3		1		2	3
K	3	1			4	3	1			4	2	2			4
L	6				6	3	3			6	3	3			6
M	4	2			6	2	1	1	2	6	2	1	2	1	6
N	2		1		3	2		1		3		1	2		3
O		2		1	3		2		1	3			2	1	3
P	1				1	1				1				1	1
Q		1			1				1	1		1			1
R		1			1			1		1			1		1
S	1				1		1			1		1			1
T	7	1	1		9	1	7		1	9	4	5			9
U	1		2		3		2		1	3	1	1		1	3
V	6				6	4	1	1		6	5	1			6
W		1		1	2	1		1		2	2				2
X	3				3	2	1			3	1	2			3
Y	1	2			3		2		1	3	2	1			3
Z	1	3	1		5	1	2	2		5	5				5
AA	1	3			4	2	2			4		2	2		4
BB	4				4	1	1	2		4		3		1	4
CC	5				5	2	3			5	3	1	1		5
DD	8	3	2	1	14	1	4	6	3	14	6	3	4	1	14
EE	3				3	2		1		3		2		1	3
FF	2				2			1	1	2		1		1	2
GG		1	1		2		2			2				2	2
HH	1	4	1	1	7	3	2		2	7	1	4	1	1	7
II	3				3	2	1			3		3			3
JJ	2				2	2				2	1	1			2
OO		1			1				1	1	1				1
Total	78	40	14	15	147	44	59	20	24	147	52	60	21	14	147

TABLE A III-10 (cont.)

	No. of Females Tested					Total No. of Subjects Tested					No. of Persons Treated in Psychotherapy				
Univ.	0	1-10	11-20	21 or above	Total	100 or less	101-150	151-200	201 or more	Total	0	1-15	16-30	31 or more	Total
B		3	2	1	6		1	1	4	6	2	4			6
C	1	2			3		1	1	1	3		2	1		3
D	2	9	1		12	3	4	3	2	12		7	1	4	12
E	1	5	1		7		4	1	2	7		6		1	7
F		7		1	8		1	1	6	8		7	1		8
G				1	1			1		1		1			1
H		1			1				1	1	1				1
I	1	1			2	2				2		1	1		2
J			2	1	3				3	3		1		2	3
K		4			4	2	1	1		4		4			4
L	2	3	1		6	5	1			6	6				6
M	2	3		1	6	3		1	2	6		1	3	2	6
N		2		1	3	1	1		1	3	1	2			3
O			2	1	3			2	1	3			2	1	3
P		1			1	1				1		1			1
Q			1		1				1	1			1		1
R			1		1				1	1		1			1
S		1			1	1				1		1			1
T	1	4	3	1	9	4	2	1	2	9		8	1		9
U	1	2			3	1			2	3		2		1	3
V	5	1			6	4	2			6		5	1		6
W		2			2		1		1	2		2			2
X		3			3	2	1			3	2	1			3
Y			1	2	3		2		1	3		3			3
Z	3	2			5	1	1	3		5		1	3	1	5
AA		3	1		4	1	2	1		4		3	1		4
BB		3	1		4	1	2	1		4		4			4
CC	2	2		1	5	2	2		1	5		1	1	3	5
DD	3	8	2	1	14		2	5	7	14		7	3	4	14
EE	1		2		3	1		1	1	3	1	2			3
FF		2			2		1		1	2			2		2
GG			1	1	2				2	2			1	1	2
HH	1	2	1	3	7	1		2	4	7	1	2	4		7
II		2	1		3	3				3		3			3
JJ		2			2	2				2	1	1			2
OO	1				1				1	1		1			1
Total	27	80	24	16	147	37	35	27	48	147	15	85	27	20	147

34

PRODUCTION MANAGER

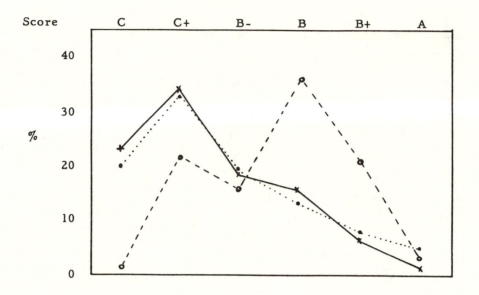

CERTIFIED PUBLIC ACCOUNTANT

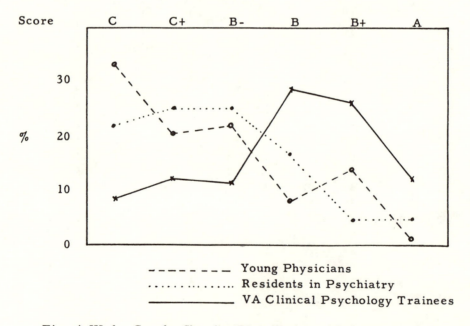

------ Young Physicians
.... Residents in Psychiatry
————— VA Clinical Psychology Trainees

Fig. A III-1. Graphs Showing Distribution of Strong Interest Scores of
63 Young Physicians, 118 Residents in Psychiatry and 129
VA Clinical Psychology Trainees When Scored on (a) Production Manager Key and (b) Certified Public Accountant
Key.

also able to secure a comparable set of scores for a group of 63 young physicians just completing their intern year at the University of Michigan Medical School.

Distribution of the scores for each group on each of the Strong Keys were prepared and the groups were compared by means of a composite graph of the three resulting distributions for each set of scores. The upper part of Figure A III-1 represents these distributions for Strong Production Manager scores. This graph is generally typical of those for all Strong scores which clearly differentiate the interest patterns of the three groups: the interest patterns of psychiatrists and clinical psychologists tend to be remarkably similar to each other and both different from the interest pattern of the group of young physicians. These differences would probably be even more striking if the young physicians planning to specialize in psychiatry were excluded from the physician group.

Six of the Strong scores show this general picture of differences. As compared with clinical psychologists and psychiatrists, the interests of young physicians tend to be much more like those of architects, engineers, chemists, production managers, farmers, and aviators. It will be noted that these are professions whose members are concerned with things, materials, ideas, and efficiency of production. Several other Strong keys show the opposite kind of differentiation of the groups: clinical psychologists and psychiatrists, when compared with physicians have interests more like those of personnel directors, public administrators, musicians, and advertising men. On the Teacher and City School Superintendent Keys, the psychologists tend to score relatively high with scores for psychiatrists falling between those of the psychologists and the physicians.

On the original Strong Psychologist Key, scores for the psychiatrists distribute themselves much like those of the clinical psychologists, but on the Physician Key, psychologists and physicians are fairly well separated with the curve for psychiatrists falling in between.

The interests of clinical psychologists and psychiatrists are clearly differentiated by only one Strong Score, Certified Public Accountant. Distribution of CPA scores for the three groups are shown in the lower part of Figure A III-1. On this Key it will be noted that the distributions of interest scores of the psychiatrists and physicians are very similar and both are quite different from that for the clinical psychologists. Since Strong CPA scores are practically uncorrelated with those based on any other Key, the interpretation of this difference is a bit difficult. While relatively few psychologists score "A" on this key, they do tend to make more B, B+, and A scores than members of the two other professional groups. Since Certified Public Accountants are interested primarily in the objective appraisal of data, this difference may reflect a somewhat more impersonal attitude on the part of trainees in clinical psychology.

CHAPTER B I

PREDICTORS

This chapter is devoted to a description of each of the many measures which served
as predictor variables. Predictor measures include: (a) University Predictions,
i. e. , judgments of university staff members as to the probable success of their entering students; (b) approximately 100 scores derived from a battery of objective
tests, and (c) clinically derived measures, i. e. , the judgments and predictions made
by assessment staff members who evaluated the subjects on the basis of a variety
of clinical procedures. Since these clinical judgments were expressed in the form
of ratings, this chapter includes a description of the basic rating scales used. Included also is a detailed description of the assessment procedures which served as
the basis of the sequential individual and group ratings of the candidates. The final
section of the chapter describes the modified assessment programs followed at
Wellesley in 1948, and in the 1949 reassessment of the 1947 cases, both of which involved making evaluations of and predictions about subjects not seen by the assessment staffs.

The Choice of Predictor Measures

The logical design for a personnel selection study involves the determination of the criterion
measures to be used, the choice of tentative predictors, and the experimental testing of the efficiency of these predictors. Our first step was not the identification of criterion measures, but
a job analysis as represented by the variables included in Scale C of the basic rating scale: these
included predicted Academic Performance, Diagnostic Competence, Professional Interpersonal
Relations, and several others (cf. Appendix I A).

In choosing our predictor measures, we had two alternatives: we might have used a few tests
and procedures which seemed to be highly promising predictors; instead we decided to include
representative procedures from each of several approaches to personality measurement. Thus
current clinical practice was represented by the interview and by several kinds of projective
tests and current personnel selection practice was represented by objective tests of intelligence,
interests, and "personality." We also used situation tests and the assessment approach, and
quantified judgments by persons actually responsible for the selection of trainees at universities.

Our decision to use many and varied predictor measures was based on the opinion that no one
test or procedure looked appreciably more promising than any other. The absence of previous
definitive research in the area of professional selection indicated the desirability of trying out a
large number of predictors selected to represent each of the several approaches to the evaluation
of personality.

University Predictions

All students studied in this project in 1946 and 1947 had already been evaluated and accepted
for training by one of the cooperating universities. Different departments followed differing procedures in selecting applicants, but in all cases some department had judged the candidate to be
worthy of admission. Since there was no available information concerning the validity of these

procedures already in use, an attempt was made to estimate their validity by systematically collecting predictions from departments as to the relative promise of selected candidates. The validity of these judgments, as determined by correlating them with criterion measures, would in
one sense serve as a baseline with which the validities of more elaborate selection procedures
could be compared: a more complex procedure would have no practical value if its validity was
not above that resulting from common practice.

For the 1946 Group

Since the project did not begin until the fall of 1946, it was not possible to collect predictions
by university staff members before those students entering in 1946 had arrived at the university.
Nevertheless, in October, 1946 each department chairman was asked to have each candidate rated
by all local staff members who had assisted in the selection of candidates. Two variables were
rated, using the eight-step rating scale adopted by the project: Academic Performance and Suitability as a Clinical Psychologist. Each university rater was asked to indicate the basis of his
ratings, e.g., credentials only, credentials plus interview, etc. Each rater was also asked to
indicate whether, before making the ratings, he had seen the student in previous academic years
and/or whether he had seen the student since he had arrived at the university that fall. Unfortunately, it was not possible to obtain these university predictions on all or even most of the students entering at that time. Furthermore, the number of students rated on the basis of any given
amount of information or personal contact was very small. Raters at some schools agreed very
closely with each other on their predictions while at other schools the raters showed almost no
agreement with each other. We assume that such differences were in part a function of the
amount of discussion between staff members about candidates.

For the 1947 Group

In the spring of 1947, the cooperating universities were asked to make predictions for the applicants whom they accepted for entrance into the program in the fall of 1947. This time ratings
were obtained on four variables: (a) Predicted Academic Performance, (b) Predicted Skill in
Diagnosis and Therapy, (c) Predicted Research Competence, and (d) Overall Promise as a Clinical Psychologist. Again each rater was asked to indicate the basis of his ratings. University
predictive ratings were obtained for only 60 of the 128 candidates assessed in the summer of
1947: some departments apparently forgot to return these ratings; one chairman declined to cooperate, stating that "it was unscientific even to attempt to make predictions of diagnostic and
therapeutic skill on the basis of the limited material available to the department at the time of
selection."

Objective Measures

The project collected many and varied objective test scores on all VA trainees studied. Table
B I-1 summarizes the tests used and the variables on which each was scored. Since it was obviously not practical to administer a comprehensive battery of all standardized tests which might
conceivably predict skill or performance as a clinical psychologist, tests were selected from each
of several areas.

Certain of the variables scored require an explanation. The VA Clinical Psychologist Key for
the Strong was developed by E. K. Strong, Jr. on the basis of data collected by this project, i.e.,
the test blanks completed in 1947 by 149 full time clinical psychologists. The five Kriedt Keys
(Kriedt, 1949) include keys for Clinical Psychologist, Experimental Psychologist, Guidance Psychologist, Industrial Psychologist and a general 1948 Psychologist Key.

The "Thrown" scores on the Strong were used as a possible measure of the ability to place

TABLE B I-1

OBJECTIVE TEST SCORES UTILIZED
AS PREDICTORS

	No. and Nature of Variables Scored	Available for Groups Entering in:		
		1946	1947	1948
Intelligence and Achievement				
Coop. General Culture Test	7 Conventional		(x)*	
Miller Analogies (Form G)	1 "	x	x	x
Chicago Tests of Primary Mental Abilities	6 "	x	x	
Interests				
Allport-Vernon Study of Values	6 "	x	x	x
Kuder Preference Record	9 "	x	(x)*	
Vocational Interest Blank (Strong)	30 "	x	x	x**
plus VA Clinical Psychologist		x	(x)*	x
plus 5 Kriedt Keys			(x)*	(x)*
plus 5 'Thrown' M-F		x	(x)*	
Personality				
Guilford-Martin Battery	13 Conventional	x	x	x
plus Facade (GAMIN only)			(x)*	x
Minnesota Multiphasic Personality Inventory	10 Conventional	x	x	
plus 7 Gough Keys			(x)*	
Total Number of Objective Scores	101			

*These scores were not available to the assessment staff.

**42 Strong Interest Scores were available for this experimental group.

oneself in the role of another. They were based on successive administrations of the Strong Blank as follows: the trainees, after answering the Blank for themselves, were instructed to answer each item on the test as they thought it would be answered by women in general; then, in a third administration, they were asked to answer each item as they thought it would be answered by men in general. These three sets of answers were each scored on the Strong Masculinity-Femininity Key. From the Masculinity scores for these three sets of answers, three derived scores were obtained. (a) The difference between a subject's Masculinity score and his Masculinity score when instructed to answer the test for women in general; (b) the difference between his Masculinity score and his score when answering the test for men in general, and (c) the sum of these two scores, i.e., the difference between his two Thrown scores.

The Facade Key was developed by Ernest Tupes on the basis of the differences between responses to the Guilford-Martin GAMIN test under normal instructions and responses under instructions to create as favorable an impression as possible. Seven empirical keys for the Minnesota Multiphasic Personality Inventory developed by Harrison Gough*, were also used in scoring the project's test blanks: these are Dominance, Social Status, Social Participation, Social Responsibility, Psychologist, Intellectual Functioning, and Graduate Student.

Several other objective tests were administered to the first assessment group (FAC). These were not repeated because it became quite clear that the testing time required for the objective tests was far in excess of that compatible with reasonable cooperativeness on the part of the subjects.

Scores on the Graduate Record Examination were collected for a part of the 1946-47 group of trainees. Since the GRE Psychology Test correlated .60 with the Miller Analogies Test and .60 and .54 with the Strong Psychologist and VA Clinical Psychologist Keys respectively, its overlap with the other tests was too great to justify the collection of further GRE data. No further analyses of GRE scores were made.

Semi-objective scoring techniques were also applied to the Rorschach and TAT protocols obtained in the assessment programs. The Monroe Inspection Technique was applied to the 1948 Wellesley assessment cases. We also made use of experimental manuals for scoring the Rorschach and TAT, developed by the companion VA Research Project on the Selection of Psychiatrists (at the Menninger Foundation).

Clinical Measures - The Assessment Programs

The major characteristics of the assessment programs used in this project are the following: (a) the use of a wide variety of different types of diagnostic procedures; (b) the use of ratings based on practical, economical combinations of procedures--in only a few instances were ratings based upon a single procedure by itself, (c) the use of both independent individual ratings and the pooled ratings agreed upon at a staff conference, (d) almost uninterrupted evaluation and observation lasting over several days.

Except for the second characteristic above, these assessment programs maintained the same general features as the major Station S program reported in the Assessment of Men (1948). One major difference, however, lay in the relative emphasis upon qualitative formulations in the Office of Strategic Services program as contrasted with the emphasis on ratings in this research program.

Three pilot assessment programs were held during the first year of the project. They served

---

*These experimental Keys were made available to the project by Dr. Gough.

primarily as testing grounds for procedures later to be used in the major assessment program
in the summer of 1947. Because the nature of each program and the rating scale used in it differed from one of these preliminary programs to the next, it was not possible to combine the
data obtained from these three programs for validational analyses. Furthermore, the subjects
assessed during the academic year, 1946-47, ranged in experience from first year graduate students with no previous clinical training to experienced clinicians who needed but a single year
to finish their doctoral degrees. Such a heterogeneous group was hardly a representative sample
of the applicants which a university department must ordinarily evaluate.

The evolution of our ratings scales throughout the first year parallelled a change in emphasis
concerning the objectives of assessment as we moved from one pilot program to the next. We
began the year by seeking to describe the trainee solely in terms of a few personality variables
judged to be related to future performance as a clinical psychologist in addition to making predictions of specific job competences. We came gradually to the conclusion that we were unwise to
trust our hypotheses about the personality traits likely to be found in potentially outstanding
trainees and clinicians. Thus while we continued to make predictions of future performance in
each assessment program, we eventually developed a rating scale with the added objective of
describing the present behavior and personality structure of the trainee. In case it turned out
that our predictions and evaluations had little or no validity, these descriptive measures could
also be treated as predictor variables.

The other major lesson gained from the three preliminary assessment programs was a necessity for close attention to staff and student tolerant thresholds. Since the students at these assessment programs knew that the evaluation of their assessment performances would have no
direct effect upon their professional careers, many were less than enthusiastic in their participation. The majority were as cooperative as could be expected under the trying conditions imposed upon them. However, it became quite clear that the physical and emotional tolerances of
trainees had to be respected. Similarly, although the staff members applied themselves to their
assessment tasks with a concentration of energy which was "above and beyond the call of duty,"
it became increasingly apparent that our earlier assessment plans underestimated the demands
imposed by the continuous evaluation process and overestimated the energy capacity of the staff.

After each of the preliminary assessment programs, two critiques were held. A member of
the staff or a visiting psychologist met with the students and in a permissive atmosphere sought
to obtain fairly frank reactions to the assessment experiences as seen by the students. Following this, each assessment staff met to criticize the assessment procedure and rationale, and to
make recommendations for future assessment programs. The opinions expressed in both of
these critiques played a major role in the revision and (we hope) improvement of each successive
assessment program.

The three preliminary assessment programs also brought out the necessity for organizing an
assessment staff which would include experts in each of the various diagnostic procedures and
demonstrated the need for training and experience with the rating scales.

The 1947 Ann Arbor Assessment Program

We shall now attempt to provide the reader with a fairly complete description of our major assessment program, which was carried out in Ann Arbor in the summer of 1947. There follows:
(a) a brief description of the physical arrangements; (b) a description of the rating scales used by
staff members in recording their clinical judgments, (c) a statement of the sequence of experience
of a candidate and (d) the sequence of duties of staff members. This statement is much less detailed than the Manual of Operating Procedures prepared for use by the staff but will, we believe,

serve to give the reader an adequate understanding of the assessment process.

The Ann Arbor assessment program was carried out during July and August, 1947. The professional staff consisted of 30 clinicians, including two VA psychiatrists and several VA psychologists. Other staff members were drawn from five different universities and several other institutions. This resulted in considerable diversity of background, training, and bias.

The students assessed were VA trainees who had already been accepted for training by one of the cooperating universities. They came to Ann Arbor in six successive classes of 24 each at nine-day intervals, each class remaining for seven days. There was no systematic assignment of students to classes, except that as far as possible each candidate was permitted to come at the time most convenient for him.

Each class was divided into six teams of four students each. Each student team was studied intensively by a staff team of three members.

The project was housed in a sorority house and a smaller residence previously converted for dormitory use. The sorority house provided living quarters for all students and a part of the staff. It also provided dining facilities for both staff and students. The other house served as staff headquarters. Interviews and other procedures were conducted at both houses.

The Rating Scales

As has been noted above, the term "assessment" refers to the making of clinical judgments, descriptive, evaluative, or predictive, on the basis of a variety of techniques and procedures. In order that such judgments be amenable to accepted tests of reliability and validity, it was necessary that they be quantified. This was accomplished by the use of an elaborate rating scale. Because the ratings based on this scale constitute the basic data of assessment, the scale is reproduced in full in Appendix I A.

This rating scale has three parts: Scale A was intended to cover primarily phenotypic variables, descriptive of the subject as seen by the staff at the time of assessment. It was constructed with the help of Raymond Cattell on the basis of his several factor studies of personality ratings and the final edition was designed to cover 22 variables. Although these variables were selected as primarily descriptive of overt aspects of behavior, some of them, e.g., "Imaginativeness" could be rated only on the basis of inference from observed behavior.

Scale B was intended to provide judgments of more genotypic variables, i.e., evaluative judgments of broader underlying variables, again as seen by the staff at the time of assessment. It includes ten variables.

Scale C includes a list of 11 skill variables on which staff members were asked to make predictive judgments relative to the future performance of each candidate as a clinical psychologist. The Scale C variables represent a kind of job-analysis of the profession of clinical psychologist.

Before rating the candidate on these variables, the staff made ratings on Variable 0, Degree of Liking. This item was included for two reasons. First, we were interested in the variable itself, and second, it seemed likely that staff members would be more inclined to make objective ratings on other traits if they had first been permitted an overt expression of the degree of their own liking or disliking of the candidate.

All ratings were made on an 8-point scale, with a suggested distribution of ratings as follows:

8. Highest   3% of a population of first year graduate students.

7. Next   7%   "   "   "

6. Next   15%   "   "   "

5. Next   25%   "   "   "

4. Next   25%   "   "   "

3. Next   15%   "   "   "

2. Next   7%   "   "   "

1. Lowest   3%   "   "   "

For Scale C, the raters were asked to use a reference population of VA trainees five years after assessment. Staff members were instructed to rate anyone who they believed would fail in the training program a 1, 2, or 3 on item 42 "Overall."

In the case of Scale A items, a rating of "1" always refers to the left end of the scale. For items on Scales B and C, a rating of "1" is low or poor and a rating of "8" high or good.

The Candidate's Schedule

With this background let us now follow a typical student, John, through his assessment.

Late in June, John received a letter from the project stating the objectives of the research and asking him to participate in the assessment program. He returned a form on which he had checked the various dates when he could come to Ann Arbor. The Project assigned him to a class and one summer morning he came to the sorority house from his home in New York. When all his classmates had arrived, the Project Director gave the group a welcoming speech, indicating the general nature of the program. Subjects were told what was expected of them and assured that strict professional confidence would be maintained for all personal material gathered by the project.

In the time remaining before lunch, John and the rest of the group took several objective tests. At lunch, as at every meal during the first five days, each team of four students sat at a specified table, along with any two of the staff who would not be evaluating that team. In the afternoon, the class continued to take group tests. Before he had been at the center for three days, John had taken the following tests: Thematic Apperception Test (ten cards), the project's form of the Sentence Completion Test, the Miller Analogies Test, the Chicago Tests of Primary Mental Abilities, the Allport-Vernon Study of Values, the Strong Vocational Interest Blank, the Guilford-Martin Battery (Inventory of Factors STDCR, Inventory of Factors GAMIN, Personnel Inventory I), and the Minnesota Multiphasic Personality Inventory. During the first day or perhaps the next, John was called out to take the Rorschach Test and the Bender-Gestalt Test, each at a separate session.

That first afternoon, John had an "Initial Interview" lasting one hour. From the questions John realized that the interviewer had little information about him, although John did not know that the interviewer knew only what was contained in his "credentials file," i. e., the materials he had submitted with his application to the university. This included the correspondence between himself and his university, the transcripts of his college grades, his Civil Service Form 57 on which he had applied for employment as a P-1 trainee, and letters of recommendation submitted in his behalf. This initial interview, while searching, was not particularly deep because the interviewer was careful not to arouse anxieties in John, whom he would not interview again.

In the evening of the first day, John filled out a Biographical Inventory, which contained over a hundred multiple-choice items about background, personal history, experiences and preferences. He also received an outline for an autobiography he was to write within the next two days (cf. Appendix I E and F).

For several hours on the third day, John took more objective tests. These included the Kuder Preference Record and the Cooperative General Culture Test. He also took the Strong Test twice more: once, he filled it out as he thought it would be answered by "women in general" and finally, as he thought it would be answered by "men in general." Although John did not know it, the scores from these three tests were not made available to the assessment staff but were filed away for later independent analyses.

Late that afternoon, John had an appointment with his "Intensive Interviewer," the staff member whom he would get to know best and the person who got to know John best. This interview was thorough and probing. They discussed his early life, his parents, his school and work records, his interest in clinical psychology. At the end of the two hours, John felt there was nothing about him which had not been covered. From the nature of the interviewer's questions, John correctly guessed that the interviewer had carefully examined his credentials, his autobiography, his Biographical Inventory, his test scores and the other materials on which he had spent so many hours during the previous days.

Since John had no appointments the next day, he and several of his classmates went to Detroit. After sharing a day of sightseeing and relaxation with him, together with the previous three days of stress in the novel assessment situation, his companions were old friends to him.

John's schedule on the fifth day looked very different from any previous one. Immediately after breakfast, he and seven classmates were seated around a table. Opposite them were six staff members with clipboards and pencils. In a relaxed and informal tone, one of them said to the students:

In your work thus far you have kindly provided the staff with a great deal of extremely important and useful personal information in the form of test scores, autobiographical data, projective materials, and interview data. Unfortunately, however, with the exception of the interview, the gathering of all this material has been done under circumstances which provided a limited opportunity to see you in action.

This might have been accomplished by allowing you and the staff members to mingle freely whenever the occasion permitted, but allowing this would have produced unequal opportunity for observation and would have invalidated much of the work being attempted here.

In order to 'control' the amount and kind of observation by staff members, therefore, the research design provides for a series of 'Standard' situations in which the staff will have more or less equal opportunity to see you be active. These situations are of three kinds--a group, or team situation, in which from four to eight of you will participate jointly; dual situations, in which you and another person will be involved; and finally, an individual situation, in which each of you will be asked to participate alone, in the presence of staff members only.

Some of the situations are easy, some rather difficult; all of them are fairly brief. The staff asks only your continued cooperation in this, which we believe will be a more interesting phase of the program.

The staff member then set an imaginary problem for the group to solve in this <u>Discussion Situation Test</u>:

You are the members of a committee of eminent citizens called together from different parts of the country by Henry Ford's executor to decide what should be done with $100,000,000 which, according to Ford's will, is to be used for the purpose of 'Attacking a basic cause of human suffering in the world today.

Your task is to reach a group decision as to how the money should be spent. Since the members of this group are eminent citizens who probably represent a number of different points of view, you will, of course, want to hear each man's opinions. You will be given five minutes to prepare a written statement on the way you feel the money should be spent.

After each man has been given a chance to read his idea, there will be time for discussing the specific proposals. At the end of 30 minutes, we should like to hear a majority report (and, if you wish, minority reports) giving your specific recommendations as to how the money should be spent.

Finally, at the conclusion of your report you are asked to discuss openly and arrive at a decision on which member of the group has contributed most to furthering the discussion.

Any questions? The meeting is in your hands.

After a self-conscious chuckle, John's friend Tom immediately organized the group, but Bob presented the most cogent suggestion. The staff watched them with interest, making notes from time to time as the discussion continued.

For their next appointment, John and Tom met together. A staff member greeted them and gave them the following orientation:

You are asked to participate in a series of interpersonal situations involving yourself and another person. You will be given directions which describe the situation in which you find yourself and who the other person is. Read these directions over twice and then enter the room to begin the situation.

As he listened, John saw, through the partly open door, two chairs half facing each other in front of a group of six staff members. If, after he had read his instructions, the staff member had told him this procedure was called "Improvisations" (cf. Bronfenbrenner and Newcomb, 1948), he would have agreed. His directions were these:

You are the Superintendent of Schools in a community with a population of five or six thousand. Mr. Green is a teacher in your high school. He is about 35 years of age and a bachelor. You have heard such persistent rumors regarding Mr. Green's sexual conduct, that you have decided something must be done. You have called Mr. Green to your office.

Tom, in the role of Mr. Green, was provided with an even less structured set of instructions:

You are a public high school teacher in a community of five or six thousand people. You are about 35 years of age and unmarried. You have just had word that the Superintendent of Schools would like to see you in his office.

The two students went in before the staff and uneasily took their places. The Superintendent brought up the rumors only to have Mr. Green become indignant and resign. The staff paid close attention but gave few clues as to their reactions. Tom and John left the room to receive their next instructions. After three different situations with Tom, John participated in three more with Jerry.

Lunch was spent in a joking spirit as the students exchanged descriptions of what they had done in these odd assignments. In the afternoon, John's team met the same staff group in the back yard. Before them were 16 especially cast cement blocks of assorted shapes and colors, all heavy! The students read together the following instructions for the Block Situation Test.

DIRECTIONS FOR TEAM FOR BLOCK GAME

(Four minutes for reading and discussion)

1. This game is played by a team of four individuals.

2. The object of the game is to place all of the blocks into 4 groups so that each of the blocks in any group is similar to all of the other blocks in that group. The score in the game is the total number of moves needed to accomplish this objective. The lower the score, the better.

3. Note the varying characteristics of the blocks which you see in front of you.

4. The way to start is as follows: You will note that one block has already been assigned to group 3. Try any one of the other blocks by moving it into group 3. If the placement is correct, the examiner will so indicate; if it is incorrect, you will be told to bring it back to the starting position. After you have succeeded in getting at least one additional block properly matched in group 3, you may proceed as follows: if you try a block and it is incorrect, you may either return it to the starting position, or you may try it in some other group.

5. Note: only one block may be moved at a time.

6. You will be allowed 30 seconds to make each move. If you do not move a block before the 30 seconds have elapsed, one move will be counted against you--you will have lost that move.

7. The blocks may be moved in any manner you wish except that they must not be dropped or thrown.

8. You are competing against all other teams from this and previous assessment classes. Get the lowest scores possible.

9. Note: all talking done by the team must be loud enough so that the observing staff may hear what is being said.

The next ten minutes were occupied by the strenuous physical exertion of carrying the blocks. Frequently John felt frustrated by the leader's impersonal verdict that a move was "incorrect." When it was all over, the staff asked questions about possible groupings of the blocks and about students' reactions to this situation. After a shower, John went on to his next appointment. He heard the following instructions for the Expressive Movement Situation Test:*

For this situation, you will first read the poem on this sheet. Read it carefully to get the feeling which the poet is trying to convey, that is, the feeling of this poem as it seems to you. In a few minutes, you will be asked, in the other room, to try to convey or express your feelings to this poem without using your voice. There are no other restrictions. You may use your body in any manner and as freely as you wish. Most people use at least three to four minutes for this task.

The poem shown him, "In Excelsis," is frankly emotional. When this unique task had been completed, the staff member spoke to him again:

John, the second part of this situation does not differ greatly from the first. The principal difference is that, whereas in the first part your stimulus was an entire poem, in this part the

*William Soskin was primarily responsible for the conception and development of this test.

stimuli will be single words presented individually. I will say a word, and as soon as I do, you will begin reacting--as you did last time--trying to convey the <u>feeling</u> which this word has for you. You are to continue as long as new feelings come to you. Most people use 1.5 to 2 minutes. Are there any questions?

John heard the word "Success" and saw it on a card. His expression of what this word conveyed to him was followed by the presentation of other words, one at a time: Mother, Father, Defeat, Authority, Hatred, and Funny. Then the staff member suggested that he be seated and quietly inquired: "Is there anything you would like to tell us about your performance either on individual words or on the poem?" This short discussion was terminated by a congenial reference to the <u>Party</u> that evening.

John probably spent the next hour with his teammates, preparing a skit burlesquing the assessment program. After dinner, the whole staff gathered with the students for an evening of relaxation, featuring skits and spontaneous singing.

After breakfast on the sixth and last morning, John sleepily dragged himself to the group testing room for his last written work. He was told that he was to complete a sociometric questionnaire concerning his reactions to his classmates and that he was to rate himself and his three teammates. The final assignment was the hardest: he was to prepare frank character sketches about the same three teammates.

John barely had time to complete these tasks before his final individual appointment with the staff member he had seen in the two hour interview. Although John went to this appointment with the hope of learning the staff's opinion of him, he came away relatively satisfied with a small amount of rather innocuous data. The final interview had also included a discussion of two or three topics barely touched in the previous, more intensive session.

John next joined the entire class in the living room and recognized the leader as a visiting psychologist who had not been on any staff team. The leader conducted a therapeutic critique which permitted the students to complain about the food and say they should have been told to wear old clothes to the Block Test. One student protested about the attitude of his interviewer but received no support from his colleagues.

The program closed with a farewell talk by the director, who repeated the assurance that the findings would be kept in strict confidence. The director thanked the group for their cooperation and shook hands with John as he left to catch his train back to New York.

The Staff Schedule

What was the staff doing when they were not observing John and Tom? Let us follow an interviewer through his duties for one class. On the afternoon of the day the students arrived, he conducted Initial Interviews with two students. Before each, he had spent an hour or more examining the credentials file, on the basis of which he had rated the student on Scales B and C of the rating scale. (There seemed little point in attempting to rate a person's behavior on Scale A variables before seeing him.) After each of the unstructured initial interviews, he made notes and rated each candidate on all scales, A, B, and C.

The next two days each interviewer had free. He returned on the fourth day to make a series of evaluations of the two candidates for whom he served as Intensive Interviewer. In this sequence, he was evaluating the students whom the <u>other</u> interviewer on his staff team had seen in Initial Interviews two days before. (Similarly, his two initial interviewees were now seen by his fellow interviewer.) For each student he examined, in order, (a) the credentials file, (b) the objective test profile and answer sheets, (c) the autobiography and the biographical inventory and (d) the projective test protocols and their interpretations. After studying each of these four sets of materials, he made ratings on Scales B and C. Thus each of the four sets of ratings was based on a cumulative collection of material, e.g., credentials file plus objective test profiles. However, he filed each set of ratings before making his next set in order to reduce any tendency to "defend" the previous ratings.

The objective tests had been scored and scores reported on profile forms. The projective tests were administered as follows: each student took both the Rorschach and the Bender-Gestalt Tests individually. Each was interpreted and summarized by the administrator of the test. The Thematic Apperception Test and the Sentence Completion Test were administered as group measures. Various staff members analyzed them. No staff member analyzed more than one projective test for any one subject. In addition to the qualitative interpretation, the projective analyst made ratings on the basis of each projective protocol plus a few items of basic identifying data, e.g., age, education, religon, etc. Thus the four complete sets of ratings were available, each based solely on one of the four projective techniques.

For half the students in each class, the person who had interpreted the Rorschach Test subsequently studied all four projective tests and interpretations for the purpose of integrating their several findings. This "Projective Integrator" wrote up the synthesis and made another set of ratings.

The interviewer usually spent about four hours preparing for the intensive interview. Like the initial interview this was unstructured. Each staff member was free to ask any questions and use whatever interviewing techniques he regarded as useful in securing a better understanding of the candidate. Because of the relatively large amount of information about the candidates already reviewed, these two hour interviews tended to be somewhat more penetrating than the initial interviews. After this interview, the interviewer again rated the student on all scales.

At this point in the schedule, the students rested and the staff worked. Each staff team held a conference to discuss each of their four students. In addition to the two interviewers, there was a third person on each team. For half of the teams, this was the "Projective Integrator." For the other teams, he was known as the "Pre-Conference" Rater, a staff member who had studied all of the paper and pencil materials available to the Intensive Interviewer, taken all together, and made a single set of ratings on all scales. Note that in both kinds of teams, the various participants came to the conference familiar with different but overlapping groups of materials about each case.

These preliminary conferences had two purposes: the first was to discuss the case and by subjectively pooling the three individual and independent ratings on each variable, to arrive at a pooled or team rating; the second was to provide for a full exchange of information and opinion about each case--with both the Initial and the Intensive Interviewers reporting on their interviews. In these conferences the Intensive Interviewer always reported last, so that the other reports would not be lost in the shadow of the more complete knowledge available to the Intensive Interviewer.

The next day, each staff team observed its four students in situation tests. Because the members already knew so much about these students, it is likely that these observations were strongly influenced by previous information about the candidates. In assessment jargon they were said to be "contaminated" on these four cases.

In order to determine the predictive value of situation tests as independent procedures, these four students were also observed by another staff team which had not seen either the students or the students' records. This second staff team was, therefore, "uncontaminated" by any previously seen materials.

Although the staff did not make separate ratings after each situation test, they usually kept detailed notes. The next day, after the four kinds of situation tests and the informal evening party, each staff team made ratings of the four students whom they had not seen previous to the situation tests. The three staff members took their individual Uncontaminated ratings to a pooling conference and arrived at a set of "Uncontaminated Pooled" ratings on each case. This completed their evaluation of those four cases.

Much remained to be done, however, with the four cases on whom they were "contaminated," the four about whom they had held their preliminary pooling conference. For each student, each staff member made a set of ratings based on his total impression up to and including situation tests. The interviewers then held Final Interviews with the students whom they had first seen in Intensive Interviews. The substance of the final interview was reported to the other two team members. The staff members then examined the tabulations of the sociometric questionnaire and studied the teammates' ratings of each as well as the students' self-ratings. They also read the character sketches to determine how each student appeared in the eyes of his teammates and to estimate the ability to judge others displayed by the author of each sketch. Also, for the first time, staff members were permitted to examine all the ratings which had previously been made on each case. These included the individual and pooled ratings of the uncontaminated team, those of each projectivist, and each of their own successive earlier ratings. In the light of this new mass of data, they were permitted to make revisions in the "Contaminated Situations" ratings they had just previously made. These last, or Final Individual ratings were then taken to the Final Team Conference at which the staff team made their best judgment about each case in the light of the entire week's assessment and agreed on Final Pooled ratings. The assessment "week" was not over, however, until each interviewer had written a report on each of the two cases he had interviewed intensively. This comprehensive report considered many aspects of the person: his emotional life, his intellectual functioning, his relations with others, his motivation for clinical psychology. From a research point of view, its most important function was to record qualifications about certain ratings: e. g., the staff might rate a certain case with the understanding that he would soon be having psychotherapy. Obviously, this consideration would influence the staff's predictions on Scale C variables. Again, when a certain variable was difficult to rate because the definition did not fit the observed personality structure, the nature of the difficulty was reported in the assessment report.

It should be pointed out that every staff member adhered to this rigorous schedule of ratings and rated on every variable even if he felt his rating was little better than a random guess. Only with this whole-hearted cooperation from the staff was it possible to obtain data satisfactory for the statistical analyses to be reported in later sections. Some of the staff members had had previous experience with the rating scales in the pilot assessments; the others were found to begin using the scales with the first class of trainees after but minimal indoctrination. Originally we had considered using the first class for training purposes only but in retrospect it was judged that the data collected for this class were sufficiently comparable with those of the second class to justify their inclusion in the analyses. Actually, it is likely that the staff's conceptions of the rated variables continued to change slightly throughout the summer.

Cost of Assessment

This assessment program was admittedly an expensive one. It was designed to serve a research function--not as a model for practical use by individual institutions. The aim was to find how well each technique functioned, independently, and how much it contributed to the final evaluation based on all techniques.

The actual operating cost of this program was about $275 per student. This included travel, board and room for the candidate and salaries of the staff during the assessment period. Staff salaries amounted to about 60% of the total, in spite of the fact that staff members worked an average of about 60 hours per week! The above figures do not include staff costs of designing the program, developing instruments, etc. An assessment program utilizing only certain selected procedures would, of course, be less expensive.

In terms of staff time invested, the projective tests were the most expensive technique used; over 30% of the total staff hours were spent in their administration, interpretation, and in making ratings based on them. The next largest investment of staff time, approximately 25%, was in the group of situation tests. Nearly 20% of the staff time was spent in staff conferences discussing the case and arriving at pooled team ratings. The remainder of the staff time was spent in interviews, in the individual analysis of other clinical materials, and in making individual ratings.

Sociometric Ratings

In addition to the approximately 1,000 staff ratings made on each assessed trainee, we developed a series of scores from the trainees' responses on the sociometric questionnaire (cf. Appendix I B). Because teammates' ratings had showed promising correlations with preliminary criterion measures, the sociometric data were further analyzed. Sociometric scores were derived on the basis of the number of times each trainee was chosen by his fellow trainees in response to each of the separate sociometric questions as well as to various combinations of questions. Scores included: (a) total number of positive choices, (b) total number of negative choices, (c) the difference between these two totals, (d) the sum of these two totals, (e) the total number of different people making positive choices of the trainee, (f) the total number of different people making negative choices of the trainee, (g) the number of different individuals to whom each subject gave positive choices, (h) the number of different individuals to whom each subject gave negative choices, and finally, (i) the sum of these last two scores. These data were subsequently treated in the same way as the scores for the objective tests.

The Assessment Staff

The reader may form his own impressions about the qualifications of the assessment staff by examining the list of names earlier presented. In seeking members for the assessment staff, we kept several criteria in mind: previous experience on assessment staffs, reputation as a diagnostician, and ability to cooperate under the trying conditions of assessment. While we were unable to arrange for the participation of some psychologists whom we very much wanted to have on the staff, we were very much pleased with the interest displayed by most of the staff members and with their willingness, in some cases, to make personal sacrifices to serve on the staff.

The 1948 Wellesley Abbreviated
Assessment Program

For reasons already indicated, the planning staff decided that the assessment program during 1948 would be on a much abbreviated scale, one which was sufficiently practical and economical for possible use by any university department. These considerations limited the materials available on each candidate to "paper and pencil" records, test scores and protocols, and an autobiography, all of which could be obtained for each candidate at geographically distributed testing centers. A new factor which differentiated the subjects of this program from previous groups studied was the fact that they had all been tested under selection conditions, i.e., before they knew whether they had been accepted or rejected for the VA training program. In essence then, the Wellesely assessment involved the clinical evaluation and rating of candidates solely on the basis of the kinds of materials available to the Intensive Interviewer before his interview in the 1947 program, i.e., an assessment without benefit of any type of face-to-face contact between staff and candidate.

No attempt will be made here to delineate the detailed research design followed at Wellesley but the major emphases will be indicated. In addition to the above noted major differences, it was decided to use only Parts B and C of the rating scale. (A new variable, No. 28b, "Motivation to Help People" was added to Part B.) There seemed little reason to collect additional data on the degree to which the traits on Part A could be rated from paper and pencil materials. This change alone markedly reduced the amount of staff time required. A staff team of three studied three students, but before the single pooling conference, each of the staff members had seen all of the material available for the candidate. This procedure also tended to reduce the length of time devoted to staff conferences and arriving at final ratings.

The Wellesley program appeared to provide a unique opportunity to collect information on several important questions which could not be answered from previously collected data: two of these were "Is there any effect of the order in which specific materials became available to the staff members?" and "What is the relative contribution of different tests or techniques of the same general type?". During the summer of 1947, staff members had all been given materials in a standard order, i.e., credentials, objective test profile, autobiographical materials and projective materials. Furthermore, they had been given the scores on all objective tests in one block, all projective test materials in another block, etc.

The actual materials available for each applicant in the Wellesley program included:

1. Credential File (transcript, letters, Form 57, etc.)

2. Autobiographical Materials

   a. Biographical Inventory
   b. Autobiography

3. Objective Test Scores (and answer sheets)

   a. Miller Analogies Test
   b. Strong Vocational Interest Blank (complete profile)
   c. Guilford-Martin (STDCR, GAMIN, O. Ag. Co.)
   d. Allport-Vernon Scale of Values

4. Projective Techniques

   a. Sentence Completion
   b. Rorschach (Previously scored by Munroe Inspection Technique) For a few cases, this was not available and the Draw-a-Person Test, which had been included in the test battery for experimental purposes, was substituted.

With the limited number of available cases, it was not feasible to try all possible combinations and sequences of techniques. As before, the decision to test or not to test a given combination or sequence was based on the practical consideration: would it be reasonable as an actual selective procedure? Thus, for instance, we did not collect additional evidence on the validity of predictions based on credentials alone, or on the Rorschach alone but in each case staff members first rated on a combination of credentials plus one other technique, e.g., Rorschach or Autobiography or a minimum objective battery such as the Miller and Strong. At the next level, the candidate was re-rated on the basis of credentials plus all projectives or all autobiographical materials. Finally, he was rated by each member of the staff team on all materials and a pooling conference was held to arrive at final ratings.

The third question on which we sought to collect data was: "Do the pooled ratings reached by a conference of three staff members predict better than pooled ratings from a team of two?" All cases were rated by three staff members but half of them were pooled by a team of three and half by a team of two staff members.

In addition to assessing all accepted P-1 applicants for whom full test data were available, the staff also evaluated a group of applicants favorably considered but eventually rejected by certain universities. This permitted a tentative answer to a fourth question: "Are some rejected applicants assessed as better training risks than some of those accepted?"

Finally, to estimate the agreement between predictions from this abbreviated assessment procedure and the longer 1947 one, it was decided to reassess 24 cases previously evaluated during the summer of 1947. Members of the assessment staff were informed that the group being assessed included rejects and also "re-do" cases, but did not know in which category any given case belonged.

Between August 20th and September 3rd, 1948, our staff (all with experience in one or more previous programs) assessed 143 cases representing 28 institutions. Of these, 98 were accepted P-1 applicants, 21 were rejected P-1 applicants, and 24 were cases previously assessed in the summer of 1947.

Although the Wellesley assessment program involved by far the lightest (i.e., most nearly normal) working schedule, staff members were not happy at having to assess candidates without seeing them. As a group, they missed the interview greatly and even after arriving at final ratings frequently expressed a desire to see what the person was really like. Some even bemoaned the lack of a photograph of the candidate. However, because they realized the importance of determining the actual validity of an "assessment without candidates," every staff member worked faithfully at his task and important data were collected.

The distributions of final pooled ratings on Overall Suitability (A 42) for the accepted and rejected applicants are shown in Table B I-2.

The 21 rejected applicants assessed were named by four of the larger training institutions as persons who were runners-up for selection but as far as we could learn, these applicants were not accepted for admission at any institution. As will be seen from Table B I-2, these rejects as a group were seen as poorer risks by the assessment staff. Note that 12 of the 21, or 57% of the rejects were rated an overall "3" or below as compared with only 27 of 98 or 27% of the acceptees so rated.

This is encouraging but note also that three out of the 21, or 14% of the rejects received an overall assessment of 6, 7, or 8, as compared with only 18% of the accepted applicants receiving these higher overall ratings. Either some promising applicants are not being recommended for training or these particular applicants who looked promising "on paper" have serious liabilities, evident to the rejecting university but not noted by the assessment staff on the basis of materials available in this type of assessment.

It was the general opinion of our Wellesley staff that the 1948 group of assessees were not quite so promising as groups of trainees previously seen in assessment. This judgment, however, is not reflected in the distribution of final overall ratings. It is true that the Wellesley distribution of Final Overall ratings is skewed, with more below than above average ratings, but

TABLE B I-2

FINAL OVERALL RATINGS (A 42) OF P-1 APPLICANTS
ASSESSED AT WELLESLEY (Summer 1948)

Final Pooled Rating on Overall Suitability (A 42)	Accepted	Rejected	Total
8	1	0	1
7	2	1	3
6	16	2	18
5	19	1	20
4	33	5	38
3	20	10	30
2	5	1	6
1	2	1	3
Total	98	21	119
Mean	4.26	3.67	
S.D.	1.31	1.36	

C.R. =1.78 (The probability of obtaining a positive CR of this size or larger by chance is .04)

it is remarkably similar to the distribution of pre-interview ratings for the summer of 1947. Apparently, an assessment staff finds it difficult to assign really high ratings before a face-to-face contact.

The general opinion that the 1948 group of trainees was not quite so good as former ones was no doubt in part due to the absence of personal contacts with the candidates. Two other factors probably contributed to the impression: (a) the 1948 group was on the average about one and a half years younger than the 1947 group and consequently appeared less mature, particularly in their autobiographies; (b) it must be remembered that the 1948 group took the test battery and wrote their autobiographies before they were admitted to graduate school, i.e., under an actual selection situation. It is not surprising therefore that many of the autobiographies were not so full or so rich as those obtained from trainees in the 1947 program.

Analyses of distributions of personality test scores suggest that there was a somewhat greater tendency for applicants to "fake good" when taking tests in the actual selection situation, but it did not appear great enough to interfere seriously with the clinical evaluation of resulting test profiles. During the winter of 1947, we had developed a "facade key" for the Guilford-Martin, which showed considerable promise in evaluating the degree of "faking good" on this test, and each candidate's score on this key was available to the staff members.

The 1949 Reassessment

During July and August, 1949, 20 VA trainees at the University of Michigan served as staff members in reassessing 100 cases from the 1947 group on the basis of data contained in the assessment files. They made ratings on the basis of a study of: credentials, objective test scores, autobiographical materials, and projective tests. For each case two judges made three successive ratings on increasing units of material before coming to the pooling conference; the two other raters examined all these materials in any order desired and made a single set of ratings before the conference. These two staff roles corresponded to the Intensive Interviewer before his interview and the Situationist or Pre-Conference rater in the 1947 schedule respectively. The entire rating scale (including parts A, B and C) was used in this program.

The second part of this reassessment program, the intensive study of ratings based on projective protocols, has already been described in Chapter A II. Findings growing out of both aspects of this program will be reported in Chapter D IV.

CHAPTER B II

ANALYSES OF PREDICTION MEASURES

This chapter is primarily concerned with the reliability of the predictor measures and the interrelationships among them. A factor analysis of the 42 variables rated by assessment staffs identifies ten factors contributing to the intercorrelations among the ratings, these ten first-order factors are later reduced to five second-order factors. Next, attention is given to the agreement between the ratings made by different judges but based on the same materials; in general, there was better agreement on general or global variables than on more specific descriptive ones. There follows an analysis of the relationships between the Final Pooled assessment ratings and those made at earlier stages on the basis of more limited materials. In a sense, these findings may be regarded as indicating the relative weights which staff members, in arriving at their Final Pooled judgment, implicitly assigned to the data provided by the several procedures. Evidence is presented to indicate that assessment ratings are in part a function of the materials or procedures on which they are based, e. g. , mean ratings tend to be less laudatory when based on procedures not providing an opportunity for personal interaction between the candidate and staff members. The last part of the chapter reports the generally low intercorrelations between assessment ratings and 82 objective test scores.

University Predictions

The reliabilities of the predictions made by university departments for applicants accepted in the spring of 1947 are presented in Table B II-1. The degree of agreement between ratings by different university members on the same student tended to be low. Of the 60 cases for whom these ratings were made, only 33 were for trainees who were not known to the department at the time of their application. The university raters agreed less well with each other than did the Initial and Intensive Interviewers in the assessment program, when their ratings were based solely on the credentials file. However, the assessment staff had a common frame of reference for interpreting the rating scale itself and the competences to be rated. While the agreement between the median department ratings and the final assessment ratings is fairly good for the total population of 60, it is quite low for the 33 cases not previously known to the university staff. The considerable disagreement between these predictions based on the credential file suggests the possibility of technical deficiencies in the selection systems then in use by departments. The validity of these university predictions, however, appears to be reasonably high (cf. Chapter D II).

The Assessment Ratings

Factor Analysis

A factor analysis* was made of the 42 variables used in the 1947 assessment program. The data were the Final Pooled ratings for each of the 128 men.

---

*This factor analysis was carried out by Mr. John Mellinger at the Psychometric Laboratory of the University of Chicago under the guidance of Dr. L. L. Thurstone. We are grateful to them for their assistance.

TABLE B II-1

PREDICTIONS BY UNIVERSITY DEPARTMENTS: THEIR
RELIABILITY AND THEIR CORRELATION WITH
ASSESSMENT RATINGS (Summer 1947)

With respect to the Prediction of:	Estimated Rater-Rater Reliability (N=60)	Comparable interjudge agreement of Assess-ment Ratings by Initial and Intensive Inter-viewers, each based on credentials only (N=127)
Academic Success	.35	.53
Diagnosis and Therapy	.21	.33*
Research	.26	.49
Overall	.23	.48

With respect to the Prediction of:	Correlations of Median Staff Ratings with Final Assessment Ratings	
	All cases for whom Department ratings were available (N=60)	Cases in which candidates were "not known" to Department staff (N=33)
Academic Success	.60	.34
Diagnosis and Therapy	.32	.21
Research	.53	.36
Overall	.38	.27

*Diagnosis alone.

Product-moment correlations were computed between the ratings on each of the 42 variables. The resulting correlational matrices are presented in Appendix III A. Before factoring, the signs of the correlations for the following variables were reflected to maximize the number of positive signs: 1, 2, 3, 6, 10, 16, 17, 18, 19, 20, 25. After six factors were extracted by the group method, three more were taken out by the centroid method. During the process of rotation, one factor appeared to be a residual factor. However, when it became apparent that the other factors omitte a considerable portion of the variance in several variables, this factor, I, was set orthogonal to the others and became the most general of the first-order factors. The oblique factor matrices and the intercorrelations among factors (for both first and second order factors) are shown in Appendix III B.

Before attempting to interpret the rotated factors, we would remind both ourselves and the reader that these factors are based on ratings of one group of persons (students) by another group of persons (staff). It is entirely possible, therefore, that the resulting factors are as much a function of the staff's mode of perceiving others as they are of the personalities of the candidates assessed. In one sense, the factors may be regarded as the common and perhaps implicit dimensions used by the staff in the assessment process.

Interpretations of the First-Order Factors

Factor A.

Loadings	Rated Variables
.66	3. Assertive
.62	22. Marked Overt Emotional Expression
.62	11. Talkative
.59	6. Gregarious
.41	4. Cheerful
.30	20. Frank
.25	12. Adventurous

The three variables which define this factor most specifically are Assertive, Talkative, and Gregarious. The person high on this factor strikes up a conversation readily and probably keeps talking without much awareness of the other person. His expansiveness is self-centered, but not necessarily selfish. This variable is unrelated to Readiness to Cooperate and to Social Adjustment. The dimension involved seems to be Social Initiative.

Factor B:

Loadings	Rated Variables
.51	15. Self-sufficient
.51	21. Independent-Minded
.44	3. Assertive
.37	12. Adventurous
.30	7. Unshakable
-.27	1. Readiness to Cooperate

The two variables with the highest loadings here have in common the tendency to be independent of others, to have no concern for other people. A large amount of this factor would be found in the self-reliant person, perhaps the person with much professional self-confidence. The location of this factor in the second-order structure suggests a tendency to approach problems critically, with no deference for the traditional or the accepted formulations. Independent-Mindedness conveys the essence of this factor, which has large correlations with Factors D (Insight) and G (Intellectual Effectiveness).

Factor C:

Loadings	Rated Variables
.65	17. Conscientious
.64	5. Serious
.44	41. Integrity of Personal and Professional Behavior
.32	10. Generous
.30	1. Readiness to Cooperate
.26	9. Trustful
-.45	19. Marked Overt Interest in the Opposite Sex

A strong super-ego is suggested by the key variables in this factor. The other significant loadings round out the idea of moral conformity. While variable No. 41 presumably predicted future Integrity of Personal and Professional Behavior, it is obvious that this prediction was based largely on evaluation of present integrity. The phrase, Ethical Sense, seems to convey the basic nature of this factor. Its highest correlation is with Factor K (Effectiveness in Interpersonal Relations), presumably because we feel we can trust the person who has Ethical Sense.

Factor D:

Loadings	Rated Variables
.56	29. Insight into Others
.49	30. Insight into Himself
.37	18. Imaginative
.29	33. Clinical Diagnosis
.26	14. Adaptable, Flexible

This factor is clearly Insight into Self and Others. The sizable loading on Clinical Diagnosis indicates that predictions of this competence were based in large part, but not solely, upon estimates of present insight. The staff seems to have felt that training and experience would not markedly alter the relative positions of trainees with respect to insight. The presence of Imaginative in this factor is probably a result of the particular definition we used: " . . . sensitive to a multitude of emotional and other possibilities not realized by the average person" vs. " . . . unresponsive to the subtleties in a situation."

Factor D is one of the few first-order factors which include variables from all three parts of the rating scale, including those from Scales B and C, which are to a large extent specific to the applied aspect of this research project. The table of intercorrelations of factors suggests that Independent-Mindedness (Factor B) may contribute to this Insight.

Factor E:

Loadings	Rated Variables
.47	7. Unshakable
.44	13. Socially Poised and Adept
.39	16. Placid
.38	6. Gregarious
.32	1. Readiness to Cooperate
.32	23. Social Adjustment

The person high on this factor is sociocentric, and perhaps sociophilic. He both wants and is able to maintain an unruffled, socially graceful demeanor. His Social Poise facilitates his Social Adjustment. While he displays no anxiety or tension in social situations, there is some suggestion that he carries his suppression a little too far; he is not noted for Appropriateness of Emotional Expression nor for being Adaptable, Flexible. The negative correlation with Factor A implies a tendency to let others take the initiative, yet a certain amount of independence (Factor B) is also associated with this Social Poise.

Factor F:

Loadings	Rated Variables
.50	20. Frank
.48	12. Adventurous

.46	11.	Talkative
.45	22.	Marked Overt Emotional Expression
.44	14.	Adaptable, Flexible
.39	4.	Cheerful
.27	9.	Trustful
.26	24.	Appropriateness of Emotional Expression

-.25	13.	Socially Poised and Adept
-.26	5.	Serious

This factor appears to concern the quality of expression. It is not impulsiveness because the expression is reasonably appropriate and thère is little sign of tensions bursting out. The core seems to be Spontaneity; the expression of emotions and feelings is natural and unreserved.

Factor G:

Loadings		Rated Variables
.61	32.	Academic Performance
.57	36.	Research
.55	39.	Teaching Psychology
.47	31.	Quality of Intellectual Accomplishments
.36	42.	Overall Suitability for Clinical Psychology
.35	37.	Administration
.31	33.	Clinical Diagnosis
.31	38.	Supervising Clinical Psychologists

The four variables whose principal loadings are on this factor suggest the label, Intellectual Effectiveness. Further investigation would be necessary to determine whether this should be restricted to the field of scholarship. It is also not clear whether originality is present. While Imaginative is not included in the pattern, Quality of Intellectual Accomplishments is present. The correlations between this factor and Factors B (Independent-Mindedness) and D (Insight) are outstandingly high.

From the loading for predicted competence in Clinical Diagnosis, we may infer that the assessment staff felt that diagnostic competence requires Insight coupled with intelligence.

Factor H:

Loadings		Rated Variable
.49	25.	Characteristic Intensity of Inner Emotional Tension
.46	2.	Consistent
.38	26.	Sexual Adjustment
.35	16.	Placid
.32	4.	Cheerful
.32	27.	Motivation for Professional Status
.27	7.	Unshakable

Freedom from Emotional Tension seems to be the appropriate description of this factor. "Emotional Adjustment" is not satisfactory because the absence of a significant loading on Appropriateness of Emotional Expression. The negative side of this factor appears to be neuroticism. We may assume that the person high on this factor has had few personal problems. If he has had problems, he has learned to deal with them.

Such a person is easy-going. Perhaps he is too Consistent and does not react sufficiently to internal and external stimuli. He is Cheerful in the sense of being good-natured but he is not exuberant.

Factor I:

Loadings	Rated Variables
.53	34. Individual Psychotherapy
.49	40. Professional Interpersonal Relations
.46	35. Group Psychotherapy
.44	42. Overall Suitability for Clinical Psychology
.43	37. Administration
.42	23. Social Adjustment
.40	14. Adaptable, Flexible
.40	24. Appropriateness of Emotional Expression
.39	38. Supervising Clinical Psychologists
.38	10. Generous
.37	41. Integrity of Personal and Professional Behavior
.35	26. Sexual Adjustment
.34	9. Trustful
.31	20. Frank
.30	12. Adventurous
.27	19. Marked Overt Interest in Opposite Sex
.26	39. Teaching Psychology
.25	30. Insight into Himself

This rather general factor is not clearly delineated. Most of the variables with high loadings involve Effectiveness in Interpersonal Relations. The fact that predicted clinical skills show the highest loadings suggests the precaution of limiting the dimension to predicted professional competence; however, the other variables have more general implications.

Interpretations of Second-Order Factors

Because of the rather sizeable intercorrelations among the factors, the table of intercorrelations for nine first-order factors was also subjected to a factor analysis. Five more general second-order factors were thus identified.

Factor AA:

Loadings	First-Order Factors
.69	E. Social Poise
.60	K. Effectiveness in Interpersonal Relations
.52	H. Freedom from Emotional Tension
-.45	A. Social Initiative

This factor is probably not specific to this particular selection situation. It appears to be Personal and Social Adjustment. Its composition suggests that the effective person is likely to be the adjusted one.

Factor BB:

Loadings	First-Order Factors
.80	G. Intellectual Effectiveness
.67	D. Insight into Self and Others
.58	B. Independent-Mindedness

With Insight and Diagnostic Competence subsumed under this factor, it might be equated with the clinician's diagnostic function. Factors B and G, however, have no other high loadings and hence a more appropriate concept seems to be Scholarship in the Field of Human Behavior.

Factor CC:

Loadings	First-Order Factors
.67	C. Ethical Sense
.66	I. Effectiveness in Interpersonal Relations
.33	D. Insight into Self and Others

Interest in Social Welfare seems to summarize this constellation.

Factor DD:

Loadings	First-Order Factors
.62	A. Social Initiative
-.36	C. Ethical Sense

This pair of first-order factors reminds us of Spranger's political type as opposed to his religious type. Egotism is the central characteristic. Since, with the exception of rated integrity, this second-order factor is composed solely of variables in Scale A, it appears to be a dimension of overt behavior.

Factor EE:

Loadings	First-Order Factors
.57	E. Social Poise
.50	F. Spontaneity

This factor is hard to interpret. Factor F is out-going, but Factor E is reserved. What do they have in common? Both involve Sociability. People possessing these first-order factors are agreeable and pleasant company. They like to be with other people and others like to be with them, but probably for different reasons.

This elaborate factor analysis was undertaken primarily as a guide for later analyses and interpretation of assessment data.

No attempt will be made here to compare these factors with those reported in other studies. The only study using similar variables is that of Cattell (1947) which differs from the present one with respect to specific variables and their definitions, in the basis of ratings, in the raters, and in the methods of rotation. Even so there would appear to be a marked similarity between the factors identified in these two studies. The first 22 variables in the rating scale had previously been factor analyzed independently (Fiske, 1949). There is also a considerable amount of similarity between the two sets of resulting factors, but since the factors for the larger analysis here reported are more fully delineated, a comparison of the two studies would not further our understanding of the rating scale.

Interjudge Reliability of Assessment Ratings

Ratings Based on Same Materials

How well did the ratings of the assessment staff members agree with each other? Let us consider first those instances where the ratings were based upon identical data. The agreement between ratings by the Intensive and the Initial Interviewer, based on the materials in the credential file alone, is relatively poor. For 10 variables in Scales B and C, the correlations range from .03 for the trait Appropriateness of Emotional Expression to .53 for the prediction of Academic Performance. There was usually better agreement on Scale C (predictive) variables than for the Scale B (evaluative) ratings. This tendency, which also appears elsewhere, is probably to be explained as a reflection of a global impression which pervaded the Scale C predictions; in general there was better agreement on this overall impression than there was upon the more specific variables.

The agreement between assessment raters appears to be in part a function of the amount of material on which the ratings were based. For 61 cases, both the Intensive Interviewer and the Pre-Conference rater made ratings based on the same total body of data: credential file, objective tests, autobiographical materials, and projective protocols and interpretations. The median correlation between the ratings made by these two staff members on the variables in Scale B was .47; the lowest correlation was .28 for Insight into Others and the highest was .68 for Quality of Intellectual Accomplishments. On Scale C, however, the median interjudge agreement was .63, the lowest correlation being .44 for Integrity of Personal and Professional Behavior and the highest being .71 for Academic Performance. The agreement on Overall Suitability for Clinical Psychology was .64. Once again we find better agreement on Scale C than on Scale B even though the Scale C ratings are predictions of future behavior.

Ratings Based on Situation Tests

The interjudge reliability of ratings made by the Uncontaminated Situationists, on the basis of observed behavior, varied widely according to the variable being rated. The average intercorrelation between these individual situationists' ratings was computed for four Scale C variables: the highest correlation was .51 for Overall Suitability, No. 42. Other values were: Research (No. 36) .45, Therapy (No. 34) .44, and Diagnosis (No. 33) .40.

It should be noted that none of these reported interjudge reliabilities indicate the estimated value for the sum or average of the several independent individual ratings. For example, the reliability of the sum of the three situationists' ratings on Variable 42 is .76 as estimated by the Spearman-Brown formula.

Reliability of Final Pooled Ratings

By the time the staff had studied the candidates for the entire assessment week, they agreed quite closely in their final individual ratings. It will be remembered that the assessment team had had one previous pooling conference on each case and that for these final individual ratings, all previous ratings were available to each judge. For each variable, the correlation between the Final Individual ratings for three pairs in the assessment staff team was obtained. The median of these correlations was .64 for Scale A variables, the median for Scale B was .69, and the median for Scale C was .76. For variable No. 42, Overall Suitability as a Clinical Psychologist, the inter-correlation of the Final Individual staff ratings was .81, which corresponds to an estimated reliability of .93 for the average of three ratings. Within each scale the reliabilities were quite homogeneous, with the exception of variable No. 2 in Scale A (Consistent-Inconsistent) and variable No. 27 in Scale B (Motivation for Professional Status). The relatively poor agreement on these two variables probably indicates a lack of clarity in their conception or definition.

Reliability of Teammates' Ratings

Comparable interjudge correlations were computed between Teammates' ratings of fellow trainees. The correlations for Scale A variables range from .37 to .68 with a median of .51. The somewhat poorer agreement between peer ratings when compared with staff agreement probably reflects the students' unfamiliarity with the rating scale or the definitions and the relatively limited sample of behavior on which the ratings were based. Furthermore, the conflict in the motivation of the students between the desire to display insight into others and the wish to avoid disparaging their fellow sufferers may have attenuated the reliability of these ratings by teammates.

Reliability of Wellesley Ratings

Since the 1948 Wellesley Assessment staff did not see the trainees they were rating, it is not surprising to find that their ratings showed less agreement than that found for the ratings made in the Ann Arbor Assessment program. The agreement between raters for their first set of ratings on Overall Suitability based on very limited materials was only .36. Even when the ratings were based on more materials the interjudge reliability remained at approximately the same level. Although the final ratings at Wellesley were based on the same materials as those available to the Pre-Conference rater and the Intensive Interviewer in the 1947 program, the Wellesley raters never reached the degree of agreement (.64) obtained by the 1947 raters. Differences in motivation of staff members is a possible but unlikely explanation. A more important consideration is the fact that the Wellesley subjects represented a younger and more highly selected group of applicants tested under different conditions.

Reliabilities of 1949 Reassessment Ratings

The pattern of reliabilities of staff ratings made in the 1949 assessment of the 1947 cases is more like that for the 1947 assessment than that for the 1948 assessment. The median reliability for the ratings based on credentials and objective tests was .31 for Scale B and C variables. The reliabilities for ratings at the next level, after seeing the autobiographical materials, are somewhat lower. However, at the third level, after the raters had examined the projective protocols and interpretations, the reliabilities are higher than those at the second level for every single one of the variables. Even so, the median reliability for the Scale B variables is .43 and the median for the Scale C variables is also .43. The agreement on Overall Suitability was .63. We believe that these trends in the reliabilities may be a function of the training received by the reassessment staff. The 1949 staff had had little experience or training in interpreting autobiographical materials of the sort used in the assessment program. However, their intensive training in projective tests may have led to the more consistent ratings at the third level.

Agreement between Ratings Based on Independent Assessments

We may also compare the agreement between the 1947 assessors and the 1949 reassessors on the same cases. For Overall Suitability (No. 42) the agreement between a random 1947 staff member and a random 1949 staff member for ratings based on the same materials was approximately . 50. For most variables the 1949 Final Individual and Final Pooled ratings correlated with the 1947 Final Pooled ratings at about this same level. For predictions of Academic Performance the 1947 and 1949 ratings agreed somewhat better; the representative value is . 64.

Reliabilities of Ratings Based on Projective Tests

An intensive study of ratings based on projective tests was carried out as a part of the 1949 reassessment program (Samuels, 1950). Each of the four raters rated each of four projective protocols for each of 20 subjects. It should be noted that each rater based his ratings solely on the protocol; the protocols had been obtained by other examiners and the 1949 rater did not see the subject, as did the 1947 rater. For each of six variables rated on the basis of each test the six interjudge correlations were computed. The median of the medians for each of the techniques was as follows: Rorschach, . 44; Bender-Gestalt, . 35; TAT, . 28; Sentence Completion, . 27. The median agreement for all ratings based on the same techniques was . 35.

Intra-Judge Agreement on Ratings Based on Different Projective Techniques

Since the same judge made independent ratings on each of the four projective protocols for each trainee, it was possible to determine how well the judge "agreed with himself," i. e. , how well his judgment based on one type of projective material agreed with his judgment of the same variable from another projective test. The median agreement between the ratings based on the four different tests, i. e. , ratings made by the same judge, was only . 13. Thus different judges agreed better in rating the same projective protocol than a single judge agreed with himself in his ratings for the several protocols produced by the same subject. For each of these six pairs of projective tests, the median agreement for 15 variables was close to zero; in no case did the median exceed . 08.

Correlations between Ratings at Different Stages

Table B II-2 presents the correlations between the Final Pooled Ratings in the 1947 Assessment program and the ratings of the same variables made at various preceding stages. These may be regarded as validity coefficients only in accordance with one's willingness to regard the Final Pooled ratings as criteria of the variables rated. Scale C predictions certainly cannot be considered as criteria. On the other hand, Scale A and B variables, made at the end of the one-week assessment program, are probably about as valid and reliable measures of personality as can be obtained for normal subjects and present day assessment techniques.

Ratings Based on Projective Tests

In view of the findings concerning the low interjudge agreement in ratings based on projective techniques, it is not surprising to discover that correlations of these ratings with the Final Pooled ratings tend to be low. For most variables the ratings made by the Intensive and Initial Interviewers after seeing the credentials alone correlate about as highly with the Final Pooled ratings as do the ratings based on a single projective test.

Successive Ratings by the Intensive Interviewer

The correlation with the Final Pooled ratings increased for each successive rating made by the Intensive Interviewer. As more material was made available to him, his ratings became closer and closer approximations of the Final Pooled rating. A striking feature of this table is the relatively small amount of increase in the correlations after the Interviews. Since great

TABLE B II-2

CORRELATIONS BETWEEN FINAL POOLED RATINGS AND RATINGS MADE AT PRECEDING STAGES IN 1947 ANN ARBOR ASSESSMENT PROGRAM

(N = 128 except as indicated)

Stage or Basis of Rating	Depressed* No. 4	Conscientious No. 17	Imaginative No. 18	Dependent-Minded No. 21	Limited Emot. Exp. No. 22	Diagnosis No. 33	Indiv. Therapy No. 34	Research No. 36	Overall Suitability No. 42
Rorschach*	.03	-.07	.36	.30	.16	.29	.25	.25	.33
Sentence Completion*	.40	.26	.41	.32	.23	.33	.26	.24	.29
TAT*	.27	.09	.39	.35	.35	.34	.27	.27	.24
Bender-Gestalt*	.21	.17	.21	.27	.19	.18	.13	.37	.22
Projective Integ. (N =67)	.37	.39	.51	.27	.45	.27	.34	.24	.37
Initial Interviewer after									
Credentials						.32	.27	.47	.29
Interview	.42	.42	.44	.55	.39	.43	.50	.63	.46
Intensive Interviewer after									
Credentials						.32	.25	.48	.40
Objective Tests						.49	.40	.63	.46
Autobiography						.62	.51	.70	.61
Projective Tests						.59	.48	.57	.57
Interview	.65	.74	.68	.57	.59	.69	.63	.68	.70
Pre-Conference (N = 61)	.62	.46	.64	.43	.42	.79	.67	.72	.68
Preliminary Polling	.69	.80	.82	.75	.59	.78	.77	.82	.80
Self	.38	.10	.30	.09	.22	.11	.03	.25	.04
Median of Teammate Ratings						.38	.38	.31	.39
Uncontaminated Pooled	.67	.35	.56	.46	.55	.59	.48	.62	.64
Contaminated Init. Inter.	.54	.83	.77	.80	.65	.79	.82	.85	.85
Contaminated Intens. Inter.	.79	.79	.81	.74	.66	.84	.85	.90	.90
Contaminated Sit.	.72	.72	.78	.87	.64	.79	.73	.81	.86
Final Individual-Init. Inter.	.83	.89	.85	.81	.76	.86	.88	.90	.91
Final Individual-Intens.Int.	.87	.83	.88	.85	.83	.88	.90	.92	.95
Final Individual-Sit.	.75	.82	.86		.73	.87	.84	.84	.87

*The projectivists made ratings on Scale A variables only when there was no Projective Integration, i.e., for the cases rated by Pre-Conference raters. Thus N = 61 for Nos. 4, 17, 18, 21 and 22.

emphasis has been placed upon the interview in both diagnosis and personnel work and since staff members were generally of the opinion that the interviews were the most valuable part of the assessment program, one might have expected it to have contributed more variance than it did to the Final Pooled ratings.*

Another noteworthy feature of the table is the size of the correlations for the Pre-Conference rater. These are about as high as the corresponding correlations for the Intensive Interviewer after his interview. (The same trend is present when the correlations are computed for just the 61 cases rated by the Pre-Conference rater.)

In interpreting the correlations between assessment Final Pooled ratings and ratings at earlier stages, we must remember that the Final Pooled ratings were made by staff members who had contributed more or less to the ratings at preceding levels. Furthermore, in the Final Pooling conference there was a definite tendency to defer to the opinions of the Intensive Interviewer on the grounds that he was the staff member who was best acquainted with each case. Hence, other things being equal, one would expect his earlier ratings to show higher correlations with the Final Pooled ratings than those for any other staff member.

Self Ratings and Teammate Ratings

The Self ratings show but little relationship to the Final Pooled ratings. The ratings made by Teammates, on the other hand, show a fair degree of relationship with the Final Pooled ratings, in fact, these agree with the Final Pooled ratings about as well as ratings made by Interviewers on the basis of credentials alone.

Ratings by Uncontaminated Situationists

The ratings made by the Uncontaminated Situationists, after seeing the candidate only in the situation tests, correlate with the Final Pooled ratings about as closely as those made by the Interviewer after the Initial Interview or by the Intensive Interviewer just before his Intensive Interview. Thus on three quite different types of materials (written records, credential file plus interview and observations of performance in a situational test), sets of ratings can be obtained which show equal correlation with relatively elaborate evaluation of a candidate.**

Wellesley Ratings

Just as the agreement between raters of the 1948 Wellesley staff did not increase when the ratings were based on increasingly more material, so we find the correlations between the Final Pooled Wellesley ratings and the ratings in preceding stages change little with increased information. Whereas for Overall Suitability the ratings based on credentials plus one other piece of information correlate .54 with the Final Pooled, the addition of another item of information of this same general type yielded a correlation of only .53. The correlations of Final Pooled ratings with those made at the 3rd and 4th stages are .59 and .66 respectively. It should be recalled, however, that the data examined by the Wellesley staff were collected under realistic selection conditions. That is, the applicants had every reason to believe that their performance on the tests would influence their acceptance at the university of their choice. Although the assessment staff was well aware of the conditions under which the test had been administered, they may well have had difficulty in determining the correct amount of influence to attribute to these conditions.

*An intensive study of the relationships between ratings made before and after the interviews and Final Pooled ratings was made by Tupes (1950).

**An Intensive analysis of the ratings based solely on the situation tests was made by Soskin (1948).

Agreement between 1947 and 1948 Predictions
on Reassessed Cases

It will be recalled that 24 cases assessed in the 1948 Wellesley program had previously been assessed in 1947. For Overall Suitability the 1948 Final Pooled ratings correlated .64 with the 1947 Final Pooled and .74 with the ratings of the Intensive Interviewer after Projectives. For predicted Academic Performance the 1948 Final Pooled ratings correlated .72 and .76 with these two 1947 ratings. These are of the same order of magnitude as the correlations between the Pre-Conference rater and the Intensive Interviewer after Projectives, both of the ratings being based on essentially the same materials as the Wellesley final ratings. (They also approximate the correlations between each of these two 1947 stage ratings and the 1947 Final Pooled ratings.)

Individual Differences between Staff Members
in Their Correlations with Final Pooled
Ratings

In our assessment program we gave but little attention to possible individual differences among staff members. At the beginning of the 1947 assessment program, the suggestion that the staff might like to take some of the tests themselves met a most unenthusiastic response. It is quite understandable that these clinical psychologists and psychiatrists should be somewhat reluctant to provide clinical material for research purposes when the staff members were personally known to the research team.

It was, however, possible to obtain some evidence regarding individual differences in staff ability by correlating certain individual ratings with the Final Pooled ratings. For example, the ratings on Overall Suitability made by 24 staff members when serving as Uncontaminated Situationists were correlated with the Final Pooled ratings of the same variable. These correlations, which are highly unstable because of the small N's (7 to 23), varied from .13 to .90 with a median value of .52. For 11 of the staff members who also served as Intensive Interviewers similar correlations were computed between their ratings after seeing the autobiographical materials and the Final Pooled ratings. The correlations, which again were highly unstable, vary from .33 to .85 with a median of .72. In effect, then, we had two "validity indices" for each of 11 staff members. The correlation between these two measures is only .29 and being based on only 11 cases is, of course, highly unreliable. The fact that it is not higher suggests that diagnostic ability (or influence upon fellow staff members) in one role has little relationship to diagnostic ability (or influence) in the second role. The possible factors which may contribute to this low correlation are the unreliability of the criteria used and the relatively restricted range of clinical competence in the staff members. As we shall see later, we find equally low agreement between other pairs of measurements which might be considered to reflect ability as a clinical psychologist.

The Liking Variable

The Liking variable (No. 0) differs from any other variable in our rating scale in several respects. It was the least explicitly defined--in fact, it was given no elaboration. It was included in the rating scale because of its potential value not as a predictor variable but rather as a "suppressor" variable. The project planning staff and the assessment staff were well aware of the problem of halo and the possibility that a staff member's personal liking for a trainee might influence his ratings. We doubted that it was possible, even for sophisticated clinical psychologists, to make ratings which were completely uninfluenced by liking. It was thought that making a rating on Liking might have a cathartic value; once the rater had expressed his personal reaction to the subject, he could, perhaps, make his ratings on other variables without being unduly influenced by his personal reactions.

The Liking rating obviously reflects the personal reaction of one man to another. The individual nature of this interaction is indicated by the size of the correlations between ratings on Liking by various staff members playing different roles: the median for 14 of these intercorrelations between roles is only .25. The average intercorrelation between Liking ratings by teammates is only .24.

The importance of the Liking variable is indicated by the fact that the sum of the Final Individual ratings on Liking correlated .77 with a Final Pooled rating on Overall Suitability. At any particular assessment stage, the correlation between a staff member's rating on Liking and his prediction of Overall Suitability was almost as high.

Evidence from another source also indicates the considerable importance of the Liking variable. When one compares, for the 1947 cases, the set of correlations between Final Pooled ratings on Overall Suitability and the Final Pooled ratings for the other 41 variables, on the one hand, and the set of correlations between the sum of the Final Individual Liking ratings and the same 41 variables on the other, one finds an almost perfect correspondence: those variables in Scales A, B and C which show a high correlation with Overall Suitability also have a high correlation with Liking.

Why is Liking so highly related to predicted clinical competence? Does Liking lead to a prediction of high clinical competence or vice versa? There can be little question that a favorable reaction to a trainee tends to elevate the ratings for that trainee. On the other hand, perhaps the staff members formed an impression of a man's potential competence and then liked him or disliked him on the basis of that impression of competence. The most plausible explanation of this relationship seems to be that well adjusted individuals who are least in conflict with other individuals in their cultural group will tend to be liked, will be more effective in their interpersonal relationships, and hence will seem to show more promise as potential clinical psychologists.

Frames of Reference for Ratings

Figure B II-1, prepared by Soskin (1948), illustrates several important characteristics of assessment ratings. It will be recalled that the rating scales used in the assessment programs were arbitrarily defined as having a mean of 4.5 and a range from 1 to 8. The reference population was "first year clinical psychology graduate students at universities accredited by the APA to offer training in clinical psychology." Inspection of the graph immediately shows that the mean ratings approximated 4.5 closely on few traits. For one variable, the mean Final Pooled rating deviated more than 1 scale point from 4.5. In Figure B II-1 the variables are arranged so that the favorable or laudatory pole for each continuum is on the right hand side and the condemnatory pole on the left. While these deviations of mean ratings from 4.5 indicate something about the staff's general picture of these VA trainees, they have only negligible influence upon the magnitude of any correlations reported.

The mean ratings made at the Preliminary Pooling conference, indicated by x's in Figure B II-1, fall in random fashion on either side of the Final Pooled means. Since the Preliminary Pooled and the Final Pooled ratings were made by the same individuals, we may infer that the observations from the situation tests and from the other material made available to the raters after the Preliminary Pooling conference had no systematic tendency to influence the degree of favorableness of the ratings.

The mean ratings of the Uncontaminated Situationists are indicated on the figure by small circles: these man ratings are for the most part lower, i.e., more condemnatory than the Final Pooled ratings. The Uncontaminated Situationists had no personal interaction with the subjects; they merely observed performance in the situation tests. Since these observations represented an

Condemnatory   5.50   5.30   5.10   4.90   4.70   4.50   4.30   4.10   3.90   3.70   3.50   Laudatory
                 3.50   3.70   3.90   4.10   4.30   4.50   4.70   4.90   5.10   5.30   5.50

Left Label		Right Label
B-27	Motiv. Status	Motiv. Status — B-27
B-25	Inner Tension	Inner Tension — B-25
B-26	Sex. Adjust.	Sex. Adjust. — B-26
A-10	Selfish	Generous — A-10
B-30	Insight Others	Insight Others — B-30
A-12	Cautious	Adventurous — A-12
A-20	Secretive	Frank — A-20
B-24	Emo. Express.	Emo. Express. — B-24
A-9	Suspicious	Trustful — A-9
A-14	Rigid	Adaptable — A-14
A-16	Anxious	Placid — A-16
B-23	Soc. Adjust.	Soc. Adjust. — B-23
B-29	Insight Self	Insight Self — B-29
A-18	Unimaginative	Imaginative — A-18
A-8	Narrow Int.	Broad Int. — A-8
A-15	Dependent	Self-Suff. — A-15
A-22	Overt Emo. Exp.	Overt Emo. Exp. — A-22
A-4	Depressed	Cheerful — A-4
A-7	Easily Upset	Unshakable — A-7
A-11	Silent	Talkative — A-11
A-19	Interest Sex	Interest Sex — A-19
B-31	Intell. Accomp.	Intell. Accomp. — B-31
A-6	Not Gregarious	Gregarious — A-6
A-3	Submissive	Assertive — A-3
A-13	Soc. Awkward	Soc. Poised — A-13
A-1	Obstructive	Cooperative — A-1
A-17	Not Conscient.	Conscientious — A-17
B-28	Motiv. Science	Motiv. Science — B-28
A-2	Inconsistent	Consistent — A-2
A-21	Depend. Mind.	Independ. Mind. — A-21
A-5	Irresponsible	Serious — A-5

Legend:
● Final Pooled
✕ Prelim. Pooled
○ Uncont. Sit. Pooled
❙ Pre-Conference

Fig. B II-1. **Mean Ratings Assigned by Raters in Different Roles**

interlude in their primary task of following their main group of subjects, there was apparently little inclination for them to have developed strong favorable biases toward the candidates seen in situation tests only.

The mean ratings made by the Pre-Conference raters, indicated by the short vertical lines in the figure, also tend to run systematically below the means for the Final Pooled. These Pre-Conference ratings were made on the basis of credentials, tests, and autobiographical materials, without seeing the subject. Thus, again, when there was no opportunity for interpersonal interaction, the mean ratings tend to be lower than when such an opportunity existed.

It must be remembered that these ratings were made by the same raters, playing four different roles. In other words, differences between the mean ratings made at each assessment stage must be attributed to differences in the materials on which the ratings were based and in the opportunity or lack of opportunity for personal interaction with the subject rather than to the differences between the raters.

If the mean ratings by Teammates were added to the figure, they would fall amost consistently to the right of the line connecting the Final Pooled means. However, the line connecting the mean Teammate ratings would not exactly parallel the Final Pooled line. For example, the mean Final Pooled and the mean Teammate ratings on Independent-Mindedness were both 5.0. On the other hand, the mean Final Pooled rating on Conscientious is 4.9 as compared to 5.8 for the Teammates. In other words, the deviations (from 4.5) of the means for Teammate ratings were not highly related to the deviations of the means of staff ratings. The two groups of raters apparently had somewhat different reference systems.

Intercorrelations between Assessment Ratings and Scores on Objective Tests

For the 1947 assessment group, correlations were computed between the Final Pooled Rating on Overall Suitability (No. 42) and 82 scores derived from objective tests. These are shown in Table B II-3. The great majority of these correlations are very low. While nearly a third of the values are significant (at the 5% level), none of them is large. The intellectual component in the Final Overall Suitability ratings is reflected by the correlations with Miller, with the General Culture Test and with the S, W, R, and M scores from the PMA. The next largest correlations are with the regular Psychologist and the VA Clinical Psychologist keys for the Strong. Most of these test scores were available to the assessment staff and in a sense these correlations are a reflection of the extent to which the assessors were influenced by the test scores.

Correlations between Ratings on Scale A and Guilford-Martin Scores

For the 1947 assessment group, the 13 Guilford-Martin scores were correlated with Final Pooled ratings for the 22 variables in Scale A.* A large number of statistically significant relationships were obtained. The highest correlation was .58 between Guilford-Martin Cycloid score and rated Marked Overt Emotional Expression. Other high correlations were .49 between the Guilford-Martin Ascendance Score and the rating on Assertive, and .40 between Guilford-Martin Social Extraversion and Gregariousness. In general, the correlations tended to be in the expected directions, although many of them were not so high as one might predict if one assumes that both the ratings and the Guilford-Martin scores have high validity. Here again, it should be remembered that these test scores were available to the assessment staff and were probably given some weight in arriving at personality ratings.

---

*This study was carried out by Walter Luszki.

TABLE B II-3

CORRELATIONS BETWEEN OBJECTIVE TEST SCORES AND
FINAL RATING ON OVERALL SUITABILITY (A 42)
N = 128 Men Assessed in Summer, 1947
Values Significant at 5% level underlined

Miller Analogies		.36	Strong		
PMA	Number	.02	Artist	.17
	Verbal	.13	Psychologist	.25
	Space	.18	Architect	.16
	Word Fluency	.18	Physician	.15
	Reasoning	.27	Dentist	.02
	Memory	.23	Engineer	.02
			Chemist	.13
Allport-Vernon	Theoretical	.18	Production Mgr.	-.04
	Economic	-.07	Carpenter	-.03
	Aesthetic	.12	Math.-Science Teacher	.06
	Social	.17	Policeman	-.13
	Political	-.20	Forest Service	.07
	Religious	-.23	Personnel Mgr.	.00
			YMCA Secretary	.01
MMPI (*indicates with K correction)			Musician	.18
	*Hypochondriasis	-.19	Accountant	-.13
	Depression	-.11	Office Worker	-.17
	Hysteria	-.16	Purchasing Agent	-.23
	*Psychopath Deviate	-.16	Sales Manager	-.15
	Masc.-Fem.	.14	Life Insurance Salesman	-.16
	Paranoia	-.20	Lawyer	.05
	*Psychasthenia	-.13	Author-Journalist	.16
	*Schizophrenia	-.04	Group I	.18
	*Hypomania	-.10	Group II	.15
	K	.04	Group V	.09
			Group VIII	-.19
Guilford-Martin	Social Intra.	-.03	Group IX	-.14
	Thinking Intra.	-.19	Group X	.13
	Depression	-.14	Occupational Level	-.04
	Cycloid Ten.	-.14	M-F	-.12
	Rhathymia	.03	VA Clinical Psychologist	.25
	General Act.	.01		
	Ascendance	.11		
	Masculinity	.20		
	Inferiority F	-.21		
	Nervousness	-.17		
	Objectivity	.02		
	Agreeableness	-.02		
	Cooperativeness	.13		

Scores Not Available to Assessment Staff

Kuder	Mechanical	-.03	General Culture: Values in parentheses are		
	Computational	-.13	with Miller Score partialled out. N = 117.		
	Scientific	-.04			
	Persuasive	-.10	I. Current Social Problems	.29	(.16)
	Artistic	.03	II. History and Soc. Stud.	.21	
	Literary	.18	III. Literature	.21	
	Musical	.03	IV. Science	.14	
	Social Service	.16	V. Fine Arts	.27	(.12)
	Clerical	-.03	VI. Mathematics	.35	(.21)
			Total Score	.32	(.12)

CHAPTER C I

THE CRITERION PROBLEM

This short chapter provides a general introduction to a series of complex problems
involved in the evaluation of professional competence. In most previous studies of
professional selection, relatively little attention has been given to the measurement
of criteria; grades or completion of professional training have been used almost exclusively. In this project, on the other hand, a large share of our efforts was devoted to the development of a variety of criterion measures. The chapter concludes
with a discussion of relative merits, liabilities and limitations of first vs. second-
order criteria and specific vs. general criteria.

Definitions

In this report, the term "criterion" is used to refer to a skill or characteristic which is considered to be an essential component of the total behavior to be predicted. Thus diagnostic skill
is a criterion. We shall use "criterion measure" to refer to any procedure for measuring any
criterion. Thus, there may be one or more criterion measures for each criterion. In some industrial situations, the total number of products finished by a worker might conceivably be the
the sole criterion measure. For most criteria, and especially as concerns professional activities,
no single criterion measure appears to be adequate.

The Background

In the history of psychometrics the two decades between 1920 and 1940 will probably be looked
back upon as the time when psychologists were concerned with the development of predictor measures. Test construction, after a fairly slow start, made increasingly more rapid advances during that period. Much progress was made in the theory of psychometrics and in solving numerous technical problems involved in the measurement of human capacities.

The decade or two after 1940 will probably be looked upon as the era of the criterion problem.
Whereas psychological tests had previously been considered, either implicitly or explicitly, as
essentially their own criteria, psychologists began to realize the central importance of criterion
measures. Their experiences during World War II sharpened this realization. Psychologists
brought to bear on problems of military selection a wide variety of psychological instruments,
but they quickly discovered that an ideal selection of the tests to be used in a particular situation
was not possible with the inadequate measures of achievement and performance then available
(cf. Bellows, 1941; Jenkins, 1946; Brogden and Taylor, 1950; and Gulliksen, 1950).

Unfortunately World War II psychologists were unable to work on the development of criterion
measures during the early stages of the war. It was only toward the end of the war, after such
measures were of little use in the practical problems of choosing among available selection tests,
that concentrated attention was paid to criterion measures. For example, Naval Aviation psychologists developed a sociometric criterion by asking aviators which of their fellow aviators they
would be willing to fly with in combat (Vaughn, 1947; Jenkins et al.,1950). The OSS Assessment
Staff (1948) attempted with dubious success to collect information on the field performance of the
candidates they studied. Since no objective measures of performance were available, the OSS
staff attempted to collect information on the candidate's performance from those who presumably

were familiar with it and then attempted to evaluate these reports objectively. The Army Air Forces (Lepley, 1947) selected a wide variety of criterion measures, mostly of the objective sort, against which to correlate their many predictor tests.

In the typical personnel selection study, the sponsor asks the investigator to predict a particular criterion, usually what Thorndike (1949, Ch. 5) has called an intermediate or immediate criterion. This is well exemplified by recent publications on professional selection (Kandel, 1940; Stuit, et al. , 1949; Johnson, et al. , 1951). In these three studies the sole criterion against which selection tests were validated was academic performance. In other words these books treat only the problem of predicting performance in professional schools and merely refer in passing to the problem of predicting success in professional work.

An Analysis of the Criterion Problem

From the beginning, the project's staff and the consultants who participated in the planning of this project were acutely aware of the fact that the criterion problem would be much more difficult than the assessment problem. Previous work had pointed out the theoretical issues and the practical difficulties involved in the criterion problem but provided little on which we could build. Relatively early, therefore, we decided that a major portion of our efforts should be devoted to criterion research.

In our early thinking about the criterion problem we were particularly concerned with the necessity for making certain that criterion measures were in no way affected by the predictor measures themselves. For example, we considered the possibility of obtaining criterion measures by bringing the trainees back together again for a criterion program somewhat like the assessment program, in this program the project staff members would evaluate the diagnostic and therapeutic work of the trainees on the basis of observation of their actual clinical performance. We agreed that we could not use the same assessment staff members for such a program, lest the correlations between assessment predictions and criterion ratings be influenced by the fact that the staff reacted to the same characteristics of the trainees on the two different occasions.

In line with this objective of keeping predictor and criterion measures completely independent, we even thought of having the fundamental policy decisions concerning the nature of and the operations for collecting criteria measures made by professional psychologists who had not participated in any way in the planning for the collection of predictive measures. As we began to work on the criterion problem, however, we decided that criterion measures which were acceptable on other grounds were of a kind not subject to influence from the actual predictor ratings and measures. For this as well as for practical reasons, no attempt was made to set up a totally independent team for the development of criterion measures.

First-Order vs Second-Order Criteria

In analyzing the criterion problem, we believe it desirable to distinguish between two types of criteria: first-order criteria, which refer to the extent to which a person actually accomplishes the job he is supposed to be doing, and second-order criteria which are indirect indications of first-order criteria. For example, a first-order criterion of therapy would be the extent to which a trainee's therapy patients actually improve, while second-order criterion would include the supervisor's opinions as to the therapeutic success of the trainee; these opinions would presumably be based, in part at least, on the extent to which the trainee's patients actually improved.

The distinction between first and second-order criteria is admittedly somewhat artificial in that most criteria fall along a continuum of relevance to the true first-order or ultimate criterion (cf. Thorndike, 1949, Ch. 5). How, for instance, in measuring the outcomes of therapy, shall one classify the patient's own report of improvement as compared with the reports of his family? Likewise measures of first-order criteria are extremely difficult to find. Although there appears to be some general agreement as to first-order criteria for success in clinical psychology we were unable to find any agreement on measures of these criteria. There is perhaps even more agreement regarding second-order criteria and suitable measures of them but even here there is still considerable difference of opinion.

The Selection of Criteria

A review of the literature on the selection of professional personnel indicates that course grades are the most frequently used criteria. This is a case of using the most convenient criterion measures. Sometimes, the investigator may attempt to improve such a "convenient criterion" by studying the grading system used and making suggestions leading to improved reliability of these measures. For example, it is often possible to construct objective content examinations as a substitute for subjective evaluations of performance in professional schools.

The selection of criteria always involves an implicit or explicit value judgment. In applied studies of personnel selection, this judgment is usually made by the person or agency supporting the investigation. The objectives of this research project, however, were formulated in such a way that these judgments were not made in advance by the sponsor. Compared to most other selection studies, we had the advantage of being free to work out these judgments in consultation with professional colleagues.

In this favorable situation, it was possible to take a somewhat different approach to the criterion problem. In this approach, one examines the job and then makes an explicit value judgment identifying the first-order criteria defining the occupation or profession. This ideal statement may deviate considerably from the functions identified in a job analysis showing what people actually do on a job. In other words, the definition of the criteria constitutes a definition of the job. Obviously such an ideal statement of job functions requires an explicit rationale.

This approach can be illustrated in an analysis of clinical diagnosis. The professional task of clinical psychology as a practice may be defined as that of helping patients. Therapy in the most general terms is the helping of patients. Therefore diagnosis should contribute to therapy, i.e., help in the management and treatment of a particular clinical case. An ideal clinical diagnosis would state how the patient would react to each of the various therapeutic or management alternatives possible. Such a statement involves a series of predictions of future behavior; e.g., if the patient undergoes a particular type of therapy with a particular therapist, his condition will improve; if he receives no therapy, his condition will get worse, and so forth. Because of the absence of neat disease entities in the neuropsychiatric domain, diagnosis in the sense of merely assigning a diagnostic label to a patient ordinarily makes no tangible contribution to the patient's welfare. (This is not to deny the possibility that for certain administrative reasons, such as official monthly reports, it may be necessary to classify the patients into diagnostic categories.) Furthermore, a purely qualitative picture of the patient's personality designed to yield an "understanding" of the patient, is of no practical value in helping the patient unless it also serves as the basis for making correct predictions about the patient's future behavior. Thus we arrived at the conclusion that the objective of diagnosis is the prediction of the patient's future behavior as it is relevant to his management or treatment. This led to the further conclusion that ideally diagnostic competence is the ability to predict the patient's behavior, and should be measured accordingly.

While we attempted to follow this approach to the criterion problem in our attempts to measure several of the competences required of clinical psychologists, the nature and magnitude of the problem forced us to use other types of criterion measures to be discussed in more detail in later sections.

Specific vs General Measures

Criterion measures may also be classified in terms of their generality. For example, we used criterion measures of Overall Clinical Competence. Such a measure has practical importance because a clinician is hired to carry out a variety of clinical functions: he is ordinarily not hired because he is able to perform one clinical function well if he is inadequate in carrying out other clinical functions. From the technical point of view, such a general measure is also valuable because it provides a focal point for interpreting the entire mass of validational data. It is, in a sense, a weighted average and possesses all of the assets and liabilities of such a statistic. However, such a general criterion measure has certain disadvantages. It is usually more difficult to discover satisfactory predictor measures for it. Furthermore, the use of such a measure assumes that the more specific skills or functions are positively intercorrelated which may or may not be true.

The use of such a general criterion measure poses a major question: how are the various job functions of the clinical psychologist to be weighted in arriving at this overall or average measure? We could have obtained a measure of overall competence by applying a set of a priori weights to measures of the several job functions, but how could we determine the correct weights? Actually, we avoided this problem by allowing both the assessment staff members and the criterion raters to weight these separate job functions as they saw fit. We recognize the weakness in such a procedure, namely that each rater has his own set of subjective weights or may even weight different functions differently depending upon the particular trainee he is evaluating. The problem of weighting specific measures to obtain a general measure is further complicated by the presence of limitations or negative characteristics. Is a measure falling a given distance below the average or below some other reference point to be combined algebraically with positive characteristics or do negative deviations receive different weights? Frequently, there is a minimum score level such that any person falling below it automatically receives a disqualifying score on the general measure.

The ratings on the general variable, Overall Clinical Competence, were presumed to reflect only actual clinical skills, with little or no weight being assigned to how the rater felt about the trainee as a person. Hence, it was conceivable that a rater would assign a high rating on Overall Clinical Competence to a trainee with whom he, the rater, would not care to work. If enough other people felt the same way about him, this trainee's potential competence would be lost because no one would hire him. For these reasons we also included a general criterion measure called "Preference for Hiring." While rated Overall Clinical Competence and Preference for Hiring were found to correlate highly, the ratings of Preference for Hiring contain a much larger component of the trainee's acceptability to others than do the ratings on clinical competence.

Specific Criterion Measures

The validation of predictors of general measures would have little theoretical value unless we could identify the components of these measures. Furthermore, in such a rapidly developing field as clinical psychology, the relative emphasis on different job functions is probably changing from year to year. In addition, we were naturally interested in the extent to which each separate job function would be predicted. Insofar as the various job components required different skills and aptitudes, predictors of one skill might not predict another skill. All of these reasons led to the parallel use of a number of more specific criterion measures.

Rejected Criterion Measures

A by-product of our criterion research was a list of possible criterion measures which we rejected for one reason or another. Many of these rejected measures will not be discussed in the subsequent chapters on the measurement of the several clinical skills because they do not fit into the developmental work leading up to the measures which we finally used. These rejected measures are summarized in Appendix II G, together with a brief statement of the reasons for rejection. This summary may help other investigators to prevent duplication of effort on unprofitable lines and may also stimulate new ideas for criterion measures in clinical psychology.

CHAPTER C II

CONVENTIONAL CRITERIA OF PROFESSIONAL SUCCESS

This chapter describes the more conventional criterion measures used in the project. These include reports of successful completion of training, objective content examinations, and evaluations of the trainee's performance by others.

Trainees were categorized in dichotomous criterion groups on the basis of annual confidential reports from the universities contributing to the project. One such dichotomy was: Successful (all trainees who had completed or appeared likely to complete the program) vs. Unsuccessful (all trainees who had been separated from the program for any reason, e.g., dismissed, voluntary withdrawal, etc.). The second dichotomy was made on the basis of overall professional promise. The Highs included only persons who had completed or were expected to complete the program with generally superior evaluations, while the Lows included not only the obviously unsuccessful candidates, but also those who had failed to secure superior evaluations.

In order to provide an objective measure of the knowledge acquired by trainees, a measure which could be independent of variations in local frames of reference or academic standards, a multiple choice content examination was developed. Part A covered the content of clinical psychology and Part B the basic fields of psychology. Intercorrelations of the subsections of this examination are positive, but relatively low.

Ratings of the competence of trainees in professional functions are regarded as valid and socially significant criterion measures. This chapter includes a description of the developmental work leading up to the Criterion Ratings Scales, and reports the findings growing out of the analysis of the ratings obtained from three groups of raters: university clinical staff members, installation staff supervisors, and colleagues. These analyses led to the decision to combine the ratings from the three groups of raters into combined criterion ratings. A factor analysis of these combined criterion ratings indicates that at least three factors are required to evaluate professional competence in clinical psychology.

In our comprehensive and eclectic approach to the problem of developing criterion measures, we included indices of administrative status. At the time of collecting the final criterion measures for the current research program, in the fall of 1950, each trainee on whom we had predictive measures was classified into one of the following categories:

1. Ph. D. Obtained. By correspondence with training universities we ascertained which trainees had been awarded the doctoral degree. (We planned to distinguish between those who received the doctorate in the field of clinical psychology and those who received it in other fields of psychology. However, of our two primary groups, those assessed in 1947 and in 1948, none had received his Ph. D. in non-clinical areas.)

2. Still in Training. The great majority of the 1947 and 1948 assessment groups were still in training in the fall of 1950 when the criterion measures were collected.

3. Voluntary Withdrawal. This category included the small proportion of the cases who left

76

the training program voluntarily. Some of them left school; others remained in school but resigned from the VA training program while remaining in the clinical field. Still others shifted to non-clinical fields of psychology or to other fields of graduate study. Through correspondence with the university directors of clinical training, it was ascertained that in almost no case of voluntary withdrawal was pressure put on the student by the school to withdraw from the program.

4. Dismissed. Data supplied in unofficial correspondence indicated that the primary basis for dismissal was academic deficiency. Personality difficulties were also responsible for a number of dismissals. In some cases academic deficiencies and personality difficulties were both present.

A number of other categories of administrative status were set up to cover all the reported reasons for leaving school, but the frequencies in these other miscellaneous categories were very small.

It should be emphasized that this classification into categories of administrative status was based upon unofficial and frank statements of the facts in each case as obtained from university clinical directors by personal correspondence, on a confidential basis. This classification probably is more psychologically accurate than the official records. Thus a student might be officially listed as having resigned from school whereas the real situation might be that he was about to be dismissed by the university. Unfortunately, the number of cases in each of the various subgroups was insufficient to justify more detailed analyses of prediction of particular types of failures.

Administrative status was used as a criterion for validational analyses in two ways. First, the 1947 and the 1948 assessment groups were divided into a Successful and Unsuccessful group. The Unsuccessful group was heterogeneous; it included those who had been dismissed, a few applicants who had been accepted for the VA program but did not enter training, and several who had left the program or had left school with or without pressure from the school. The Successful group included all other cases, i. e. , all those for whom there was any reason to believe they would complete their doctorate in clinical psychology.

There was some question whether all of the trainees in the Successful group were more competent clinical psychologists than all in the Unsuccessful group. We therefore tried a dichotomy splitting the total group at a higher level, on the basis of Professional Promise. In this dichotomy, the high group contained trainees receiving a Composite rating on Clinical Competence of 6, 7, or 8: these included some cases who had left the VA training program voluntarily (e. g. , to get clinical experience with children) and some who had received their doctoral degree. (If 1950 ratings were not available, 1949 ratings were used). The low group, in terms of professional promise, contained all other cases, i. e. , did not enter, failures, withdrawals, and those rated below 6 on Clinical Competence.

The Content Examination

Objective examinations, developed in collaboration with the American Board of Examiners in Professional Psychology, were administered in the fall of 1950. These multiple-choice tests were in two parts: Part A, Clinical; and Part B, General Psychology. The first section of Part A was composed of 123 questions on the content of clinical psychology; theory, method, standard clinical practice, and research findings were all included.

The second part of the clinical section included a detailed case history covering four single-spaced pages. The clinical materials included social history and results of physical, neurological, and mental status examinations. The 117 questions following these case materials asked for opinions concerning the diagnosis and the desirable treatment of the case but also asked a number of questions pertaining more to this type of patient or to patients in general than to this particular case. The key for this section had to be developed on the basis of a consensus of experts. Whereas there was little possibility for questioning the correctness of the key in all other sections of these examinations, it is quite possible that another panel of experts would have keyed some items for this case differently.

Part B was designed to measure the student's background in the basic fields of psychology: (1) Learning, (2) Human Development, (3) Personality Dynamics, (4) Tests and Measurements, and (5) Experimental Methods and Statistics. There were 225 items in Part B.

Table C II-1 presents the intercorrelations among the various sections on the Content Examination. The two sections of Part A (Clinical) correlate only .37 with each other. The first section, covering the general content of clinical psychology, correlates higher with the total score on Part A than does the second section. Although detailed analyses of these scores have not been made, we may assume that Section I was considerably more reliable than Section II based on the case history.

TABLE C II-1

INTERCORRELATIONS OF SUBSCORES ON CONTENT
EXAMINATION
(N = 170)

	A2	At	B1	B2	B3	B4	B5	Bt
A1 Clinical Content	37	92	32	46	41	56	49	63
A2 Clinical Case Study		63	12	29	22	25	22	32
At Clinical Total			30	48	42	55	48	63
B1 Learning				34	40	31	46	65
B2 Human Development					34	32	36	57
B3 Personality Dynamics						27	43	61
B4 Tests and Measurements							59	78
B5 Experimental Methods and Statistics								83
Bt General Total								

All of the intercorrelations among the five sections of Part B are of approximately the same magnitude. The highest intercorrelation (.59) is between Tests and Measurements (4) and Experimental Methods and Statistics (5). These two sections also show the highest correlations with a total score on Part B. As will be noted, the correlation between Part A and Part B total scores is .63; interestingly enough, the correlation between the Clinical Content section of Part A and the total score on Part B is the same value.

Previous analyses of data collected from a comparable group of subjects indicate that this Content Examination is fairly reliable: e.g., the split-half reliability of the Content section of Part A, estimated for the full length of this section, is .90. The relatively low correlations between sections therefore suggest that the different sections are measuring different types of academic achievement in psychology.

Subjective Evaluations as Criteria

One set of criterion data was purely qualitative. The installation and university supervisors were asked to describe their trainees' performance in clinical work and in research respectively, their descriptions being guided solely by a few general headings (see Appendix II-B). Since the objective in gathering these criterion materials was to collect qualitative impressions, these were not used to order the trainees on any continuum or set of categories. They were, however, used in a matching study where judges were asked to decide which of two sets of qualitative criterion descriptions belonged with a given assessment report (see Chapter D I).

Ratings

General Considerations

In view of the well known objections to ratings and the difficulties involved in their collection, analysis, and interpretation, we shall begin by giving the reasons for using ratings as criterion measures in this research project. In the first place ratings are very commonly used in the administrative evaluation of professional personnel. The hiring of a professional person and his promotion or dismissal are frequently based upon ratings. It should be noted, however, that the ratings used in this research as criterion measures were not Civil Service ratings made by the trainees' supervisors: our ratings were gathered with the assurance that they would be kept confidential and would not be used for any administrative purposes. We cannot generalize from the findings based on our criterion ratings to officially collected ratings which are designed to be used in administrative decisions.

The second reason for including ratings among our criterion measures was that we wanted to be sure to have acceptable measures of all relevant criterion variables, of all types of clinical competence, even those which we were also attempting to measure by other techniques. We did not feel that any of our non-rating criterion measures, such as those based on work samples, could be considered completely acceptable criterion measures on a priori grounds alone. Even if some measures were acceptable to us as investigators, we felt obligated to consider those colleagues who might not accept such work sample measures as adequate criterion measures of a particular type of clinical competence.

A third and perhaps the most important justification for the use of ratings was that they provided the only available type of measure for such variables as interpersonal relations and integrity. Our interest in these variables and our desire to measure them required that we use ratings. If a rating scale was to be used at all, it demanded little extra effort for the raters to rate several other variables at the same time as they rated these variables which could not be measured by any other type of measure.

The Criterion Raters

Our criterion ratings were made by university and installation supervisors and by fellow trainees. The supervisors were experienced clinicians or university instructors, all with professional training in psychology. We may reasonably assume that they were familiar with rating scales, with their uses, and with the hazards to be avoided in their use. We feel that the ratings made by these supervisors were about as good as any ratings which could have been collected under these conditions, except for one defect: the raters were not given specific training in the use of this particular rating scale and they had no opportunity to develop a common set or frame of reference.

We could not, however, justify the expense of bringing the raters together from all parts of the country or of sending out staff representatives to train these raters in the use of this particular rating scale.

The ratings by fellow trainees were made by young psychologists with adequate training but with considerably less experience in the use of rating scales and considerably less professional maturity than our other criterion raters. Nevertheless, it is likely that these colleagues were in the best position to make ratings of Integrity and Professional Interpersonal Relations, since any deficiencies which trainees possessed in these areas would more likely be known to colleagues than to supervisors.

The Frame-of-Reference Problem

This research project has the somewhat unusual feature of studying a national group. Our subjects were not a sample of VA trainees but rather were an almost complete sample of all VA trainees entering training in certain years. This wide geographical distribution permits us to make generalizations to all VA trainees. On the other hand, the several universities offer a variety of training and emphasize different features of the training program and different kinds of clinical experiences (cf. Chapter A III). Many of our correlations and other findings therefore represent a sort of averaging effect, possibly obscuring certain higher degrees of relationship in some training centers because of the absence of these relationships in other training centers. For the problem of criterion ratings, however, the important consequence of using a national sample is that the supervisors who evaluated trainee performances represent many diverse points of view. Hence, it is to be expected that these criterion raters interpreted the criterion skills somewhat differently in different parts of the country.

Development of Criterion Rating Scales

Although an intensive attack on the criterion problem was not made until the latter half of the project's existence, we began to collect criterion ratings at the earliest possible date. These early ratings were collected for three purposes. First, we used early interim ratings of performance as an opportunity to pretest criterion rating scales, just as we ran three assessment programs before the major program in 1947. By means of such pretesting we hoped to develop an entirely adequate scale by the time we were ready to collect our final criterion ratings. The second purpose in collecting these ratings was to obtain preliminary data on the validity of various predictor measures. Since the value of validation studies against interim criteria was purely transitory, the data losing their intrinsic worth as soon as later criterion measures were collected, these preliminary validational analyses could only serve to give a rough approximation to the trends found in the final analyses. However, these preliminary results did contribute significantly to the planning of our selection of final criterion measures, to their collection, and to their analysis. Finally, we had hoped that these preliminary criterion ratings would serve as adequate terminal criterion measures for cases which dropped out of training before the collection of the final measures for the entire group. However, it quickly became apparent that we could not use the data for this purpose because of successive revisions of the rating scale.

In the spring of 1947 we asked the supervisors in VA installations to rate the VA trainees under their supervision on eight criterion variables. In the instructions for these ratings the reference population was indicated to be clinical psychologists employed in the VA at the P-3 level or above, excluding trainees. Subsequent analyses indicated that these instructions were unsatisfactory because most of the supervisors were not in a position to use such a national frame of reference. Presumably they used as their frame of reference those VA employees with whom they were acquainted, a reference group which varied greatly from installation to installation.

In May 1948 we again collected criterion ratings, but this time we called upon the cooperating universities to help us. We felt it was more likely that the cooperating universities would be acquainted with the trainees' clinical competence than that the installation supervisors would be acquainted with the academic performance and research competence of trainees. To simplify the task of the raters, we asked for ratings on only three variables: Academic Performance, Research Competence, and Clinical Competence. This time we asked raters to use as a reference population VA trainees at all levels in the training program. As might be expected the resulting distributions of ratings were all badly skewed; in fact, there was but little differentiation between trainees.

Even more significant was the finding that the average rating varied considerably from one university to the next. Thus the trainees at one university would all be rated 6, 7, or 8, while at another university the trainees would be rated 4, 5, or 6. These inter-university differences in ratings were significant at the 1% level. Furthermore, it was obvious that there was no consistent relationship between the mean rating at a given university and the probable average caliber of trainees at that university. While we had no objective criterion against which to compare these average ratings for the different universities, we did not feel that we dared rely on each university's own impression as to the average standing of its trainees against a national frame of reference as a valid basis for ordering the different universities. Therefore, in our preliminary validation studies, we adjusted these ratings in such a way that the mean rating for the trainees at one university was the same as that for all other universities. (These preliminary validational analyses confirmed the highly tentative results obtained with the previous year's criterion ratings: it became clear even at this time that the general order of magnitude of our validity coefficients would be relatively low but positive.)

In the spring of 1949, we made a major effort to collect usable criterion ratings. This time, we asked university supervisors, installation supervisors, and the trainees to make ratings. In order to avoid some of the difficulties encountered in the two previous years we decided to use rankings rather than ratings. In analyzing these rankings we converted each ranking to a percentile and thus obtained a somewhat arbitrary or forced discrimination among the ratings. The use of these percentiles automatically equated the mean rating for each institution.

We also provided the rater with an opportunity to indicate his degree of confidence in his ranking of any trainee on any variable, with a place to indicate whether he felt that it was difficult to rank a trainee because his performance in any particular respect was highly variable, and we left space for comments or qualifying remarks. While these opportunities for qualifications may have improved the morale of the raters, they used them very infrequently.

To obtain each rater's evaluation of the competence of his trainees against a national frame of reference, we asked the rater to indicate which of his trainees he would classify as unusually competent and which relatively deficient, these points being defined as approximate thirds of the distribution of advanced trainees throughout the country. The data collected from this last procedure could not be subjected to intensive analysis because many raters overlooked or failed to follow the instructions. This 1949 criterion rating scale included a series of clinical skills and in addition two new variables: Liking and Preference for Hiring. We felt that Preference for Hiring might be a more realistic indication of a trainee's general standing as a clinician than the more impersonal variable of Overall Clinical Competence.

Intercorrelations were computed among all variables as rated by each of three types of raters. Colleagues, University Supervisors and Installation Supervisors. The agreement between ratings on the same variable ranged from .27 for the correlation between Installation and University ratings on Liking to .75 for the correlation between University and Colleague ratings on Clinical Diagnosis. This level of agreement was considered satisfactory in view of the estimated reliability of the ratings of any one source, based on the intercorrelation between separate raters. However, we discovered that the raters from different sources were not interpreting the variables in the same way. The correlation between ratings from different sources was frequently as high when different variables were considered as when the same variable was rated by the two sources. For example, the University and Installation ratings on Professional Interpersonal Relations correlated only .40 with each other while the Installation rating on Professional Interpersonal Relations correlated with the University rating on Group Psychotherapy .47. Again, the University rating on Group Psychotherapy correlated .59 with the Colleagues' rating on Research, whereas the University and Colleague ratings on Group Psychotherapy correlated only .50 with each other. It was thus apparent that the agreement among the ratings from different sources was in terms of some general factor and not in terms of specific competence.

Separate factor analyses of the ratings from each source clearly demonstrated that each contained a sizeable general factor and also revealed differences in the factorial structures of the ratings from each source. In other words, the three sets of raters apparently made differing interpretations of the rated variables.

The Final Criterion Rating Scale

The criterion rating scale used in the fall of 1950, as a part of the battery of final criterion measures, was quite different from those used in previous years. While we wished to retain the information provided by a ranking procedure (as opposed to a rating procedure where numerous ties might be present), we also wanted the ratings to contain information as to each trainee's absolute scale position, instead of the arbitrary scale position derived from the ranks provided by the 1949 rating scale. To achieve these objectives we used a Thurstone type of scaling method to scale a series of descriptive statements pertaining to competence in each of the various areas of clinical functioning.

As the first step in this procedure, we drew up lists of 10 to 42 statements descriptive of varying degrees of competence for each variable. These lists were sent to VA area chief clinical psychologists and to the chief clinical psychologists in all VA field installations. These judges were asked to assign each statement a scale value on an eight-point scale where intervals 1 and 2 were defined as showing less that P-4 (GS-11) competency in the particular skill being described and points 7 and 8 were described as showing P-5 (GS-12) competency, with 3 to 6 covering the range of P-4 competency. A distribution was made of the 76 judgments made for each statement. We then selected for each variable 10 to 15 statements which had been assigned median scale values at diverse points on the rating scale and which showed a relatively small degree of variability within the 76 judgments.

In the final rating scale, (see Appendix II A) the page for a given variable first provided a general definition; then the center of the page contained a long column, on the sides of which the selected descriptive statements were placed at the appropriate scale positions. The scale values were not recorded on the rating blank. Raters were instructed to write, in the appropriate position in the column, the code numbers of the trainees, using the descriptive statements as guideposts. Thus each rater ranked his ratees and at the same time assigned them an absolute scale position.

Each of the installation and university supervisors was given a list of trainees who had worked at his institution. Each supervisor rater indicated his degree of acquaintance with each trainee and indicated (on a 4 point scale) his estimate of the validity of his ratings for that trainee. For each trainee the three raters at VA installations who indicated the highest degree of acquaintance with the trainee were selected to provide a basis for an average rating from the Installation. The same procedure was carried out for the University ratings. For the Colleague ratings, we had to avoid the possibility that colleagues would refuse to rate fellow trainees of whom they held a low opinion. Therefore each trainee was asked to rate a group of seven fellow trainees arbitrarily assigned to him. Since trainee raters also indicated their degree of acquaintance with their fellow trainees and their estimate of the validity of their ratings, it was possible to select the five colleague raters who were in the best position to provide meaningful criterion ratings for each trainee. By these operations, University, Installation and Colleague ratings were obtained for each clinical skill and for Overall Clinical Competence, Preference for Hiring, and Liking. University supervisors were asked to rate Academic Performance in addition to these other variables.

Interjudge Agreement on Criterion Ratings

The estimated reliabilities of the criterion ratings of each source are presented in Table C II-2. These estimates were made by computing the average intercorrelation between all possible pairs of raters of the same source: university supervisors, installation supervisors, or colleagues. These estimates are slightly elevated because some trainees had less than three university raters, three installation raters and five colleague raters. These intra-source reliabilities are all reasonably high, indicating at least general agreement among judges. Furthermore, reliabilities from one source are of the same magnitude as those from another source. These reliabilities are about the same for all variables, although Clinical Competence, Preference for Hiring, Academic Performance, and Research tend to be rated somewhat more reliably than other variables.

TABLE C II-2

ESTIMATED INTRA-SOURCE RELIABILITIES OF 1951
CRITERION RATINGS

	University (n = 3)* N = 150	Installation (n = 3)* N = 90	Colleague (n = 5)* N = 360
C32 Academic Performance	78		
C33 Diagnostic Competence	66	66	68
C34 Individual Psychotherapy	56	60	56
C35 Group Psychotherapy	51	53	61
C36 Research Competence	68	73	69
C38 Supervisory Competence	68	40	58
C40 Professional Interpersonal Relations	57	38	62
C41 Integrity	68	57	54
Ccc Clinical Competence	74	73	67
Cph Preference for Hiring	75	68	65
C0 Liking	56	56	63

*These estimates are somewhat elevated: On Ccc, 56% had 3 university raters, and 65% had 3 installation raters; (the balance had 2 raters). On Ccc, percentages of trainees with 2, 3, 4 and 5 colleague raters: 3, 8, 18 and 70, respectively.

84

Intercorrelations of Criterion Ratings

As noted in the previous section the correlations between variables as rated by any one source were found to be relatively high. The median intercorrelation between judges for the University ratings was .61 while the medians for the Installation and Colleague ratings were .52 and .51 respectively. Each of the three sets of intercorrelations between ratings of different pairs of sources were of the same general order of magnitude. The University-Colleague correlations tended to be slightly higher than the University-Installation correlations, which in turn were a trifle higher than the Installation-Colleague correlations.

A careful and extended analysis of these data (including separate factor analyses of each set of ratings) gave us no basis for regarding the ratings from any one source as superior criterion measures. There appear to be slight differences in the interpretations of some variables and in the frames of reference used by the different groups of raters, but the similarities and overlap are even more marked. Therefore it was decided to develop composite ratings for each variable by averaging the median ratings from each of the three sources. Since these mean Composite ratings had somewhat less variability than the original ratings, they were recorded on an 8 point scale for use in all subsequent validational analyses. Academic Performance was rated only by University supervisors, hence, the Composite ratings on this variable have a slightly different meaning than on the other criterion variables.

The intercorrelations between the Composite Criterion ratings are presented in Table C II-3. These range from .26 to .84. The median intercorrelation is .60 which indicates either a considerable lack of specificity of clinical skills or an inability on the part of our judges to evaluate these skills independently.

Factor Analysis of the Composite
Criterion Ratings

The matrix of correlations appearing in Table C II-3 was subjected to a factor analysis. Three centroid factors appear to account for practically all of the correlation among these rated criterion variables. These centroid factors were subjected to a series of rotational solutions in an effort to arrive at the factor pattern which permitted the most logical interpretation of the three factors. The solution selected for presentation here was carried out by plotting the centroid loadings on the surface of a sphere and (by inspection) locating a new spherical triangle which provided the best "psychological fit" of the data.

This factor solution yields three orthogonal, i.e., uncorrelated factors with augmented loadings as shown in Table C II-4. (Augmented loadings assume a communality of 1.00 for each of the variables--i.e., that the measure is perfectly reliable and contains no specific variance.)

Graphically, these loadings are represented by points on a spherical triangle as shown in Figure C II-1. In this figure, the distances between any two points is inversely proportional to the correlation between the variables represented by the points (again assuming complete reliability and the absence of specific factors for each of the measures.) Thus, it will be noted that C34 and C35, Individual and Group Therapy, which are highly intercorrelated, appear close together in the figure. None of the points are separated by 90°, indicative of a zero correlation, but the relatively low correlation of .31 between Research Competence and Group Therapy is reflected by the wide separation of the points, C36 and C35.

TABLE C II-3

INTERCORRELATIONS OF COMPOSITE CRITERION
RATINGS
(N = 188)

		C33	C34	C35	C36	C38	C40	C41	Ccc	Cph	C0
C32	Academic Performance*	55	33	36	60	50	47	33	62	51	26
C33	Diagnostic Competence		70	53	47	72	68	55	79	71	56
C34	Individual Psychotherapy			64	39	65	65	56	73	70	57
C35	Group Psychotherapy				31	60	61	45	59	59	52
C36	Research Competence					58	56	52	58	54	38
C38	Supervisory Competence						81	64	79	77	62
C40	Professional Inter-personal Relationships							68	78	79	67
C41	Integrity								61	69	62
Ccc	Clinical Competence									84	61
Cph	Preference for Hiring										72
C0	Liking										

*Rated only by University Supervisors

   In view of the positive intercorrelations among all of the criterion variables, it is obvious that a better fitting set of factors could have been arrived at by permitting the factors to be correlated. For example, Factor B could have been located at C35 and Factor C at C41. However, at least a portion of the correlations among the related variables may be assumed to be a function of halo; hence it seems reasonable to suppose that the underlying factors are somewhat less correlated than the obtained ratings which aid us in locating the factors.

TABLE C II-4

ROTATED FACTOR LOADINGS OF
CRITERION RATINGS

Criterion Variable	Factors		
	A	B	C
C32 Academic Performance	99	11	09
C33 Diagnostic Competence	70	62	36
C34 Individual Therapy	39	85	36
C35 Group Therapy	30	90	33
C36 Research	81	58	08
C38 Supervision	65	51	56
C40 Interpersonal Relations	47	56	68
C41 Integrity	37	40	84
Ccc Clinical Competence	64	63	44
Cph Preference for Hiring	44	62	65
C0 Liking	20	55	81

Before attempting to identify or name these factors, let us remember that both the table of intercorrelations and the resulting factors are based, not on actual measures of professional skills, but on ratings of these skills by supervisory staff members and colleagues. In a sense, then, the resulting factors may be thought of as relatively independent dimensions, which these judges used implicitly in making the ratings.

Factor A is almost identical with rated Academic Performance, hence may be thought of as the Intellectual Factor or component of professional competence. The relatively high loadings of Individual and Group Therapy on Factor B suggest that it is the essence of reputed therapeutic competence; perhaps we might call it Effectiveness in Close Interpersonal Relations. Factor C is not well identified; its highest loadings are with C41, Integrity of Personal and Professional Behavior, and C0, Liking. It would therefore seem that Factor C might tentatively be regarded as the Personal Integrity essential to all professional functioning.

With this factor solution, the two general criterion variables, Clinical Competence and Preference for Hiring, fall near the center of the spherical triangle, suggesting that they are made up of more or less equal amounts of the three component factors. Interestingly enough, Supervisory Competence (C38) and Interpersonal Relations (C40) fall in this same cluster of general criterion variables. Rated Research Competence (C36) on the other hand is correlated only with Factors

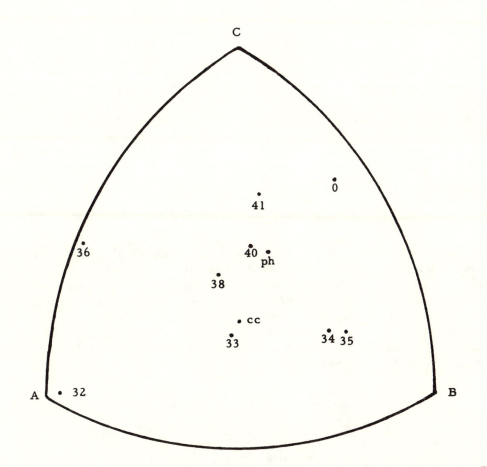

Fig. C II-1. Graphical Representation of Factor Loadings of Criterion Ratings.

A and C while Liking (C 0) shows but very little correlation with Factor A. Diagnostic Competence (C33) has about equal loadings on Factors A and B but a relatively low loading on Factor C.

An alternative solution to this problem resulted in a general factor with high loadings for the general competence variables and the remainder of the variance accounted for by two additional factors, one of which was bi-polar. These factors did not appear to be as meaningful as those presented above.

CHAPTER C III

THE MEASUREMENT OF DIAGNOSTIC COMPETENCE

Although it had been found that judges agree reasonably well in the evaluation of a trainee's diagnostic competence, there was no basis for judging the validity of such evaluations. Do clinicians regarded as "good diagnosticians" more often arrive at a "more accurate formulation" of a patient's dynamics than those less highly evaluated? Because of the social importance of this question, this project devoted considerable effort to the development of a first-order criterion of diagnostic competence. On the basis of several exploratory studies, it was decided to define diagnostic competence as the ability to predict patient behavior.

This chapter begins by describing in considerable detail the rationale for and the procedures used in developing the Test of Diagnostic Prediction. The estimated reliability of the test for a single patient is .61; the correlation between two cases is .23, indicating that it would have to be used with a number of cases in order to arrive at a stable measure of the diagnostic competence of an individual clinician. The test is regarded as a promising technique for the evaluation of diagnostic competence, in spite of an obtained correlation of .00 between scores on the test and ratings of Diagnostic Competence by judges.

An Approach to the Problem

A Definition of Diagnostic Competence

Diagnosis continues to be a major function of most clinical psychologists in this country today. Despite the central role of diagnosis in the clinical psychologist's daily activities, no objective measure of diagnostic competence is available and in general use at this time. The judgments of supervisors and professional colleagues continue to be almost the sole criterion of diagnostic competence. Such judgments are based on two aspects of a diagnostician's work. One aspect involves procedures which are relatively standardized and relatively available to observation, such as the trainee's performance in the administration and scoring of tests. While one may hold that skill in this aspect of diagnostic work is a necessary condition to skill in diagnosis, it is certainly not a sufficient condition.

The second part of a diagnostician's work on which judgments of competence are usually based is his description of the patient's personality. The adequacy of the diagnostic report is usually evaluated in terms of the extent to which the diagnostician interprets various clinical signs in the ways accepted by the evaluator, in terms of the internal consistency of the report, and in terms of agreement with the conception of the case as formulated by the supervisor or colleague. Thus a diagnostic report which is well written from a literary point of view, which includes references to well accepted diagnostic signs from the test protocols, and which presents an internally consistent picture of a patient's personality is likely to be considered a good report. Such an evaluation of a diagnostic report does not consider the extent to which the personality portrait provides a basis for accurate predictions of those future behaviors which are relevant to the administrative and therapeutic management of the patient.

What does constitute an acceptable criterion measure of diagnostic competence? At present, we have no direct method for validating descriptions of personality dynamics. While we could obtain for diagnostic patients who later undergo therapy the therapist's formulation of personality dynamics, we would still have no acceptable means of determining the correctness of this latter formulation. Even if a reasonably accurate description of the patient's personality could be obtained from some expert source, there is no ready method for determining the congruency between it and the diagnostic formulation being compared with it. If the reader questions this point we suggest that he examine the sample assessment reports and qualitative descriptions by supervisors presented in Appendices I-C and II-B.

For these reasons we worked out the rationale, presented in Chapter C I, leading to the definition of diagnostic competence in clinical psychology as the ability to predict a patient's responses to subsequent management and treatment. When for practical reasons, we measure the ability to predict other behaviors of the patient, e. g., test responses, we are, of course, using a second-order criterion. Let us first analyze the prediction situation and then discuss the prerequisites for an adequate measure of predictive ability.

The components of the diagnostic prediction situation would seem to include:

A. The Predictor or Judge. A number of investigators have studied the personality characteristics of the good judge of others (e. g., Adams, 1927; Wolf and Murray, 1947; Taft, 1950). However, for our immediate purpose of developing a criterion measure we are interested in measuring an individual's ability to make correct predictions, rather than analyzing his personal characteristics as a predictor.

B. The Bases for Prediction of Behavior. This is something about which little is known. The following hypotheses appear tenable: (a) accurate prediction requires information indicating the major cultural and subcultural groups to which the subject belongs; (b) accuracy of prediction is probably correlated with the relative heterogeneity of the past behavior samples on which the prediction of future behavior is based, (c) since consistency of behavior is an obvious assumption underlying all predictions of behavior, it is reasonable to believe that the closer the similarity between the behavior to be predicted and the behavior on which the prediction is based, the more accurate the prediction. We shall see later the extent to which these hypotheses are supported by the findings of the present research project.

C. The Subject Being Predicted. Subjects seem to differ in their predictability (see Estes, 1938; and Dymond, 1950).

D. The Predictive Procedure. The most important element in this component is the relevance of the behavior predicted. One can predict that a patient's handwriting style will be the same tomorrow as it is today, but such a prediction may have little value in the administrative and therapeutic management of the patient.

E. Interaction between Components. Although but little research has been done on these interactions, there is some evidence suggesting that certain judges can predict the behavior of certain patients better than other judges, that certain judges can make more accurate predictions on the basis of specific psychological procedures, and that certain types of behavior are more predictable for certain subjects.

It might be assumed that the authors regard diagnosis as a purely intellectual task with little or no allowance for the possible contributions of non-intellectual factors. This conclusion does not necessarily follow; it may be that the diagnostic process is as much or more a function of intuitive or empathic factors as of cognitive ones. Regardless of the abilities or aptitudes required and regardless of the nature of the process itself, the important thing is to determine whether or not what the diagnostician does and says is related to the subsequent behavior of the patient, and hence worthy of consideration in decisions regarding the handling of the patient. We are under the impression that much of what presently passes for diagnosis does not "make any difference" to the patient or to his handling. Only after we have a measure which differentiates among varying levels of true diagnostic competence will it be possible to determine the relative importance of the aptitudes required, the nature of the diagnostic process and the types of training and experience which contribute to the improvement of diagnostic skills.

Requirements for a Test of Ability to Predict
Behavior

The most important feature of a prediction test to be used as a measure of diagnostic competence in clinical psychology is the behavior to be predicted. Ideally such behavior should be related to questions arising concerning the management or treatment of a particular case. However, certain types of questions were not practical in a prediction test for this research project: for example, one could ask for a series of predictions of future performance or adjustment but this would require waiting for weeks, months or even years to obtain the correct answers. This limitation would make the test impractical in a research setting such as the present one. Furthermore, one cannot adequately weight the extent to which inaccuracies of such long term predictions are a function of contingent factors and intervening events, concerning which the predictor could not be expected to have any information. On the other hand, questions concerning the patient's immediate status such as, "is this individual ready for discharge from the hospital?" do not have any fully objective answer in most cases.

In our attempts to develop an adequate measure for predictive ability, we formulated a number of prerequisites for such a measure:

1. The behavior to be predicted must be such that different judges make different predictions concerning it. In psychometric terms, each behavioral prediction item should have a degree of difficulty between .10 and .90, after correction for chance success. This same requirement can be formulated in a different way: the behavior to be predicted must reflect individual differences in patients. In other words, confronted with the same situation different people must react differently. Thus there is no point in asking questions which can be answered solely on the basis of a knowledge of the culture or subculture in which the subject lives. For example, it would be useless to ask whether a male subject wore trousers when he came to the clinic. On the other hand, such a question might be asked concerning female patients attending clinics in certain sections of the country.

2. The behavior to be predicted must be psychologically meaningful or socially relevant. This prerequisite needs little elaboration. While one may well argue that all behavior showing individual differences is psychologically meaningful, it is certainly true that certain types of behaviors are considered to have greater psychological significance than others. Thus the fact that a man's collar and cuffs were dirty on a particular afternoon may not be particularly significant whereas the fact that he struck another man with his fist might well be of considerable significance.

3. The scoring of a test of predictive competence must be completely objective. There must be no question as to the fact that the correct alternative (if one is using a multiple-choice form of test) must accurately describe the subject's behavior in such a way that there would be no disagreement among a series of judges.

The reader may ask at this point why we did not use the judgment of experts to provide a key to tests of diagnostic competence. Even if we could find that experts agreed with each other very well on the behavioral description of general trends in the patient's personality, we would be unwilling to use these judgments since the degree of their accuracy would not be known. The consensus of experts itself is not enough. While certain experts may be highly competent predictors of behavior, we could not select experts on the basis of reputation achieved by clinical work or on the basis of the number of papers published. Theoretically we could have developed empirical methods to identify experts who could predict behavior correctly and then we might assume that their dynamic formulations were correct. One might argue that if a person is able to predict behavior correctly, then he should be able to state accurately the grounds on which he bases his predictions. However, the theoretical development of clinical psychology at this time does not appear to justify such an assumption; moreover this process did not appear to be practicably feasible. We conclude, therefore, that the behaviors to be predicted must be capable of highly impersonal and reliable description such that there can be no question concerning the correctness of the keyed answer. Furthermore, in this rationale it is assumed that the setting in which the criterion behaviors occurred will be part of the basis for the prediction. It is essential that the setting in which the behavior to be predicted takes place be fully delineated. One cannot be expected to predict specific behavior with accuracy if one does not have a fairly complete picture of the situation in which the subject finds himself at that time and perhaps also some information as to his mood or emotional state at that time, etc.

4. The extent to which a test of predictive ability should have face validity is a matter of opinion. We adopted the point of view that the procedure must have a rationale which would be acceptable to competent psychologists who were practicing clinicians as well as to competence psychologists whose major interests were in psychometric methods.

While one might argue that scores on such a test should show some agreement with reputed diagnostic competence, we have little evidence that reputation is an adequate criterion for diagnostic competence. Certainly a high degree of agreement between reputed diagnostic skill and scores on our test of diagnostic prediction would be reassuring. A satisfactory correlation between these two types of criterion was obtained in small samples where the supervisors were known to be well acquainted with the trainee's work; however, the correlation between scores on our test of diagnostic prediction and rated diagnostic competence for the national group of VA trainees turned out to be .00. Given the fact that the ability to predict behavior (e. g. , a patient's self-description) is independent of reputation, two explanations are possible: either reputation is a meaningless criterion or different abilities are involved in our prediction tests and in ordinary clinical function (these abilities being uncorrelated in our group perhaps because of its narrow range of skill). We are not willing to accept the alternative explanation that the rationale for measuring diagnostic competence through prediction ability is faulty.

5. The prerequisite that the test be reliable seems acceptable on a priori grounds. At least two types of reliability need to be considered. The test should have intra-case reliability: in other words the ability to make correct predictions of certain items on the test should be correlated with the ability to make correct predictions on other items. This prerequisite is based on standard psychometric theory. In a test designed to measure a single aptitude, the items should have some correlation with each other. However, it must be noted that if the prediction test involves the prediction of several different types of behavior, the requirement of inter-item correlation should be applied only to correlations between items predicting the same type of behavior. One might well find that the ability to predict one type of behavior is not necessarily related to the ability to predict behavior of another sort.

Again it is reasonable to ask for some degree of inter-case reliability. If the ability to predict the behavior of one patient is completely unrelated to the ability to predict the behavior of another patient, then our measure is worthless as a criterion of diagnostic competence: we cannot order our subjects in terms of any hypothetical underlying predictive ability. On the other hand, it is obvious that many factors work together to reduce the intercorrelation between cases. Unless one standardizes the type of patient (or even the patients for whom the predictions are to be made), the materials on which the predictions are to be based, and the types of behavior to be predicted, one could hardly expect to obtain a high degree of inter-case reliability.

6. We had to establish certain administrative prerequisites in order to meet the requirements of our experimental design. Our diagnostic competence test had to be administered nationally, in at least 50 different installations. Furthermore, since we could not put an unreasonable burden upon local supervisors, and since we did not wish to provide a test administrator to give the tests, the test had to be almost self-administering. Group administration would have been desirable and scoring in a central place was necessary.

Furthermore, since the training programs differed from place to place, the test had to be one which would not penalize trainees who had not received training on one or two specific clinical instruments, or trainees who were not familiar with a particular theoretical position, or who had learned a particular scoring system (e.g., for the Rorschach). Other things being equal, we wanted the test to be as acceptable as possible to both supervisors and the trainees. Also, preliminary and rather unsystematic studies had failed to identify any specific diagnostic procedures which might contribute materially to accuracy of prediction (cf. later section on the Final Form of the Diagnostic Prediction Test).

Prediction and Postdiction

Throughout the preceding discussion we have used prediction to cover both prediction and postdiction. The rationale for measuring diagnostic competence in terms of ability to predict behavior holds equally well for the ability to postdict behavior, i.e., to choose, from among several alternatives, that one which correctly states how the patient has behaved at some previous time. Postdiction has many advantages over prediction. Better items can be constructed when the particular situations that confronted the subject in the past and his responses to those situations are already known. Furthermore, the determination of the accuracy of "prediction" can be made immediately, without waiting for particular behaviors to appear at some future date. For these reasons all of our diagnostic tests were based on postdiction. However, we shall continue to use the term prediction because it conforms to the subjective experience of the person taking such a test.

Statistical and "Cultural" Chance

One problem in measuring the ability to predict behavior is the determination of a base line from which to measure the degree of success. The usual psychometric method for determining chance success does not apply to this type of problem. For example, if the prediction test contains a hundred items, each with two alternatives, one might assume that a chance prediction score is 50. However, a component which we might call "cultural chance" must be considered. To the extent that there is consistency of behavior within a cultural or subcultural group, predictions of an individual's behavior can be made with an accuracy above statistical change. Thus one can ask the judge to predict behavior on the basis of such limited information as age, sex, and socio-economic status, and the judge will be likely to obtain a score above statistical chance. Gage (1951) had students untrained in psychological methods observe fellow students in a series of tasks and then attempt to predict their responses to the Kuder Preference Record. Previously he had asked the same judges to fill out the Kuder as they thought it would be filled out by the typical student at that school. He found that when the responses predicted for the typical student were matched against the actual responses of his experimental subjects, the "prediction" scores tended to be higher than when the predictions for a specified subject were compated with the subject's own responses. In other words, the brief period of observation or some related process in the observer-judges made a negative contribution to the prediction of the behavior of specific individuals.

Developmental Work on the Diagnostic Prediction Test

Predictions without Face-to-Face Interaction

Prediction of Supervisor Rating by 1949 Assessment Staff

The 1949 Reassessment program had as one purpose the derivation of a criterion measure of diagnostic skill of the trainees who served as staff members. Since these trainee staff members predicted the success in training of cases on whom 1949 criterion ratings were available, we attempted to measure their clinical competence in terms of their ability to predict supervisors' ratings. While the trainee-assessors showed marked differences in their correlations with supervisors' ratings, no stable measure could be obtained. The measured ability to predict University Supervisors' ratings was not related to the measured ability to predict Installation Supervisors' ratings. Several factors led to this negative result: the agreement between the two sets of Supervisor ratings was low; the correlation between a trainee's predictions and the supervisors' ratings was quite unstable because it was based on a small number of cases; and it was also influenced by the "range of talent" of the cases assessed.

Prediction of Patient Behavior

We began our preliminary efforts to develop a predictive instrument by using as behavior to be predicted information from social histories, psychiatric intake interviews, therapeutic interviews, court records and military records. The materials provided to the clinician on which he could based his predictions were standard clinical procedures, such as the Rorschach, TAT, free drawings and Wechsler-Bellevue. Questions were asked concerning the type of approach the patient had made toward his therapist during the first hour, the patient's presenting symptoms, his sumptomatology, statements the patient made about his family and statements which members of his family made about him. We worked successively with one patient who had been "sentenced to psychotherapy" by the court for pedophilia, one patient who had confirmed brain damage, and one psychoneurotic student with peptic ulcers. Predictive items were written, tested, and re-written several times. Considerable time and effort were spent on item-writing and re-writing. However, for none of these three cases could we find test items which yielded scores with sufficient range and inter-item correlation to warrant further work along these lines.

We came to the tentative conclusion that our difficulty lay in the source of the test items. We had been attempting to write test items on the basis of information which had been collected for other purposes, information which might not be sufficiently valid or relevant for our purposes. At this point we were fortunate to have the collaboration of Dr. William Soskin who was developing a similar procedure for another purpose. He had obtained the cooperation of a subject, "David." This subject was given a battery of projective tests which included the Rorschach, TAT, free drawings, Sentence Completion, and word associations, together with several objective tests including the Wechsler-Bellevue, the Guilford-Martin and the Allport-Vernon. Intensive interviews were held with David and after obtaining his permission, with his wife.

Three types of behavior were included in our predictive procedures for the David case. One was David's responses to the GAMIN part of the Guilford-Martin test. The second was his self-description in terms of his sorting a set of descriptive statements. These statements sampled 38 variables in the personality questionnaire published in Explorations in Personality (Murray, 1938). In this procedure, the subject was asked to sort 76 statements into a series of piles, the piles being points along a continuum from "most applicable" to "least applicable": thus the subject was asked to place in the one extreme pile the statement which he felt was most applicable to himself; in the next pile the five statements which he felt were next most applicable to himself, and so on to the last pile which included one statement which the subject felt was least descriptive of himself. For ease in handling these self-descriptive judgments, the subject was asked to place a predetermined number of statements in each pile, such that the total distribution approximated a normal curve (Stephenson, 1950). The third type of behavioral prediction concerned a number of actual incidents in David's recent life. Only those incidents were included on which several persons agreed as to David's actual behavior. Multiple choice items based on these incidents were assembled into what was called the "David Test."*

The entire David case was pre-tested on 39 VA trainees at the University of Michigan. Each trainee was provided with all of David's test protocols and with a brief account of the impressions of the psychological examiner during the testing period. The trainees were given an entire day to study these materials and to make the three types of predictions. Since the David Test included a brief description of the setting in which each behavioral incident took place, this test itself provided additional information which could serve as a basis for prediction.

The correlations between the split halves of the three prediction tests were as follows: .12 for the David Test, -.12 for the sorting test and .83 for the GAMIN test. The sorting score and the GAMIN score correlated .19, while the David Test correlated .30 and .32 respectively with the other two measures. These values cannot be considered to be representative of these three types of prediction tests in all situations. For example, in unpublished investigations by Soskin, similar tests seemed to have some internal consistency when the judges made their predictions on the basis of observations of role-playing situation tests. However, the small numbers of judges in these exploratory studied render any definite conclusion impossible. In certain other preliminary studies, the reliability of the sorting test had usually been fairly high. In still other studies of the predictions of GAMIN-type items, the reliability seemed to be quite satisfactory.

To ascertain whether these results were in part a function of the predictability of David himself, we made one last effort to use this type of test, i.e., one requiring "blind predictions" where the judge does not see the subject whose behavior is to be predicted. We abbreviated the David case and the David Test, and used David and three other cases: patients who had made self-descriptive card sorts and one patient had also taken the GAMIN test. Since all previous evidence had shown no relationship between the accuracy of prediction and the amount of time spent by the clinician on a case or the amount or kinds of material he had on which to base his predictions, each of the four cases was designed as a two-hour test. The judges in this experiment were 33 trainees at the University of Chicago.

The results were again unsatisfactory. The series of four scores based on predictions of each subject's self-sort had zero intercorrelations with each other. The intercorrelations among the three David prediction scores were essentially zero for this group which was given less material and less time to make predictions. The only promising finding was a correlation of .43 between scores on the GAMIN predictions which were available for two cases. The scores on each of the several prediction tests were also correlated with supervisors' ratings on diagnostic competence. All correlations were low but the sum of the self-sort prediction scores correlated .28 with supervisor ratings and the sum of the two GAMIN prediction scores correlated .29.

In another exploratory study, 28 University of Michigan trainees predicted the GAMIN responses for each of four cases on the basis of hearing the autobiography of the subjects read aloud. The corrected split-half reliabilities ranged from .53 to .94 for the four cases. The average intercorrelation between one case and the next was .21 or .33, depending upon the particular score used.

---

*William F. Soskin was responsible for the conception and development of this test.

From these preliminary investigations, we reached the tentative conclusion that a prediction test could not be expected to have internal consistency (reliability) if the behavior to be predicted occurred in a situation which was unknown or unfamiliar to the predictor; on the other hand, some degree of item intercorrelation was obtained when the various items of behavior to be predicted occurred in a familiar, fairly definitely structured situation, such as a mental hygiene clinic. Furthermore, it was beginning to appear that scores based on predictions for cases whom the judge had not seen face-to-face would have low intercorrelation. Luft (1949, 1950) has supported this last finding.

We also speculated on the problem of motivation. Might it be that successful prediction of patients' behavior requires a high degree of effort and that the necessary energy and attention were not mobilized by these predictions on cases used for research purposes only? For these reasons we decided to use a prediction test in which the trainees predicted the responses of patients whom they were testing as part of their routine diagnostic work. Exploratory work indicated that better predictions and higher inter-case correlations might be expected when the patients were living realities rather than a series of mimeographed pages containing a case history and test protocols. The use of real cases would seem to produce greater ego involvement on the part of the clinician making the predictions.

Measures of Diagnostic Competence Used as Criteria

The Final Form of the Diagnostic Prediction Test

In the Diagnostic Prediction Test in its final form (see Appendix II-E), the trainee predicted the responses of a patient routinely assigned to him for diagnostic testing. The behavior to be predicted consisted of the patient's self-description in terms of 40 forced-choice and 40 multiple-choice items. The yes-no items were selected by item-analysis of predictions for the whole GAMIN test. The forced-choice items were drawn from self-sort statements in the set discussed above and from a set developed by the Counseling Center at the University of Chicago based on clients' self-descriptive statements made during therapy.

In a preliminary form of the test, five sets of 20 statements each were used. Some of the groupings were homogeneous: e.g., one set contained items each of which showed relatively high variability in patients' responses to it, one set contained items which were relatively easy to predict, etc. Predictions for 33 patients were used in a pre-test. The scores for the five sets were intercorrelated and the one set showing the lowest intercorrelations was dropped. The median inter-set correlation for the four parts retained for the final form of the test was .49.

Are Prediction Scores a Function of Either Diagnostic Experience or the Diagnostic Procedures Used?

An analysis of the Diagnostic Prediction scores indicated that our 1947 assessed group did not make a significantly higher mean score on this test that did the 1948 group. Since the 1948 group was more highly selected and was trained somewhat differently, we cannot conclude that one year of additional training at this level makes no difference in diagnostic competence as measured by this test. On the other hand, we have no evidence that diagnostic competence, so measured, improves with training.

When prediction scores were classified on the basis of the procedures utilized by the diagnostician, only negligible differences were found in the distributions. In other words, the mean score for predictions based on one procedure, such as the Rorschach or an interview, was not significantly higher or lower than the mean for predictions on more than one procedure. No single procedure or combination of procedures seemed to provide a superior basis for prediction of patient behavior.

The Reliability of the Diagnostic Prediction Test
───

Table C III-1 presents the intercorrelations between the scores for the two parts of the Diag-nostic Test and between the scores for two patients predicted by the same trainee. The forced-choice part correlates .40 with the yes-no part for one patient and .48 for another patient. (These two correlations were computed separately since it was possible that the reliability was different for the first case that the trainee predicted from that for the second case.) If the Spearman-Brown formula is applied to .44, the median of these two coefficients, the estimated reliability of the total score for the prediction of a single patient is .61. Thus the test would appear to have reasonable internal consistency.

Each of the two parts shows some internal consistency. The forced-choice part (I) has a reli-ability of .32 when two of the four sets of items are correlated with the other two (estimated as .48 for the entire section). This is probably a minimal estimate of reliability because the pair-ings were arranged so as to put together the more dissimilar sets. The correlation between the first 20 yes-no items and the second 20 yes-no items in part II is .40 (estimated as .57 for the entire section). From these data, we may conclude that the Diagnostic Prediction Test has ade-quate intra-case reliability or internal consistency.

TABLE C III-1

RELIABILITY COEFFICIENTS FOR THE
DIAGNOSTIC PREDICTION TEST
N = 100

(Intercorrelations between scores for each part and between scores
for predictions for two patients.)

	Part I (forced choice) Patient 1	Part II (yes-no) Patient 2	Total Parts I and II Patient 2
Part I (Forced Choice) Patient 2	.23	.40	
Part II (yes-no) Patient 1	.48	.04	
Total Parts I and II, Patient 1			.23

The inter-case reliability is not so satisfactory. Correlation between the case 1 score and the case 2 score for Part I (forced choice) is only .23; the corresponding correlation for the yes-no (Part II) is only .04, and the correlation between the total scores for one patient versus the second patient is again .23. Thus the estimated reliability of a score based on the sum of the scores for two separate cases is only .37. These values are considerably below those obtained in the pilot study using a more homogeneous group of trainees. Whether these lower values reflect a less serious approach to the task by the national sample is not known. It has been reported that some trainees regarded the test as an inappropriate way of measuring diagnostic competence and such persons undoubtedly gave the task less than maximal effort.

Inspection of the scatter plots for the reliability coefficients indicates that some trainees made a score on one case which was below statistical chance, but no trainee made scores on both cases which were below statistical chance.   In other words, a trainee might be systematically wrong in his predictions of one case (perhaps because his conception of the case contained some fundamental error), but he was never systematically wrong in his predictions of both cases.   On the other hand, a number of trainees were able to predict two cases clearly above chance levels.   If one is willing to take the position that a score below chance on this test has no more meaning than a negative score on an intelligence test where the score is corrected for chance successes, then one would say that all scores below statistical chance should be recorded as being at statistical chance.   Rescoring in accordance with this rationale, the inter-case correlation for the forced-choice part is raised from .23 to .26, the intercorrelation for the yes-no part is raised from .04 to .09, and the intercorrelation between the total scores for the two patients is raised from .23 to .30.   This would correspond to an estimated reliability of .46 for the trainee's score based on his prediction for two patients.

This low degree of inter-case reliability can be accounted for in terms of the various factors discussed in the preceding section.   Another factor which may have been working in this particular situation was the practice effect.   This prediction test represented a new task for the trainees and it is possible that the trainees learned from predicting on one case how to make better predictions on the second case.   We do not know how many trainees checked the accuracy of their predictions on their first case: such a procedure should make it easier for them to obtain a high prediction score on the second case.   Whatever the sources of this unreliability, it is obvious that predictions for at least four or five cases should be combined, not only to increase the reliability of the prediction score, but as a check on competence in differential diagnosis.   Unfortunately, time did not permit us to undertake the collection of additional criterion materials, so in our validational studies we have had to use these relatively unreliable scores based on only two cases.

Facade Set as an Attenuating Factor

It seemed desirable to explore the possibility that the prediction score was primarily a function of the extent to which the diagnostician is able to predict the number of socially acceptable or socially desirable answers given by the patient.   We established an a priori key by choosing what seemed to us the most socially desirable or the more complimentary responses.   Using this key to score both the patient's self-descriptions and the trainee's predictions, we obtained two facade scores.   These scores had a high degree of internal consistency (of the order of .70) within the forced-choice part.   The fact that facade score is predictable is indicated by a correlation of .49 between the patient's facade score and the facade score for the predictions by the diagnostician.   Ability to predict facade score on the forced-choice part correlated in the order of .45 with the ability to predict the facade on the yes-no part.   Further evidence that the diagnostician was able to make this discrimination is indicated by the fact that the facade score for his predictions for one case was uncorrelated with the facade score for his predictions for the second case. This evidence suggests that a major component in prediction scores is the ability to predict the general set which the patient will take toward the scale.   It is obvious that any further investigation of the ability to predict this type of behavior should use sets of items which are equated on social desirability.

However, the study of facade set did not help us in our search for the basis of the low inter-case reliability.   Ability to predict facade on the forced-choice part of the prediction test correlated only .12 between the two cases.   For the yes-no part the inter-case coefficient was negative. We therefore attempted to determine the reliability of the prediction score when facade was partialled out.   Given the facade score of the patient and the facade score of the diagnostician's prediction for any one set of items, there is a maximum number of possible correct item predictions. We thus developed a score which compared the obtained number of items correctly predicted with the maximum possible number. But once again we found no inter-case reliability.

In light of these findings, perhaps we should be happy to have obtained an inter-case correlation as high as .23. Luft (1950) found no significant correlation between prediction scores for two cases, for either trained or untrained judges. Bender and Hastorf (1950) had 33 students in intermediate psychology predict the test responses of one or two members of the class whom they knew well. There was no relationship between a student's relative ability to predict his first case and his relative ability to predict a second case.

Correlation of Scores on Diagnostic Prediction Test with
Rated Diagnostic Competence

The obtained correlations between scores on the Diagnostic Prediction Test and the rating on Diagnostic Competence is exactly .00 (N = 122)! We can only conclude that they are almost, if not completely, independent measures of diagnostic ability. The reader is asked to suspend relative evaluations of them as measures of diagnostic competence until he has learned more about each measure from the validational analyses.

As one measure of therapeutic competence (cf. Chapter C IV), trainees predicted the responses of their therapy patients to Part I (forced-choice) of the Prediction Test. The correlation between prediction scores for therapy patients and scores for diagnostic patients is .16. Since this is lower than would be estimated from the reliabilities of the two tests, it suggests that the ability to predict the responses of diagnostic patients is relatively independent of the ability to predict for therapy patients.

THE MEASUREMENT OF THERAPEUTIC COMPETENCE

Although therapeutic competence can be defined as the ability to facilitate improvement in the adjustment of patients, there is no adequate measure or definition of improvement. A number of indirect approaches to measuring therapeutic competence were made, all based on the assumption that the essence of therapy is the relationship between therapist and patient. The therapist's understanding of the patient may contribute to this relationship. Therefore the ability to predict the responses of therapy patients on the Diagnostic Prediction Test was used as one criterion measure. This test had higher inter-case reliability for therapy patients than for diagnostic patients.

Again it was assumed that an effective therapeutic relationship is one that gives the patient freedom to communicate to the therapist the feelings and emotions which have interfered with his adjustment. A procedure was developed for scoring therapy progress notes which yields an index of the extent to which such crucial topics were discussed in the therapeutic interviews conducted by trainees. In addition to this Progress Note Score, a subjective rating of therapeutic competence was made by the judges who scored the progress notes. Satisfactory interjudge and inter-case reliabilities were obtained.

Another approach was based on the assumption that the therapist's feelings toward his patient affect the therapeutic relationship. Measures were developed of the extent to which the therapist felt his patient to be similar to or different from himself. The low inter-case correlations for these measures made it doubtful that they were measuring any lasting attitude or skill of the therapist.

Recordings of of therapy interviews were collected from some trainees. Judges' ratings of therapeutic competence, based on these recordings, showed low but significant interjudge and inter-case correlations.

Composite ratings of Therapeutic Competence were also obtained. The intercorrelations between the several different measures of competence in therapy were so low that the measures seemed almost independent of each other. Much fundamental research on the nature of therapy must be carried out before satisfactory measures of therapeutic competence can be constructed.

An Approach to the Problem

Identification of Competence

The problem of evaluating therapeutic competence seems more difficult than that of evaluating diagnostic skill. The ideal (first-order) criterion would, of course, be an objective measure of the "improvement" in the adjustment of a patient as a result of the efforts of a particular therapist. Since there is as yet no general agreement among psychotherapists as to acceptable measures of "improvement" it was impossible within this project to develop a measure of therapeutic competence based on patient improvement. In fact, the very definition of improvement involves a value judgment, and different psychotherapists may make different value judgments. Although intensive research on this problem is underway at the moment (e. g. , the current research program of the Counseling Center at the University of Chicago), these studies in progress were not ready to provide us with measures which we could use at the time that we had to collect our criterion measures.

Some previous research in this area has compared the adjustment of patients by means of tests administered both before and after therapy. Such work involves an a priori definition of adjustment. Furthermore, the results obtained from such pre- and post-tests are rather difficult to interpret and the studies of different investigators do not always agree (Muench, 1947; Carr, 1947; Reader, 1948; and Siegel, 1951). Furthermore, such procedures would be difficult to apply in VA installations because of the considerable time span between the beginning and end of therapy, because some patients leave the VA installation and could not be brought back for retesting, and because both patients and therapists frequently change installations during any given interval.

Whatever the definition of improvement, it is clear that the evaluation of a therapist's competence cannot be based on the improvement in a single patient. Some persons are apparently not capable of benefiting from therapeutic contacts with anyone. Again, it is likely that for certain definitions of adjustment, the degree of improvement may well be related (positively or negatively) with the degree of the patient's maladjustment at the time he enters treatment. In view of these and similar considerations any measure of therapeutic competence will obviously be unstable unless it is based upon the therapist's work with more than one patient.

On theoretical grounds one might argue that a good therapist will produce a given amount of improvement in his patients in a shorter time than that required by a poor therapist. However, it is obvious that length of time required for therapy cannot be used as a criterion measure unless the severity of the patient's maladjustment and amount of improvement can be measured or controlled. For example, it is common experience to find that students are not able to keep their first therapeutic cases as long as later ones: patients of beginning therapists break off treatment because they feel they are not receiving sufficient benefit to justify continuation of treatment.

Although there is no accepted operational measure of adjustment or improvement, decisions must be made every day as to the competence or incompetence of a particular therapist, and as to the relative therapeutic competence of groups of therapists or student therapists. Because of these practical administrative necessities, we devoted considerable thought and energy to the development of temporary and tentative measures of therapeutic competence.

Requirements for Measures of Therapeutic Competence

To be useful to this research project, an adequate measure of therapeutic competence should satisfy the following conditions:

1. It should be standardized to a degree which would permit practicable administration under varying conditions in many different clinical installations.

2. It should be relatively independent of differences in training or in theoretical orientation. As the analyses of the Training Experience Inventories showed (Chapter A-III), training in psychotherapy varied greatly from school to school and from installation to installation. In some places trainees were encouraged to treat patients, while trainees in other places were discouraged or were not permitted to treat patients. Again, the degree of supervision varied from a very superficial level to one approximating the intensity of a controlled analysis.

3. The measure should be objective: i. e. , it should be independent of the judgments of supervisors.

4. It should have sufficient reliability to yield a relatively stable measure of the competence
of each trainee. There is usually a relationship between the stability of a measure and the length
of time required to obtain that measure. We had to arrive at a compromise between the ideal of
high reliability and the practical fact that we could expect only a reasonable amount of cooperation
from supervisors and trainees over the country as a whole, that amount of cooperation represented
roughly by several hours of each trainee's time.

5. Other things being equal, the measure should correlate with other presumptive criteria such
as supervisors' ratings. While it is theoretically possible to develop a series of criteria each of
which measures an independent aspect of the criterion skill under consideration, such a series of
independent measures is much less plausible than a series of measures which show a certain
amount of overlap. Especially in a situation where one is unwilling to accept any one criterion as
absolute, one is inclined to prefer measures which are somewhat related to each other rather than
completely independent measures.

6. The criterion measure should be relatively independent of the type of patient the therapist
happens to be treating at that time. It should also be independent of the particular phase of treatment in which each of the therapist's patients happen to be at the time of measurement. If the
measure is influenced by the type of patient or the phase of treatment, then the score for each
therapist would have to be based upon several patients or systematic corrective factors should be
used.

7. It is obvious that the evaluation measure should not interfere in any way with the therapist's
primary responsibility toward his patient. Until we have a definitive and unquestionable measure
of therapeutic competence, we could never justify the application of such a measure if it is likely
to interfere with the treatment process. Even under such conditions the use of such an ideal measure would be justifiable only if it were sincerely believed that an accurate evaluation of a therapist's competence would avoid undesirable results for later patients of that same therapist.

Since it was obviously impossible to develop, within this project, a true first-order criterion
measure of therapeutic competence in terms of actual improvement in patients, the most feasible
and efficacious approach seemed to be to try to measure such competence through therapeutic processes. Such an approach has the disadvantage that it has to be based primarily upon a general
theory of therapy, a theory which has not been empirically verified as yet. Furthermore, in such
an approach we are forced to utilize the opinions of experts as to the competence of certain criterion groups used in developing the measures. Thus we may postulate that therapy is effective if and
only if the therapist takes a certain attitude or uses a certain technique. The validity of such an
assumption becomes dubious if it turns out on the basis of empirical evidence that the possession
of this attitude or the use of this technique does not discriminate between the reputedly good and
poor therapists. On the other hand, if such discrimination is found, it is only supporting evidence:
it cannot be considered definite proof of the validity of the postulates on which the measure is
based.

A Rationale for the Indirect Measurement of Therapeutic
Competence

The conventional situation in which psychotherapy is carried out involves one therapist and one
patient. The relationship between therapist and patient is regarded by many as the essence of
therapy. The success of the therapy is, in turn, believed to be a function of the type of relationship

which the therapist is able to develop. A therapeutically beneficial relationship is allegedly one which permits the patient to work on his problems, particularly the problems involving his relationships with other people. Perhaps the task of the therapist can be considered to be one of aiding the patient in his learning how to form more satisfactory interpersonal relationships. He does this by providing the patient with the experience of a "good" interpersonal relationship. Presumably the fact that the patient has experienced one adequate interpersonal relationship with his therapist contributes to the likelihood of his being able to form better interpersonal relationships with other people afterwards.

Experimental Approaches to Measuring Therapeutic Competence

Experimental Measures Based on the "Ideal" Therapeutic Relationship

Fiedler (1950) has shown that there is a high degree of agreement upon the nature of the ideal therapeutic relationship with respect to some dimensions. Not only did expert therapists of different theoretical orientations agree on this concept but laymen also showed a high degree of agreement with each other and with expert therapists as to the nature of the ideal therapeutic relationship. Such agreement, of course, does not guarantee the validity of this general impression. However, it is possible to measure the extent to which the therapeutic relationship observed in any therapeutic hour approximates this ideal relationship. By combining the descriptions of this ideal relationship provided by expert therapists into a single composite description, Fiedler obtained a scale which could be correlated with the description of the relationship in any particular therapy hour as provided by one or more judges who listen to a recording of that hour. In fact, Quinn (1950) has shown that it is possible to evaluate the adequacy of a therapist, i.e., the extent to which the therapist is able to develop a relationship approximating the ideal, on the basis of the therapist's remarks alone: he re-recorded the therapist's remarks during several therapy hours and had judges make their evaluations solely on the basis of this re-recording.

Unfortunately, this possible measure of therapeutic competence could not be used by us to measure the competence of trainees because we could not be sure of obtaining recordings from a sufficiently large proportion of our experimental groups. Furthermore, preliminary evidence suggested that this technique would not discriminate sufficiently well between trainees having a somewhat limited range of therapeutic skills. We also tried asking a few trainees to describe their conception of the ideal therapeutic relationship, these conceptions being scored in terms of their correlation with the composite ideal. The variability in the scores of the trainees was insufficient to warrant further investigation of this approach.

The Therapist's Understanding of His Patient
as a Determinant of the Relationship

In descriptions of therapeutic relationships, Fiedler (1950 a) found that experts could be distinguished from non-experts on the basis of the degree to which they were judged to have the "ability to understand the patient." We therefore investigated the possibility of developing a measure based on the postulate that an effective therapeutic relationship required that the therapist understood the patient. In attempting to develop a test of ability to understand a patient in a therapeutic session, we used a recorded psychoanalytic interview. At various natural breaks in the session, the recording was stopped and the judge was asked what happened next, "what were the patient's reactions?" In other words, we again defined understanding as the ability to predict subsequent behavior. While the test had considerable face validity and elicited the enthusiastic cooperation of subjects as judges, it showed little promise of discriminating between therapists and non-therapists, to say nothing of discriminating between good and poor therapists. One of the major difficulties was the problem of writing satisfactory multiple-choice items on which experts would agree regarding the correct answer.

A Measure of Understanding as Ability to Predict

As part of another approach, we asked the trainee therapists to predict the responses of their therapy patients on the form used to measure diagnostic competence. For 83 trainees who made predictions on two therapy patients the inter-case correlation between prediction scores was .43. This inter-case reliability coefficient is substantially higher than the .23 obtained for inter-case reliability of diagnostic predictions. The therapy prediction score based on both therapy cases, where two were available, correlated only .16 with the prediction score for diagnostic cases. (These correlations are based on the prediction of responses to the forced-choice part of the scale only.) These last two findings are consistent with the widely held notion that therapeutic understanding may possibly involve different attitudes and skills from those required in diagnostic understanding. A diagnostic relationship may involve a temporary and rather impersonal relationship as contrasted to the more enduring and affective relationship involved in therapy.

Expressed Feelings as a Measure of the Relationship

Rationale for Scoring of Progress Notes*

Many therapists believe that if a therapeutic relationship is to be effective, it must not only give the patient the experience of a "good" interpersonal relationship; but must also give the patient freedom to communicate to the therapist the feelings and emotions which have hitherto interfered with his interpersonal relationships. They further believe that, in the course of psychotherapy, the patient must somehow come to experience a relationship between himself and his therapist which permits him to restructure his perception of himself and his perceptions of others. We may postulate that improvement in therapy is directly related to the extent to which these topics are discussed. A more conservative formulation would be that little or no therapeutic progress can be made unless such crucial topics are discussed.

The most direct and presumably the most fruitful attack a patient can make on his problems of relating to others is to discuss with the therapist his feelings toward the therapist. Such discussion permits the patient to test the reality of his perceptions and to evaluate the types of interaction which result in most anxiety or most comfort. A similar result is achieved when the patient discusses the feelings he has toward himself. Here again he is able to evaluate his own part in the relationship and he is in a position to modify his reactions toward other persons in view of his changed perceptions.

A much less direct attack on his problems is for a patient to discuss his feelings toward other people significant to him, that is, to persons on whom he depends for emotional gratification (parents, siblings, spouse or other sexual partners, children, and in certain cases, parents-in-law, stepbrothers or stepsisters, or parent surrogates.) By discussing with the therapist his feelings toward such significant others he can restructure his feelings toward them and his perceptions of them.

Another group of topics, also indicative of the therapist-patient relationship would include intimate details of the patient's life which he would not ordinarily communicate to anyone else: e.g., sexual aberrations, anti-social acts, phantasies, etc.

Still other topics such as discussions of work, sports, co-workers, school, etc. may at times be important to therapeutic progress but presumably do not contribute so directly to the improvement in the patient's interpersonal relationships as the topics discussed in the above paragraphs.

*Fred E. Fiedler was primarily responsible for the conception and development of this approach to the measurement of therapeutic competence.

The patient's boss may be a father figure, his co-workers may be sibling surrogates, but unless he can place his displaced feelings back onto the original source of the difficultues, the secondary relationships are not likely to improve; even if the secondary relationships do improve, the primary relationships will remain unimproved.

Is there any relationship between therapeutic improvement and a score based upon the extent to which crucial topics are discussed in the interviews and recorded in progress notes?

While we cannot give a definitive answer to this question, one preliminary study suggests that such a relationship exists. Siegel (1951) collected the records of 80 psychoneurotic patients who had undergone psychotherapy. By having two judges apply a carefully worked out method for estimating degree of improvement during therapy from the case records, he was able to provide us with the progress notes for the ten most improved and the eight least improved cases. These progress notes were scored with an a priori key which weighted different topics in accordance with the rationale outlined above. There was no difference between the mean scores of the groups for all therapy sessions but the groups did differ significantly when compared on the basis of selecting the highest progress note score for each case. These limited data tend to support the rationale for scoring progress notes and for the use of the highest interview score rather than an average interview score.

Let us make explicit the several steps involved in the rationale for scoring progress notes. The basic postulate is that a good therapist develops a therapeutic situation in which the patient is more likely to discuss therapeutically important topics. When we used progress notes to indicate the extent to which important topics are discussed we are also postulating that a good therapist is able to recognize such topics as important ones. Furthermore, we assume that the therapist, regardless of his competence, will be able to recall the content of the therapy hour. It seems reasonable to believe that if a therapist recognizes important topics when they are discussed in the therapy hour, he will be able to recall these when he is making his notes immediately after the hour. A further assumption in this rationale for scoring progress notes is that the therapist will not consciously or unconsciously falsify his record of the topics discussed in the therapy hour. A study by Covner (1944) supports the belief that therapists are likely to be accurate in their reported recollection of therapy hours although they may not recall the total content of the hour.

The Collection of Progress Notes

The ideal method for ascertaining the extent to which these crucial topics occupied the content of therapy interviews would involve the analysis of full recordings of transcripts of the entire therapy sequence, an exceedingly expensive approach. We therefore studied progress notes to determine their adequacy as a record of the content of the therapy hours. In our preliminary studies we used the notes which therapists had recorded for their own purposes. We found that such notes varied considerably in form, length and relative emphasis, particularly from installation to installation. We therefore developed a simple standardized form for recording progress notes with the following instructions:

Please summarize the major content of each of your next five treatment hours with each patient. Do not use more than 100 - 150 words, but be sure to include all major topics you covered. Use one blank for each interview.
Please write this account immediately following the treatment hour.
(This note will be kept strictly confidential.)

We were able to collect notes for two to ten interviews with one to three therapy patients from each of 200 trainees.

The Procedure for Scoring Progress Notes

The full manual of instructions for evaluating progress notes is given in Appendix II F. The note for each interview was scored independently by two raters. The scorer tallied the number of topics or themes which could be classified as: (a) feelings toward therapist or feelings toward self, (b) feelings toward significant others or intimate details and finally (c) all other topics. Each reference to feelings toward the therapist or feelings toward self was arbitrarily given a weight of three. Each theme concerned with feelings toward significant others or intimate details, a weight of one, and all other topics were given zero weight. From these weighted scores a ratio was obtained: the numerator was the sum of the weights assigned to each topic or theme (e.g., one theme involving feelings toward therapists and one theme involving feelings toward significant others would yield a sum of four); the denominator was the total number of topics discussed, regardless of weight. As noted above preliminary studies had indicated the advisability of using the highest value resulting from a series'of interviews as the index of therapeutic success. In an arbitrary sample of ten interviews, with one or more patients, conducted by the same therapist, there might be as many as four to six where little therapeutic progress was made, i.e., where few important topics were discussed. However, in such a series, a therapist who was able to develop a relationship such that his patients could discuss important topics would be likely to have two or three interviews where important content was brought out. For this reason, we decided to use a maximum measure rather than any measure of central tendency. However, because of the possible instability of a ratio based on a single interview, we identified for each trainee the two interviews which had the highest ratios, and then obtained a new ratio where the numerator was the sum of the two numerators for the single interviews and the denominator was the sum of the two denominators. This value seemed somewhat more stable than an average of the two ratios.

The decision to use a score based on the two interviews with highest scores was largely determined by theoretical considerations of reliability. The highest score for any single interview had a very high relationship with the score based upon the two interviews with the highest scores (not an unexpected result for a part-whole correlation).

Because the scorers felt that the standardized scoring procedure sometimes yielded a value which did not agree with their objective impression about the therapist's competence, the scorers also rated the general therapeutic competence of each trainee, the rating being based on their general impressions from reading and scoring the series of progress notes for each trainee. The correlation between the progress note score and the progress note therapy ratings was .64. This indicates that the scorers based their ratings in part on those elements which were reflected in the score and in part on something else. High ratings were never assigned to trainees who received low objective scores: on the other hand, the scorers sometimes felt that a high score represented an over-estimation of the therapeutic competence of a trainee and accordingly assigned him a lower general rating.

Analyses of the Scores and Ratings Based on Progress Notes

One person, Judge A, scored and rated all the progress notes and each of two other judges scored and rated half of the notes, so that the notes for any one trainee were scored and rated by two judges. The correlation between the two sets of scores of the judges was .73. While this coefficient represents reasonably satisfactory inter-judge reliability, it is attenuated by the fact that the two scorers who each scored only half the notes had average scores which were different from each other and from that of the scorer who scored all the notes. To correct for these differences, the scores for each rater were converted into percentiles, and these two percentile scores were averaged to arrive at a final score for each trainee.

The inter-judge correlations for ratings of therapeutic competence were .52 for Judge A versus Judge B and .60 for Judge A versus Judge C. The reliability of the average rating of any two judges is estimated to be at least .68. Thus the judges agreed better in their scores based on explicitly defined procedures than they did in their global ratings. No explicit definition of therapeutic competence was used by these judges since the three judges had worked together in a clinic and in research studies over several years and felt that they had very similar conceptions of therapeutic competence.

To estimate the reliability of a Progress Note Score based on a single interview, the scores for all trainees who had submitted notes on more than one case were further analyzed. Using the scoring of Judge A, the highest score received by a trainee for any interview correlated .67 with the second highest score per interview (the second interview might or might not be from the same case). Presumably a score based upon a combination of these two scores would have a reliability higher than .67. When this same highest interview score for a single trainee as compared with the highest interview score received by the trainee for his second case, the correlation dropped to .49. This then is our best estimate of the inter-case reliability of the Progress Note Score. This evidence for higher consistency within a case than between cases is to be expected, in view of the considerations discussed earlier concerning differences between patients.

Is the highest interview score related to the number of cases on whom notes were submitted and the serial order of the interview? In these analyses, we again used only the scoring of Judge A. For 38 trainees submitting notes on only one case (on two to ten interviews) the median highest interview score was 1.10 and the range was the maximum of 0 to 3.00. For 38 randomly selected trainees who submitted notes on two therapy cases the median highest interview score was 1.71 and the range was from .75 to 3.0. In other words, trainees who submitted notes on two cases received somewhat higher Progress Note Scores than those supplying notes on a single case. However, using only one case selected at random from each of the 38 pairs yielded a median highest score of 1.50, not significantly different from 1.20 for the trainees submitting only one case. Those trainees submitting notes on more than one case may have been better therapists than those who submitted notes on only one case; probably the better therapists seek the opportunity and are permitted to treat more cases.

Is there any relationship between highest interview score (for any case) and the serial number of the interview in the treatment series? When the highest interview score came from interviews numbered 2 - 5 the median score was 1.30. When the score came from interviews 6 - 11 the median was 1.60 and when the interview number was 12 or greater the median was 1.85. (This relationship cannot be satisfactorily represented by a Pearson correlation coefficient because the distribution of interview numbers is highly skewed.) This relationship between highest interview score and the serial number of the interview is to be expected for two reasons: topics given high scores in this scoring system are less likely to be discussed in the first few interviews than in later interviews; furthermore, good therapists are more likely to carry their cases over a longer number of interviews than poor therapists, and therefore it is likely that their highest scored interview would be some interview other than the first few.

Measures of the Therapist's Feeling Reactions
toward his Patients

In the study by Fiedler referred to above (1951 a), another factor which differentiated expert and non-expert therapists involved the therapist's feeling of personal security in the therapy session. We may postulate that more secure therapists are more likely to develop therapeutic relationships conducive to the improvement of their patients. Our rationale for this approach begins with the postulate that the therapist's perception of his patient is determined in part by the therapist's own needs. Consciously, the therapist may perceive the patient as someone coming to him for help, for emotional gratification, for understanding and support; unconsciously he may or may not perceive the patient as someone toward whom he can feel psychologically close, i.e., as someone who essentially is a person like himself or like the kind of person he might easily be. Or he may perceive the patient as someone entirely different from himself, someone whom he cannot really understand and toward whom he cannot have warm feelings.

One approach to the measurement of these attitudes involves asking the therapist to describe himself and to predict how his patient will describe himself. Then if the patient's actual self-description is also obtained we may compare the actual similarity between the self-description of the patient and the self-description of his therapist and the similarity between the therapist's self-description and the therapist's prediction for his patient. The basic postulate is that a good therapist will perceive his patient as being relatively similar to himself whereas a poor therapist will perceive his patient as being relatively different from himself (Fiedler, 1951). A parallel rationale has been developed in which the therapist's self-description is replaced by his description of his ideal, of the way he would ideally like to be. In our data measures of the therapist's estimation of the similarity between himself and his patient correlated highly with measures of the therapist's estimate of the similarity between his patient and his (the therapist's) ideal. For this reason we confined our analysis to relationships involving the therapist's self-description and his prediction of his patient.

In our preliminary studies using this general approach, we asked both the therapist and the patient to provide the several descriptions by means of successive sortings of 76 cards, each containing a self-descriptive statement. The degree of similarity between any pair of sorts was expressed as a correlation. It did not seem practical to attempt to utilize this rather elaborate sorting procedure in the large scale administration of criterion measures involving several hundred trainees in some 50 installations. With reluctance, we decided to substitute the forced-choice part of the Diagnostic Prediction Test for the card sorting procedure, using the successive instructional sets previously employed with the cards. It is not known to what extent this change in procedure was responsible for the generally low relationships found between the derived therapy measures and other criteria of therapeutic competence.

When the self descriptions are collected in the form of forced-choice responses, as in the first part of the diagnostic prediction test, it is possible to classify each of the items on the test into one of the four classifications indicated on Figure C IV-1. The column classification is based upon the real similarity or overlap between the therapist's self-description and the patient's self-description. The row classification is based upon the similarity between the therapist's self-description and the therapist's prediction for his patient. Whenever the therapist's prediction for an item corresponds with the patient's self-description, the therapist has made a correct prediction. Such correct predictions may be classified into those resulting from predicting the patient's response to be the same as or different from the therapist's self-description. The same sub-classification may be made of the therapist's errors in prediction. Thus the upper right and lower left sections of the figure represent correct predictions and the other two sections represent errors in prediction.

We explored a number of different measures of the extent to which the therapist assumed that the patient was like himself. On logical grounds, we concluded that the most useful measures would be those which are independent of the real similarity between the therapist and the patient and are also independent of the degree to which the therapist is successful in predicting his patient's self-description. While it may be that success in therapy is related to the actual similarity of self-descriptions of the therapist and patient, we were not in a position to investigate this problem. The decision to partial out the therapist's ability to make correct predictions was based on the fact that we were deriving a separate measure of that ability. The measures which seemed

Relation between Therapist's Self-Description
and Patient's Self-Description

		Real Difference Patient is not like therapist	Real Similarity Patient is like therapist	
Classification based on Comparison of Therapist's Self-Description and Therapist's Prediction.	Assumed Similarity (Therapist assumes patient is like therapist.)	AS, RD False Assumed Similarity (FAS) Errors in Prediction	AS, RS True Assumed Similarity (TAS) Correct Predictions	Total AS
	Assumed Difference (Therapist assumes patient is not like therapist.)	AD, RD True Assumed Difference (TAD) Correct Predictions	AD, RS False Assumed Difference (FAD) Errors in Prediction	Total AD
		Total RD	Total RS	

$$TAS\% = \frac{TAS}{TAS + TAD} = \frac{TAS}{Total\ Correct\ Predictions}$$

$$FAS\% = \frac{FAS}{FAS + FAD} = \frac{FAS}{Total\ Errors\ in\ Predictions}$$

$$SAS\% = \frac{TAS\% + FAS\%}{2}$$

Fig. C IV-1. Diagram Illustrating Various Measures of Assumed Similarity
Derived from Forced Choice Descriptive Tests (2 alternatives)

most promising were these: TAS%, the proportion of correct predictions which involved the therapist's assuming similarity between himself and his patient; FAS%, the proportion of errors in prediction which involved the therapist's assuming erroneously that the patient was similar to himself; and SAS%, the average of TAS% and FAS%.

Analyses of Measures of Therapist's Feeling-Reactions

The correlation between TAS% and FAS% proved to be approximately zero. Since both of these values depend in part on the degree of actual similarity between the therapist and patient, this lack of relationship is not surprising. The average of the two values (SAS%) corrects for most but not all of the effects of differences in real similarity, and hence is theoretically a more promising measure.

The reliabilities of these measures, defined as the inter-case correlations, present a puzzling situation. Measures based upon the errors in therapeutic predictions such as FAS, FAS%, and FAS I% (the extent to which the therapist falsely assumes the patient to be like his ideal) show zero or even slightly negative correlations between cases. In some of our preliminary analyses we had found that measures such as FAS show definite relationships with rated competence in therapy. For some variables the low inter-case reliability was a function of the fact that no therapist received high scores on both cases, although some therapists received low scores on both their cases. We have already noted the possibility that a good therapist may be able to help some patients but not other patients, due to the differences between patients. To the extent that this is true, the foregoing rationale which assumes that the therapist would have a general tendency to take a particular attitude toward all patients may be faulty.

Measures based upon the therapist's correct prediction of the patient's responses, on the other hand, show some inter-case reliability. We have previously stated that the total prediction score for one case correlated .43 with the total prediction score for a second case. TAS% has an inter-case correlation of .31. Perhaps the factors contributing to successful prediction in one case are more similar to those contributing to successful prediction in a second case than are the sets of factors contributing to errors in prediction in two cases. SAS%, the sum of TAS% and FAS%, shows some inter-case reliability when the 1947 and 1948 samples are combined. However, there is little evidence of reliability within either of these groups and the correlation for the combined block appears to be a result of combining two dissimilar groups.

Whether or not the good therapist is the one who can make the most accurate prediction of his patient's response to forced-choice itest items is, of course, a moot question. On theoretical grounds, it would be answered differently by therapists with varying theoretical positions. The actual correlations among these and several ɔner possible measures of therapeutic competence are reported in a later section of this chapter.

Recordings of Therapy

Because we were far from sanguine about the adequacy of the other measures of therapeutic competence, described above, we decided to collect recordings of therapeutic interviews from each trainee. Each trainee was asked to submit two recordings either from the same patient or one recording from each of two patients. Where therapy sessions were routinely recorded we suggested that the trainee should select two recordings which, in his opinion, represented his best therapeutic work. Due to practical difficulties and to the fact that some installations had a policy against making recordings of therapy we obtained only 120 recordings from 80 trainees. Since some recordings were of very poor quality and some were on very unusual media we had only about 100 usable recordings from approximately 65 trainees. In this group there were less than 20 trainees from each of our major experimental populations, our 1947 and 1948 Assessment Groups! Obviously this was not enough cases to permit us to use the measures based on the recordings as criteria of therapy in the validational analysis, but we were in a position to study the relationship between these and other criteria.

Two advanced graduate students in clinical psychology listened to these recordings and made ratings on Overall Therapeutic Competence and on several aspects of therapeutic skill. These included components of therapeutic competence which we hoped to measure by other procedures. Some of these judgments were descriptive rather than evaluative. For the one judge who listened to all of the interviews an inter-case correlation of .49 was found for rated Overall Therapeutic Competence (N = 42). For 37 interviews submitted by 30 different trainees the inter-judge correlation on ratings of Overall Therapeutic Competence was .43. These rather unsatisfactory reliability coefficients are probably due in part to the fact that the raters were not given any special training in rating therapy recordings: they were merely provided with a typed definition of each variable and a description of the scale to be used. Inspection of the correlation plot suggests that the judges agreed somewhat better upon the trainees who were rated high than upon the trainees who were rated low by one or the other of the two raters.

The rating scale for rating Overall Competence is reproduced below:

OVERALL COMPETENCE AS A THERAPIST

Consider the therapist's overall competence in terms of the interpersonal relation-ship between him and the patient: i.e., rapport, spontaneity, mutual respect, and 'emotional warmth.'

1 2 3	4 5 6	7 8
Would discourage anyone from consulting him. An extremely poor therapist.	Would refer certain selected cases to him for treatment of maladjustment problems.	Excellent therapist. Would go to him myself or refer members of my family to him.

Measures of Therapeutic Competence Used in Subsequent
Validational Analyses

Let us summarize the measures of therapeutic competence which seemed, on the basis of preliminary studies, to be worth further investigation. Note that these are all second-order criterion measures. For each measure, we have indicated the number of cases used in analyses of the measure. These N's are usually smaller than the total number of trainees for whom the measure was obtained.

1. Composite Criterion Rating of Therapeutic Competence. N = 92 for 1947 group; 81 for 1948 group.

2. Progress Note Score: an index based on the therapist's record of the extent to which the patient discussed topics considered essential to therapeutic progress. N = 42 for 1947 group; 42 for 1948 group.

3. Progress Note Rating: a rating on therapeutic competence made by the judges who scored the progress notes. N = 41 for 1947 group; 42 for 1948 group.

4. Prediction Score for Therapeutic Patients: a score based on the extent to which the therapist predicted the patient's self-description on Part I of the Diagnostic Prediction Test. N = 33 for 1947 group; 39 for 1948 group.

5. Ratings Based on Recordings: each of two judges rated each trainee's therapeutic competence after listening to one or two recordings of therapeutic interviews conducted by the trainee. N = 55 for all groups.

6. TAS%: the percent of correctly predicted items on the Prediction Test where the therapist had predicted that his own self-description and the patient's self-description would correspond. N = 33 for 1947 group; 38 for 1948 group.

7. SAS%: the average of TAS% and FAS% (FAS% is the percent of items incorrectly predicted where the therapist had wrongly assumed that his self-description and the patient's self-description would correspond). N = same as for TAS%.

Intercorrelations between Measures
of Therapeutic Competence

Although some of our data suggests that some of the generally accepted principles concerning reliability may not apply to certain measures of the clinician's skill in handling different patients, we were unwilling to use measures which showed no inter-case reliability. Any score which is a function of a particular therapist interacting with a particular patient and has no generality from patient to patient is not a measure of any general characteristic of the therapist and is of no value in the theoretical analysis of therapeutic skill.

Table C IV-1 presents the intercorrelations between those measures of therapeutic competence which had inter-case reliabilities greater than zero. The inter-case and inter-judge reliabilities have been discussed in the preceding sections. Inspection of the table shows the following pattern of relationships: the Composite Criterion Rating on Individual Psychotherapy is positively related to the scores and ratings based on progress notes; these in turn show a slight positive relationship with ratings based upon the recordings; finally, these ratings based upon recordings show some relationship to the therapy prediction score. The other relationships in the table are essentially negligible or even negative. For example, we cannot complete the chain of relationships just stated because the therapy prediction score has a negative correlation with the Composite Criterion Rating of therapeutic competence.

The positive relationship between Composite Ratings and progress note measures is easy to understand: both are based primarily upon the trainee therapist's reports of the content of his therapeutic sessions. Since it is rare for therapy supervisors to observe the therapeutic sessions conducted by their trainees or even to listen to recordings of these sessions, the supervisors must base their evaluations of their supervisee's therapeutic competence upon the trainee's report, oral or written. The major difference between these two measures is that the progress notes represent only one part of the evidence upon which the supervisors (or the colleagues) base their evaluation of therapeutic competence.

The relationship between Progress Note Scores and ratings based on recordings is not quite so easy to interpret. Why should the recording ratings correlate with progress note measures but not with Composite Ratings? The explanation may lie in the manner and setting in which the recording ratings were made. It will be recalled that the recordings were listened to and rated by two graduate students trained at the same institution. Furthermore, the Overall Competence ratings which they made were embedded in a much longer rating scale which included the task of judging the extent to which certain important topics (those used in the progress note scoring), appeared in the interviews. Furthermore, this particular rating scale was drafted by Fiedler, the man primarily responsible for the technique of scoring progress notes. While the judges who listened to the recordings were not familiar with the rationale for scoring progress notes, it is entirely possible that these judges were somehow influenced by the form of the rating scale itself and the definitions embodied in it.

On the other hand, the definition of therapeutic competence used in the rating scale for recordings emphasized the interpersonal relationship between therapist and patient. If the judges emphasized this aspect of the definition, it may support the hypothesis that the extent to which the patient is able to talk about significant topics is a function of his relationship with the therapist.

The relationship between the Therapy Prediction Score and recorded therapy rating is also not an obvious one. Both are based upon accurately recorded responses of the therapist toward his patient, and so in one sense are the progress notes. Perhaps the type of interpersonal relationship which was emphasized in the definition of therapeutic competence used in rating the

TABLE C IV-1

INTERCORRELATIONS BETWEEN MEASURES OF
THERAPEUTIC COMPETENCE

(N varies from 28 to 152) The basic group includes all available cases
from the 1947 and 1948 groups.

	Reliability* inter-case	inter-judge	C34	PNS	PNR	Recordings Rater A	Rater B	Pre-diction	TAS %	SAS %
Composite Ratings (C34)		56**	–	29	26	-13	-10	-26	11	13
Progress Notes Score (PNS)	49	73	29	–	64	18	40	01	-20	-32
Progress Notes Rating (PNR)		52,60	26	64	–	18	19	10	-13	-02
Recordings - Rater A	49	43	-13	18	18	–	43	16	-21	01
Recordings - Rater B		43	-10	40	19	43	–	38	-02	-45
Prediction Test (Part I only)	43		-26	01	10	16	38	–	-07	-02
TAS%	31		11	-20	-13	-21	-02	-07	–	62
SAS%	29		13	-32	-02	01	-45	-02	62	–

*Case 1 vs. Case 2 (plotted as interchangeable variables) or Judge 1 vs. Judge 2, uncorrected for combined score.

**Median intra-source reliability.

Note: Because all measures were not available on all cases, the above correlations are not strictly comparable with each other.

recordings is developed more frequently by therapists who seek to understand their patients, in the sense of arriving at a diagnostic formulation from which it is possible for them to predict the test behavior of their patients.

The absence of certain relationships, however, is a more important finding than the presence of other relationships. Here are four measures of therapeutic competence, developed independently, each with a reasonably sound rationale. Which one measures therapeutic skill? Is therapeutic skill composed of several elements, some of which are entirely uncorrelated with other elements? To put the problem in practical terms, which, if any, of these measures reflects the objectives of training in therapy? Again, to what extent are these measures susceptible to explicit training? It may be that once a trainee has conducted a few therapeutic interviews to become acquainted with the role of therapist, his scores on some of these measures would remain essentially unchanged over time.

In our preceding discussion we have not mentioned the measures based upon the therapist's reactions toward his patient. It will be noted that neither TAS% nor SAS% shows an appreciable relationship with any of the other criterion measures of therapy. In fact, in some of our preliminary analyses, some measures with no inter-case reliability (such as FAS) showed even higher relationships with other criterion measures than those reported in this table for TAS% and SAS%. While the AS measures may have a valid rationale, they do not seem to measure any aspect of therapeutic competence which is involved in the other measures.

It will be recalled that the judges who listened to the recordings also made estimates of the percentage of the therapeutic hours which were devoted to the various topics utilized in scoring progress notes, and ranked these five types of topics in the order of the degree of intensity with which the content in each of these areas was discussed by the patient. Inspection of the relationships between these estimates based upon recordings and the Progress Note Score reveals a fair degree of agreement. Trainees whose progress notes received high scores submitted recordings in which the patients spent relatively more of the hour discussing topics which were weighted in the progress note scoring and less of the hour discussing unweighted topics. On the other hand, there may not seem to be any trend toward a relationship between Progress Note Score and intensity of the feeling with which the patient discussed weighted topics.

In the absence of any acceptable criteria of therapeutic success, we undertook this series of studies in an effort to develop objective measures of certain components of the therapeutic process generally agreed to be essential to good therapy. While certain of these measures were found to show some generality, i.e., inter-case reliability, the generally low intercorrelations among them force us to conclude either that therapeutic competence is a complex of relatively unrelated skills or that some of these measures of the process are not related to skill in therapy.

CHAPTER C V

THE MEASUREMENT OF RESEARCH COMPETENCE

Starting with the assumption that, since the ultimate purpose of science is to build and improve theory, the value of a research product is a function of its eventual impact on theory, a rationale is developed for evaluating research products. Since it was obvious that most of the subjects studied would not have completed research products in time to permit a direct evaluation of them for this project, no actual measures of research products were developed.

In addition to Composite Criterion Ratings of Research Competence, two indices of reported research activity were utilized: (1) progress toward completion of dissertation; (2) number of research studies in which the trainee had been engaged. Both seem to be fairly adequate indices of interest in research but neither is necessarily related to research productivity or creativity.

Some Studies of Research Competence

The evaluation of research competence is in essentially the same position as the measurement of diagnostic or therapeutic competence: there are no generally accepted procedures available. At the present time the Manpower Branch of the Human Resources Division, Office of Naval Research is carrying out a program of research on scientific productivity (Hogan, 1950). As a part of this program, Flanagan (1949) has utilized his Critical Incident Technique to develop a "check list of critical requirements for the evaluation of scientific personnel." This is essentially a refined and detailed form of a rating scale. It is to be hoped that this research program will provide future investigators in this area with leads toward ways of objectively evaluating research competence.

Hart (1947) developed a scale for rating verifiability of research reports, a scale giving the highest weights to statistical or enumerative data. The intercorrelations between the ratings of students applying this scale to various articles in psychological and sociological journals ranged between .71 and .94. Meltzer (1949) studied the productivity of 266 instructors in social science at 30 leading universities. He arbitrarily assigned a weight of 1 for each article and a weight of 18 for each book in computing his productivity measure. He found that publication output was related to the rate of educational progress through graduate training and to early publication (both age at first publication and number of early publications). He found no relationship between research productivity and a number of other measures. A sociometric reputation index showed a significant relationship to his productivity measure.

In an exploratory study, we examined the research productivity of people who received their Ph. D. 's in psychology in the year 1940, counting the number of times an abstract of one of their publications appeared in Psychological Abstracts within each of three periods: 1938-39; 1941-42; and 1949-50. We found significant relationships between publication in any one of these periods and publication in each of the other periods. This study and that of Meltzer indicate that social scientists are rather consistent over time in their tendency to publish.

None of the work mentioned above provided us with anything approximating what we considered to be a first-order criterion of research competence. Our practical problem was complicated by

114

the fact that few trainees had published articles, not many trainees had completed their dissertations, and many trainees had not had an opportunity to demonstrate their research competence because of the pressure of academic requirements and internship requirements. While we were unable to develop a satisfactory measure of research competence, our approach and our efforts in that direction are summarized below.

A Rationale and a Procedure for the
Evaluation of a Research Product

Our basic postulate was that psychological research* has as its ultimate purpose the construction and development of theory which will permit the description, prediction, and control of behavior. The more a piece of research contributes to theory, the more valuable it is; the more a piece of research changes existing theory by reversing, modifying, supporting, or detracting from it, the more valuable it is.

If the above postulate is accepted, the social value of a research product is a function of its eventual impact on the theory current at the time the research is published. This is a first-order criterion. A crude operational measure of this criterion would be the number of references to the given research product found in the subsequent papers of other research workers (perhaps with a special weight for references in theoretical papers). Using this criterion measure, an accurate evaluation of a research paper could be made only many years after publication. However, it appears likely that a sufficiently valid and reliable appraisal of probable impact might be made by examining certain characteristics of the research product itself.

It is suggested that impact of a research product is a function of three dimensions:

A. The generality of the area in which the work was done and to which the findings apply. Importance to science is a function of generality. Generality is admittedly a rather subjective matter. Yet a diverse group of judges should be able to arrive at reasonably close agreement on generality and therefore on importance to the science itself. For example, a contribution to the theory of personal adjustment is more important than one to a theory limited to the development of a particular individual. Within the field of clinical psychology one could assume that a theory of psychotherapy is more important than a theory confined to the selection of TAT pictures.

This dimension can be made more explicit. For simplicity's sake let us limit the definition of psychology in the following discussion to the study of human behavior. To evaluate generality we may ask to what proportion of human beings do the results apply? Do they apply to all human beings, all people in a particular sub-cultural group, or to some other specifically defined subgroup? Unfortunately, many of the research findings in psychology today can be safely generalized only to sophomore students in psychology.

We may also ask what proportion of the variance in human behavior is accounted for by the findings of a specific research? Do they account for all behavior, all psychogenic behavior, all behavior of a specified type or only all behavior in a highly specific situation such as a laboratory? The final evaluation of the generality of a research product in psychology should probably be based on the product of weights on each of these two sub-dimensions: (a) the proportion of human beings to whom the results are applicable and (b) the proportion of variance accounted for in the behavior to which the findings are applicable.

Many social scientists may feel that a third aspect of generality should be specified: the

---

*Our definition of Research Competence (see rating scales in Appendix II A) was centered around experimentation because few graduate students make primarily theoretical contributions to science.

importance of the phenomena studied in terms of social relevance. We feel that such a component is not relevant to the measurement of contribution to a science. Furthermore, it is probably covered in large part by the two other components of generality discussed above.

Preliminary investigation indicated that while some agreement could be obtained between judges in evaluating generality, the degree of agreement was relatively low. It seems likely that different judges use different value systems in making such judgments.

B. The type of contribution made by the product. The contribution or contributions of a research product may be categorized as contributions to theory, concepts, methods, variables, or applications. A series of 13 statements descriptive of possible types of research contribution were prepared and presented in a paired comparison form to 29 staff members in the psychology departments at the University of Chicago and the University of Michigan.* Analysis (by the Law of Comparative Judgment, Case V)** yielded scaled values for these statements as shown in Table C V-1.

In general, statements dealing with contributions to theory were assigned high values, statements dealing with factual contributions received low values and statements dealing with methodological contributions fall in between. However, there is considerable overlap; for example, some statements dealing with contributions pertinent to theory fall below statements dealing with factual and methodological contributions. While the general order of value, theory-method-fact, is present, novelty or originality obviously makes a substantial contribution to the scale values. A new theory, a new method or a new fact is given more importance than a confirmation of previous content.

Although no definite conclusion can be reached on the basis of such limited data, a cursory analysis of them suggested the possibility that these statements fell along a single dimension; this is rather surprising in view of the heterogeneity of the statements.

These scale values should not be taken too seriously. Each represents a scale point obtained by averaging the values assigned by different judges, and their distributions are in some cases rectangular and for one statement even bi-modal. Furthermore, the individual judges had quite diverse conceptions as to the relative importance of contributions to theory, methods and fact. While more than half the judges rated theory as more important than method or fact, one-quarter of the judges did not value theory as clearly more important than method or fact. Some judges felt that there was no distinction between the value of theory and method or method and fact. These detailed analyses indicated that there was no clear consensus among these judges on the scale values. In additon, the judges who contributed to arriving at these scale values were few in number and were not a randomly selected sample. For these reasons, we did not feel justified in applying this scale in the evaluation of the research products of trainees. Furthermore, this scale should not be used to evaluate the products of any individual researcher, except perhaps for exploratory research purposes.

C. Degree of conviction created by the paper. No research has impact unless its findings are more or less scientifically credible. This dimension has two subsidiary components: (a) demonstrated technical competence in applying research methods. This component would include evidence pertaining to: accuracy in observation and analysis, the use of appropriate measuring devices, the use of an appropriate experimental design, and skill in communicating procedures,

---

*We are indebted to Mr. Thomas Johnson and to Dr. William Schutz for their work on this study.

**Cf. Guilford, J. P. Psychometric Methods, 1936, Chapter 7.

TABLE C V -1

OBTAINED SCALE VALUES FOR VARIOUS TYPES
OF RESEARCH CONTRIBUTIONS

Scale Value

3.58	1.	A theory is proposed; is shown to account for existing fact, and is in such form that it can be tested.
2.90	2.	A prediction derived from existing theory is tested and confirmed in a new experiment.
2.68	3.	A prediction derived from existing theory is tested, but is not confirmed, in a new experiment.
2.44	4.	It is experimentally demonstrated that a proposed method gives information which is relevant and non-obvious.
2.39	5.	An experimental test of an existing theory is repeated, the results not agreeing with the results of the previous test.
2.23	6.	A method is derived logically and it is shown that it could give information which is relevant and non-obvious.
1.87	7.	An experiment, completed outside of any formal theoretical context, clarifies the nature of the variable.
1.85	8.	The information yielded by a particular method is found to be subject to previously unrecognized influences which make the method less useful.
1.79	9.	A logical analysis is made of the structure of an existing theory.
1.66	10.	An experimental test of an existing theory is repeated, the results agreeing with the previous test.
1.42	11.	An experiment, completed outside of any formal theoretical context, relates variables.
1.32	12.	An experiment, completed outside of any formal theoretical context, presents new facts.
0.00	13.	An experiment, completed outside of any formal theoretical context, is repeated.

results and conclusions. Related to this, but we believe worthy of separate evaluation is (b) the relative unambiguity of the findings, i.e., the definiteness with which the factual conclusions can be stated, the assurance with which a known hypothesis can be considered to have been disproved or shown to be tenable.

Although we have not attempted to develop procedures for measuring the degree of conviction created by a research paper, we feel that this dimension would present fewer problems than either of the other two dimensions. These three dimensions are probably not independent and much research will be required before it is possible to evaluate a research paper on the basis of them. The final summary score for any given research paper should probably be a function of three scores, one for each of the three dimensions. Perhaps it should be the product of these scores since impact is a function of mass. If a product is "thin" on one dimension, a high score on another dimension does not necessarily compensate for that weakness!

We have not attempted to develop a method for arriving at a measure of the total research contribution of an individual, which would obviously be some function of the quantity and quality of his research products plus the almost intangible variable, personal influence upon other research workers.

Criteria of Research Activity and Productivity

Although we used no work sample measure of research competence, we did obtain data regarding the research activity and productivity of subjects studied. While the amount of research activity is probably more a function of motivation than ability, it may be assumed to bear at least some positive relationship to the quality of research contributions.

Our measures of research activity were obtained from the Training Experience Inventory (cf. Chapter A III and Appendix II-D). These data were provided by the trainees and may therefore be subject to some distortion or exaggeration; however, since the reported facts could be readily verified, these data are probably reasonably correct. In the Training Experience Inventory each trainee was asked to indicate how far along he was toward completing his dissertation. After more than three years in graduate training one third of the 1947 group had not yet selected the title for the dissertation and only 23% had collected their data. Only 5% of the 1948 group, in their third year of training, had collected data for a dissertation (see Table C II-2). It develops that if we had constructed a scale for evaluating research products, we could have applied it to the dissertations of only 5% of the 1947 group and only 1% of the 1948 group. At one point we considered using the research proposal itself as a basis for estimating research competence but felt such measurement would be too indirect and inferential.

Even if more of our experimental group had completed their dissertations, the use of doctoral dissertations as research work samples would have been questionable. The contribution of the sponsor and other faculty advisors to a dissertation probably varies widely from student to student, and perhaps from department to department. Since the extent of such contribution in any particular case would be difficult to ascertain, the quality of the dissertation itself is a doubtful index of the graduate research competence of a young Ph.D.

Progress toward completing the dissertation is, however, an acceptable measure of research interest and motivation. As we have seen above, Meltzer found that rate of progress through graduate training is related to the rate of research productivity. Still a better measure of research interest may be the amount of research a student does above and beyond that required for the degree. We therefore asked each trainee to "list all research in which you have been engaged . . . . Include minor research (e. g. , exploratory studies, projects to fulfill course requirements, research done on the job,) but omit papers based on library research only unless accepted for publication." Because these instructions were worded in such a general manner, they were no doubt interpreted somewhat differently by different trainees. We felt, however, that the total number of titles of research studies listed by each trainee would provide a fairly adequate index of his research activity. Table C V-2 indicates that 53% of both 1947 and 1948 groups had engaged in two or more research studies. It is interesting to note that the 1948 group, which has had one less year of graduate training, reports as much or more research activity as the 1947 group. Note, too, that only 14% of the 1948 group as compared with 23% of the 1947 group report no research titles. Whether this represents a difference in the selection standards utilized by universities in 1948 as compared to 1947, or a change in the attitude of university departments in the direction of encouraging research activity on the part of clinical trainees, we cannot determine

TABLE C V-2

MEASURES OF RESEARCH ACTIVITY

	Progress toward Completing Dissertation		
	1947 Group (N = 71)	1948 Group (N = 76)	All Available Cases* (N = 279)
No title reported	34%	78%	42%
Title only	14%	9%	8%
Design completed	28%	8%	15%
Data collected	18%	4%	11%
Dissertation completed	4%	1%	20%
Dissertation published	1%	0%	4%

	Number of Titles of Research Studies		
	1947 Group (N = 71)	1948 Group (N = 76)	All Available Cases* (N = 279)
0	23%	14%	24%
1	24%	33%	23%
2	27%	17%	20%
3	10%	17%	15%
4	4%	4%	5%
5	6%	9%	8%
6 or more	7%	5%	6%

*Includes 1947 and 1948 experimental groups plus trainees entering in 1946, trainees entering in 1947 and 1948 at 2nd or 3rd year levels, trainees entering in 1947 and 1948 who were not assessed, etc.

from our data. Probably both factors had some influence.

The trainees were also asked to indicate those research projects which had resulted in a publication and those which had resulted in a paper delivered before a professional society. Only 1% of each of the two groups reported having presented papers before professional societies. Twenty percent of the 1947 group and 13% of the 1948 group reported published papers. Neither of these two measures were used as criteria in validational analyses.

Rated Research Competence

For the reasons outlined above, we were not able to develop and apply any direct measures of research competence. In the validational analyses, therefore, it has been necessary to depend primarily on the Composite Ratings of Research Competence as a criterion measure. To the extent that trainees had not yet completed any research, these ratings reflect little more than another evaluation of research promise. However, since they were made by judges who had observed the trainee in settings where research activity is encouraged, these ratings are likely to be highly correlated with future research productivity. As already reported in Chapter C II, the inter-judge reliabilities of criterion ratings of Research Competence were among the highest values obtained.

CHAPTER C VI

THE EVALUATION OF OTHER PROFESSIONAL QUALIFICATIONS

The three major functions of the clinical psychologist today are generally agreed to be diagnosis, therapy and research. Our efforts at measuring these competences have been described in the last three chapters. This brief chapter discusses other less specific but nevertheless important criteria of professional competence.

Competence as a Supervisor

Most clinical psychologists are called on to assist in the training of students and younger staff members. Such supervising duties are normally carried out by the chief psychologists or more mature staff members of an installation, but because of a shortage of full time staff members during the last five years, many advanced trainees have had an opportunity to serve in at least minor supervisory roles. Thus in some installations, the first level supervision of P-1 trainees is sometimes assigned to P-3-3 or P-3-4 trainees, who are in turn supervised by a staff psychologist.

Although competence in supervision is necessary for a fully qualified clinical psychologist, we did not attempt to develop any objective measure of this skill. We did, however, obtain ratings on this skill from installation supervisors, from university staff members, and from colleagues. For trainees who had not had an opportunity to function in a supervisory role, ratings on this variable are admittedly more nearly estimates of "aptitude for" than "measures of success in" this professional function.

Two other variables appearing in the Criterion Rating Scale deserve brief mention. These are: Professional Inter-Personal Relations and Integrity of Personal and Professional Behavior. Although neither of these variables refers to specific professional competences, both are regarded as essential to all aspects of professional competence.

Professional Inter-Personal Relations

It is our impression that, among clinical psychologists, outright failure on a job, i.e., dismissal or request for resignation, rarely if ever results from a lack of competence in specific job function. On the other hand, such professional "failures" may result if the psychologist is not able to get along with his professional colleagues, whether in psychology or in the related professions. In fact, we strongly suspect that good inter-personal professional and social relationships have enabled many persons with relatively inadequate clinical skills to survive professionally or even to achieve promotion on the job. Whether or not this is a desirable state of affairs is a debatable question; but if we are realistic, we must accept the fact that the ability to get along with colleagues in the working situation is an important and perhaps the major determinant of professional success. Because of the social nature of this variable, it seemed that ratings by installation supervisor, university staff, and colleagues would give us the best possible measure of it. No attempt was made to develop any other measure of Professional Inter-Personal Relations.

Integrity of Personal and Professional Behavior

Although a relatively young profession, clinical psychology is rapidly maturing with respect to the problems of ethical practice. With all other professions, it shares the common responsibility of serving individuals by providing some kind of a service which they are unable to provide for themselves. In other words, the individual asks for some kind of help. In so doing, he places himself, at least in part, within the power of the person whose professional help he seeks. The ethics of all professions demand that the interest and welfare of the client or patient be kept paramount in all professional behavior.

Because of the personal nature of the problems brought to members of the mental hygiene profession, as well as the general dependence of the patients who bring them, it is inevitable that psychiatrists, social workers, and clinical psychologists are frequently confronted by decisions involving ethical considerations. While ethical codes may provide a guide to such decisions, it is generally agreed that ethical professional behavior is primarily a function of the character structure of the practitioner. Supervisors, staff, and colleagues' ratings promised to provide us with the most valid index of this vague but important variable, Integrity of Personal and Professional Behavior.

CHAPTER D I

THE PREDICTION PROBLEM

The prediction problem involved in this study is examined both theoretically and empirically. The numerous components of the assessment predictions and of the criteria are made explicit to show the possible sources of errors in the predicting process and in the descriptions of the individual at the time of assessment and at the time the criterion measures were made. Then the problem is approached from a technical point of view with an evaluation of factors influencing the size of all the validation coefficients.

The next part of the chapter presents data on the agreement between descriptive ratings made at the same two points in time, findings which provide a frame of reference against which to compare agreement between predicted performance and later measured performance. While the two sets of descriptive ratings show relatively low agreement with each other, the predictions of performance and the subsequent performance measures reach the same level of agreement.

Since the prediction of future professional performance cannot be expected to be any more accurate than the consistency of personality and behavior over time, it seemed desirable to obtain an estimate of the degree of this consistency. The last sections of the chapter report studies on the matching of individuals on the basis of two personality evaluations obtained three years apart. It was found that judges were able to match with fair success independent qualitative descriptions written more than three years apart. Profiles based on two sets of descriptive personality ratings were about equally often matched by a statistical procedure.

Components in the Prediction Problem

Before presenting the results of our validation studies, it seems well to examine the several components of the complex prediction process involved in assessment. Figure D I-1 presents a rough schematic diagram of these components. The horizontal dimension represents time: the left-hand end indicates Time I, the time of initial assessment or testing, and the right hand end Time II, at which our criterion measures were obtained. For each trainee we postulate a Personality I as of Time I and a Personality II as of Time II. Personality II is assumed to be identical with Personality I except for the influence of certain factors operative during the intervening time period: these factors would include normal growth and experience factors, the effects of graduate training in clinical psychology, and for at least one-quarter of our experimental subjects, the effects of personal psychotherapy. The degree to which these factors individually or jointly operated to produce changes between Personality I and Personality II cannot be accurately determined.

Let us now examine the left-hand column. We postulate the existence of certain potentially true predictive data (B) determined by Personality I (A). By definition, if these true prognostic data were known, it should be possible to predict true future performance. The accuracy of such a prediction would be perfect except for the influence of the variables referred to as operating during the intervening years and such contingent and unpredictable factors as are unique to the university or installations in which the subject received his training.

124

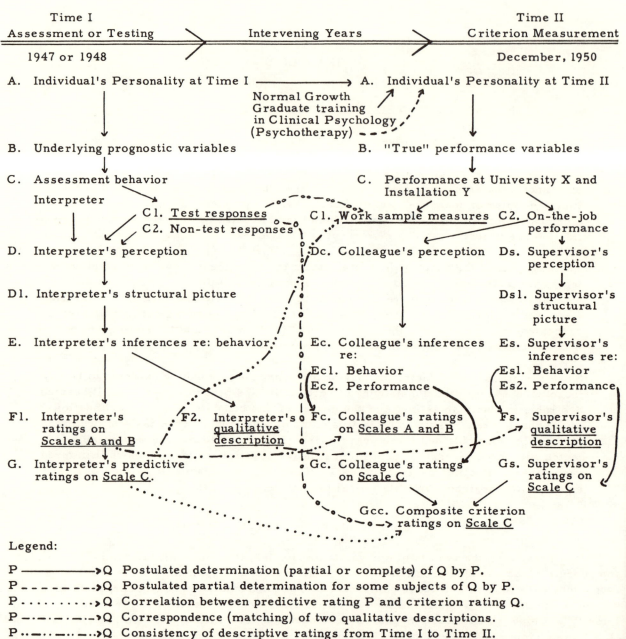

Time I
Assessment or Testing   Intervening Years   Time II
Criterion Measurement

1947 or 1948   December, 1950

A. Individual's Personality at Time I ⟶ A. Individual's Personality at Time II

Normal Growth
Graduate training
in Clinical Psychology
(Psychotherapy)

B. Underlying prognostic variables   B. "True" performance variables

C. Assessment behavior   C. Performance at University X and
    Interpreter   Installation Y

       C1. Test responses   C1. Work sample measures   C2. On-the-job
       C2. Non-test responses   performance

D. Interpreter's perception   Dc. Colleague's perception   Ds. Supervisor's
                                                         perception

D1. Interpreter's structural picture   Ds1. Supervisor's
                                                          structural
                                                            picture

E. Interpreter's inferences re: behavior   Ec. Colleague's inferences   Es. Supervisor's
                                            re: inferences re:
                                         Ec1. Behavior   Es1. Behavior
                                         Ec2. Performance   Es2. Performance

F1. Interpreter's   F2. Interpreter's   Fc. Colleague's ratings   Fs. Supervisor's
     ratings on   qualitative   on Scales A and B   qualitative
     Scales A and B   description   description

G. Interpreter's predictive   Gc. Colleague's ratings   Gs. Supervisor's
    ratings on Scale C.   on Scale C   ratings on
                                                                  Scale C

                                   Gcc. Composite criterion
                                        ratings on Scale C

Legend:

P ⟶ Q Postulated determination (partial or complete) of Q by P.
P - - - - - - ⟶ Q Postulated partial determination for some subjects of Q by P.
P . . . . ⟶ Q Correlation between predictive rating P and criterion rating Q.
P -·-·-·-·-·⟶ Q Correspondence (matching) of two qualitative descriptions.
P ··-··-··-··⟶ Q Consistency of descriptive ratings from Time I to Time II.
P - ● - ● - ●⟶ Q Correlation between assessment test response P and criterion rating Q.
P ●● - ●● - ●●⟶ Q Correlation between assessment test responses P and work sample measure Q.
P . . . - . . . - . . .⟶ Q Correlation between predictive rating P and work sample measure Q.

Fig. D I-1 Components in the Validation of Assessment Procedures*

*We are indebted to Lee J. Cronbach for the idea of depicting this problem in graphic form.

Continuing to the next level of derivation, in the left hand column we come to the behavior of trainees at the time of assessment (C). Our record of this behavior is far less complete than would have resulted if hidden sound cameras had been used to follow the trainee through every second of the assessment program. The assessment behavior of each trainee can be divided into the test responses recorded by the trainee on answer sheets (C1), and other responses which were observed but only partially recorded by staff members (C2). These latter responses were reported in more or less detail and with more or less accuracy by staff members (e.g., the Rorchach protocol, the interview notes, and notes on behavior in situation tests). From these various responses, in one combination or another, were derived the interpretive perceptions of these responses (D1). We have not complicated the diagram by adding the personality of the staff members (judge) as one determinant of these perceptions, a determinant which continues to influence the data of each of the successive stages or levels in this column.

From his perceptions of the candidate's behavior, the interpreter formulates a conception of the candidate and from this makes certain inferences regarding his personality. These inferences were recorded in the form of ratings on the variables in Scales A and B (F1) and in the form of a qualitative description of the personality structure (F2). From these inferences the interpreter then made predictions as to the future behavior of the candidate. These predictions were systematically recorded in the form of predictive ratings on Scale C (G).

It is evident that errors in the Scale C predictions could have resulted from distortions or loss of information occurring at any one of several levels or stages in this derivational process. For example, we can never know the extent to which assessment behavior corresponded to the hypothetical prognostic data. There is every reason to believe that the behavior of the candidates in the assessment situation was more or less influenced by their perceptions of that situation. In the case of the 1947 group they had been brought voluntarily but not of their own initiative to a strange place with only strangers around them. Although they were told that their assessment records would never be used for official purposes, they knew that their behavior, feelings, attitudes and phantasies were being carefully scrutinized. The 1948 group believed that at least some of their test responses were to be used in determining their acceptability for graduate training. Thus for neither group is it likely that assessment behavior was a representative sample of general behavior. Each trainee's assessment behavior was a function of both his general behavior and his reaction to the assessment situation. Different trainees probably perceived the assessment situation to be more or less stressful, more or less punishing or gratifying, and behaved accordingly.

We have already commented upon the possibility of a degree of distortion in the interpreter's perceptions of the trainees' assessment behavior. In addition to this effect we have errors produced by the interpreter's attempts to develop a structural picture of the trainee and to make generalizations or inferences about his behavior. In writing the qualitative description the interpreter attempted to communicate to professional colleagues his picture of the individual. The extent to which the picture seen by the interpreter coincided with the picture derived by a reader of this qualitative description would be a function both of the interpreter's idiosyncrasy of style and vocabulary and of certain characteristics of the reader.

From his inferences regarding the characteristics of the trainee, the interpreter made ratings on Scale A and B variables. These ratings were obviously influenced by the interpreter's conceptions of these variables. During assessment staff team conferences, it was not uncommon for two staff members to conclude that they perceived the trainee in the same way but still have difficulty in agreeing about the numerical rating to be assigned to him because of their individual interpretations of the variable being rated.

Even if two interpreters had agreed perfectly on their formulation of the personality of the trainee at the time of assessment, they could still have made quite different predictions regarding the trainee's future behavior. Assessment staff members naturally disagreed to some extent in their views as to the degree to which a particular trainee's personality would be modified by four years' experiences in a particular university, and by contact in one form or another with the content of clinical psychology and possible changes in self-insights from such experiences. Furthermore, the assessment staff members were quite uncertain as to the skills and traits which would be required, several years hence, for a trainee to be judged as high in specific clinical skills, e. g., diagnostic or therapeutic competence.

While we can never determine accurately the amount of distortion introduced by each level of abstraction or interpretation, several indirect approaches are possible. Our analyses indicate that by the time they made their final individual ratings the assessment staff agreed very closely with each other in their evaluation of a trainee. There is the possibility that certain staff members may have tended to dominate their fellow staff members in the pooling conferences, but since staff members were rotated on teams, it seems unlikely that the final pooled assessment ratings were greatly influenced by individual differences among the personalities of the different staff members. By comparing the relationship between test responses and criterion measures, with the relationship between predictive ratings and criterion measures, we are able to obtain an estimate of the amount and nature of the variance introduced by the process of making qualitative inferences from test scores. Finally, the relationship between descriptive ratings on Scales A and B at time of assessment and again at time of criterion measurement can be compared with the relationship between predictive ratings at these same two times in order to determine the degree of error introduced in the interpreter's inferences regarding the trainee's future behavior.

The successive steps in the right hand column of Figure D I-1 closely parallel those in the left hand column. We can postulate an underlying Personality II(A) as of the time of performance measurement and the corresponding set of "true" performance and behavior data (B), which is independent of the unique situation of assessment. At the next stage we have the performance at a given university and at a given installation (C) which could potentially be recorded with precise accuracy. Actually we were forced to rely on colleagues' perceptions of this performance (Dc) and their derived inferences regarding the trainee's behavior (Ec), inferences which are recorded in the form of colleagues' ratings on Scales A and B (Fc); and colleagues' inferences regarding the trainee's professional performance which in turn are recorded in colleagues' ratings (Gc) on Scale C. We also indicated the installation supervisors' perceptions of the trainee's clinical performance and the university supervisor's perceptions of the trainee's research and academic performance (Ds). These perceptions determine the supervisor's inferences (Es), his qualitative descriptions (Fs), and his ratings of clinical competence variables (Gs). Finally, the colleagues' ratings and those from each type of supervisor were combined into Composite Criterion ratings (Gcc).

Actual performance in training may be considered to be a function of true performance modified by the trainee's reactions to the demands of the specific situation as he perceives it at university X and at VA installation Y. Criterion measures based on work samples are a function of his performance in a particular situation plus his reaction to our request that he take time from his routine responsibilities to carry out the particular task requested by this project. These measures were not distorted by any other person's perception of his performance, except where the derived criterion measure required the use of a judge in arriving at a quantitative measure of the work sample.

Analyses of the criterion ratings, as reported in Part C, indicate a fairly satisfactory degree of agreement among raters with the same general orientation but a much less satisfactory degree of agreement among raters representing different points of view, e. g., colleague versus installation supervisor. From these data we may conclude that the individual criterion ratings were affected much less by the personalities and the resulting idiosyncratic perceptions of raters than they were by the points of view from which groups of raters viewed the trainee. Each group of raters had a particular role, a particular set of values, and a given set of opportunities to observe the trainees.

There are two indirect ways of estimating the degree of distortion introduced in criterion measures based upon the perceptions and reports of observers. First, we may compare the relationship between assessment test responses and work sample measures with the relationship between assessment test responses and criterion ratings. Furthermore, we can compare the relationship between predictive ratings on Scale C with work sample measures on the one hand and with composite criterion ratings on the other hand. The interpretation of differences in the relative magnitudes of such relationships must be made with extreme caution: the magnitude of any correlation with the specific criterion measure is a function not only of the true correlation and of such attenuating factors as reliability of the criterion measure but also of the homogeneity or generality of the criterion measure. For example, we may anticipate that the correlation between the Miller Analogies Test and the Content Examination will be relatively high not only because both tests measure certain aspects of academic performance but also because both have high internal consistency (reliability).

Most of the relationships to be reported may be located on this diagram. Only the major validational analyses, however, have been explicitly diagrammed. For example, the relationships between colleagues' criterion ratings and supervisors' criterion ratings could be indicated by a line between Gc and Gs. The correlations between assessment test scores and prediction of Scale C variables could be represented as a line between C1 and G (on the left side of the figure). However, this diagram was not prepared as a visual guide to the mass of data to be reported. Its principle purpose is to make explicit the major determinants of the covariance and the error variance in the various validational studies to be reported. The core of the prediction problem is the classification and measurement of behavior at the time of prediction and the classification and measurement of performance at another point in time. Increasingly accurate predictions may be expected to result only with reduction in the amount of error variance involved in both sets of measures.

A Psychometric Analysis of the
Validational Problem

The preceding discussion is a generalized theoretical exposition designed to point out a number of possible sources of error variance in the assessment process. In general we have seen that our validity coefficients may have been reduced by: (a) the fact that both the predictive ratings and the criterion ratings were based on incomplete or distorted samples of the individual's "true" behavior, (b) errors of inference on the part of the judge who evaluated either assessment behaviors or the later behaviors on which criterion measures were based, or (c) influences affecting the individual between the time the predictions were made and the time the criterion measures were collected.

What other factors may have attenuated or magnified the true correlations between prediction measures and criterion measures? Correlations are generally more susceptible to attenuation than to spurious magnification, but it is necessary to ask whether any factors may have operated to elevate the magnitude of an obtained correlation above its proper value. One such potential factor is the influences of the prediction itself upon the criterion measure. For example, a university staff member might recall how he had evaluated a candidate at the beginning of training and his subsequent evaluation of the trainee's performance might be affected by selective perceptions confirming his original predictions. However, as we shall see in the next chapter, university predictions of Academic Performance, where the criterion measure was university ratings, are no better than the university predictions of the composite criterion ratings on Research, to which the university raters contributed only about one-third of the ratings. The only other predictive measures which we believe may have affected criterion measures were scores on the Miller Analogies Test and the Strong Interest Blank which were returned to universities in 1948. To the degree that later perceptions and ratings of trainee performance were influenced by a knowledge of these scores, the validity coefficients of these test scores for the 1948 group could have been elevated. We have no definite evidence which suggests that this factor caused a spurious elevation of correlations. Neither do we know to what extent those universities which did not ordinarily use these scores as part of their selection program made use of them in selecting 1948 trainees. Actually, the use of these scores seems to have resulted in less variability on these measures in the 1948 group and this probably lowered the validities of these and related measures.

Another factor which could operate to produce spuriously high validities is differences between the mean ratings of trainees at different geographical locations. This problem can best be illustrated by the example of university predictions. Suppose certain universities consider their students to be relatively more promising as compared to the national population of trainees whereas other universities perceive their trainees as relatively inferior. Suppose these opinions persist over the four-year period between the time university staff members make predictions and the time they make criterion ratings of the same students. Even if there were no correlation between university predictions and the university criterion ratings at individual institutions, the covariance of the mean predictions and the mean criterion ratings would generate a positive correlation for the total sample. The best estimate of the true correlation would be the median of the correlations between predictions and criterion ratings within universities. Unfortunately the number of trainees at the same university on whom both measures were available was never large and in most cases was under ten. However, we did compare the mean predictive rating on Overall Suitability for each school several years later and found no definite relationship. We conclude therefore that this factor probably did not elevate the correlations between university predictions and composite criterion ratings.

It is conceivable that inter-university differences may have influenced other validational coefficients. For example, if the assessment staff tended to rate trainees high because they were going to a school with a good reputation, and if this reputation with the assessment staff agreed to any considerable extent with the estimate of those local psychologists (supervisors and trainees), who provided the criterion ratings on these trainees, then validational coefficients involving assessment ratings might also be affected by this factor.

It appears more likely that our validational correlations were attenuated than elevated by different perceptions of the nature of the criterion skills being rated in both assessment and criterion measurement. Although it is possible that correlations between predictive and criterion ratings might be raised if both sets of raters shared the same stereotype of a "good clinician," e.g., a warmhearted, congenial trainee with limited aptitude might be overestimated by both assessors and criterion raters, it seems reasonable to assume that different raters conceive of the same clinical skill, such as diagnosis, in different terms and do not entirely agree on the aptitudes required for the development of a particular skill. For example, some staff members may have felt that diagnosis was primarily the solving of intellectual problems, while others may have believed that diagnosis was primarily a matter of utilizing one's empathic abilities. In making predictions of diagnostic competence, the first group would have weighted the applicant's intelligence scores highly whereas the second would have looked for evidences of sensitivity in the trainee's behavior. Fortunately, this problem was not serious so far as assessment predictions are concerned, since the assessment staff members were able to talk over their interpretations of the variables and reach a fairly satisfactory consensus. Moreover, the correlation between the university predictions and the assessment final pooled ratings was essentially as high as the reliability of the two separate measures would permit. Hence we must conclude that the university staff members and the assessment staff members agreed as well with each other as the members of each group agreed among themselves.

Criterion raters do not appear to be so uniform in their interpretation of the criterion variables. Although there is reasonably close agreement among the raters from any one source, for most variables, the correlation between the median rating from one source and the median rating from another is sufficiently lower than would be estimated from the inter-judge reliabilities to suggest that somewhat different definitions are involved. For example, either the connotations of diagnostic competence are not the same for installation supervisors as they are for colleagues, or the supervisors and the colleagues base their ratings on different samples of each trainee's diagnostic performance. Probably both alternatives are in part correct.

The major source of attenuation in validational correlations is, of course, unreliability. In the following paragraph, we will use reliability to refer to the agreement between identical, interchangeable judges observing the same phenomena. The basic principle can be stated in terms of the formula.

$$r_{pc \, (obt)} = r_{pc \, (true)} \sqrt{r_{pIpII} r_{cIcII}}$$

In other words, the obtained correlation between the predictor and the criterion is equal to the true validity of the predictor times the square root of the product of the reliabilities of the predictor and the criterion. The same principle may be stated in another way: the maximum correlation between a predictor and a criterion is equal to the square root of the product of their reliabilities. To apply this formula, one must know the reliability of each predictor and criterion measure. For certain measures this information is easily obtained: e.g., the reliability of the median university prediction varies from .40 to .61, depending upon the variable. On the other hand, it is impossible to estimate the true reliability of the Final Pooled assessment ratings. The correlations between the Final Individual ratings are not adequate for this purpose since these Final Individual ratings were made after previous staff conferences about a candidate. A crude estimate of the reliability of Final Individual ratings can be obtained by correlating the ratings made by the Intensive Interviewer after examining projective tests with those made by the Pre-Conference rater on the basis of studying the same materials. These correlations vary from .44 to .71 for Scale C variables. From these data we can estimate that the reliability of ratings based on the arithmetical pooling of three such independent judgments would vary from .70 to .88. Since the Final Pooled ratings were based on considerably more information than that available at this stage of assessment, it is reasonable to believe that the Final Pooled ratings have reliabilities above these values. It is certainly true that staff members making ratings on the basis of less information, for example, on the basis of credentials alone, show less agreement (.33 to .53.). Perhaps the most important point to be noted in this discussion is the rather obvious fact that the reliabilities of different predictive ratings vary greatly: differences between validity coefficients involving the same criterion measure may, therefore, be in part a function of the differential reliabilities of the predictors. We have not, however, corrected obtained validities for attenuation. The values reported are our best estimates of the validity of the predictive measures with their varying reliabilities.

When we come to the problem of the reliability of our criterion ratings, we are faced with the question of identifying the appropriate values of the various inter-source and intra-source correlational analyses. Our Composite ratings were based upon the combination of three sets of only relatively homogeneous ratings, and it is doubtful whether the assumptions of the Spearman-Brown formula hold for this situation. Hence we cannot take a typical inter-source correlation and raise it by the Spearman-Brown formula to estimate the reliability of a "test" three times as long because we are not pooling homogeneous ratings. An approximation involves correlating one university rater with one installation rater selected at random. For Diagnostic Competence and Research, these values are .22 and .33 respectively. Correcting for the number of raters, we would predict that the median University ratings should correlate with the median Installation ratings .46 and .60 respectively. These values are higher than the obtained inter-source correlations of .31 and .49. If one is willing to consider the composite ratings as representing a pooling of approximately ten sets of ratings, the estimated reliability of the composite ratings on these two variables becomes .74 and .83 respectively. These are probably overestimates of the "true" reliabilities.

Not only does reliability vary with the particular predictor and the particular type of criterion measure involved in a validity coefficient, but reliabilities of both the predictor and the criterion also vary for different variables.

We must also recognize the possibility that any curvilinear relationships between predictors and criterion measures would not be adequately reflected by product moment correlations. We did not attempt to plot the hundreds of validating coefficients because our earlier analysis had failed to indicate any markedly curvilinear trends. In summary, because a number of different factors may affect the value of a specific correlation between a predictor and criterion variable, not too much weight should be given to the interpretation of individual coefficients of validity. In the discussions to follow, therefore, we shall emphasize the trends of the values obtained for the various techniques and procedures when used as predictors of different criterion measures.

Agreement between Sets of Personality Ratings Made Three Years Apart

Since the prediction of future competence involves a time interval between the predictive and criterion measurements, we need some measure of the consistency of personality measures over time. The correlations between two sets of ratings of the same variables, ratings made 3 1/2 years apart, provide an estimate of the maximum predictive coefficients we could possibly obtain. For example, if the highest correlation over time between ratings on the same personality variable is .47, we can hardly expect predictions of job-functions to have validities above that value.

The ideal design to answer this question would estimate the consistency over time of both the predictive and the criterion measures. We should establish the consistency of the predictor measures: to what extent do the several determinants of the prediction change with time? We should also ascertain the stability of the criterion measure. Moreover, it is quite possible that the ceiling above which a validational coefficient cannot rise is different for different variables.

The term "consistency" in this section refers not to any hypothetical absolute invariability, but to the position of a person in a group relative to the average and the variability of that group. Thus an entire group might improve their competence in diagnosis or some other skill while the relative positions of the members were not changed.

Few experimental studies of consistency of personality measures over time have been published. Strong (1951) has recently reported a median correlation of .84 between profiles on the Vocational Interest Blank from college seniors retested after five years and a median of .75 for college seniors retested 22 years later! Similar test-retest reliabilities for other types of personality measures are apparently not available.

The small number of studies bearing on this problem can be explained in part by the fact that such research obviously requires many years to complete. It is also likely that such studies have not been carried out because of widely held beliefs about the consistency of the mature personality. Relatively high consistency is postulated in almost all psychological theories as well as in lay generalizations based on "common sense." Such diverse views as analytic and constitutional theories hold that major determinants of behavior endure relatively unchanged through the years. Again, the layman believes in the consistency of the individual personality for several reasons. A person's physique, voice, and expressive movements appear much the same one year as the next, unless some trauma has occurred. Furthermore, people tend to generalize any consistency which may exist to almost complete consistency because this assumed principle provides the simplest basis for social intercourse.

Our basic experimental design did not provide for estimating the consistency of personality. Our efforts were focused on collecting data on a wide variety of predictor measures and on the later measurement of clinical skills. Since this design already necessitated the expenditure of many hours' work by each subject, we did not feel justified in collecting retest or reassessment data. It is possible that any attempt to collect such data would have reduced the value of our crucial criterion measures because of negative effects from lowered motivation.

We did, however, ask fellow-trainees to rate each subject on Scale A and B, at the same time as they rated them on clinical skills. Fellow-trainees were assumed to be in the best position to rate these variables because they presumably saw the trainee in a wide variety of situations--at work, at rest, in class, etc. The same raters were used for Scales A, B, and C; it will be recalled that median Colleague ratings were based on ratings selected from the several sets of obtained ratings--those made by the trainees reporting the most extensive acquaintance with the subject rated.

Correlations were computed between each of two sets of assessment ratings made on candidates during the summer of 1947 and ratings on the same variables by fellow trainees in the fall of 1950. The resulting values are shown in Table D I-1a for Scale A variables and in Table D I-1b for Scale B variables. It will be seen at once that the general order of magnitude of these correlations is low. The highest value in the two tables is .47 between Final Pooled assessment ratings on Talkativeness and ratings on the same variable by colleagues three years later. For some variables there is no relationship between the ratings made at these two different times.

Let us first compare the relative consistencies for each type of assessment ratings. One would expect that the 1947 assessment staff Final Pooled ratings would show higher inter-judge reliability than the ratings made by the 1947 teammates, since the staff had more data on which to base their ratings and because they were devoting several days solely to this task. Although this tends to be true the differences are not as great as might have been expected. On Scale A variables the median for the Final Pooled staff ratings is slightly higher than for the Teammates' and the Final Pooled ratings have higher coefficients for most variables. On Scale B variables the median reliability for Teammate ratings is as high as that for the staff Final Pooled ratings (not shown in table). While the trend is clear-cut, the differences are not of large magnitude. On the basis of this comparison we can probably eliminate one possible explanation for the low correlations of personality ratings over time, i.e., that many or most of the trainees put on a consistent front or facade while in the presence of assessment staff members. It does not seem likely that they maintained this front or facade when no staff members were present, yet the Teammate ratings do not in general correlate quite as high with Colleague ratings as those made by the staff. This may be related to the fact that ratings by teammates were in general more favorable than the assessment staff ratings and tended to have somewhat less variability.

These same tables report comparable correlations for ratings from the 1949 reassessment program. In comparing the findings for the 1947 and 1949 Final Pooled ratings, two factors should be kept in mind. The 1949 staff did not see the candidates. These Final Pooled ratings were based solely on those written materials regarding the candidate collected in 1947. The other

TABLE D I-1a

CORRELATIONS OF 1950 COLLEAGUE RATINGS ON SCALE A WITH RATINGS FROM VARIOUS
ASSESSMENT SOURCES; AND RELIABILITIES OF 1947 ASSESSMENT RATINGS

Variable	Scale A Label	1947 Teammate Median* (N = 78)	1947 Final Pooled (N = 78)	1949 Final Pooled (N = 60)	Reliability of 1947 Teammate Median* (N = 128)	Reliability of 1947 Final Pooled** (N = 128)
0	Liking			18		
1	Cooperative--Obstructive	00	17	32	69	80
2	Consistent--Inconsistent	27	26	29	65	72
3	Assertive--Submissive	32	45	39	82	89
4	Depressed--Cheerful	21	30	25	76	85
5	Irresponsible--Serious	36	24	07	70	81
6	Gregarious--Non-gregarious	30	32	32	69	79
7	Easily Upset--Unshakable	15	25	-01	74	84
8	Narrow--Broad, Interests	30	36	22	76	92
9	Suspicious--Trustful	-04	22	22	70	81
10	Generous--Self-centered, Selfish	17	18	25	71	85
11	Silent--Talkative	43	47	29	86	92
12	Cautious--Adventurous	23	19	07	78	84
13	Socially Poised--Socially Clumsy	16	31	01	68	79
14	Rigid--Adaptable, Flexible	14	07	-11	79	84
15	Dependent--Self-sufficient	07	08	30	64	85
16	Placid--Worrying, Anxious	42	17	03	79	84
17	Conscientious--Not Conscientious	-05	18	10	70	86
18	Imaginative--Unimaginative	17	40	28	81	90
19	Overt Interest in Opposite Sex, Marked--Slight	22	31	27	81	85
20	Frank--Secretive	15	15	31	81	79
21	Dependent--Independent Minded	27	21	39	70	86
22	Overt Emotional Expression, Limited--Marked	24	44	15	83	79
	Median	21	25	25	75	84

*Rank order correlation between (a) reliabilities of 1947 Teammate Median (5th column) and (b) correlation between 1947 Teammate Median and 1950 Colleague Median (2nd column) is .34.

**Calculated from intercorrelation between Final Individual Ratings.

TABLE D I-1b

CORRELATIONS OF 1950 COLLEAGUE RATINGS ON
SCALE B WITH TWO ASSESSMENT RATINGS
ON THE SAME VARIABLE

(N = 78)

Colleague Variable	Scale B Label	1947 Teammate Median	1947 Final Pooled
23b	Social Adjustment	20	29
24	Appropriateness of Emotional Expression	09	16
25	Characteristic Intensity of Inner Emotional Tension	20	-01
26	Sexual Adjustment	21	17
27	Motivation for Professional Status	-09	15
28	Motivation for Scientific Understanding of People	31	31
29	Insight into Others	08	17
30	Insight into Himself	15	13
31	Quality of Intellectual Accomplishments	16	28
Median:		16	17

difference was in the composition of the staff. The 1949 reassessment staff was composed solely of VA trainees whereas the 1947 assessment staff were more experienced clinicians.

In general, the 1949 staff, without personal contact with the candidates, made ratings of Scale A variables which correlate with ratings made three years later about as well as the ratings made by the 1947 assessment staff. The median r's are identical, but the 1949 group has higher coefficients on only six of the 22 variables. We must not overlook the possible influence of varying motivation of the raters on the validity of these ratings. The 1949 group were striving to do as well as they possibly could on the basis of the materials provided to them; they knew that their predictive ability would be compared to that for the more experienced staff of the 1947 assessment program.

How else can we account for the low degree of consistency of two sets of ratings three years apart? We can rule out the consideration that the variables were so vaguely defined that different raters interpreted them differently. The reliabilities of the 1947 Final Pooled and the 1947

Teammate ratings are relatively high ranging from .64 to .92 for Scale A variables. Thus two raters looking at the same person from the same point of view and at the same time agree quite well on their ratings. We must emphasize the difference between the two situations in which the earlier and later ratings were collected. The assessment ratings were based upon the observations in a unique situation, the trainees being among a group whom they had never seen before and being there solely for the purpose of being studied by the staff. The 1950 fellow-trainee ratings were based upon various formal and informal contacts on the job, in classrooms and, to some extent, in social situations outside of the clinic or hospital. The behavior which the candidate showed at the time of assessment to his fellow candidates was probably a biased or atypical sample of his general behavior. Unfortunately, our data do not permit us to prove or disprove this hypothesis concerning the influence of the total situation upon the rated behavior of the trainees.

Up to this point we have been implicitly assuming that ratings made three years apart should agree as well as ratings made at the same time, that personality or at least overt behavior is relatively consistent from year to year. We would not expect such marked personality changes in a group whose median age at the time of assessment was 27 years as we would in a younger group. Nevertheless, we cannot entirely ignore the possible influence of general growth factors. Therefore, a plausible explanation of these findings is that the particular nature of the training program in clinical psychology may lead to considerable change in behavior. Perhaps, the study of theoretical material which tends to stimulate self-evaluation, and clinical experience with patients results in more differential growth among students than we have suspected.

Let us consider one other interpretation. Our experimental group is obviously not a random sample of the general population. It is composed of individuals of superior intelligence, highly motivated toward a specific type of study and service, individuals who chose to prepare for the profession of clinical psychology. While such persons may maintain their same relative standings in the general population on certain descriptive variables, are we asking too much to expect these VA trainees to maintain the same relative standing over time within such a relatively homogeneous group?

However, if homogeneity were a major factor in explaining the low consistency over time, we should expect to find relatively lower consistency for those variables on which the group is presumably more homogeneous. Two such variables are Broad Interests and Imaginative (No. 8 and No. 18 respectively), yet these variables are rated relatively consistently over time. Again, if homogeneity is important, we should expect the inter-rater reliabilities to be lower for the variables on which this group was selected. Our data do not confirm this expectation; the reliabilities of the ratings would seem to be more a function of the ease with which the variables can be observed and the clarity of the definition of them than of the variability of the group on the variable. We must conclude that even with this more or less homogeneous group the assessment staffs were able to make adequate discriminations among the trainees on all variables.

It is, however, true that the relative magnitude of the coefficients over time is in small part a function of the reliability with which the variable can be rated. For the Scale A variables there is a correlation of .35 (rho) between the rank order of the reliability of the 1947 Teammate ratings and the rank order of the size of correlations between 1947 Teammate medians and 1950 Colleague medians. This correlation helps us to interpret the differences between the coefficients over time but does not assist in the explanation of their low average magnitude.

One quarter of this group underwent personal therapy during the intervening three years. Definite changes in the behavior of this part of the total sample might well have the effect of markedly reducing the coefficients over time for the entire group.

Table D I-2 compares the correlations over time for trainees who had undergone personal therapy in the interval and for those who had not. For Scales A and B, the agreement between 1947 and 1950 ratings is slightly higher for those who had personal therapy. This difference may be due to the fact that the 1947 ratings for these therapy cases tended to be somewhat more variable than the 1947 ratings for those who had no therapy. Thus intervening personal therapy did not systematically lower the consistency between the sets of descriptive ratings. We shall see later, however, that personal therapy had a marked effect on the accuracy of predictions of clinical performance.

Which variables show the highest consistency over time? We can roughly classify the relatively more consistent variables into three clusters. The first is a dimension characterized by intellectual orientation and ability. This group would include Broad Interests (No. 8), Imaginative (No. 18), Independent Minded (No. 21), Motivation for Scientific Understanding of People (No. 28), and Quality of Intellectual Accomplishments (No. 31). The variables related to this component are rated relatively consistently over time, perhaps because these variables are related to Intelligence, which probably changes little over time. Also these variables have fairly clear definitions and can be rated rather impersonally--they do not involve the rater's personal interactions with the subject.

Another group of variables rated relatively consistently includes: Consistent, Cheerful, and Marked Overt Emotional Expression (Nos. 2, 4, and 22). These variables may be related to some underlying dimensions of temperament.

In still a third group are such variables as: Assertive, Attentive to People, Marked Overt Interest in the Opposite Sex, Talkative, and Social Adjustment (Nos. 3, 6, 11, 19, and 23b). These four variables reflect an active social orientation, our tentative labels are Social Extroversion and Social Initiative.

A Comparison of Qualitative and Quantitative Matching

The basic design of the assessment phase of this project emphasized the use of ratings rather than qualitative descriptions. This decision was based in part on the relative ease with which ratings can be analyzed and in part on the difficulties involved in the scientific utilization of qualitative materials. We did, however, ask the Intensive Interviewers to prepare qualitative reports on all cases studied in the 1947 program. This qualitative report usually included a discussion of the trainee's personality structure, his assets and liabilities, and any qualifications or reservations concerning the Final Pooled ratings made by the assessment staff team. Our original purpose in obtaining these reports was to provide material which might help in understanding cases where assessment predictions were unusually poor or good.

As the research progressed, several professional colleagues expressed the opinion that our analyses did not provide any estimate of the accuracy of the clinical pictures obtained by the assessment staff. They argued that the assessors might have an accurate description of the candidate's personality but might have failed to translate this picture into correct ratings or predictions. The same criticism was relevant to the use of ratings to describe qualitatively different aspects of clinical competence.

In the light of these opinions, we decided to collect qualitative descriptions of the trainees' performance in clinical and research work (see Appendix II B-1 and 2). We gave considerable thought to the development of a research design which would provide an evaluation of the accuracy of such qualitative descriptions but found it difficult to formulate testable hypotheses relevant to this general problem.

The accuracy of predictive ratings on Scale C may be compared with the accuracy of descriptive ratings on Scales A and B, by noting the correlations of each with the appropriate measures obtained three years later. But this is only one aspect of the problem. We may also ask whether the

TABLE D I-2

COMPARISON OF CORRELATIONS BETWEEN 1947 FINAL
POOLED ASSESSMENT RATINGS AND 1950 COLLEAGUE
RATINGS FOR TRAINEES WITH OR WITHOUT
INTERVENING PERSONAL THERAPY

	Trainees Who Had Therapy (N = 22)	Trainees Who Had No Therapy (N = 56)	Total Group (N = 78)
Scale A			
1 Cooperative--Obstructive	20	17	17
2 Consistent--Inconsistent	32	20	26
3 Assertive--Submissive	63	36	45
4 Depressed--Cheerful	53	24	30
5 Irresponsible--Serious	30	22	24
6 Gregarious--Non-gregarious	29	35	32
7 Easily Upset--Unshakable	33	21	25
8 Narrow--Broad, Interests	62	27	36
9 Suspicious--Trustful	22	24	22
10 Generous--Self-centered, Selfish	-07	29	18
11 Silent--Talkative	70	41	47
12 Cautious--Adventurous	05	25	19
13 Socially Poised--Socially Clumsy	58	21	31
14 Rigid--Adaptable, Flexible	14	05	07
15 Dependent--Self-sufficient	30	00	08
16 Placid--Worrying, Anxious	-09	29	17
17 Conscientious--Not Conscientious	13	21	18
18 Imaginative--Unimaginative	56	35	40
19 Overt Interest in Opposite Sex, Marked--Slight	10	39	31
20 Frank--Secretive	17	15	15
21 Dependent--Independent, Minded	48	15	21
22 Overt Emotional Expression, Limited--Marked	61	36	44
Median for Scale A	30	24	24
Scale B			
23b Social Adjustment	35	28	29
24 Appropriateness of Emotional Expression	37	05	16
25 Characteristic Intensity of Inner Emotional Tension	-10	04	-01
26 Sexual Adjustment	20	17	17
27 Motivation for Professional Status	48	12	15
28 Motivation for Scientific Understanding of People	11	40	31
29 Insight into Others	02	21	17
30 Insight into Himself	13	12	13
31 Quality of Intellectual Accomplishments	27	28	28
Median for Scale B	20	17	17

qualitative assessment report is sufficiently accurate to permit this matching of the qualitative report with the qualitative descriptions written by the trainee's installation and university supervisors three years later. In order to be able to evaluate the absolute value of the accuracy of such qualitative matching, we formulated a single design for a matching study in which the accuracy with which judges could match qualitative descriptions would be compared with the accuracy with which profiles of ratings could be matched by a statistical technique.

Case Materials and Design Used in Matching Study

We first selected all 1947 assessment cases (a) who were not known to the trainees who would serve as judges and (b) for whom reasonably adequate assessment reports and qualitative criterion descriptions were available. For example, we rejected all cases on whom we obtained no report of research performances by the university supervisor. For the remaining group, we selected 20 cases at two extremes of predictive accuracy on the basis of scatter plots of the 1947 Final Pooled ratings on Overall Suitability correlated with the Composite Criterion Rating on Clinical Competence and Preference for Hiring. We were able to select ten cases for whom the predictive ratings were relatively accurate and ten for whom they were relatively inaccurate. This was done in order to determine whether the qualitative reports could be matched as well for cases where rated predictions were wrong as for cases where predictions were more nearly correct.

Once the 20 cases had been selected, the two sets of reports were carefully edited. Biographical data were eliminated. Also cut out were physical descriptions such as "a tall blond Southerner with a marked drawl." Our purpose was to prevent identification of the case by judges who might happen to have met the trainee, and to avoid any correct or incorrect matching by a judge because both reports referred to such irrelevant cues (see Appendix II-C for a sample of our edited assessment report).

Since the assessment reports had been written with the assumption that the predictive ratings would be available to the reader, we attached to each assessment report a profile of the Final Pooled ratings on Scale C, i.e., predictions of future competence.

The design called for 380 triads in each of which an assessment report for a given case was grouped with the criterion description for that same case and with the criterion description of another case. Thus, the assessment report for Case A was placed with the criterion descriptions for Cases A and B, forming one triad. Other triads were formed by substituting each of the other 18 cases for Case B. Similarly, for Case B the criterion description for every other case was successively grouped with B's assessment and criterion sketches. The design is illustrated in Figure D I-2.

Sketches	Triad		Triad		Triad	
Assessment	A		B		C	
Criterion	A	B	B	A	C	A
Assessment	A		B		C	
Criterion	A	C	B	C	C	B
Assessment	A		B		C	
Criterion	A	D	B	D	C	D

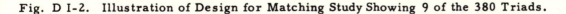

Fig. D I-2. Illustration of Design for Matching Study Showing 9 of the 380 Triads.

The 380 triads were divided into 38 sets of ten, following a pattern such that no descriptions appeared twice in the same set. For the triads in each set, the correct matches were randomly assigned to first or second position. Thirty-eight local staff members, VA staff psychologists and VA trainees served as judges. The median number of correct matches was seven out of ten and the range for individual clinicians was from zero to ten. However, only two judges made fewer than five correct choices. The lowest score was made by one of the relatively more experienced clinicians in the group of judges. Combining all judgments, 70% of the 380 triads were correctly matched. This proportion is significantly different from the chance value of 50%.

Each judge indicated on a three-point scale the degree of confidence he felt in each judgment. A positive relationship was found between accuracy and confidence: the percentages of correct matches were 80%, 73%, and 50%, for "Much," "Some," and "Little" confidence respectively.

The 38 judgments involving each case were analyzed by a 2 x 2 table and phi coefficients were computed for each case. These coefficients ranged from .69 to -.05, with a median value of .44. We may conclude that the qualitative materials for some cases were easier to match than those for others.

The cases also differed in the number of times they were chosen as the correct match. One case was chosen every time when it was correct and one-third of the time when it was the wrong choice. Another case was chosen only seven times out of 19 when it was correct and just twice when it was wrong. We cannot say whether the individual differences between cases reported in the last two paragraphs are due to the personalities of the subjects or to the qualitative descriptions written about them.

The accuracy of matching was the same for those cases whose general clinical competence was correctly predicted by ratings as it was for cases incorrectly predicted. Since there was no relationship between the accuracy of prediction by ratings and the accuracy of matching of qualitative materials, errors must have been made or information lost in some cases in the translation of the personality picture into predictive ratings.

Of the 20 cases used in the matching study, eight reported that they had had personal therapy between 1947 and 1950, 11 reported they had not, and no report was obtained from the last case. The median phi coefficient for the eight cases who had had personal therapy was .44, exactly the same as that for all 20 cases. We may conclude that the factor of intervening personal therapy had no effect upon accuracy of matching of the two sets of qualitative materials.

The Objective Matching of Profiles of Ratings

To provide a comparison between the extent to which the individuality of a case is conveyed by ratings and by qualitative materials, we compared the profile of ratings made on Scale A (phenotypic) variables by 1947 assessment teammates with the profile on the same variables made in 1950 by colleagues. The same general design using the same cases and the same triads, was used as in the qualitative matching study. If the true match yielded a higher index of relationship than the false match, we recorded a hit, if the relationship was lower, we recorded a miss.

We first applied the coefficient of profile similarity r_{ps} developed by Du Mas (1949) to the raw ratings. Hits were obtained for 75% of the triads: i. e., the profiles for the same person were more similar in 75% of the triads than the profiles for different people. While this value indicated that the individual could be identified as well by his ratings on 22 variables as by qualitative descriptions, we were dissatisfied with this rather rough method for comparing profiles. We had, of course, reversed the poles of some variables so that the favorable poles were all on the same side. But there were still objections: The means and variabilities for the different variables had not been equated, as the formula requires. Hence, we converted all the ratings to standard scores. Even more important, the Du Mas coefficient utilized only N-1 of the possible N (N-1)/2 slopes of all possible comparisons. We therefore decided to compute r_{ps} for all possible slope comparisons.*

For each set of ratings on each individual, the variables were assigned ranks on the basis of the standard scores. Tau coefficients were computed for the true and false matches, hits being recorded when the true match yielded a higher tau than the false match. From this complex analysis, 74% correct quantitative matchings were obtained. Thus the more simple but less precise method of profile matching yielded the same results as the more complex and precise method.

When the eight cases who had had personal therapy were analyzed by themselves, we obtained 72% correct matchings. Again we find that personal therapy did not significantly reduce the correspondence between the two pictures of the individual obtained three years apart. However, we shall see later that predictions of future performance were less successful for those cases who had had therapy than for other cases.

Before interpreting these findings, let us examine carefully the data involved. Each assessment report was written by one person, although it was based on an extensive array of data about the trainee and reflected to a varying degree the viewpoints of the other members of the assessment staff team. The criterion descriptions of performance were provided by one installation supervisor and one university supervisor. In contrast, the assessment teammate medians were based on three sets of ratings and the fellow-trainee ratings were based on four or five sets. Thus one can argue that the ratings were more reliable, that they were influenced less by a single observer's impressions, than were the qualitative materials.

The two sets of personality ratings were made by different raters and were based on observations in quite different situations. However, the variables rated were the same. In neither case were the raters familiar with the rating scale used and the validity of the ratings of assessment teammates was probably attenuated by the conflicting situation under which they were obtained, i.e., trainees were anxious to rate their fellow trainees accurately in order to show how good they were as judges of others, but were at the same time loath to rate a fellow trainee low on any variable. On the other side, the assessment reports described the trainees' personalities and made few predictions about future performance; the supervisors' descriptions were structured to emphasize performance. Thus the two kinds of qualitative materials were written from different points of view. However, in both, the quality of the trainees' relationships with others, his aptitudes, and his work habits were usually discussed.

It is evident that any comparison of these findings concerning the success of matchings from qualitative and from quantitative data must be interpreted with considerable caution. Nevertheless, we feel safe in concluding that a profile of ratings by assessment teammates is about as idiosyncratic and individualistic as a qualitative assessment report. Stated in another way, although the teammate ratings and the assessment reports contain different information, both seem to provide about equal amounts of information as measured by the extent to which they permit the individual to be identified at a later time. Note, however, that we compared qualitative

---

*We find that this revised coefficient of profile similarity turns out to be the "tau coefficient" developed by Kendall (1948). Kendall refers to tau as a coefficient of disarray or ranks. Like rho, it uses ranks; but unlike rho, it does not use the absolute difference between ranks. A separate paper will be published on the relationship between r_{ps} and tau.

descriptions as matched by judges with rated profiles matched objectively. In this comparative study, the content and the matching method were not separate.

The findings of this investigation of matching individuals over time are, of course, relevant to the problem of consistency of personality over time. We find that in spite of relatively low correlations of ratings of single personality variables over time, roughly three out of four persons of this group of highly similar persons can be correctly identified on the basis of the pattern of ratings. This pattern of rated variables provides a more idiosyncratic picture of the individual than ratings on any single variable.

CHAPTER D II

THE VALIDITY OF UNIVERSITY PREDICTIONS

An examination of the limited data on predictive ratings for 46 entering students made by staff members at about half of the universities reveals a relatively high level of validity for predicting the general level of subsequent performance. Predictions from the records usually provided by applicants for graduate training were as valid as predictions based on these records plus such observations as are made in interviews or in classroom contacts.

The relationships between the predictions made by university staff members in the spring of 1947 and the Composite Criterion ratings three and a half years later are presented in Table D II-1. The level of agreement between these predictions and our criteria is generally high. The more intellectual variables were predicted considerably better than the clinical skills. However, there is a considerable lack of differentiation between the variables. For example, university predictions of Diagnosis and Therapy actually predict rated Research Competence somewhat better than they predict either Diagnosis or Therapy! Predicted Research Competence correlates as well with Academic Performance as it does with rated Research Competence: this finding may have resulted from the fact that the ratings on Academic Performance were based solely on the university staff supervisors' ratings, whereas the criterion ratings on other skills were based on a composite or pooling of ratings from three separate sources. Again, the university predictions of Overall Suitability actually predict Research and Academic Performance better than they predict rated Clinical Competence. Looking at the table the other way, rated Diagnostic Competence is predicted better by the predictions of Academic Performance and Research than by the more logical predictor, Diagnosis and Therapy.

Before discussing the values reported in Table D II-1, a number of qualifications must be introduced. In the first place, these correlations are based upon only 46 cases. To be sure, these are all available cases which meet the following requirements: university staff members made predictions on them; they entered at the P-1 level; they were assessed in 1947; and finally, they were still in training in December 1950 so that criterion ratings could be obtained for them. Since this group includes no cases who discontinued training for any reason, these correlations represent discriminations within the range of competence of students who are almost certain to complete their graduate training.

In comparison with validity coefficients to be reported later, the outstanding feature of this table is the number of values above .5. However, we have some reason to believe that the criterion measures were somewhat easier to predict for these 46 cases than for those constituting the total 1947 group. For this group the correlation between the Final Pooled assessment ratings on Overall Suitability and rated Composite Clinical Competence is .53 as compared with only .20 for the remaining 46 cases in the total group. Similarly, for this group, the Intensive Interviewers' ratings based on a study of the credential file only, yielded a validity of .39 (against the same criterion) as compared with .31 for all cases. Thus it would appear that this subgroup of cases for whom University Staff predictions were available was either composed of more predictable trainees, or of trainees for whom more predictable criterion ratings were obtained, or both. It seems not unlikely that those departments which cooperated in providing staff predictions may differ systematically from those not cooperating in this phase of the project in ways which affected the reliability or the validity of the criterion ratings for their students. We simply do not

141

TABLE D II-1

CORRELATIONS BETWEEN PREDICTIONS BY UNIVERSITY STAFF
MEMBERS (1947) AND CRITERION RATINGS (1950)

A. Correlations between University Predictions and Composite Criterion Ratings (N = 46)

University Predictions (Median of 1-5 raters)	C32 Academic Performance*	C33 Diagnostic Competence	C34 Individual Psychotherapy	C36 Research Competence	Ccc Clinical Competence
Academic Performance	63	41	25	57	42
Diagnosis and Therapy	30	30	29	40	27
Research	65	53	20	62	46
Overall Suitability	51	42	28	55	40

*Criterion Academic Performance was rated only by University raters.

B. Comparison of Correlations between University Staff Predictions and University Criterion Ratings on Academic Performance (C32).

1. Individual Staff ratings, 43 trainees, 116 ratings: $r = .45$

2. Cases where rater had seen trainee in class or in admission interview, 19 trainees, 48 ratings: $r = .40$

3. Cases where rater had not seen trainee, 24 trainees, 68 ratings: $r = .44$

4. Assessment Prediction for same 24 trainees based on credential file only:
   a. By Initial Interviewer $r = -.03$
   b. By Intensive Interviewer $r = .45$

know how well staff members at the other universities could have predicted future criterion measures of their students. We do know that criterion measures for students from the universities which did not choose to cooperate in this phase of the project are not as well predicted by assessment ratings.

Several other factors may have operated to produce these relatively high coefficients. The predictions were made by raters who contributed to the criterion ratings. Similarly, the local connotations and expectations for each skill were probably similar for staff members making the predictions and the criterion ratings, i.e., the predictors knew what the university would demand of the trainees. Furthermore, it is not unlikely that the general point of view of the university staff members concerning values of varying kinds of clinical competence is picked up by the students and staff members of nearby VA installations and hence served as a frame of reference for the criterion ratings of colleagues and university supervisors.

We were able to eliminate one factor which might have contributed to these high relationships. It was conceivable that, in many cases, the university predictions were based upon such adequate and extended contacts with the applicants (e. g. , trainees who were former students of the raters), that the university predictions had higher true validities than other comparable predictions. However, as Part B of Table D II-1 indicates, essentially the same degree of relationship between prediction and criterion was obtained for those individuals whom the university staff member had never seen before as that obtained for applicants whom he had had as former students, as colleagues, or whom he had seen in admission interviews.

There is a possibility, which we could not check, that a certain degree of "contamination" is present in this analysis; the university staff members may have formed favorable or unfavorable biases toward the applicants on the basis of the selection materials, and these biases may have influenced the subsequent success or failure of the student in his graduate training.

It should be noted that the median rating of the several university raters has a validity coefficient of .63 for Academic Performance whereas the validity for the individual ratings plotted separately is only .45. This is perhaps the most marked increase in validity due to the mathematical pooling of ratings in any of our data (cf. , last section of Chapter D IV). It is possible that in those cases where the university predictive ratings agreed with each other, the various effects which we have been discussing as possibly contributing to the high magnitude of these correlations were intensified; for example, if the university staff members held the same favorable or unfavorable impression of an applicant, that applicant would be much more likely to have his graduate career affected by these impressions than would a trainee about whom different staff members had different impressions. That this does not seem to have happened is suggested by the fact that a detailed analysis showed that university predictions correlate as highly with the Composite Criterion ratings as with University Criterion ratings.

In summary, we may say that the rated evaluation of beginning students by university staff members, even when not based on previous personal contact with the students, yields comparatively high validities against rated performance three years later. These obtained values are probably higher than would be the case if predictions were made by university staff members at University X for students at University Y, since staff members of a given university are most familiar with the demands of the training program and expectations of clinical competence in the local sub-culture.

CHAPTER D III

THE VALIDITIES OF OBJECTIVE TESTS

Approximately 1400 correlations between objective test scores and criteria are reported for the 1947 group of trainees. For this group each criterion measure was
predicted at a statistically significant level by several scores from objective tests.
Academic achievement and research skill, two kinds of intellectual performance,
were predicted well by scores on several tests, especially by the Miller Analogies
Test and the Strong Vocational Interest Blank. Skills in interpersonal relations were
predicted fairly well by tests which seem to reflect an interest in interacting with
people as opposed to a desire to manipulate people. Measures of competence in
diagnosis and psychotherapy were also predicted with moderate success.

In general, criterion measures for the 1948 group were not well predicted by any
objective test scores. Possible reasons for these lower validities are discussed.

At the time we selected the tests for our objective test battery, there were no tests especially
designed to predict clinical competence. In fact, about the only measure specifically aimed at
predicting success in psychology was the psychologist key for the Strong Interest Blank. This
key was based on the modal responses of prominent psychologists in the 1930's; the standardiza-
tion group included almost no clinical psychologists. With the exception of the VA Clinical
Psychologist key for the Strong, we did not attempt to build any special tests or scales to measure aptitude for clinical psychology. Instead, we selected and used typical psychological tests
which enjoyed a favorable reputation, which were constructed on sound psychometric principles,
and which represented varying conceptual approaches to personality measurement.

In this section we shall focus our attention upon analyses based on the 1947 assessment group.
This group is more homogeneous than the 1946 group and at the time criterion measures were
obtained had completed more than three years of training. By using the 1947 group, we can compare objective tests and assessment ratings in terms of their relative predictive efficiency. Correlations are reported for the 1948 group between criterion ratings and scores on those objective
tests which had shown most promise for the 1947 group. However, the coefficients for the 1948
group were generally lower than those for the 1947 group. This difference probably results from
the fact that the 1948 group was (a) more carefully selected, i.e., had a narrower range of intellectual ability, (b) had been subject to a somewhat different training program (cf. Chapter A III),
and (c) had had a shorter time to develop their clinical skills.

The Problem of Identifying Significant Validities

While the correlations between objective tests and composite criterion ratings are in general
low, there are a number of significant correlations and some high ones. The correlation of each
of the objective test scores with each of the criterion measures resulted in some 1400 correlations. In each table presented, coefficients significant at or beyond the 5% level of confidence
are underlined; however, it must not be forgotten that one out of each 20 coefficients would be expected to reach this value by chance. Actually, even this is an underestimate of chance expectancy, since the several criterion measures are inter-correlated and there is also considerable
correlation between many of the predictor measures. We know of no way by which to arrive at
an accurate estimate of chance expectancy for these tables and shall therefore rely on the logic

of the relationship as well as the patterns of relationships in reaching conclusions regarding the validities of individual test scores as predictions of the criterion measures used.

Each of the several criterion variables can be reasonably well predicted by some test. Tests which show significant validities may be categorized into two groups: (a) tests measuring intellectual achievement or theoretical orientation, and generally predictive of Academic Performance, Research Competence, and Overall Clinical Competence; and (b) other tests measuring qualities of interpersonal relationships predictive of Overall Clinical Competence.

Tests of Intellectual Abilities

Most intelligence tests have not been designed to discriminate at the level of ability required for graduate training. Furthermore, there was some question in our minds as to whether measured intelligence would be related to performance in clinical psychology especially with a selected group of graduate students. Table D III-1 presents the validational analyses for the Miller Analogies Test and the Chicago Tests of Primary Mental Abilities. The Miller Analogies Test predicts rated Academic Performance ($r = .47$) and scores on both parts of the Content Examination ($r = .58$). While it predicts these variables better than any other objective test, it also predicts Research Competence, Clinical Competence and Supervisory Competence about as well as any other test. All things taken together, it is the most useful test in our battery for predicting both academic and clinical performance. Eight of the 13 validities for the Miller scores are significant.

We used the Tests of Primary Mental Ability to determine whether certain types of mental ability were related to academic and clinical competence. Thirteen of the 60 correlations with Criterion ratings are significant at the 5% level of confidence. The score on Number Ability (N) shows positive correlations with all Composite Criterion Ratings. Its highest correlations are with Clinical Diagnosis, Supervision, Interpersonal Relations, and Clinical Competence. These correlations are not easy to interpret. Perhaps speed in carrying out simple arithmetical operations is related to speed in reacting to any kind of cue, personal or impersonal. Also it is possible that Number Ability may be related to a general type of intellectual efficiency, a freedom from internally generated distraction.

Word Fluency (W) scores are significantly related to the scores on both the Clinical and General parts of the Content Examination and also to the scores on the Diagnostic Prediction Test. Although the Content Examinations had no time limits, there would seem to be some relationship between the recall of information required by the Content Examination and the ability to think of any words which fulfill certain specified requirements (such as beginning with a particular letter). The relationship between Word Fluency scores and the Diagnostic Prediction Test is somewhat unexpected and may be due to chance factors. One possible interpretation may be found in the work of Carol Pemberton (1951) who found a relationship between the First Letter subtest of the W factor and a tendency to rate oneself as socially outgoing. Perhaps the scores on the Diagnostic Prediction Test are related to a tendency to accept people as they are.

The Reasoning (R) scores also showed several significant relationships: to rated Academic Performance, Research, Supervision, Clinical Competence, Preference for Hiring, and to scores on the General part of the Content Examination. This pattern is essentially the same as that for the Miller Analogies Test but at a definitely lower level. Both tests require the subject to find relatively simple underlying relationships among concepts.

The Memory score of the PMA battery is based on the ability to recall first names, given the last names, immediately after a brief learning period of the whole series. This score was

TABLE D III-1

CORRELATIONS BETWEEN SCORES ON TESTS OF INTELLECTUAL
ABILITY AND CRITERION MEASURES
1947 Group

| | Miller Analogies | N | \multicolumn{5}{c}{Primary Mental Abilities} |
			V	S	W	R	M
Ratings							
C32 Academic Performance	<u>47</u>	14	12	04	18	<u>27</u>	14
C33 Diagnostic Competence	<u>24</u>	<u>31</u>	09	14	07	19	06
C34 Individual Psychotherapy	02	15	-16	-02	-04	00	-06
C36 Research Competence	<u>38</u>	11	-03	-02	08	<u>21</u>	09
C38 Supervisory Competence	<u>34</u>	<u>25</u>	13	11	14	<u>23</u>	<u>24</u>
C40 Professional Interpersonal Relations	18	<u>25</u>	01	00	15	16	<u>21</u>
C41 Integrity	16	16	-06	09	04	15	16
Ccc Clinical Competence	<u>35</u>	<u>25</u>	10	11	13	<u>27</u>	<u>22</u>
Cph Preference for Hiring	<u>20</u>	15	00	05	09	<u>21</u>	20
C0 Liking	11	07	-05	00	07	07	11
Content Examination							
A_t Clinical Total	<u>58</u>	17	05	-02	<u>30</u>	21	09
B_t General Total	<u>58</u>	14	12	05	<u>24</u>	<u>33</u>	21
Diagnostic Predictions Test							
Σ Sum for 2 cases	14	10	-15	01	<u>37</u>	09	09

Coefficients significant at or beyond the 5% level of confidence are underlined.

N for Ratings = 93
N for Content Examination = 76
N for Diagnostic Predictions = 53

related to Supervision, Interpersonal Relations, Clinical Competence, and Preference for Hiring. These four criterion ratings all involve good interpersonal relationships. The correlation of .21 with scores on the General part of the Content Examination is of course not surprising.

Scores on both the Space factor and the Verbal factor show no correlation with composite ratings, with scores on the Content Examination, or with scores on the Diagnostic Prediction Test. For this group of subjects, the Verbal test had an inadequate ceiling, i.e., most subjects scored near the maximum score. It may well be the restricted range accounts for the absence of significant relationships between this score and Academic Performance and scores on the Content Examination.

Personality Tests

Guilford-Martin Battery

The correlations of each of the several Guilford-Martin scores with the criterion measures are shown in Table D III-2. Although only about 8% of the values are significant at the 5% level of confidence, most of them are in the expected direction. Furthermore, eight of the 14 significant values are for two of the 14 scores, Freedom from Cycloid Tendencies (C) and Thinking Extraversion (T). The C score is the best single test predictor of Preference for Hiring and the T score the best test predictor of rated Integrity. Also of interest is the fact that the two significant correlations of Social Extraversion (S) are with Diagnostic and Therapeutic Competence, criteria which are generally less well predicted by either test scores or assessment ratings.

TABLE D III-2

CORRELATIONS BETWEEN SCORES ON GUILFORD-MARTIN
BATTERY AND CRITERION MEASURES
1947 Group

	S	T	D	C	R	G	A	M	I	N	O	Ag	C0	Gamin Facade
Ratings														
C32 Academic Performance	06	05	-07	00	02	14	05	-03	-09	-01	07	-13	-07	05
C32 Diagnostic Competence	_23_	17	14	14	12	14	06	08	00	-07	13	00	06	11
C34 Individual Psychotherapy	_22_	09	10	11	09	13	06	-11	08	-18	04	07	09	04
C36 Research Competence	-04	05	-04	-03	04	15	09	00	-09	-10	09	-17	-05	-03
C38 Supervisory Competence	05	_20_	02	09	10	10	-12	-05	-17	_-20_	-02	-08	00	-16
C40 Professional Inter- personal Relations	07	_20_	11	16	15	12	-05	-09	02	-10	07	06	07	-03
C41 Integrity	13	_30_	19	_20_	09	12	10	-03	06	-07	15	06	19	07
Ccc Clinical Competence	11	19	14	18	08	12	-04	-05	02	-06	10	-03	05	04
Cph Preference for Hiring	06	_24_	20	_30_	04	07	-04	-06	08	02	17	10	16	07
C0 Liking	-06	_21_	13	_24_	-10	-03	-16	-16	-06	-13	06	06	09	-11
Content Examination														
At Clinical Total	-12	10	-02	08	08	-13	_-26_	08	-17	01	-02	-07	-14	-14
Bt General Total	-20	10	-05	03	-01	01	-28	16	-09	-03	-03	-06	-07	-16
Diagnostic Prediction Total														
C Sum for 2 Cases	21	05	-08	-02	17	02	14	-02	06	19	-08	-18	-08	01

N for Ratings = 93
N for Content Examination = 76
N for Diagnostic Predictions = 53

Coefficients significant at or beyond the 5% level of confidence are underlined.

It will be recalled that a "Facade" key was developed for the Guilford-Martin test. While Facade scores showed relatively high relationship with favorable scores on other Guilford-Martin keys at the time of assessment, these scores are not significantly related to any Composite Criterion ratings.

Minnesota Multiphasic Personality Inventory

The regular scales of the Minnesota Multiphasic Personality Inventory yielded only a chance number of relationships with criterion measures (cf. Table D III-3). However, certain of the scores based on the special keys developed by Gough, on other groups, show promising validities for certain of the criteria. Although scores on the Intellectual Functioning (IF) scale show practically no correlation with rated Academic Performance or Research, they have significant validities for six other criterion measures: Diagnostic Competence, Individual Therapy, Professional Interpersonal Relations, Clinical Competence, Preference for Hiring, and Liking. The Graduate Student (Gr) and Psychologist (Psy) scores also show significant correlations with several of the criterion measures. The Social Status (SS) scores yield two interesting validities; .34 for rated Research Competence and .39 for scores on the Diagnostic Predictions Test, the latter being the highest validity obtained for this particular criterion measure. The other three of Gough's keys, Dominance (Do), Social Participation (SP), and Social Responsibility (SR), show no significant correlations with any of the criteria.

Interest Tests

The Strong Interest Blanks

Fifty-nine scores were obtained from the Strong Vocational Interest Blank. It seems best to approach the resulting mass of correlations with criterion ratings by taking up each group of occupations separately.

Strong Group I scores were significantly related to rated Academic Performance, Research, Clinical Competence, Preference for Hiring, and scores on both parts of the Content Examination. Group I includes such occupations as Artist, Architect, Physician, Dentist, and Psychologist. These separate occupational keys tend to show the same general patterns as the group key. Scores on Group I probably indicate the extent to which the trainees have the interests of professional people in general.

Strong Group II scores are significantly related to rated Research Competence, Academic Performance, and scores on the two parts of the Content Examination, but not to rated Clinical Competence or Preference for Hiring. This is one of the few instances where we find a predictor related to criteria of intellectual achievement without being related to criteria of general clinical competence. Since the occupations in Group II include Mathematician, Physicist, Engineer, and Chemist, the Group II score measures similarity to the interest of quantitatively minded scientists. It is interesting to note that Rated Competence in Individual Psychotherapy shows generally negative correlations with scores for Group II occupations.

Group V scores are significantly and positively related to rated psychotherapeutic competence and negatively to the Content Examination scores. This might be called the "Service Group" of occupations; it includes YMCA Secretary, Public Administrator, Social Science High School Teacher, Minister, etc. Presumably people with high scores on these keys go into clinical psychology in order to help other people and are not necessarily interested in the scientific content of the field. Note that these particular predictors are related to a specific rated clinical skill but not to Overall Clinical Competence.

TABLE D III-3

CORRELATIONS BETWEEN SCORES ON THE MINNESOTA MULTIPHASIC INVENTORY AND CRITERION MEASURES

	Regular MMPI Keys										Gough's Keys*						
	D	Hs	Mf	P	K	Hy	Pd	Pt	Sc	Ma	Do	SS	SP	SR	Psy	IF	Gr
Ratings																	
C32 Academic Performance	-01	-09	26	-24	-03	-01	-04	-12	06	06	10	20	-02	00	16	04	14
C33 Diagnostic Competence	-09	-12	-05	-10	09	-12	-05	-08	01	-02	05	12	03	09	22	21	17
C34 Individual Psychotherapy	-08	-02	03	-01	06	-16	05	-04	-09	-03	04	22	10	06	15	32	16
C36 Research Competence	02	-23	04	-22	-14	-15	-17	-22	-13	-06	16	34	04	-09	15	05	11
C38 Supervisory Competence	-02	-16	03	-17	01	-15	-15	-10	-04	-10	-07	15	00	-05	12	16	08
C40 Professional Interpersonal Relations	-04	-11	08	-07	10	-09	-08	-05	-06	00	01	22	-04	-02	23	28	23
C41 Integrity	01	-08	-15	-04	17	-05	01	05	-06	-06	-06	08	-04	05	25	19	16
Ccc Clinical Competence	-09	-09	01	-16	11	-12	-04	-04	03	01	08	14	03	13	25	23	24
Cph Preference for Hiring	-08	-09	-06	-13	19	-03	-03	00	-01	-09	02	11	-03	06	26	24	21
C0 Liking	-08	-19	-09	-13	10	-04	-03	05	-08	-07	-01	14	-14	00	18	23	21
Content Examination																	
A$_t$ Clinical Total	10	-09	15	-16	-02	01	-08	-05	15	-06	08	19	09	02	23	11	22
B$_t$ General Total	16	00	06	-14	-06	05	-07	03	28	-05	15	09	-08	06	09	00	06
Diagnostic Predictions																	
Σ Sum for 2 cases	-09	-07	18	-08	-26	02	-14	-29	-14	10	00	39	20	-20	-15	-05	-14

N for Ratings = 93
N for Content Examination = 76
N for Diagnostic Predictions = 53

Coefficients significant at or beyond the 5% level of confidence are underlined

*Do = Dominance
 SS = Social Status
 SP = Social Participation
 SR = Social Responsibility

Psy = Psychologist
IF = Intellectual Functioning
Gr = Graduate Student

TABLE D III-4

CORRELATIONS BETWEEN CRITERION MEASURES AND GROUPS I, II, AND V SCORES
OF THE STRONG VOCATIONAL INTEREST BLANKS, 1947 GROUP

	Group I	Artist	Psychologist	Architect	Physician	Osteopath	Dentist	Group II	Mathematician	Physicist	Engineer	Chemist	Group V	YMCA Physical Director	Personnel Director	Public Administrator	YMCA Secretary	Social Science H.S. Teacher	City School Supt.	Minister
Ratings																				
C32 Academic Performance	26	19	33	27	18	-05	02	23	22	24	06	17	-14	-16	-03	-07	-16	-16	05	07
C33 Diagnostic Competence	04	04	03	07	-04	-12	-11	-09	00	-04	-19	-17	11	11	-02	-01	04	12	17	08
C34 Individual Psychotherapy	06	11	-02	07	-01	-01	-05	-19	-13	-15	-26	-22	21	21	01	01	18	19	15	15
C36 Research Competence	30	28	43	34	22	-05	05	32	36	36	19	27	-15	-15	-01	02	-19	-15	09	04
C38 Supervisory Competence	18	15	18	15	15	08	07	08	11	12	00	08	00	03	-06	-03	-04	-02	-03	12
C40 Prof. Interpersonal Relations	10	14	10	10	04	-04	-07	-06	05	01	-21	-10	08	06	-07	-05	06	13	10	20
C41 Integrity	06	01	01	06	00	04	07	00	02	00	-02	00	04	08	-02	-01	06	01	-02	08
Ccc Clinical Competence	21	22	18	22	10	-02	01	00	09	06	-12	-04	06	03	-03	-02	-02	02	07	18
Cph Preference for Hiring	22	20	18	23	15	07	13	05	13	09	-08	-01	07	10	-05	-10	-01	04	08	15
C0 Liking	18	19	14	17	16	03	10	02	17	07	-16	-05	09	16	-13	-11	07	09	08	19
Content Examination																				
At Clinical Total	28		37	27	26			29	32				-32							
Bt General Total	32		43	31	29			44	42				-39							
Diagnostic Predictions																				
Σ Sum for 2 Cases	05		04	01	06			-03					-03							

N for Ratings = 93
N for Content Examination = 76
N for Diagnostic Predictions = 53

Blank spaces indicate values not computed.

Coefficients significant at or beyond 5% level of confidence are underlined.

The Strong Group VIII key shows negative relationships with Academic Performance and Research, with Clinical Competence, and with the Content Examination scores. This group includes such occupations as Office Worker, Accountant, Banker, and Mortician, occupations in which the way the job is done, e. g. , accuracy, is crucial and the content is of secondary importance. The key for Purchasing Agent, one occupation in this group, shows the basic pattern and, in addition, is negatively correlated with acceptance by professional colleagues, i. e. , Liking. Does this perhaps mean that compulsiveness and the economically important values of efficiency and economy tend to be rejected by clinical psychologists?

The Strong Group IX key shows negative correlations with Research and the General part of the Content Examination. Perhaps persons with interests like those of salesmen are not motivated to seek scientific proof through research.

The keys for Lawyer, Author-Journalist, and Advertising Man fall in Group X. The key for this group shows positive relationships with Academic Performance, Research, Scores on the Content Examination, and also with Diagnostic Competence, Interpersonal Relations, and Clinical Competence. We can perhaps characterize people with this interest pattern as being interested in convincing others by rational argument.

The keys for occupations in Group IV show generally negative correlations with criterion ratings. The only sizable ones are negative correlations between the Carpenter key and rated Academic Performance and Clinical Diagnosis; and negative correlations between the Policeman key and rated Academic Performance and Research.

Strong Production-Manager scores (Table D III-6), like those for Purchasing Agent show negative correlations with all rated criteria. These negative values are especially significant for rated Diagnosis, Therapy, Interpersonal Relations, Preference for Hiring, Liking, and Clinical Competence. Purchasing Agent scores show somewhat lower negative correlations with specific clinical competences but higher negative correlations with criteria of academic achievement. We shall note later that scores based on the Strong-Kriedt Industrial Psychology Key yield a pattern of validities very much like that for the Strong Production Manager Key.

Musician scores are significantly correlated with rated Therapeutic Competence and with Preference for Hiring and Liking.

Certified Public Accountant scores show positive relationships with Academic Performance and Research, much like those shown by Group I keys, but are also significantly related to rated Diagnostic Competence.

Among the non-occupational keys, the Occupational Level score shows positive correlations with academic achievement, both as rated and as measured by the Content Examination. On the other hand, Interest Maturity scores are negatively correlated with achievement on the Content Examination. Apparently trainees with low Interest Maturity scores are more inclined to undertake the mastery of content materials than those whose interests are more crystallized at the time they enter training.

Scores based on the regular Strong Psychologist key (cf. Table D III-4) predict rated Academic Performance, rated Research Competence, and scores on the Content Examination with relatively high validities. The VA Clinical Psychologist key, an ad hoc key developed within this project, while yielding a number of significant correlations, does not predict intellectual criteria as well as the original Strong Psychologist key. Scores based on the VA key had correlated somewhat higher with criterion ratings obtained on this 1947 Group after only two years of training. Among

TABLE D III-5

CORRELATIONS BETWEEN CRITERION MEASURES AND GROUPS VIII, IX, X AND IV SCORES
OF THE STRONG VOCATIONAL INTEREST BLANK, 1947 GROUP

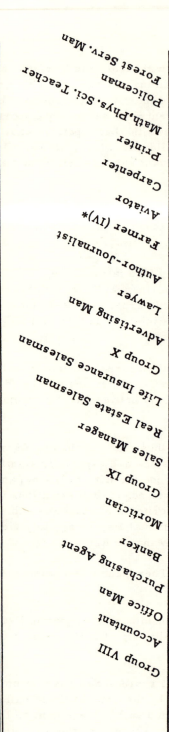

	Group VIII	Accountant	Office Man	Purchasing Agent	Banker	Mortician	Group IX	Sales Manager	Real Estate Salesman	Life Insurance Salesman	Group X	Advertising Man	Lawyer	Author-Journalist	Farmer (IV)*	Aviator	Carpenter	Printer	Math,Phys,Sci, Teacher	Policeman	Forest Serv, Man
Ratings																					
C32 Academic Performance	-23	-14	-26	-21	-18	-24	-07	-05	-08	-12	27	25	27	26	-18	-06	-21	-12	-09	-31	-17
C33 Diagnostic Competence	-09	-05	-13	-10	-14	04	18	14	11	09	22	25	29	16	-15	-10	-24	-12	-19	-13	-11
C34 Individual Psychotherapy	-10	-13	-15	-14	07	14	15	05	11	13	15	22	13	12	-02	-07	-05	00	-15	-01	02
C36 Research Competence	-27	-13	-30	-25	-27	-34	-22	-21	-17	-24	24	15	23	27	02	08	-05	00	00	-29	-02
C38 Supervisory Competence	-16	-13	-17	-19	-07	-01	-02	-07	00	00	14	17	15	17	-02	03	-06	02	-10	-06	-01
C40 Prof. Interpersonal Relations	-11	-12	-15	-20	04	04	09	-02	10	05	20	24	19	18	-06	-11	-13	-04	-16	-14	-09
C41 Integrity	-03	-04	-04	-06	05	08	04	-04	01	-03	00	06	-01	-02	05	03	07	07	00	04	08
Ccc Clinical Competence	-22	-15	-24	-23	-08	-08	07	04	01	02	26	35	24	27	-10	-07	-16	-03	-16	-18	-03
Cph Preference for Hiring	-18	-16	-20	-24	-05	-02	-01	-10	00	-07	18	23	14	18	05	01	-07	03	-05	-09	05
C0 Liking	-12	-16	-15	-21	05	05	-02	-15	02	-06	15	14	12	16	10	-07	-05	06	-04	-01	07
Content Examination																					
At Clinical Total	-40			-33			-07				40	41	44						-39		
Bt General Total	-33			-32			-23				28	27	32						-36		
Diagnostic Predictions																					
Σ Sum for 2 Cases	-17			-10			13	15			18	05	21							-05	

N for Ratings = 93
N for Content Examination = 76
N N for Diagnostic Predictions = 53

*Group Number

Coefficients significant at or beyond the 5% level of confidence are underlined.

TABLE D III-6

CORRELATIONS BETWEEN CRITERION MEASURES AND MISCELLANEOUS SCORES ON THE STRONG VOCATIONAL INTEREST BLANK, 1947 GROUP

	Production Manager (III)*	Musician (VI)	CPA (VII)	Pres. Mfg. Concern (XI)	Occupational Level	Interest Maturity	VA Clinical Psychologist	Psychologist (Kriedt Psychologist Keys)	Clinical	Experimental	Guidance	Industrial	Masculinity (M)	Thrown Masculine (TM)	Thrown Feminine (TF)	TM minus TF	TM minus M	M minus TF
Ratings																		
C32 Academic Performance	-14	06	35	14	28	-12	15	27	10	10	-14	-17	-10	-01	-04	04	11	-07
C33 Diagnostic Competence	-25	03	22	12	15	-04	12	04	23	-18	12	-11	-14	01	00	01	15	-10
C34 Individual Psychotherapy	-29	20	-02	-03	-06	01	17	01	23	-17	09	-06	-18	01	16	-10	15	-20
C36 Research Competence	-10	17	28	10	14	-19	22	38	01	16	-22	-22	-05	02	08	-05	04	-09
C38 Supervisory Competence	-14	14	07	08	01	-16	14	15	08	04	-09	-17	-10	05	08	-05	11	-10
C40 Professional Interpersonal Relations	-30	16	04	11	04	-10	17	11	20	-13	04	-16	-23	01	06	-04	17	-21
C41 Integrity	-02	05	04	03	-06	-04	08	07	04	-03	02	-02	-02	04	08	-04	01	-03
Ccc Clinical Competence	-25	18	12	12	13	-08	24	20	26	-08	00	-21	-21	-03	02	-04	15	-16
Cph Preference for Hiring	-28	25	03	-05	01	-07	20	20	17	01	-04	-26	-20	04	08	-04	16	-17
C0 Liking	-32	23	-04	-12	-10	-14	15	15	17	-01	-04	-31	-20	19	14	02	22	-18
Content Examination																		
At Clinical Total	-05				30	-36	24	41	19	13	-29	-15	05	06	-01	05	02	02
Bt General Total	-03				22	-36	12	46	01	29	-37	-24	17	03	-01	04	-10	13
Diagnostic Predictions																		
Σ Sum for 2 Cases	09				09	-08	15	00	18	-09	02	07	-11	04	02	-02	11	-14

N for Ratings = 93
N for Content Examination = 76
N for Diagnostic Predictions = 53

*Group Number

Coefficients significant at or beyond the 5% level of confidence are underlined.

153

the six psychologist keys developed by Kriedt (1949) is a revised general psychologist's key, and keys for special subgroups of psychologists. Scores based on these keys yielded a number of significant validities. Kriedt Clinical Psychologist scores correlate significantly with Diagnostic and Therapeutic Competence, Interpersonal Relations, and Overall Clinical Competence. These scores also correlate .41 and .46 with Content Examination scores. On the other hand, scores based on Kriedt's Guidance Psychologist key show a negative correlation with rated Research Competence and with scores on the Content Examination. As has already been noted, the Kriedt Industrial Psychologist shows generally negative relationships with all criterion ratings. It would appear that trainees with interests like those of Industrial psychologists are not likely to be engrossed with the content and methods of clinical psychology; furthermore, such trainees are not likely to be accepted by clinical psychologists as indicated by the -.31 correlation with Liking.

The Masculinity score of the Strong shows negative correlations with Interpersonal Relations, Clinical Competence, Preference for Hiring, and Liking. This tendency probably reflects the fact that clinical psychologists prefer associates with aesthetic, i.e., non-masculine, interests.

The Thrown scores on the Strong, derived from the trainees' attempts to answer items as men in general or women in general answered them, appear to have almost no predictive value.

In summary, each of our several criterion variables is predicted reasonably well by at least one Strong key. There is every reason to expect that from the large pool of items provided by the Strong Vocational Interest Blank it would be possible to develop keys for specific job functions which would have even higher predictive value than the standard keys which we have used. However, in view of the relatively fluid state of clinical psychology as a profession today, it seems unwise to develop for practical application any such keys on the basis of the responses of the trainees tested more than four years ago.

The Kuder Preference Inventory

Several scales from the Kuder Preference Record also show significant relationships to criterion variables. (see Table D III-7). The scientific scale shows significant negative correlations with rated Diagnostic and Therapeutic Competence and with rated Clinical Competence. "Scientific" in this context probably refers to an interest in the physical and biological sciences rather than in the social sciences.

The Kuder Persuasive Scale shows significant negative correlations with Research. The Artistic and Musical Scales show significant positive relationship with Academic Performance, Clinical Competence, and Preference for Hiring. Does this represent an interest in the study of personality as an aesthetic phenomenon or simply a type of interest pattern which other clinical psychologists find highly acceptable?

The Allport-Vernon Study of Values

Turning now to the Allport-Vernon Study of Values (see Table D III-8), the Theoretical scores are significantly related to rated Research and Academic Performance and also to scores on the Content Examination. Scores on the Religious key show the reverse pattern and, in addition, a negative correlation with rated Clinical Competence. Political scores are negatively related to Academic Performance and Research while Aesthetic scores are positively related not only to these variables but also to Clinical Competence. Notice that the value scores of the Allport-Vernon test predict best those criterion measures reflecting intellectual achievements.

TABLE D III-7

CORRELATIONS BETWEEN CRITERION MEASURES AND SCORES ON
THE KUDER PREFERENCE RECORD, 1947 GROUP

	Mechan-ical	Compu-tational	Scien-tific	Persua-sive	Artis-tic	Liter-ary	Musi-cal	Social Service	Cleri-cal
Ratings									
C32 Academic Performance	06	14	-03	-17	_23_	05	_20_	-17	-06
C33 Diagnostic Competence	-14	-06	_-25_	07	11	09	11	02	-02
C34 Individual Psychotherapy	-14	_-21_	_-33_	04	15	06	17	15	-15
C36 Research Competence	02	_20_	00	_-24_	18	03	11	-12	-02
C38 Supervisory Competence	-01	-12	-07	00	12	06	16	_-20_	-19
C40 Professional Interpersonal Relations	-12	-14	-19	02	12	09	08	04	-03
C41 Integrity	02	-16	-01	08	02	-11	-06	16	-05
Ccc Clinical Competence	-10	-18	_-30_	00	_31_	13	_23_	-02	-15
Cph Preference for Hiring	-11	-10	-17	-04	_26_	-01	_24_	-02	-09
C0 Liking	_-21_	00	-11	-02	-04	05	07	01	05
Content Examination									
At Clinical Total	03	-03	-04	-18	11	_26_	11	-16	-10
Bt General Total	06	18	08	_-27_	06	18	-11	-15	07
Diagnostic Predictions									
Σ Sum of 2 Cases	06	09	07	-25	05	10	09	00	-02

N for Ratings = 93
N for Content Examination = 76
N for Diagnostic Predictions = 53

Coefficients significant at or beyond the 5% level of confidence are underlined.

TABLE D III 8

CORRELATIONS BETWEEN CRITERION MEASURES AND SCORES ON THE
ALLPORT-VERNON STUDY OF VALUES

1947 Group

	Theoretical	Economic	Aesthetic	Social	Political	Religious
Ratings						
C32 Academic Performance	20	00	25	-04	-18	-29
C33 Diagnostic Competence	-06	-04	07	01	03	-15
C34 Individual Psychotherapy	-16	03	10	03	02	-07
C36 Research Competence	26	03	25	03	-20	-39
C38 Supervisory Competence	00	-02	17	-05	-04	-16
C40 Professional Interpersonal Relations	00	01	13	00	-08	-11
C41 Integrity	00	16	-02	05	-04	-13
Ccc Clinical Competence	00	00	22	-06	-06	-23
Cph Preference for Hiring	-03	-02	19	-03	-07	-15
C0 Liking	-04	-04	13	00	-12	-02
Content Examination						
At Clinical Total	24	-15	24	13	-27	-33
Bt General Total	38	-09	11	11	-29	-32
Diagnostic Predictions						
Σ Sum of 2 Cases	10	-09	05	20	-11	-07

N for Ratings = 93
N for Content Examination = 76
N for Diagnostic Predictions = 53

Coefficients significant at or beyond the 5% level of confidence are underlined.

Best Test Predictors

What consistent patterns do we find in these analyses of the validities of objective test scores? Table D III-9 summarizes what may be regarded as the "best bets," i.e., the three test scores showing the highest correlation with each of the 13 criterion measures for the 1947 subjects. In this table, we have arranged the criterion measures in three clusters suggested by the factor analysis presented in Chapter C II; these are listed in the left hand column of the table.

By all odds, the best predictor of what might be termed the group of intellectual criterion measures is the Miller Analogies Test. Scores on this test show the highest correlations with three of these four criterion measures and third highest for the fourth. The next most predictive scores are those based on the Strong Vocational Interest Blank: the Kriedt Psychologist Scores, the Author-Journalist Scores and the original Psychologist Scores.

For the four more general criterion variables listed in Group II, Miller scores again turn out to be the best predictor of one of them with a tie for another. Other promising test predictors of these variables are Strong Advertising Man and Strong Production Manager scores, the latter showing two negative validities. As has already been noted, the Guilford-Martin C score is the best single predictor of Preference for Hiring. The relatively strong intellectual component of rated Supervisory Competence is indicated by the fact that next to the Miller, the PMA Number and Memory scores are the best predictors of this skill.

Looking next at the five more specific criterion measures in Group III of the table, we note immediately the appearance of a wide variety of measures among the 17 best bets. Six of these are Strong scores but based on four different keys. Three of the seven MMPI-Gough scores also appear in the list. Perhaps even more interesting is the finding that two of the PMA subtest scores are among the best test predictors of two uncorrelated criteria of diagnostic skill. Interesting also is the fact that the best test predictor of Therapeutic Competence is the Scientific score on the Kuder Preference Inventory--with a negative validity coefficient.

A tally shows the following box score for these 45 first, second, and third places:

	First	Second	Third	Total
Miller Analogies Test	5	0	1	6
Strong (10 different keys)	3	7	9	19
MMPI (1 key)	0	0	1	1
MMPI-Gough (3 keys)	1	3	1	5
Guilford-Martin (2 keys)	2	0	2	4
PMA (3 subtests)	1	2	2	5
Kuder (2 keys)	1	0	3	4
Allport-Vernon (1 key)	0	1	0	1
	13	13	19	45

Obviously multiple r's somewhat higher than the above validities could have been computed by combining two or more tests in a predictive battery. We have not allowed ourselves to follow this temptation because of the lack of any really comparable group of subjects on which to determine how well the multiple is held up. For reasons already indicated, the 1948 group is far from comparable with the 1947 group and the criterion measures for this group, after only two years of

TABLE D III-9

SUMMARY SHOWING THE THREE OBJECTIVE TEST SCORES YIELDING THE HIGHEST CORRELATIONS WITH 13 CRITERION MEASURES

1947 Group

Criterion Measure	r	Highest Validity Test	r	Next Highest Test	r	Third Highest Test
I. Intellectual Criteria						
C32 Academic	47	Miller	33	Strong (Psychologist)	-31	Strong (Policeman)
C36 Research	43	Strong (Psychol.)	-39	A-V (Religious)	38 / 38	Miller / Strong (Kriedt-Psychol.)
At Content Exam., Clin.	58	Miller	44	Strong (Author-Journ.)	41 / 41	Strong (Kriedt-Psychol.) / Strong (Lawyer)
Bt Content Exam., Gen.	58	Miller	46	Strong (Kriedt-Psychol.)	44	Strong (Group II)
Mdn.	52		41		39	
II. General Criteria						
C38 Supervision	34	Miller	25	PMA (Number)	24	PMA (Memory)
C40 Interpersonal Rel.	-30	Strong (Production Mgr.)	28	MMPI (Gough IF Key)	25	PMA (Number)
Ccc Clinical Competence	35	Miller	35	Strong (Advertising Man)	31	Kuder (Artistic)
					-26	Strong (Kriedt-Industr. Psych.)
Cph Preference for Hiring	30	Guilford-Martin (C)	-28	Strong (Production Mgr.)	26 / 26	Kuder (Artistic) / MMPI (Gough-Psychol.)
Mdn.	32		28		26	
III. More Specific Criteria						
C33 Diagnosis	31	PMA (Number)	29	Strong (Lawyer)	-25 / -25 / 25	Strong (Production Mgr.) / Kuder (Scientific) / Strong (Advertising Man)
C34 Therapy	-33	Kuder (Scientific)	32	MMPI (Gough IF Key)	-29	Strong (Production Mgr)
C41 Integrity	30	Guilford-Martin (T)	25	MMPI (Gough Psy. Key)	20	Guilford-Martin (C-Lack of Cycloid
C0 Liking	-32	Strong (Production Mgr.)	-31	Strong (Kriedt Ind. Psy.)	-24	Guilford-Martin (C) Tend.)
Σ Diagnostic Predict.	39	MMPI (Gough-Soc. Status)	37	PMA (Word Fluency)	-29	MMPI (Psychasthenia)
Mdn.	32		31		25	

training, are probably not yet as predictable as those for the 1947 group.

An indication of the generally lower objective test validities found for the 1948 group (Wellesley) is shown in Table D III-10 which lists for both groups the corresponding correlations between the 13 criterion measures and the previously listed best test predictors for the 1947 group. The only

TABLE D III-10

COMPARABLE VALIDITY COEFFICIENTS FOR 1947 AND 1948
GROUPS FOR BEST TEST PREDICTORS OF 13
CRITERION MEASURES

Criterion Measure	Best Test Predictor	r	Validity
I. Intellectual Criterion	1947	1947	1948
C32 Academic Performance	Miller	47	16
C36 Research Competence	Strong (Psychol.)	43	09
A$_t$ Content Exam (Clin.)	Miller	58	43
B$_t$ Content Exam (Gen.)	Miller	58	52
II. General Criteria			
C38 Supervisory Competence	Miller	34	-09
C40 Prof. Interpersonal Relations	Strong (Production Mgr.)	-30	-04
Ccc Clinical Competence	Miller	35	-11
Cph Preference for Hiring	Guilford-Martin (C)	30	13
III. More Specific Criteria			
C33 Diagnostic Competence	PMA (Number)	31	not used
C34 Individual Psychotherapy	Kuder (Scientific)	-33	not used
C41 Integrity	Guilford-Martin (T)	30	16
C0 Liking	Strong (Production Mgr.)	-32	-07
Σ Diagnostic Prediction	MMPI-Gough (Social Status)	39	not used

correlations of the same general magnitude are those between scores on the Miller Analogies Test and scores on the objective Content Examination. Since a similar pattern of lower validities was found for assessment predictions for the 1948 group, we can only conclude that the previously noted factors interacted in such a manner as to make the prediction of criterion measures for this group extremely difficult. This matter will be discussed more fully in the next chapter.

CHAPTER D IV

THE VALIDITIES OF ASSESSMENT RATINGS

The predictions made by the 1947 assessment staff in the form of Final Pooled Ratings show a median validation coefficient of .34. This median correlation is somewhat higher than that for the consistency of descriptive ratings over the same time interval. However, both in Final Ratings and in ratings made at previous stages of the assessment process, the staff was frequently unable to differentiate the several criterion skills; predictions for one variable often correlated higher with criterion measures of another variable. The criterion variables predicted best by assessment ratings were Academic Performance and Research Competence. The criterion skills, Competence in Diagnosis and in Therapy, were predicted least well by assessment ratings.

For almost every criterion variable, predictions based on limited materials are about as valid as those based on all materials available to the assessment staff. Thus rated Clinical Competence and measures of academic achievement are predicted from Credentials plus Objective Tests as well as they are from Final Pooled Ratings. With one or two exceptions, the validities for predictions made on the basis of records only and without face-to-face contact are as high or nearly as high as any other validities for a given variable. Most predictions based upon projective tests had insignificant validities. For most variables, interviews did not contribute to the validity of predictions.

Predictions for the same cases were made by the 1949 reassessment staff without face-to-face contact. Validities for predictions of intellectual achievement, Diagnostic Competence, and Interpersonal Relationships were as high as those made in 1947 on the same materials and were almost as high as the validities for the 1947 Final Pooled Ratings.

Assessment predictions based on similar materials for the 1948 group showed considerably lower validities. Since similarly lower validities were found for objective test predictors we must attribute them to differences in the selection and training of the two groups, to the fact that the assessment materials were collected under conditions of actual selection, to the fact that the trainees were not well differentiated on the criterion measures after only two years of training, or a combination of these factors.

Some significant correlations were found between descriptive ratings (Scale A) and criterion ratings of Academic Performance and Overall Clinical Competence.

The use of multiple judges or assessors and the pooling of predictions in a clinical conference were found to add little to the validities of predictions.

The Validity of the 1947 Final Pooled Predictions of
Overall Suitability for Clinical Psychology

The correlations between the 1950 Composite Criterion ratings and other criterion measures and the 1947 Assessment Final Pooled Predictions for Scale C are presented in Table D IV-1. For the moment let us confine our attention to the column for A42, Final Pooled Prediction of Overall Suitability. This global assessment prediction correlates positively with all criterion measures, especially high with rated Clinical Competence, Preference for Hiring, Supervisory Competence,

TABLE D IV-1

CORRELATIONS BETWEEN 1947 ASSESSMENT FINAL POOLED
PREDICTIONS AND CRITERION MEASURES

	A32	A33	A34	A35	A36	A37[1]	A38	A39[2]	A40	A41	A42[3]	A0*
Criterion Ratings												
C32 Academic Performance	46	36	24	16	51	18	25	42	12	13	27	17
C33 Diagnostic Competence	21	16	29	14	18	08	14	16	09	18	22	11
C34 Individual Psychotherapy	09	14	24	12	07	14	07	07	09	20	18	11
C35 Group Psychotherapy	24	21	26	20	21	15	19	19	11	16	22	13
C36 Research Competence	46	40	32	26	52	28	33	49	19	15	36	20
C38 Supervisory Competence	33	27	39	31	32	34	33	40	24	25	41	25
C40 Professional Interpersonal Relations	22	25	39	28	24	30	29	33	26	28	37	27
C41 Integrity	23	23	38	33	25	35	37	32	34	30	37	30
Ccc Clinical Competence	45	32	36	27	38	32	26	40	25	25	38	22
Cph Preference for Hiring	29	30	40	30	14	33	32	32	35	32	37	26
C0 Liking	13	23	43	33	11	27	27	18	34	31	35	30
Content Examination												
A_t Clinical Total	42	25	14	-01	33	15	08	33	07	-04	20	00
B_t General Total	45	43	28	16	54	19	24	51	21	17	37	12
Prediction Tests												
Σ Diagnostic Cases	29	35	18	18	38						21	05
TP Therapy Cases	09	33	21	22	26						26	15
Research Activity (from Training Inventory, Biserial r's)												
No. of Titles Cited	19	21	22	21	22	27	07	14	04	02	26	06
Progress on Dissertation	30	12	-12	01	24	15	03	20	01	-08	04	-09

N for Ratings = 92 (except A0 column, where N = 89).
N for Content Examination = 75.
N for Diagnostic Prediction Test = 55 (except A0 column, where N = 52).
N for Therapeutic Prediction Test = 33.
N for Research Activity Measures = 71 (Dichotomies for biserial r's were close to median).
Correlations significant at or beyond the 5% level of confidence are underlined.

[1] A37 - Administrative Competence.
[2] A39 - Competence in Teaching
[3] A42 - Overall Suitability for Clinical Psychology

Interpersonal Relations, Integrity, Research, and Liking. In general the Assessment Overall Suitability rating predicted both Interpersonal Professional Relations and the intellectual criteria better than it predicted specific clinical skills. Not shown in the table, but of considerable interest, is the fact that this assessment rating (A42) predicts the Composite rating on Clinical Competence substantially better than it predicts ratings on this criterion made by homogeneous groups of raters: i.e., university staff, supervisors or colleagues.

The Final Pooled Overall Suitability Assessment Rating also predicts other criteria fairly well. It predicts the general section of the Content Examination much better than it predicts the clinical section. Perhaps the assessment staff tended to overweight general intellectual ability and underestimate the importance of other aptitudes for clinical work. Again, Overall Suitability correlates with scores on the Diagnostic Prediction Test, for patients seen for both diagnosis and therapy, about as well as it predicts rated Diagnostic or Therapeutic Competence. Thus this general Overall Suitability rating seems to have predicted a common core of all of our various criterion measures.

The Validities of 1947 Final Pooled Predictions on
Other Scale C Variables

Academic Performance

The assessment prediction of Academic Performance (A32) correlates quite well with rated Academic Performance but its correlation with Clinical Competence is about equally high. In fact, the assessment prediction of Academic Performance predicts Composite Clinical Competence better than does the assessment prediction of Overall Suitability. As one might expect, A32 also shows a high correlation with scores on both the Clinical* and General Sections of the Content Examination. The correlation between predicted Academic Performance and scores on the Diagnostic Prediction Test is higher than with similar scores for Therapy Patients.

Research

The picture for predicted Research Competence (A36) is quite similar to that for predicted Academic Performance. Not shown in the table, but again of some interest, is the finding that assessment predictions of Research predicted both the University and the Colleague criterion ratings of Research as well as they predicted the Composite Rating on Research. However, Installation ratings of Research were less well predicted.

The assessment prediction of Research Competence is more highly related to rated Research Competence than to either of the two measures of research activity, whether the trainee reported more than one research study on the Training Experience Inventory, or whether this progress toward completing his dissertation was equal to that reported by the more advanced half of the group.

The similarity between the patterns of validities for predicted Academic Performance and predicted Research Competence is somewhat confusing. There is no evidence in these data that either the assessors or the criterion raters were able to distinguish between these two types of competence. Is the trainee who gets high grades on preliminary examinations necessarily the same as the trainee who plans, carries out, and writes up a good doctoral research problem? While the true relation between these two criterion variables is probably high, we doubt that the variables are as nearly identical as these findings suggest. The most likely explanation is that at the end of three and a half years the trainees have not spread themselves out very well on research competence

---

*Neither assessment ratings on A32 nor on any other Scale C variable predicts scores on the Case Study part of the Clinical Section of the Content Examination.

with only the most able and the most highly motivated having given any demonstration of their technical skill in research and their capacity for creative thinking.

In general, we may say that predictions of intellectual achievements were relatively successful and it would appear that the assessment staff was able to discriminate between intellectual achievement and such clinical skills as diagnosis and therapy.

Supervisory Competence

Although assessment predictions of Supervisory Competence (A38) correlate fairly well with rated Supervisory Competence, they predict the criterion variable, Integrity somewhat better, and to a lesser extent, Preference for Hiring and Research Competence. It will be recalled that in the factor analysis of the 1947 assessment ratings, predicted Supervisory Skill showed high loadings on two factors: Factor G, Intellectual Effectiveness and Factor I, Effectiveness in Interpersonal Relations.

Teaching and Administration

Two variables were included in the assessment prediction scale that were not included in the criterion rating scale, Administration (A37) and Teaching (in a university, A39). No criterion ratings were collected for these variables at this time because few if any trainees had had an opportunity to demonstrate their competence in these fields. Correlations between the predictions on these two variables and criterion ratings have been included in Table D IV-1. The pattern of validities for predicted Teaching Skill corresponds very closely with that of predicted Research, with the exception of a higher correlation with Preference for Hiring. Predicted Administrative Skill correlates significantly with rated Research Supervision, Interpersonal Relations, Integrity, Clinical Competence and Preference for Hiring.

Validities of Predictions on Specific Clinical Variables

Diagnosis

Assessment predictions of specific clinical skills in general show lower correlations with all criterion variables. Predicted Diagnostic Competence (A33) shows significant correlations with almost all criterion variables except rated Diagnostic Competence! Its highest correlations are with rated Academic Performance, Research, Composite Clinical Competence, Preference for Hiring and scores on the General section of the Content Examination. From these data one is forced to conclude that the assessors had a different conception of the nature of diagnostic competence than did the criterion raters. The assessment staff seems to have felt that diagnostic competence required a combination of intellectual skills similar to those needed for high academic performance. In this connection, it is of interest to note that predicted Diagnostic Competence correlates quite well with the Diagnostic Prediction Test scores for patients seen for either diagnosis or therapy. It will be recalled that there is no relationship between rated Diagnostic Competence and scores on the Diagnostic Prediction Test $(r = .00)$. We shall return later to the probable bases for the ratings of Diagnostic Competence.

Psychotherapy

Predicted Competence in Individual Psychotherapy (A34) correlates only .24 with rated Competence in Psychotherapy. Note, however, that this is the highest correlation with the particular criterion measure. It correlates much higher with several other criterion measures: Liking, Preference for Hiring, Interpersonal Relations, Supervising, Integrity, Clinical Competence and Research. Aptitude for Psychotherapy seems to have been assessed as a rather global variable.

Since predicted Competence in Group Therapy (A35) correlated highly with predicted Competence in Individual Therapy, the pattern of correlations with the criterion measures is quite similar for these two assessment predictors, with predicted competence in Group Therapy yielding generally lower coefficients.

Thus we are confronted with the fact that predictions on the two more specifically clinical skills predict other rated skills better than the ones which they were expected to predict. The explanation cannot lie in the unreliability of either the predictions or the criteria because these have been shown to be reasonably satisfactory. We can only conclude that the conceptions of the assessment staff of the nature of these skills differed considerably from those of the criterion raters. In this connection it is worth comparing the two rows of Table D IV-1 for criterion Diagnosis and criterion Therapy with the two columns for predicted Diagnosis and Therapy. Whatever skills or competences are involved in rated Diagnostic and Therapeutic Competence were not predicted to any appreciable extent by any of the assessment predictions. On the other hand, whatever the assessment staff used as a basis for predictions of diagnostic and therapeutic competences was related to several criterion skills. In other words, the assessors understood the trainees well enough to be able to predict something correctly by their ratings on these two variables, but the criterion ratings on these two skills are apparently based primarily on variables not adequately represented in any of the assessment ratings. One possibility is that the nature of these two functions has changed somewhat during the three years between assessment and criterion measurements. Such a change in the field may account for part, but only part, of these findings. It is much more likely that the principal source of the discrepancy lies in the criterion ratings; there is considerable evidence, at least in the case of therapy, that different individuals hold quite different notions of what constitutes therapeutic competence, especially people from different schools and different parts of the country.* We are firmly convinced that the objective evaluation of therapeutic success and of therapeutic competence and of the personality requisites for each is a major problem in clinical psychology today.

Validities of Predictions on Other Variables

Integrity and Inter-Personal Relations

Assessment predictions of Integrity (A41) correlate most closely with rated Integrity, Preference for Hiring, and Liking. The assessment predictions of Interpersonal Relations (A40) show an almost identical pattern of validities. These patterns are similar to those for predicted Competence in Therapy and Liking, but with somewhat lower coefficients than those for Therapy.

Liking

Since Liking of one person for another is properly an individual matter, the assessment staff did not attempt to arrive at a group judgment on the variable. However, the median of the Final Individual assessment ratings on Liking is seen to have a correlation of .30 with the median Liking ratings by the criterion raters. It also correlates significantly with rated Integrity, Supervision, Interpersonal Relations, Clinical Competence, and Preference for Hiring. It must be recalled that these ratings were not predictions, but simply descriptions of the feelings of the assessors toward trainees at the time of assessment. For this reason, it is reassuring to find that the correlation between Liking as rated at assessment and as rated at the time of criterion

*One only has to listen to a few of the recordings of therapy submitted by the trainees as samples of their work to realize the tremendous variability in what is called therapy from one installation to another. The samples submitted included hours representing almost every conceivable therapeutic orientation: non-directive, analytic, positive suggestion, exhortation, as well as others which sounded like awkward social conversations between relative strangers.

measurement is no higher than .30. If this correlation had turned out to be as high as .50 or .60, we should have to consider the possible interpretation that halo effects were operating, i. e., that the assessors' and the criterion raters' Liking for a candidate so influenced the ratings of each on specific skills as to have generated the correlations between assessment and criterion predictions on them. Even so, the high level of the intercorrelations among the assessment predictions and among the criterion ratings indicates that some halo or generalizing effect was probably operating in each case. It is likely that each set of raters had a general impression of a man's overall efficiency in a clinical situation (future or present) and that this general impression modified their ratings of specific skills.

It is clear that the assessors were able to discriminate between good social relations and good potential intellectual performance, but they apparently had difficulty in distinguishing Integrity from Interpersonal Relations. It appears that the feeling of trustworthiness involved in high ratings of Integrity is an important component in high ratings of Interpersonal Relations.

In interpreting intercorrelations between Scale C predictions and criterion ratings, one must bear in mind the possibility that the particular order in which Scale C variables appeared on the rating scale may have influenced the patterns of validational coefficients. Because Predicted Diagnostic Competence followed Predicted Academic Performance in the assessment rating scale, the staff may have weighted intellectual capacity too heavily as a component in diagnostic skill. Similarly, the estimated contribution of diagnostic skill to therapeutic competence and the estimated contribution of intellectual capacity (evaluated in rating research) to supervising skill may be too great. While little is known about rated Integrity, the fact that this variable was placed after Interpersonal Relations may help to explain the pattern of correlations found for predicted Integrity.

The Effect of Personal Therapy upon Validities
of 1947 Final Pooled Predictions

We saw in Chapter D I that the general consistency of descriptive ratings (Scales A and B) over time was not affected by the fact that certain trainees had had personal therapy in the interval. On the other hand, personal therapy did lower the accuracy of prediction of clinical performance. As shown in Table D IV-2, the validities of predictions for trainees who subsequently had therapy are generally lower than those for other trainees. These lower validities do not appear to be a function of differences in intra-group variability.

We note that the predictions of Academic Performance and Research Competence are as accurate for trainees with intervening therapy as for those without. In contrast, the validity coefficients for the predictions of clinical skills are all low or even negative for trainees who had therapy. This evidence suggests that such a major intervening experience may make impossible the accurate prediction of certain types of professional performance. The job functions most affected are those involving personal interactions.

Intervening personal therapy obviously did not have the same effect on all trainees; if it had systematically raised the general level of clinical competence, the correlations for the therapy cases would be positive, not zero. There is the possibility, even the probability that the trainees who went into therapy represent a group, either more difficult to assess or less predictable. It is also likely that personal therapy may have interfered with other training activities for some of the trainees. Finally the lower validities for the therapy group may have resulted from the fact that the assessment staff did not know which individuals would enter therapy. At the time of assessment some candidates reported their intention to enter therapy, while others did not make the decision until later.

TABLE D IV-2

COMPARISON OF VALIDITY COEFFICIENTS FOR 1947 TRAINEES
WITH OR WITHOUT INTERVENING PERSONAL THERAPY

Assessment Prediction and Corresponding Composite Criterion Rating	Trainees Who Had Therapy (N = 22)	Trainees Who Had No Therapy (N = 70)	Total Group (N = 92)
32 Academic Performance	<u>46</u>	<u>45</u>	<u>46</u>
33 Diagnostic Competence	-21	<u>27</u>	16
34 Individual Psychotherapy	-14	<u>33</u>	<u>24</u>
35 Group Psychotherapy	08	<u>26</u>	<u>20</u>
36 Research Competence	<u>61</u>	<u>51</u>	<u>52</u>
38 Supervisory Competence	-13	<u>46</u>	<u>33</u>
40 Professional Interpersonal Relations	00	<u>33</u>	<u>26</u>
41 Integrity	04	<u>37</u>	<u>30</u>
42 Overall Suitability vs Clinical Competence	17	<u>46</u>	<u>38</u>
42 Overall Suitability vs Preference for Hiring	15	<u>45</u>	<u>37</u>
0 Liking (N = 20, 69, and 89)	57	<u>30</u>	<u>30</u>
Median for Variables Nos. 32-42	06	41	32
No. of Values Significant	2	11	10

Correlations significant at or beyond the 5% level of confidence are underlined.

From these data, we conclude that the intervening personal therapy of some trainees was one of the factors limiting the validities of assessment predictions of clinical performance. Note that the median validity of the assessment ratings for those trainees without intervening therapy is .41 and the correlations are significant for all criterion variables.

Assessment Predictions of Criterion Competences
Based on Limited Materials

We have found that the ratings made by the staff team at the end of an elaborate assessment program predict, with considerable but varying accuracy, ratings and other criterion measures obtained three years later. Was such an expensive assessment program necessary in order to achieve predictions at this level of accuracy? It will be recalled that the correlations between ratings made by staff members who had not yet seen the candidate and Final Pooled Ratings were sufficiently high to lead us to try an assessment program in 1948 in which the assessors did not see the trainees. We may therefore expect that predictive ratings made at early stages in the assessment program will have validities comparable to those of the Final Pooled rating. In general, this expectation is borne out.

Preliminary analyses of our data based on criterion ratings obtained at the end of two years of training had suggested the possibility that beyond a certain point, the addition of new materials might result in a slight decrement in the validities of predictive ratings (cf. Kelly and Fiske, 1950). The more definitive analyses here reported show no indication of an actual decrement in validity with increasing amounts of information, but rather suggest that the relationship is markedly non-linear, at least for the sequence of materials employed in the 1947 assessment program.

It has already been noted that the assessment prediction for a particular variable frequently predicts some other criterion variables better than the designated one. However, since we are interested at the moment only in determining the relative usefulness of predictions made at various assessment stages, we shall limit our discussion to correlations between predictions on a particular variable and criterion ratings on the same variable. Tables D IV-3a and b present a summary of the relevant correlations. These are admittedly complex tables but are well worth the readers' careful study. The general organization of the tables is as follows: on the extreme left are listed the 12 criterion variables. In the next column under "Predictor" is shown the Scale C assessment rating used as a predictor for each criterion measure. The successive columns indicate the resulting validities for ratings made by various staff members on the basis of varying kinds and amounts of data about, and contact with, the trainees. (The reader may find it useful to review the general design of the Ann Arbor assessment in Chapter B I.)

Sequence I in Table D IV-3a refers to the sequential ratings made by the Initial Interviewer (A), the Intensive Interviewer (B), and the team of three (including the Projective Integrator or the Pre-Conference Rater). Sequence II in Table D IV-3b refers to the sequential ratings made by the Rorschacher-Projective Integrator for half of the cases and by the Pre-Conference Rater for the other half of the cases. The non-sequential ratings are those based on single techniques or procedures or ratings by the trainees.

Because the N's for different rows and columns of these tables vary somewhat, we have followed the previous practice of underlining the significant correlations. With the realization that the individual coefficients reported are all subject to sampling errors, wherever possible, we have based sequential values on the same cases. This seemed necessary since, for example, the previously reported correlation of .46 between Final Pooled Prediction of Academic Performance (A32) and rated Academic Performance (C32) based on an N of 92 drops to .33 for the common N of 76 used in the first three rows of the tables now under discussion.

Because of the instability of the individual coefficients here reported, we shall give most weight to the data presented in the bottom two rows of each table, i.e., the median validities and the number of significant validities for each column. In the subsequent chapter devoted to the prediction of specific criterion variables, we shall have occasion to refer to the trends in the rows of Tables D IV-3a and b.

The Validities of Assessment Ratings as a Function of the Role of the Assessor and the Material Available to Him

Sequence I

Ratings Based on Credential File

Independent assessment ratings based solely on a review of the credential file were made by the Initial and Intensive Interviewers. The validities of these ratings range from -.06 to .41 for different criterion measures, with median values of .24 and .22. Approximately half of these validities are statistically significant.

Ratings after Objective Tests

The Intensive Interviewer next examined the candidate's profiles of objective test scores. Although many staff members expressed little confidence in the value of these data for the group being assessed, it will be noted that the median validity of the Intensive Interviewers' ratings increases from .22 to .29, this being the largest increment in the entire sequence. The number of significant values increases from 6 to 7. The range of validities is now from .04 to .51.

TABLE D IV-3a

VALIDITIES OF ASSESSMENT RATINGS BASED ON SEQUENTIAL
APPRAISALS OF CUMULATIVE DATA

(1947 Assessment)

Sequence I

Variable / Criterion	Predictor	Cred. File A	Cred. File B	Obj. Tests A	Obj. Tests B	Auto-biog. A	Auto-biog. B	Proj. Tests A	Proj. Tests B	Inter-view A*	Inter-view B	Prel. Pool. Team	Situa. Tests A	Situa. Tests B	Final Ind. A	Final Ind. B	Mdn. Final Ind. Team	Final Pool. Team	N
C32 Academic Performance	A32	13	26		36		36		38	13	32	32	30	31	30	32	34	33	76
At Clinical Total	A32	40	41		51		40		40	25	39	40	33	41	36	40	32	39	76
Bt General Total	A32	36	29		42		33		40	35	35	45	47	43	46	43	41	43	76
C33 Diagnostic Competence	A33	-06	20		17		12		05	09	02	03	02	-03	03	-04	-02	-01	53
Σ Diagnostic Prediction	A33	28	22		30		24		26	26	22	22	32	33	32	33	36	35	53
C34 Individual Psychotherapy	A34	11	03		10		20		13	25	10	21	18	20	19	23	24	26	93
C36 Research Competence	A36	38	31		44		45		41	46	47	51	56	48	55	46	53	55	76
C38 Supervisory Competence	A38	26	17		19		07		13	27	12	27	29	20	40	25	36	33	93
C40 Prof. Inter. Relations	A40	-02	23		14		24		13	14	14	17	19	34	25	29	33	26	93
C41 Integrity	A41	13	18		04		18		14	27	34	28	28	30	28	25	28	29	93
Ccc Clinical Competence	A42	33	31		37		40		40	31	37	42	35	39	39	41	35	37	93
Cph Preference for Hiring	A42	22	17		28		33		34	23	31	37	33	34	39	37	31	36	93
Median Validity		24	22		29		28		30	25	31	30	31	33	34	32	33	34	
No. of Significant Values		7	6		7		8		6	8	7	9	9	11	10	11	11	11	

A = Initial Interviewer

B = Intensive Interviewer

* = Initial Interview Rating was based on credentials and interview only.

Team = Initial Interviewer, Intensive Interviewer, and Projective Integrator or Pre-Conference Rater.

Correlations significant at or beyond the 5% level of confidence are underlined.

TABLE D IV-3b

VALIDITIES OF ASSESSMENT RATINGS BASED ON SEQUENTIAL APPRAISALS OF CUMULATIVE DATA
AND VALIDITIES OF RATINGS BASED ON SPECIFIC PROCEDURES

(1947 Assessment)

Variable Criterion	Predictor	Sequence II					Predictions Based on Specific Procedures							
		Ror-schach	Proj.[1] Integ.	Pre-[2] Conf.	Situa. Tests	Final Ind.	TAT	Sent. Com.	Bender-Gestalt	Self	Team-mate Mdn.	Uncon. Mdn.	Situa. Pooled	N
C32 Academic Performance	A32	07	05	**36**	31	**32**	08	15	15	**25**	13	**23**	19	76
At Clinical Total	A32	03	-22	**43**	**35**	**31**	10	**32**	21	**26**	**30**	12	17	76
Bt General Total	A32	03	00	**45**	**36**	**34**	08	**29**	20	**24**	**31**	**25**	**26**	76
C33 Diagnostic Competence	A33	15	07	08	06	00	24	18	**33**	05	23	04	02	53
Σ Diagnostic Prediction	A33	04	-18	30	**37**	**36**	20	19	-07	05	09	**41**	**37**	53
C34 Individual Psychotherapy	A34	-12	-05	05	09	09	16	**26**	02	-02	**28**	09	19	93
C36 Research Competence	A36	-02	20	**37**	**48**	**49**	07	**29**	**41**	**38**	**29**	**40**	**40**	76
C38 Supervisory Competence	A38	03	23	27	**36**	**35**	18	12	11	-07	**25**	19	16	93
C40 Prof. Inter. Relations	A40	10	17	26	**29**	**26**	10	**22**	08	-04	08	08	17	93
C41 Integrity	A41	18	**36**	00	18	23	-01	17	-03	-03	16	18	**22**	93
Ccc Clinical Competence	A42	04	08	16	**29**	**25**	15	18	**32**	00	**25**	**22**	**24**	93
Cph Preference for Hiring	A42	08	16	24	**32**	**29**	12	**20**	**20**	-15	**26**	19	**26**	93
Median Validity		04	07	26	31	30	11	19	17	03	25	19	20	
No. of Significant Values		0	1	4	9	10	0	6	4	4	7	5	6	

[1]Half of cases evaluated by Projective Integrator--ratings based on all projective tests.
[2]Half of cases evaluated by Pre-Conference Rater--ratings based on credentials, projective tests, objective tests, autobiography, and interview.

Correlations significant at or beyond the 5% level of confidence are underlined.

Ratings after Autobiography

The study of the candidates' Biographical Inventories and autobiographies appears to have made no contribution to the validity of the Intensive Interviewers' ratings. In fact, the median validity drops from .29 to .28; 8 of the 12 validities are, however, large enough to be significant. They range from .07 to .45.

Ratings after Projective Tests

The Intensive Interviewer next examined the protocols and interpretations of the four projective tests for the candidates. His ratings at this point show a median validity of .30, but only 6 of the 12 are now statistically significant. The range of validities at this point is .05 to .40.

Ratings after Interviews

It will be remembered that two types of interviews were used in the assessment program: a one hour interview by the Initial Interviewer immediately following his examination of the credential file and a two hour interview by the Intensive Interviewer after he was already reasonably "well acquainted" with the candidate on the basis of other assessment materials. Neither of these interviews appears to have made an essential contribution to the assessment process. In each instance the median validity increases by only .01 over the previous value and there is an increase of only one significant value in each column. The range of validities is still large: .09 to .46 for the Initial Interviewer and .02 to .47 for the Intensive Interviewer. Note, however, that the range for this and succeeding columns in Sequence I is considerably extended by the very low validities for Diagnostic Competence (C33).

Ratings at Preliminary Pooling Conference

At this point in the program the Initial Interview, the Intensive Interviewer and the third member of the staff team (Projective Integrator or Pre-Conference Rater) met for their first staff conference on each case. In this session, they arrived at what we called the Preliminary Pooled Ratings. These turn out to have a median validity of .30, and a range of .03 to .51 but nine of the 12 values are now sufficiently high to be significant at the 5% level of confidence.

Ratings after Situation Tests

All three members of the staff team spent the next day observing their four candidates in a series of situation tests after which each member of the team again rated the candidates. The median validities of the three staff members at this point are: Initial Interviewer, .31; Intensive Interviewer, .33; third member, .31 (from Sequence II in Table D IV-3b). A larger proportion of these values are significant but the range of values is still quite large -.03 to .56. For the Initial Interviewer and the third team member the post-situation medians validities represent sizable increments over those for the previous individual ratings. How much of this increment resulted from the pooling conference and how much of it was contributed by the situation tests cannot be determined from our data.

Final Individual Ratings

Before the final pooling conference all three members of the staff team were given an opportunity to study all materials thus far accumulated on each case. Materials already seen were the credential file, the objective test profile, the biographical materials, the projective tests and interpretations, and notes on the two interviewers, the preliminary pooling conference and situation tests. New data made available to staff members at this point included the following: all ratings previously made on the candidate by staff members, by the Uncontaminated staff team, by teammates, self-ratings by trainees; a tabulation of the sociometric choices of the class; and character sketches about each candidate written by his three teammates. On the basis of all of these materials each staff member made his Final Individual Ratings for each candidate. These have median validities of .34, .32 and .30 for the three staff members. The range of validities is still great--from -.04 to .55. With the exception of predictions of future Diagnostic and Therapeutic Competence, the validities are all statistically significant.

Median Final Individual Ratings and Final Pooled Ratings

We may now ask whether or not the final pooling conference was worthwhile. The only new information introduced in this conference was the Intensive Interviewers' report on his Final Interview with each of his two candidates. Considerable time was spent in attempting a final integration of all data on the case and arguing out points of difference still remaining among the team members. As can be seen, however, this conference made practically no additional contribution to the validities. The median validity of the Final Pooled ratings is .34,   just .01 higher than that for the Median Final Individual Ratings (cf. concluding section of this chapter).

Predictions Based on Specific Procedures

Projective Techniques

It will be remembered that four different projective techniques were used in the 1947 assessment program, the Rorschach, the Bender-Gestalt, 10 TAT cards, and a Sentence Completion Test. The first two were administered individually. These were scored and interpreted by the person who administered them. The last two, the TAT and Sentence Completion, were administered as group tests and interpreted "blind." In each case, the staff member who analyzed the protocol made ratings on the basis of the materials provided by the single technique.

The median validities of these ratings for each of the four techniques are generally low: Rorschach, .04; Bender-Gestalt, .17; TAT, .11; and Sentence Completion, .19. Note that personal contact with the candidate in administering the Rorschach and Bender-Gestalt tests does not seem to have contributed to the validities of the ratings based on them. Neither the Rorschach nor the TAT yielded a significant validity coefficient with any criterion measure, but 6 of the 12 based on the Sentence Completion and 4 of the 12 based on the Bender-Gestalt are significant.

As will be noted later, ratings based on the Bender-Gestalt yielded the most valid prediction of rated Diagnostic Competence, and similarly ratings based on the Sentence Completion are among the best predictions of Therapeutic Competence as rated three years later.

Another estimate of the validities of predictions based on individual projective techniques was provided by the 1949 reassessment program. Four clinicians (advanced VA trainees) each made separate predictions based on each of the four projective techniques for 20 of the 1947 cases. These judgments were, of course, made without seeing the subject and all protocols were coded so that staff members did not know which Rorschach went with which TAT, etc. Criterion measures are available for only 15 of these 20 cases. Table D IV-4 summarizes the validities of these predictions and presents comparable data for the 1947 assessment predictions. As will be seen, there is practically no consistency between the two sets of values. For these 15 cases, none of the ratings based on projective techniques is promising and the relative magnitude of the validities for the different techniques has shifted. These differences may reflect the effect of personal contact with the candidate, differences in the relative skills of the two groups of staff members with the four techniques, or they may be merely a function of sampling errors.

172

TABLE D IV-4

COMPARISON OF THE VALIDITIES OF PREDICTIONS BASED ON
FOUR PROJECTIVE TESTS

	A42 (Overall Suitability) vs Ccc (Clinical Competence)			
	Rorschach	TAT	Sent. Comp.	Bender
Predictions by 1949 Reassessors on 15 Cases* (N = 4 x 15)	.19	.16	.03	.00
Predictions by 1947 Staff (N = 93 Cases)	.04	.15	.18	.32
	A33 vs C33 (Diagnostic Competence)			
Predictions by 1949 Reassessors on 15 Cases (N = 4 x 15)	.18	.18	.07	-.13
Predictions by 1947 Staff (N = 53 Cases)	.15	.24	.18	.33

*As far as can be determined, these 15 cases were a random sample from the 100 non-Michigan 1947 assessment cases reassessed in 1949.

Self-Ratings

By a small margin, the Self-Ratings of trainees at the time of assessment turn out to have the lowest median validity (.03) of any set of ratings available. It is of interest, however, that four of the 12 values are significant and that all four of them concern the self-evaluation of intellectual promise.

Teammate Ratings

Teammate ratings, on the other hand, are found to have a median validity of .25 and are significant for seven of the 12 criteria. This median validity is the highest of all those based on single techniques or procedures, and is of all the more interest in view of the limited contacts on which the ratings were based and the conflict producing nature of the task of rating teammates. Perhaps the candidates were as talented in the processes of assessment as were the staff members!

Ratings Based Solely on Situation Tests

Each trainee was observed throughout the series of situation tests by a team of staff members who had no previous information about him. Thus we are able to estimate the validities of predictions based solely on observation of a day's overt behavior and inferences based on these observations. The median of these predictions made by three staff members for each candidate shows a validity of .19 and that of the ratings agreed upon in a pooling conference of this "Uncontaminated Team" is .20. About half of the validities in each of these columns are significant.

The Validities of Assessment Ratings Made Without Personal
Interaction

For the reasons presented in Chapter A II, it was decided that the Wellesley assessment of trainees entering universities in the fall of 1948 should be carried out in a modified program involving no personal contact between staff and trainees. As has already been noted, this 1948 group of trainees differs from the 1947 group in several ways: the candidates were younger, they were a more selected group in terms of measured intelligence and, of course, at the time the criterion measures were collected, had completed one year less of training than the 1947 groups. As a result, it did not seem wise to depend on a comparison of the resulting validities of the two groups as an estimate of the relative efficiency of the very different assessment programs.

In the summer of 1949, a staff composed of VA trainees in clinical psychology at the University of Michigan reassessed a large portion of the cases previously assessed in the 1947 assessment program. For obvious reasons, the University of Michigan trainees were not reassessed. This staff made ratings and predictions on the basis of the credentials, objective tests, autobiographical materials, and projective tests; these were the same materials available to the Intensive Interviewer before his interview and to the Pre-Conference Rater in the 1947 program.

In Table D IV-5 are summarized the validities which may be appropriately compared for predictions growing out of the three assessment programs, 1947, 1948, and 1949. For the 1948 and 1949 programs the validities are presented for only the final pooled ratings. For the 1947 program this table also includes validities for the ratings made by individual staff members on the basis of the same kinds and amounts of materials as were available to the 1948 and 1949 staffs. In general, this table is organized much as the preceding table, with this important difference-- the validities to be compared are not based on the same cases. There is no overlap between the 1947-49 cases and the 1948 cases. And while the entire 1949 group is included in the 1947 group it comprises only about 75% of this latter group. This means that in comparing any two validity coefficients appearing in this table we must remember that each coefficient is subject to a sampling error. Again, therefore, it appears safest to give our major attention to the median validities, and the numbers of significant correlations shown in the two bottom rows of the table.

Validities for 1948 Wellesley Ratings

As was anticipated, the validities of the predictive ratings for the 1948 group are considerably lower than those for the 1947 group. The median validity is only .15 as compared with a median of .34 for the 1947 group. Five of the 13 values are significant and four of these concern intellectual achievement. We cannot account for these generally low validities in terms of the amount of material available to the assessment staff. The 1948 assessment staff had essentially the same materials as those available to the Pre-Conference Rater and the Intensive Interviewer for his Post-Projective ratings in 1947. It is true that the 1948 staff had only two projective tests instead of four, and some objective test scores were omitted. However, it seems unlikely that these omissions had more than slight effect upon the validity coefficients.

The reader will recall that the materials used by the 1948 assessment staff were collected under selection conditions; at the time the 1948 group was tested, the candidates did not know if they had been accepted by their university for training in clinical psychology and hence they presumably believed that the universities would use these materials for selection. Support for the argument for the importance of this component is provided by the differences among the validity coefficients; the one criterion variable on which the 1948 predictions are as good as any others is Academic Performance, the prediction for which is based primarily upon transcripts and grades, and on intelligence test scores, data which can hardly be affected by the trainee's desire to appear to the best possible advantage. All the other predictor ratings were based in part on materials which might well be affected by the trainees' attempts to present the most favorable possible pictures of themselves. For example, the mean on the GAMIN Facade key for the 1948 group is much higher than that for the 1947 group (CR = 2.97).

TABLE D IV-5

COMPARISON OF CORRELATIONS BETWEEN CRITERION MEASURES AND
CORRESPONDING ASSESSMENT RATINGS (1947, 1948 and 1949)

Criterion Measure	Predictor	1948 Final Pooled	1949 Final Pooled	1947 Final Pooled	1947 Int. Interviewer Post-Projective	1947 Pre-Conf.
Ratings						
32 Academic Performance	A32	<u>42</u>	<u>45</u>	<u>33</u>	<u>38</u>	<u>36</u>
33 Diagnostic Competence	A33	15	15	-01	05	08
34 Individual Psychotherapy	A34	15	14	<u>26</u>	13	05
36 Research Competence	A36	<u>27</u>	<u>48</u>	<u>55</u>	<u>41</u>	<u>37</u>
38 Supervisory Competence	A38	14	17	<u>33</u>	13	27
40 Prof. Interpersonal Relations	A40	14	<u>28</u>	<u>26</u>	13	26
41 Integrity	A41	<u>26</u>	04	<u>29</u>	14	00
A42 vs. Ccc Clinical Competence	A42	12	<u>29</u>	<u>37</u>	<u>40</u>	16
A42 vs. Cph Preference for Hiring	A42	09	19	<u>36</u>	<u>34</u>	24
N		(81)	(72)	(53-93)	(53-93)	(28-42)
Content Examination						
A_t Clinical Total	A32	<u>40</u>	<u>48</u>	<u>39</u>	<u>40</u>	<u>43</u>
B_t General Total	A32	<u>37</u>	<u>43</u>	<u>43</u>	<u>40</u>	<u>45</u>
N		(73)	(59)	(76)	(76)	(38)
Diagnostic Predictions						
Σ Sum for 2 Cases	A33	-01	26	<u>35</u>	26	30
N		(58)	(42)	(53)	(53)	(28)
Mdn. Validity		15	27	34	30	26
No. of Significant Values		5	6	11	6	4

Correlations significant at or beyond the 5% level of confidence are underlined.

There is some evidence to suggest that the lower validities are not merely a function of performance at the end of two years of training being less predictable than performance after three years of trainees. Criterion ratings were collected for the 1947 group in the spring of 1949. Correlations between these 1949 criterion ratings and various ratings of the 1947 assessment program have been previously reported (Kelly and Fiske, 1950). For the 1947 group criterion measures at the end of two years of training were reasonably well predicted, but in these analyses, trainees separated from the program were assigned low criterion ratings, which may have tended to elevate the validities reported.

Neither can the relatively low validities for the 1948 group be explained by its greater homogeneity with respect to various clinical skills since the means and standard deviations on the composite criterion ratings are quite similar for the 1947 and 1948 groups. While the 1947 group tends to have slightly higher mean ratings and tends to be slightly more variable, the differences are not of sufficient magnitude to account for the low validities for the 1948 group.

A few members of the 1948 staff had had little clinical experience and little or no previous experience in assessment. However, in view of the lack of any evidence that clinical experience or training increases the validity of assessment ratings, we do not believe that the lower validities for the 1948 group were a function of the composition of the assessment staff.

The 1948 assessment staff made ratings after successively increasing amounts of materials were made available to them. A detailed analysis of the correlations between the predicted Overall Suitability ratings at each of the several stages and composite ratings on Clinical Competence and Preference for Hiring indicates that the ratings made on the basis of smaller amounts of material were, like the Final Pooled ratings, of very low validity.

We pointed out in the previous chapter that objective test scores did not predict the subsequent performance of the 1948 group as well as that of the 1947 group. Since we find reduction in validities for both objective tests and assessment ratings, we conclude that the primary causes for the reduction were, (1) the fact that the 1948 group were more highly selected and, (2) the fact that the test materials were collected under selection conditions.

1949 Reassessment Ratings

We shall now return to Table D IV-5 (page 174) to ask how the validities of the 1949 reassessment ratings compared with those based on 1947 ratings for largely overlapping groups of subjects. We note that the median validity of the 1949 ratings is .27. This value is definitely lower than the median of .34 for the 1947 Final Pooled ratings but of the same magnitude as the medians for the 1947 ratings made by staff members using the same materials as a basis for ratings. This increase from .27 to .34 represents our best estimate of the contribution to the validity of assessment ratings made by all of the techniques involving personal interaction between an assessment staff and a candidate being assessed. This included interviews, situation tests, sociometric choices and staff conferences, etc.

It would appear that the 1949 staff comprised of trainees utilized the materials as effectively as the more mature 1947 staff. Perhaps the fact that they were themselves in training gave the 1949 staff members a somewhat better frame of reference for interpreting the criterion variables and this offset any possible difference in amount of training and/or experience. Note that the highest validities for the 1949 ratings are those predicting intellectual achievement.

A detailed stage by stage analysis of the validities of the 1949 ratings against 1949 criterion ratings showed a pattern of validities very similar to that previously discussed for Sequence I of the 1947 ratings.

The Prediction of Criterion Ratings from Descriptive and Evaluative Ratings

One of the chief reasons why the assessment staffs were asked to make ratings on the various descriptive variables in Scales A and B of the rating scale was that we wished to provide for the possibility that the predictive ratings would turn out to have little or no validity. There was the possibility that the assessment staff could describe or evaluate the personality of each trainee with reasonable accuracy but yet would not be able to make correct inferences from this personality picture to the trainees' future performance in clinical psychology. Let us now examine the relationships between Scale A and B variables and the later Criterion Ratings shown in Table D IV-6. As will be seen, there are no high correlations between personality variables as rated at the time of assessment and ratings on the selected criterion variables three years later. Only 8 of the 124 coefficients are significant at the 5% level and nine of these involve the criterion, Academic Performance. None of the rated personality variables yield a significant correlation

TABLE D IV-6

FINAL POOLED SCALE A AND B RATINGS vs SELECTED
1950 CRITERION RATINGS
(1947 Group, N = 93)

			C32 Academic Perform.	C34 Individual Psychotherapy	C41 Integrity	Ccc Clinical Competence
A	1	Obstructive--Cooperative	-01	-07	18	08
A	2	Inconsistent--Consistent	-01	-04	09	05
A	3	Submissive--Assertive	23	-07	-07	17
A	4	Depressed--Cheerful	03	-17	03	01
A	5	Irresponsible--Serious	01	00	16	02
A	6	Non-Gregarious--Gregarious	09	17	-02	14
A	7	Easily Upset--Unshakable	-05	05	-05	-03
A	8	Narrow--Broad, Interests	31	04	09	25
A	9	Suspicious--Trustful	-03	-02	10	-01
A	10	Self-Centered, Selfish--Generous	-10	03	17	05
A	11	Silent--Talkative	22	-07	-02	14
A	12	Cautious--Adventurous	07	04	09	12
A	13	Socially Clumsy--Socially Poised	05	07	14	18
A	14	Rigid--Adaptable, Flexible	17	08	26	20
A	15	Dependent--Self-Sufficient	10	-09	04	-01
A	16	Worrying, Anxious--Placid	-12	05	01	00
A	17	Not Conscientious--Conscientious	-04	03	16	04
A	18	Unimaginative--Imaginative	34	09	14	26
A	19	Overt Interest in Opposite Sex, Slight--Marked	-07	01	-18	00
A	20	Secretive--Frank	17	-04	09	12
A	21	Dependent--Independent, Minded	19	05	05	16
A	22	Overt Emotional Expression, Limited--Marked	26	-05	-09	16
B	23b	Social Adjustment	-04	07	17	14
B	24	Appropriateness of Emotional Expression	03	-06	15	13
B	25	Characteristic Intensity of Inner Emotional Tension (High-Low)	-12	-09	12	-09
B	26	Sexual Adjustment	-04	-05	14	14
B	27	Motivation for Professional Status	03	-11	-09	01
B	28	Motiv. for Scientific Understanding of People	32	17	32	33
B	29	Insight into Others	22	10	09	19
B	30	Insight into Himself	21	06	13	22
B	31	Quality of Intellectual Accomplishments	38	-05	21	33

Correlations significant at the 5% level or beyond are underlined.

with the Composite Criterion ratings of Therapy. The personality variables which correlate significantly with two or more of the four criteria are, Broad Interests, Adaptable, Imaginative, Motivation for Scientific Understanding of People, Insight into Others, and Quality of Intellectual Accomplishments. In some instances assessment ratings of these variables show higher correlations with the criterion ratings than with ratings on the same variables by colleagues after three years.

Consistency of Ratings Versus
Accuracy of Prediction

Let us now compare the agreement between personality ratings on Scales A and B made three years apart with the agreement between predictions on Scale C and rated performance on Scale C, again made three years apart. (These data are reported in Tables D I-1a and 1b, and D IV-1.) The 1947 Final Pooled predictions on Scale C variables have a median correlation with Composite Criterion ratings of .32; this may be compared with the median of .25 for 1947 Final Pooled ratings on Scale A versus 1950 colleague ratings, and also with the median of .17 for the same comparison on Scale B variables. In contrast the 1949 Final Pooled ratings showed higher median correlation over time for Scale A variables (.25) than median validity for Scale C variables (.18). In spite of the fact that Scale A variables are "phenotypic" they were in general more validly rated without face-to-face contacts by the 1949 staff than were criterion variables.

Why are the predictions on Scale C, made by people in 1947 who saw the trainees, higher than the consistencies on Scale A? The explanation may lie in the "criterion" measure: for Scale A, we are using here ratings made only by colleagues, whereas for Scale C we are using a composite of ratings from three different sources, There is reason to believe that the composite ratings have higher reliability than do the ratings from colleagues alone. This factor might account for the slightly higher median correlations for Scale C than for Scale A variables.

These data suggest that the relatively low predictive coefficients for Scale C variables cannot be attributed to the failure of the assessment staff members to translate their impressions of the trainees' personalities into correct predictions of future performance. Since they were able to "predict" Scale C variables as well as or better than Scale A variables, we must conclude that they were able to make reasonably efficient inferences from their observations of the trainees in assessment. The low level of the median correlation between all 1947 ratings (both descriptive and predictive) and corresponding 1950 ratings must be explained by more general factors, such as inherent difficulties in the process of assessment, inadequate criterion measures, and actual changes in the "true" personalities of the trainees as a result of various influences impinging upon them during the three year time interval (cf. Chapter D I).

Clinical Pooling of Ratings as Compared with Arithmetical
Pooling and with Individual Ratings

A considerable part of the 1947 assessment staff's time was spent in staff conferences. There was a Preliminary Pooling Conference after the interview, a Final Pooling Conference at the end of the week, and a pooling conference for the Uncontaminated Situationists. At each of these conferences, the participating staff members reviewed the ratings which each of them had assigned the candidate on each variable and, where differences of opinion existed, reviewed the relevant evidence. They remained in conference until arriving at a pooled rating on each variable. Only in the Preliminary Pooling Conferences was new information provided to the staff members. Here the interviewers each reported on their interviews. The primary goal of the other conferences was the pooling of ratings.

Of what value was this pooling process? Did the pooled ratings, in which individual biases of single staff members were presumably eliminated, have higher predictive validity than the individual ratings? Did the medians of the individual ratings have as high validity as the pooled ratings?

We have already noted (page 171) that the Final Pooling Conference contributed very little to the validity of assessment ratings. Referring again to Table D IV-3a (last two columns) it will be seen that the median validity increased from .33 to .34. For only two of the 12 criteria do the Final Pooled ratings correlate as much as .05 higher than the median of the Final Individual ratings. For one criterion measure, Professional Interpersonal Relations, the pooling resulted in the validity dropping from .33 to .26.

Let us next examine the effects of the pooling conference held by the Uncontaminated team after observing the situation tests and making Individual Uncontaminated Situation ratings. The relevant data are found in the last two columns of Table D IV-3b. Again the median validity was increased by only .01 from .19 to .20 and none of the specific gains is impressive.

Corresponding analysis of the data for the 1948 and 1949 assessment programs yielded similar results--i.e., little or no superiority of pooled ratings over the arithmetic median of individual ratings.

While definitive data are not available, there is considerable evidence to suggest that the ratings by a single rater have predictive validities not greatly below those for ratings pooled either clinically or arithmetically. For example, the predictions based solely on the Credentials plus Objective tests are about as valid as the Preliminary Pooled ratings (cf. Table D IV-3a). Until some of the major sources of error in predictions are eliminated, the replications of assessors and the use of staff conferences hardly seems justified for this type of prediction.

In general then, we find that the validity of assessment ratings based on a staff conference are not consistently higher than those for a single participant in the conference. As a means of increasing the validity of ratings the time spent in pooling ratings was probably wasted. However, we must not overlook the fact that those conferences helped the assessment staff to develop a common frame of reference for interpreting the rating scale and the definitions of the variables. Also because of the intrinsic interest of staff conferences, they contributed greatly to the staff morale.

CHAPTER D V

THE PREDICTION OF SPECIFIC CRITERION SKILLS

The preceding chapters have discussed the relationships between various types of predictive measures and the several criterion measures. The present chapter has two purposes: (a) it summarizes the findings concerning the best predictors of each of the several types of job functions of clinical psychologists; (b) it also examines the correlates of each job function to see what light they throw upon the nature of the job function. This discussion is based on the correlations for the 1947 group reported in the tables of Chapters D II, D III, and D IV.

Academic Performance and Research Competence are predicted better than any other criterion variables. The highest validities for rated Academic Performance are for the Miller Analogies Test and for assessment predictions made on the basis of Credentials plus Objective Tests. For rated Research Competence the highest validities are for Final Pooled ratings. The Miller Analogies Test, several other objective test scores, and predictions from early assessment stages also have considerable validity as predictors of Research Competence.

While rated Diagnostic Competence was not well predicted by any measure, somewhat higher validities against scores on the Diagnostic Prediction test were found for a number of assessment ratings and objective test scores. Criterion ratings of Therapeutic Competence were predicted somewhat better than those for Diagnostic Competence. Criterion ratings of Integrity were not well predicted by either assessment ratings or test scores. Rated Overall Clinical Competence and other more global ratings are about equally well predicted by assessment ratings and single scores on objective tests.

Four selected Composite Criterion Ratings were correlated with descriptive ratings by contemporary colleagues. Overall Clinical Competence was associated with the favorable pole of most variables in Scales A and B. Rated Academic Performance was related to ratings reflecting intellectual capacity and interest as well as general drive. Therapeutic Competence was associated with traits indicating easy social relations. Integrity was related to seriousness of purpose.

Attempts to predict the dichotomous criterion of success vs. failure in the training program highlighted the heterogeneity of the failure group; the diverse reasons for leaving the program seem to have reflected highly dissimilar patterns of abilities.

Since many of the criteria, especially those based on ratings, are highly intercorrelated, we shall discuss them in groups suggested by the factor analysis reported in Chapter C II. The reader will have noticed that all prediction measures were not correlated with all criterion measures. For the most part, we confined ourselves to computing the correlations between variables where there was some reason to expect a relationship. One major exception was that each of the objective test scores was correlated with each criterion variable.

The Prediction of Academic Achievement

Three of the criterion measures used in the project may be regarded as relatively "pure" measures of academic achievement: Academic Performance as rated by University supervisors and

scores on the two parts of the Content Examination. Analysis of the relevant tables shows that
these criteria are reasonably well predicted by a variety of predictors as follows:

Rated Academic Performance (C32)   r

    Best Assessment Predictor   Final Pooled[1] A36 (Research)   .51

    Other Promising Assessment Predictors[2]   Credentials plus Objective Tests A32   .36
                                            Self Ratings A32   .25

    Best Test Predictors   Miller Analogies   .47
                                          Strong (Psychologist)   .33

Content Examination (General)

    Best Assessment Predictor   Final Pooled A36 (Research)   .54

    Other Promising Assessment Predictors   Credentials plus Objective Tests A32   .42
                                          Credentials Only A32   .36,.29

    Best Test Predictors   Miller Analogies   .58
                                          Strong (Kriedt: Psychologist)   .46

Content Examination (Clinical)

    Best Assessment Predictor   Credentials plus Objective Tests A32   .51

    Other Promising Assessment Predictors   Credentials A32   .40
                                          Sentence Completion A32   .32

    Best Test Predictors   Miller Analogies   .58
                                          Strong (Author-Journalist)   .44

Although not high, the above values are roughly of the same magnitude as ordinarily reported
for the prediction of academic performance of much less homogeneous groups. They are based,
it will be remembered, on variations in academic achievement among advanced doctoral students
in one specialized field.

From this summary, as well as a more detailed analysis of the other predictor-correlates of
these criterion measures, it would appear that the measured differences in academic performance
of the trainees are a function of (a) intellectual ability and, (b) motivation toward the use of that
ability in achieving academic success. Within the relatively narrow range of ability found in our
experimental group, motivation as measured by interest patterns appears to account for as much
variance in academic achievement as does intellectual ability. This may result in part from the
fact that the training program in clinical psychology involves a variety of non-academic activities
which may be more appealing to and more highly valued by trainees who do not share the interest
patterns of academic psychologists.

---

[1]In this and similar summaries to follow, all validities for "Final Pooled" are taken from
Table D IV-1 where the N for all ratings discussed here is 92. The N's for other stages are indicated in Table D IV-3 a and b.

[2]"Other Promising Assessment Predictors," here and in the following summaries includes ratings selected not only on the basis of the size of the validity coefficients, but also with respect to
the "cost" of the procedures on which the rating was based.

Reference to Table D IV-6 shows that rated Academic Performance is significantly related to a number of assessment ratings on Scale A and B variables: Assertive, Broad Interests, Talkative, Imaginative, Marked Overt Emotional Expression, Motivation for Scientific Understanding of People, Insight into Self and Others, and Quality of Intellectual Accomplishments.

The Prediction of Research Competence

Rated Research Competence (C 36)		r
Best Assessment Predictor	Final Pooled A36	.52
Other Promising Assessment Predictors	Bender-Gestalt A36	.41
	Self Rating A36	.38
Best Test Predictors	Strong (Psychologist)	.43
	Allport-Vernon (Religious)	-.39

While rated Research Competence was best predicted by Final Pooled ratings on A36, it is relatively well predicted by several other assessment ratings based on limited materials. It is also relatively well predicted by several objective test scores. Like rated Academic Performance, rated Research Competence appears to be a function of both ability and interest, with interest accounting for a major portion of the variance in these criterion ratings.

Measures of Research Activity

For two measures of research activity, Research Studies Reported and Progress on Thesis, correlations were computed with Final Pooled Assessment Ratings (Table D IV-1): We find that the number of research studies reported by the trainee is predicted equally well (but at a uniformly low level) by assessment ratings on the intellectual variables (A32 and A36), on clinical variables (A33, A34, and A35), and on Overall Suitability (A42). This criterion measure seems to reflect a general factor of efficient job performance which is not specific to research. Progress on dissertation is correlated significantly with only one of the assessment predictors, Academic Performance. This criterion measure probably reflects the interests and aptitudes of the scholar rather than those of the experimental scientist. These results illustrate the difficulty in finding appropriate objective measures of professional competence; a measure selected on the basis of a priori analysis often turns out to be too specific or too broad for use in evaluating a job-function. And as has already been pointed out, it is too early in the professional lives of the subjects studied to permit a meaningful evaluation of their research productivity.

The Prediction of Therapeutic Competence

Whereas all criterion measures of academic achievement and research competence were reasonably well predicted by a variety of predictive measures, neither the assessment ratings nor objective tests were highly correlated with rated Therapeutic Competence which, it will be recalled, is relatively uncorrelated with rated Academic Performance.

Rated Therapeutic Competence (C34)		r
Best Assessment Predictor	Teammate Median A34	.28
Other Promising Assessment Predictors	Sentence Completion A34	.26
	Credentials plus Initial Interview A34	.25
Best Test Predictor	Kuder (Scientific)	-.33
	MMPI (Gough: Intellectual Functioning)	.32

Not only was the assessment staff relatively unsuccessful in predicting therapeutic competence, but note that the best predictions were those based on relatively little material or brief contact with the candidate. Reference to Table D IV-6 shows that none of the Scale A or B assessment ratings shows a significant correlation with rated Therapeutic Competence. It would thus appear that many different kinds of individuals may earn the reputation of being good therapists. This is not surprising when one recalls the general lack of agreement as to what constitutes good therapy.

Some hint about the characteristics of the trainee rated as a good therapist may be gleaned from the objective test correlates of these ratings. Significant positive relationships are found not only for the MMPI-Gough IF scores noted above but for several other Strong scores including Strong-Kriedt Clinical Psychologist score; YMCA Physical Director and Advertising Man scores; and for the Guilford-Martin Social Extraversion score.   Significant negative relationships are found for the Strong Engineer, Chemist and Production Manager scores and for Kuder Scientific and Computation interest scores. These low but significant relationships suggest that trainees rated as good therapists have an orientation toward people rather than things and their interest in people is based on a desire to serve rather than to manipulate them.

None of several experimental measures of therapeutic competence developed within the project (cf. Chapter C IV) was any better predicted by assessment ratings than were the composite ratings (cf. Table D V-1). Since we do not have an acceptable measure of therapeutic competence, it is not surprising that we are not able to predict it!

TABLE D V-1

CORRELATION OF ASSESSMENT PREDICTIONS AND CRITERION
MEASURES OF THERAPEUTIC COMPETENCE

| | Final Pooled Assessment Predictions | | | |
| | 1947 | | 1948 | |
Criterion Measures*	Predicted Therapy (A34)	Predicted Overall (A42)	Predicted Therapy (A34)	Predicted Overall (A42)
Composite rating on Competence in Individual Psychotherapy (C34)	<u>24</u>	18	15	03
Progress Notes Score	14	15	10	02
Therapy Prediction Test (Score on Part I only)	21	26	-09	20
TAS%	-03	-10	-10	-16

*Ratings based on recordings are omitted because of the small N's.

Correlations significant at the 5% level or beyond are underlined.

The Prediction of Diagnostic Competence

Let us now examine the degree to which measures of diagnostic competence were predicted. It will be remembered that we used two uncorrelated measures of this criterion: Composite Ratings of Diagnostic Competence and Scores on the Diagnostic Prediction Test. In view of the lack of correlation between these criterion measures, we shall treat them separately and then ask whether or not, on the basis of their correlates, there appears to be something common to both measures.

Rated Diagnostic Competence (C33)		r
Best Assessment Predictor	Bender-Gestalt A33	.33
Other Promising Assessment Predictors	TAT A33	.24
	Teammate Median A33	.23
Best Test Predictors	PMA (Number)	.31
	Strong (Lawyer)	.29

As was the case for rated Therapeutic Competence, rated Diagnostic Competence was not well predicted by any measures. Only a few of the assessment ratings are significantly correlated with this criterion measure and many of the values are near zero or are slightly negative. The best Final Pooled predictive ratings are those for Therapy (A34) rather than Diagnosis (A33). Two of the best of the relatively low validities are for assessment ratings based on single projective techniques. Furthermore, so few objective test scores are significantly related to rated Diagnostic Competence that it is very difficult to identify the bases of the ratings on this criterion variable. We are confronted by the fact that both assessment ratings and criterion ratings of Diagnostic Competence have reasonably high inter-judge reliabilities, yet have but very low intercorrelations. Either the prediction of future performance as a diagnostician is extremely difficult or the assessment and criterion raters held different conceptions of diagnostic competence. One possible explanation is that there are marked local differences in the conception of diagnostic competence, from one training center to another, i. e., different judges representing a given university— installation frame of reference might agree with each other much better than judges with different frames of reference. This would result in both the reasonably high inter-judge reliability and generally low predictability of the composite ratings of diagnostic competence.

Diagnostic Prediction Test Scores		r
Best Assessment Predictor	Situation Tests (Uncontam. Median) A33	.41
Other Promising Assessment Predictors	Credentials plus Objective Tests A33	.30
	Credentials only A32	.28,.22
Best Test Predictor	MMPI (Gough: Social Status)	.39
	PMA (Word Fluency)	.37

We see immediately that scores on the Diagnostic Prediction Test are more predictable than ratings of Diagnostic Competence; this in spite of the known low reliability of these scores. Even though lacking in reliability, these scores have the advantage of being relatively objective, i. e., uninfluenced by local differences in the conception of the role of the diagnostician. Had they been based on several, rather than only two cases, it is probable that these scores would have been even more predictable.

Furthermore, it is of interest that performance in the Diagnostic Prediction Test seems to be much more closely related to the assessment staff's conception of diagnostic competence than are the criterion ratings of this skill. Final Pooled assessment ratings on Diagnosis (A33) correlate .35 with scores on the Diagnostic Prediction Test as compared with only .16 with rated Diagnostic Competence.

While 12 of the 26 assessment ratings of A33 are significantly correlated with scores on the Diagnostic Prediction Test, the best predictions of this criterion measure were made by staff members who saw the candidate only in situation tests. That this finding reflects more than just a favorable sampling error is suggested by the fact that post-situation ratings by members of the "contaminated" staff team are considerably more valid than those made before observing the situation tests.

Since scores on the Diagnostic Prediction Test show no correlation with rated Diagnostic Competence, it is not surprising to find little overlap in the correlates of these two criterion measures. Unfortunately, neither have sufficiently high correlates to permit accurate characterization of persons who may be expected to rank high on the measure. We do not know the bases of the assessment predictions of A33 except for Final Pooled ratings and these are not among the best predictors of either criterion measure. Let us then attempt a tentative characterization on the basis of the test correlates of each measure.

Rated Diagnostic Competence correlates highest with PMA Number Scores. These scores seem to be more indicative of arithmetic skill than of arithmetic reasoning. For example, such scores are correlated with counting backwards and repeating digits backwards. Rated Diagnostic Competence also shows significant positive correlations with Strong scores for Lawyer, Advertising Man, Certified Public Accountant and a significant negative correlation with Strong Production Manager Scores. This would seem to point to a person interested in a detailed, orderly, and analytic approach to problems, perhaps accompanied by an interest in the preparation of a systematic and convincing report.

High scores on the Diagnostic Prediction Test on the other hand show a relatively high correlation with scores on the PMA Word Fluency Test. This test calls for the ability to think of words rapidly as in anagrams and rhyming, i. e., going beyond the stimulus word. For example, these scores are not related to the ability to select the correct synonym from several choices. In addition, to MMPI-Gough Social Status scores, (about which little is yet known), scores on the Diagnostic Prediction Test are significantly negatively correlated only with MMPI Psychasthenia scores. Correlations significant at the 10% level include negative values for MMPI K scores (-.26) and Kuder Persuasive scores (-.25). To the writers, this suggests that the person who does well on the Diagnostic Prediction Test may be tentatively characterized as follows: an individual whose overall adjustment is sufficiently good that it does not interfere with good intellectual functioning; one who is sufficiently secure that he does not need to be defensive and does not have strong needs to influence the opinions of others. It is likely that such an individual would have appeared in a good light in the situation tests in which a good performance was probably, in part, a function of the candidate's ability to predict the behavior of his fellow students, especially in the role playing situations.

The absence of correlation between these two criterion measures of diagnostic competence and the corresponding lack of overlap between the characteristics of persons standing high on each would appear to be of more than academic interest. Further research is needed to determine whether either or both are functionally related to helping patients

Interrelation of Assessment Predictions and Criterion Measures of Diagnostic and Therapeutic Competence

To summarize and compare predictions of skill in these two primary clinical functions, we analyzed the data for all trainees for whom all of the following data were available: 1947 Final Pooled Assessment predictions on A33 and A34; 1950 Composite Criterion Ratings on C33 and C34; Diagnostic Prediction Test Scores; Predictions for Therapy Patients; and Progress Note Scores. Unfortunately, this complete set of measures was available for only 27 cases. The intercorrelations of these measures, presented in Table D V-2, differ somewhat from correlations between the same variables but based on larger N's, reported in Chapter C IV.

TABLE D V-2

INTERCORRELATIONS OF ASSESSMENT PREDICTIONS AND CRITERION
MEASURES OF DIAGNOSIS AND THERAPY
(N = 27)

| | Diagnosis | | | Therapy | | | |
| | Prediction | Criterion | | Prediction | Criterion | | |
	1947 Final Pooled A33	Composite Criterion Rating C33	Diag. Pred. Test	1947 Final Pooled A34	Composite Criterion Rating C34	Therapy Pred. Test	Progress Notes Score
Diagnosis							
1947 Final Pooled A33	--	07	32	73	-03	35	35
Composite Criterion Rating C33	07	--	-10	03	57	03	06
Diagnostic Prediction Test	32	-10	--	06	09	09	10
Therapy							
1947 Final Pooled A34	73	03	06	--	11	22	16
Composite Criterion Rating C34	-03	57	09	11	--	-14	08
Therapy Prediction Test	35	03	09	22	-14	--	-02
Progress Notes Score	35	06	10	16	08	-02	--

Certain trends noted previously are again found for this small sample. Assessment predictions of diagnostic and therapeutic competence (A33 and A34) have a high correlation with each other, and so do the two criterion ratings of these competences (C33 and C34). Both assessment predictions, however, have low correlations with the corresponding criterion measures. Neither assessment rating predicts the corresponding criterion rating any better than it predicts the other criterion rating.

For this group, the non-rated criterion measures of therapy (Therapy Prediction Test and Progress Note Scores) are predicted better than the composite criterion ratings; note, however, that assessment ratings of Diagnosis (A33) predict them better than do assessment ratings of Therapy (A34).

It is also of interest that, for each of these clinical skills, the assessment prediction correlates higher with the criterion measures of the skill than the criterion measures correlate among themselves. In other words, these assessment predictions tend to have positive (but low) validities against any criterion, even though the criterion measures are apparently independent variables! In this respect, they appear to reflect somewhat more global evaluations than the criterion ratings of these clinical skills.

The Prediction of Personal and Professional Integrity

The only criterion measure of this aspect of professional competence is the composite rating on C41.

Rated Integrity (C41)		r
Best Assessment Predictor	Final Pooled A34 (Therapy)	.38
Other Promising Assessment Predictors	Projective Integration A41	.36
	After Intensive Interview A41	.34
Best Test Predictors	Guilford-Martin (Thinking Extraversion)	.30
	MMPI (Gough: Psychologist)	.25

Rated Integrity is generally better predicted by assessment ratings than by objective test scores although the pattern of assessment validities is a strange one. Reference to Table D IV-1 will show that Final Pooled assessment ratings for six other Scale C variables correlate higher with C41 than do ratings on A41. Furthermore, several assessment ratings based on limited materials and some personal contacts seem to predict better than do the Final Pooled ratings. The validity for A41 ratings based on all four projective techniques is .36 yet ratings by the Pre-Conference rater based on these and other materials have zero validity. Probably more than for any other criterion measure, even moderately successful prediction appears to require face-to-face contact with the candidate.

The Prediction of General Clinical Competence

We shall now turn to the several variables which formed a cluster near the center of the spherical triangle illustrating the factor loadings of the criterion ratings. Two of these, Overall Clinical Competence (Ccc) and Preference for Hiring (Cph), are obviously general or global criterion ratings. From both the table of intercorrelations and the factor analysis, we are forced to conclude that the criterion variables, Supervisory Competence (C38) and Professional Interpersonal Relations (C40), were similarly interpreted by the raters. In rating these general variables each judge was permitted to weight each of the more specific skills and competences in the manner he regarded as most appropriate. Since each of these composite criterion measures was based on ratings by three groups of judges, we can say that a trainee scoring high on any one of them could have resulted only from his being generally well regarded by all three groups of raters: his university faculty members, his installation supervisors, and his peers.

Because of the high intercorrelation of these four criterion measures, we have summarized the best predictors for all of them in one table, D V-3. Each of these global criterion ratings is predicted somewhat better by Final Pooled assessment ratings than by assessment ratings based on more limited materials or contact with the candidate. Note, however, that each of the four is predicted better by an assessment rating on a different variable: Overall Clinical Competence by ratings of Academic Performance (A32), Preference for Hiring and Interpersonal Relations by ratings of Individual Therapy (A34) and Supervisory Competence by ratings of Overall Suitability (A42). This may be a function of sampling errors or it may reflect the lack of congruency in the conceptions of the all around clinical psychologist on the part of the assessment staff and the criterion raters.

In general, the Final Pooled ratings for each variable correlate only slightly higher with the criterion ratings for the same variable than do assessment ratings based on relatively limited materials. Finally each of these global variables is predicted about as well by any of two or three objective test scores as by the assessment ratings for the variable.

We have already noted (Table B II-3) that the Final Pooled ratings on Overall Suitability (A42)

TABLE D V-3

BEST PREDICTORS OF CRITERION RATINGS OF GENERAL CLINICAL COMPETENCE

Criterion	Best Assessment Predictors[1]	r	Other Promising Assessment Predictors[2]	r	Best Test Predictors	r
Overall Clinical Competence (Ccc)	Final Pooled A32 (Academic Performance)	45	Credentials plus Object-ive Tests A42	37	Miller Analogies	35
					Strong (Advertising Man)	35
	Final Pooled A42 (Overall Suitability)	38	Credentials A42: Initial Interviewer	33	Kuder (Artistic)	31
			Intensive Interviewer	31		
Preference for Hiring (Cph)	Final Pooled A34 (Individual Psychotherapy)	40	Credentials plus Object-ive Tests A42	28	Guilford-Martin (Freedom from Cycloid Tendencies)	30
	Final Pooled A42 (Overall Suitability)	37	Above, plus Autobiography	33	Strong (Production Manager)	-28
			Teammate Median A42	26	Strong (Kriedt:Industrial Psych.)	-26
					Kuder (Artistic)	26
					MMPI (Gough: Psychologist)	26
Supervisory Competence (C38)	Final Pooled A42 (Overall Suitability)	41	Teammate Median A38	25	Miller Analogies	34
	Final Pooled A38	33	Credentials A38: Initial Interviewer	26	PMA (Number)	25
			Intensive Interviewer	17	PMA (Memory)	24
Professional Interpersonal Relations (C40)	Final Pooled A34 (Individual Psychotherapy)	39	Sentence Completion A40	22	Strong (Production Manager)	-30
	Final Pooled A40	28	Credentials plus Object-ive Tests plus Auto-biography A40	24	MMPI (Gough: Intellectual Functioning)	28
					PMA (Number)	25

[1] For comparison purposes the assessment variable which, on the basis of its name, might be expected to correlate best with the criterion variable is included, although it may not be a "best predictor." All values in this column are taken from Table D IV-1.

[2] These values are taken from Table D IV-3a and b.

had but low correlation with any of the objective test scores. However, an indication of the characteristics most heavily weighted by staff members in arriving at Final Pooled ratings on A42 is shown in the extreme right column of the master table of intercorrelations in Appendix III-A. With only one exception (Motivation for Status, A27), all of the Scale A and B variables are positively correlated with A42. Correlations of more than .50 are found for Cooperativeness (1), Broad Interests (8), Generous (10), Socially Poised (13), Adaptable (14), Frank (20), Social Adjustment (23), Motivation for Scientific Understanding of People (28), Insight into Others (29), Insight into Self (30), and Quality of Intellectual Accomplishments (31).

Criterion ratings of general clinical competence show many more significant correlations and higher correlations with objective test scores than did assessment predictions on Overall Suitability. These test correlates of global criterion ratings yield a general characterization of the person later seen as a good clinical psychologist as follows: he is a person of superior intellectual ability and strong intellectual interests. He likes people and prefers to interact with people in terms of verbal communication rather than as objects to be manipulated. He is relatively uninterested in activities which emphasize detail, accuracy and efficiency. He is likely to have broad interests including interests in art and music. Finally, he is likely to be generally well adjusted and not subject to marked mood changes.

These two characterizations of the "good bet," the one based on assessment ratings and that based on objective test scores are in essential agreement in pointing to a paragon who might be equally likely to succeed in any of the several types of professional training. This suggests that clinical psychology will have to compete actively with other professions for good candidates for training.

Personality Variables Associated
with Clinical Skills

In an effort to secure still further evidence regarding the personality correlates of specific clinical skills, trainees were asked to rate each other on Scale A and B variables at the same time (1950) they rated each other on the criterion variables. While trainees were assured that their ratings would be kept confidential, we may expect them to be biased in a favorable direction. However, such a bias should not in itself influence the pattern of the correlations between these ratings and criterion variables shown in Table D V-4. The medians of colleague ratings on Scale A and B variables were correlated with composite criterion ratings on Clinical Competence, Academic Performance, Individual Psychotherapy, and Integrity. These variables were picked to represent the factors in the Composite Criterion ratings.

Composite Criterion ratings on Clinical Competence are, in general, associated with the favorable pole of Scale A and B variables as rated by colleagues. The higher correlations are with Socially Poised, Quality of Intellectual Accomplishment, Motivation for Scientific Understanding, Motivation for Professional Status, Warmth, Social Adjustment, Imaginative, and Insight into Self and Others.

The pattern of correlations of Scale A and B variables with rated Academic Performance is more distinctive than the patterns of correlation for other variables. Academic Performance correlates most highly with Quality of Intellectual Accomplishments, Motivation for Scientific Understanding of People, Motivation for Professional Status, Imaginative, Broad Interests, Independent-Minded, Serious, Talkative, and Assertive. This pattern corroborates our expectations on the basis of the validational analyses; rated Academic Performance is a function of intellectual capacity and interest on the one hand, and of general drive and expressiveness on the other.

Individuals rated high on Therapeutic Competence tend to be rated as socially oriented but not

189

TABLE D V-4

CORRELATIONS OF 1950 COLLEAGUE RATINGS ON SCALE A AND B
VARIABLES WITH SELECTED 1950 CRITERION RATINGS
(N = 78)

Colleague Ratings	C32 Academic Perform.	C34 Individual Psychotherapy	C41 Integrity	Ccc Clinical Competence
A 0 Dislike- Like	03	37	39	31
A 1 Obstructive--Cooperative	03	31	50	31
A 2 Inconsistent--Consistent	00	13	41	24
A 3 Submissive--Assertive	29	-07	-22	13
A 4 Depressed--Cheerful	-01	20	20	28
A 5 Irresponsible--Serious	32	19	37	31
A 6 Non-Gregarious--Gregarious	-06	38	25	22
A 7 Easily Upset--Unshakable	07	17	-03	13
A 8 Narrow--Broad, Interests	35	23	14	30
A 9 Suspicious--Trustful	10	19	36	31
A10 Self-Centered, Selfish--Generous	-08	30	38	20
A11 Silent--Talkative	30	04	-07	19
A12 Cautious--Adventurous	-08	12	-25	12
A13 Socially Clumsy--Socially Poised	11	47	26	44
A14 Rigid--Adaptable, Flexible	00	20	10	23
A15 Dependent--Self-Sufficient	20	11	14	31
A16 Worrying, Anxious--Placid	-10	24	09	20
A17 Not Conscientious--Conscientious	18	17	56	26
A18 Unimaginative--Imaginative	46	27	13	35
A19 Overt Interest in Opposite Sex, Slight--Marked	-08	12	-12	-07
A20 Secretive--Frank	26	05	-05	17
A21 Dependent--Independent, Minded	34	09	09	23
A22 Overt Emotional Expression, Limited--Marked	28	12	05	24
B23a Warmth	06	33	26	36
B23b Social Adjustment	01	33	35	34
B24 Appropriateness of Emotional Expression	15	35	32	32
B25 Characteristic Intensity of Inner Emotional Tension (High-Low)	-13	19	03	16
B26 Sexual Adjustment	-08	07	23	21
B27 Motivation for Professional Status	38	15	27	37
B28 Motiv. for Scientific Understanding of People	53	13	41	45
B29 Insight into Others	19	41	23	34
B30 Insight into Himself	09	35	26	34
B31 Quality of Intellectual Accomplishments	61	26	37	47

Correlations significant at or beyond the 5% level of confidence are underlined.

socially aggressive, and appear to get along easily with other people. The variables showing the highest correlations with this criterion skill include Insight into Self and Others, Socially Poised, Gregarious, Readiness to Cooperate, Generous, Warmth, and Social Adjustment, and Appropriateness of Emotional Expression. The person rated as a good therapist would thus seem to be the individual who is perceived as having few or no problems in the area of interpersonal relations.

Rated Integrity shows relatively high correlations with Conscientious, Readiness to Cooperate, Motivation for Scientific Understanding of People, Consistent, and several other variables in Scales A and B. Persons rated high on these variables might be characterized by seriousness of purpose, easy relationships with others, and a generally objective interest in people.

In view of the fact that these four criterion variables are not uncorrelated it is to be expected that several of the personality variables which are significantly correlated with one of the criteria are also associated with one or more of the other three. Thus Quality of Intellectual Accomplishments is significantly correlated with all four criterion variables. The variables, Liking, Readiness to Cooperate, Serious, Gregarious, Broad Interests, Socially Poised, Imaginative, Warmth, Social Adjustment, Appropriateness of Emotional Expression, Motivation for Professional Status, Motivation for Scientific Understanding of People, Insight into Self, and Insight into Others are all significantly correlated with three of these four criteria. Variables Consistent, Assertive, Trustful, Generous, Conscientious, Independent-Minded, and Marked Overt Emotional Expression are significantly correlated with two of these four criterion variables. Of the 33 Scale A and B variables rated by colleagues exactly two-thirds are thus correlated with at least two of these four criteria.

The Prediction of Dichotomous Criteria

Thus far our analyses of validities have all been concerned with the prediction of relative standing on criterion measures of trainees who have completed the program or who are practically certain of obtaining the Ph.D. We shall now turn briefly to the question of how well the various predictor measures predict overall success or failure in the program.

Although the prediction of probable failure in the program is of high potential significance to individual applicants, to departments of psychology and to the Veterans Administration, the problem is far from simple in that the criterion of success or failure (like other criterion measures) is a "fuzzy" one. Of the 128 P-1 trainees assessed in 1947, it appears that 95 are likely to complete the VA training program. However, at least seven others and probably more are obtaining Ph.D.'s (some in clinical psychology) either at the institution they first entered or at some other one. Of the 25 cases which might be technically termed "failures," there is still considerable diversity of reasons for separation from the program. A few cases were clear-cut academic failures; a few discovered that they did not like clinical psychology and resigned from the program (usually early); a few more had to discontinue the program because of ill health or family responsibilities. Finally a small group of students were dismissed from the program because of lack of aptitude for clinical work. Here, however, the criterion seems to be an extremely variable one; one trainee was dropped from University A but after transfer to University B was rated as distinctly superior in all respects among a large group of trainees.

None of the above sub-groups were sufficiently large to justify separate analyses of them. Although the sub-groups of "Failures" were far from comparable, we have computed bi-serial correlations for Final Pooled assessment predictions using a pass-fail dichotomy. These values, shown in the first row of Table D V-5, are generally lower than correlations of the same assessment predictions against other criterion measures. We can only presume that these lower validities result from the non-homogeneity of the failure group. In order to test this hypothesis, a second set of bi-serials was computed for a pass-fail group eliminating 25 cases for which either a

TABLE D V-5

BI-SERIAL CORRELATIONS FOR FINAL POOLED ASSESSMENT PREDICTIONS AND SELECTED TEST SCORES AGAINST DICHOTOMOUS CRITERION GROUPS

Criterion Group	N	Assessment Prediction on Variables											Test Scores						
													Miller Anal.	Strong Psy.	Allport-Vernon VA	Aes.	Rel.	Pol.	Rorschach Index*
		32	33	34	35	36	37	38	39	40	41	42							
I. Pass (all cases)	95	28	33	23	25	30	20	24	22	20	09	12	0						$\phi = .13$**
Fail	32																		
II. Pass (omitting "doubtfuls")	77	43	51	44	44	40	49	47	42	38	16	39	26	38	28	36	06	-23	08
Fail	25																		
III. High Professional Promise	44	21	08	12	05	16	02	05	14	-03	11	09	08						$\phi = .39$
Low Professional Promise	83																		

I. Pass includes: Ph.D. received or certain. Still in training, out of program but still in school. Fail includes: Did not enter, failure for any reason, resignation, and any other separation. (Does not include one case dismissed on a loyalty charge.)

II. Pass includes only 4 or above on Clinical Competence, Ph.D. received or certain. Fail includes all failures listed in I above except voluntary withdrawals.

III. High Professional Promise includes all cases rated 6 or above on clinical competence by supervisors in 1949 or 1950. (Does not include one case dismissed on a loyalty charge.)

*See text for details.

**N = 106 after eliminating records for trainees familiar with the Rorschach.

Correlations significant at or beyond the 5% level of confidence are underlined, except in row II where the omission of the "doubtful" cases makes the estimate of signficance questionable.

pass or fail designation was doubtful. Although the elimination of such "indeterminate" cases may have produced a somewhat spurious elevation of the bi-serial r, the resulting values, shown in the second row of Table D V-5, may be more accurate estimates of the validities of the prediction for the Pass-Fail criterion than those in the first row. It will be noted that the highest validity coefficient here is .51 for assessment prediction of Diagnostic Competence (A33), followed by other relatively high values for predicted Administration (A37), Supervision (A38), and Therapeutic (A34, A35) and Academic (A32) skills. Predicted Overall Suitability (A42) correlated .39 for this criterion, only slightly higher than the objective scores on the Miller and the Strong VA Key.

One other dichotomous criterion was applied to the entire group of 127 cases. In this analysis we were interested in determining how well assessment ratings would identify those who are later rated as of "high" Professional Promise. The "low" group in this analysis included not only failures and other separations from the program but also trainees who failed to receive a superior rating on Overall Clinical Competence (C42). As is obvious from the correlations shown in the third row of Table D V-5, the assessment ratings do not predict this dichotomous criterion nearly as well as they predict the relative standing of persons still in training (cf. Table D IV-1).

Rae Carlson, a member of the project's technical staff, devoted considerable effort to the derivation of a rational and objective index from the Rorschach as a prediction of dichotomous pass-fail criteria. The index was used to categorize trainees into "promising" and "non-promising" groups. To be regarded as "promising" a trainee's Rorschach had to meet all of the following criteria using Klopfer's scoring system:

(a) $M \gtreqless C$

(b) $M + FC \gtreqless 1/2 \ F$

(c) $FC \gtreqless CF + C$

(d) $F\% < 50\%$

(e) At least one FC and one Fc response

Approximately 40% of the trainees are categorized as "promising" by this index. It is not related to the overall Pass-Fail criterion ($X^2 = 1.83$) but does show a very significant relationship ($X^2 = 18.8$; $\phi = .39$) for criterion groups III of Table D V-5 categorized as High or Low Professional Promise.

CHAPTER E I

SUMMARY AND DISCUSSION

Preceding parts of this volume have been devoted to a detailed account of the methods used in the investigation and to a systematic report of the findings. This final chapter includes: a brief summary of the major findings, an evaluation of the more general outcomes of the project and a brief discussion of the implications of the findings.

Summary and Major Findings

Method

The primary purpose of this five-year research was the evaluation of a variety of procedures as predictors of later success in graduate training and professional functioning in clinical psychology. The overall design of the project was as follows: in 1947 and 1948, several hundred college graduates seeking admission to or just entering the four-year VA training program in clinical psychology in some 40 universities were evaluated by a wide variety of techniques, and predictions were made concerning their probable success in training and their future professional competence. The predictive techniques used included a battery of objective tests and another battery of more clinical diagnostic procedures. The objective test battery included tests of intelligence, social and emotional adjustment, and measures of values and interests. The second group of procedures was used primarily to provide assessment staff members with bases for making descriptive, evaluative, and predictive judgments about the candidate. This battery included four projective tests, two interviews, and a series of situation tests.

The second half of the project was devoted to (a) the development of criterion measures of the several functions which clinical psychologists are expected to perform in VA installations, (b) the administration of these measures to trainees near the end of the four-year training program, and (c) the analyses of the interrelationships among the predictor and criterion measures.

Major Findings

A. Regarding the Subjects and Their Training

1. Graduate students in psychology participating in the VA program are remarkably similar to other graduate students in psychology not majoring in the clinical area. Both are highly selected groups of students, not only in intelligence but also in terms of their measured social and emotional adjustment. Both show a pattern of interests and values characteristic of professional and scientific persons. The VA students differ slightly from the others primarily on the basis of interests more characteristic of the professions which involve contact with people, social welfare, and persuasive activities; the interests of the non-clinical students are somewhat more similar to professions which are primarily concerned with things and ideas.

2. Groups of trainees enrolled at different training institutions show significant differences on measures of ability and achievement.

3. Trainees report wide differences in emphases of training programs at different universities and in their clinical experiences in field training.

4. Ninety-five of the 128 P-1 trainees assessed and entering the four-year program in 1947

will probably complete their training in the VA program. For this group, then, the total attrition is about 20%. However, at least seven more of the original group are known to be completing their Ph. D. 's in psychology, some with clinical specialization but not as VA trainees.

5. About one third of the trainees studied report having received some personal therapy during their training.

6. The Strong Vocation Interest patterns of young clinical psychologists were found to be much more similar to those of young psychiatrists than to those of young physicians. The psychiatrists and clinical psychologists were much more similar in pattern of interests than were psychiatrists and other physicians.

B. Regarding Criteria of Professional Success

1. There is no satisfactory single criterion of success in training for or practicing clinical psychology. University staff members and supervising clinical psychologists show wide individual differences in their conceptions of successful academic performance and of professional skills.

2. There are three general components of success in clinical psychology: (a) intellectual accomplishments, (e. g. , academic achievement and research productivity), (b) the clinical skills of diagnosis and therapy, and (c) skills in social relations. In general, judges agree much better on the first than on the latter two components.

3. Supervisors' ratings do not adequately differentiate the various job functions of the clinical psychologists.

4. Ratings of clinical competences appear to be as much a function of the role of the rater (e. g. , teacher, supervisor, colleage) as of the person being rated.

5. No completely acceptable objective measures of competence in the purported functions of the clinical psychologist are available, but certain promising techniques for evaluating clinical skills were developed within this project. However, further developmental work on these measures is necessary before they can be used in the routine evaluation of clinical competence.

In summary, we may say that there are several varied and alternative criteria of success in clinical psychology. However, the rated criteria showed sufficiently high intercorrelations to identify a common core of what might be called "perceived clinical competence. "

C. Regarding the Prediction of Success in Clinical Psychology (for the 1947 subjects)

1. Accuracy of prediction of success in clinical psychology is a function of the job component being predicted.

2. The intellectual aspects of success in graduate training and also the general aspect of overall clinical competence can be predicted surprisingly well in view of the fact that the group of students entering training is already highly selected. Validities for these criteria range from .35 to .60 even when the range of talent is further restricted to those completing this doctoral program. Furthermore, the validities are based on a national sample; known inter-institution and inter-installation differences in caliber of students and emphases of training presumably lower the obtained relationships.

3. Prediction of relative standing within the group completing professional training is generally more accurate than the prediction of outcome of training (Success/Failure). This is probably due to (a) the diversity of causes for leaving the program: e. g. , academic failure,

health, preference for other fields, etc. and to (b) differences in the criteria applied by
various universities for continuing in the program.

4. The more clinical aspects of professional competence, being less tangible, and therefore
not as readily evaluated, are less predictable than the intellectual component of professional success. Each of several criteria of diagnostic and therapeutic competence is predicted
by one or more predictors, but different criteria of these skills tend to be predicted by different predictors.

5. Those aspects of professional success involving social skills are also predictable byond
chance but because measures of these skills are in part a function of the persons evaluating them, they tend to be less predictable than intellectual aspects of professional success.

6. For the group of trainees who entered training in 1948, the validities of both objective test
scores and assessment ratings based on a modified assessment program were found to
be much lower for the group entering in 1947. These lower validities may be a function of
any one or any combination of the following factors:

   (a) Test data and other materials were obtained for the 1948 group before action was taken
   on their applications for admission to graduate school.
   (b) The 1948 group is younger, intellectually more able, and more homogeneous with respect to both age and intellectual ability.
   (c) The 1948 group had been in training only 2 1/2 years at the time criterion measures
   were collected.

D. Regarding the Relative Efficiency of Various Predictors

1. The potential validity of all predictors is apparently limited by inadequacies in available
criterion measures. All criterion measures used and considered are more or less fallible
because of one or more of the following characteristics. They may

   (a) have low reliability
   (b) be too general or too specific
   (c) be lacking in validity, i. e. , not relevant to actual competence
   (d) be too provincial, i. e. , reflect only the degree to which professional behavior conforms
   to that expected in a sub-culture.

2. Each of the several criterion measures can be predicted about equally well by any one of
several techniques or procedures. This is especially so for the criteria of intellectual
performance (e. g. , rated Academic Performance, scores on Content Examination and rated
Research Competence).

3. In general, only a small proportion of the objective test scores were found to correlate significantly with the criterion measures. However, one or two scores from standard psychological tests predict most of the criterion measures about as well as the best of the assessment ratings by professional staff members. Although assessment ratings and objec-
tivestest scores were found to be about equal in predictive efficiency, objective tests are,
of course, much more economical in terms of time and cost. The most generally useful
of the objective tests were the Miller Analogies Test and the Strong Vocational Interest
Blank. Scores on one or both of these tests predicted most of the several criterion measures with fair efficiency.

4. With respect to the descriptive, evaluative and predictive ratings made by assessment staff
members, it was found that:

   (a) Predictive ratings show fair to high interjudge reliability when based on the same materials.

(b) The relationship between the accuracy of assessment prediction and the amount of materials on which the predictions are based is markedly non-linear. In general, assessment predictions based on the credential file plus the objective test profile tend to be almost as accurate as those based on more materials including an autobiography, projective tests, interviews, and situation tests.

(c) The findings do not reveal any clear-cut superiority in the validity of pooled ratings made in a "staff conference" or of arithmetical ratings over those of the individual staff members.

(d) Self-ratings by the candidates have some predictive value for criteria of intellectual success but show no relationship to other criteria of professional success.

(e) Judgments made by assessment teammates and judgments by staff members on the basis of observing the candidates only in situation tests both have some predictive value; in general they are about as valid as staff ratings based on the credential file alone.

(f) Predictions of success in clinical psychology made on the basis of single projective techniques tend to have very low correlations with any of the criterion measures. The same is true for predictions based on an integrative study of the protocols for the four projective techniques.

5. Predictions of success in the training program made by university staff members on the basis of procedures conventionally used by departments in the selection of students tended to correlate as well with criteria of academic performance and research competence as any assessment predictions. This was true even where the candidate had not been seen by the university staff member at the time of making the predictions. However, the generality of this finding is limited by the fact that University Staff Predictions were available for only half of the subjects, and criterion measures for this sub-group were more predictable than those for the total group of subjects.

E. Other Findings:

1. Qualitative assessment evaluations for 20 trainees were clinically matched with qualitative evaluations of on-the-job functioning made three and one half years later with an accuracy of 72% where the chance value was 50%. The median phi coefficient for individual cases was .44. The same 20 cases were matched objectively, on the basis of the profiles of personality ratings by teammates at the time of assessment and profiles of ratings made on the same variables by colleagues three and one half years later, with an accuracy of 74%. The median phi coefficient was .60. Both of these matchings are significantly better than chance.

2. Ratings on all personality variables by staff and teammates at the time of assessment tend to show low correlations with ratings on the same variables made by colleagues three and one half years later. These correlations are lower than those between the final staff predictive ratings at the time of assessment and criterion measures obtained three and one half years later. Whether these data indicate a lack of consistency of personality among the subjects over the period of graduate study reflect different frames of reference for different raters, or merely reflect the relative atypicality of the behavior displayed by candidates at the assessment, is not known.

3. None of the rated criterion measures of clinical competence or scores on the objective Content Examination were found to differentiate the skills of trainees with three and one half as compared with two and one half years of training. This finding may be the result of the latter group having been more highly selected or better trained. However, a number of lines of converging evidence lead us to question whether present advanced training procedures, or additional years of experience lead to any currently measurable improvement in clinical skills. This may be a function of the nature of the training and/or experience,

or it may merely reflect the inadequacy of available criterion measures of clinical skills.

The Need for Follow-Up Studies

In evaluating the findings of this project, it must be remembered that all of the criterion measures were collected relatively early in the professional lives of the subjects studied, and that the findings here reported are based on these early criteria of professional success. It is, of course, entirely possible that predictors which look unpromising at this time may have greater validity for predicting later criteria of professional accomplishment and vice versa. Although the writers have no immediate plans for further follow-up studies, they hope to be able to obtain even more meaningful criterion measures of the subjects after 10, 15, or 20 years and to analyze the validities of all predictors against criteria of mature professional success. The relationships between criterion measures collected near the end of training and subsequent indices of professional performance should have important implications for both the selection and training of clinical psychologists.

More General Outcomes

In addition to the above summary of the specific findings growing out of the project, it seems desirable to attempt a statement of what appear to be the more general outcomes of this series of investigations. The following list of outcomes includes some based on so-called negative findings, but in our opinion there are some situations in which even "the discovery of ignorance" may be regarded as a positive contribution.

1. The identification of the salient characteristics of the oncoming members of the developing profession of clinical psychology. In spite of its youth, clinical psychology is probably better informed as to the characteristics of its members than any other profession.

2. The collection of factual information concerning the nature of and the degree of variation in training programs in clinical psychology.

3. The collection of similar factual information regarding the nature of and variation in the current practices of clinical psychology.

4. The development of an awareness of the social importance as well as the inherent difficulties in developing valid, reliable and objective measures of professional competences in psychology. Since this problem is presumably of equal importance to all other professional groups, our analysis of the criterion problem may have considerable generality.

5. A promising beginning in the development of objective criterion measures of clinical skills.

6. The discovery that it is possible to predict success in professional training, and individual differences in the performance of professional functioning several years later about as well as permitted by the limitations of current criterion measures.

7. The further discovery that such prediction is possible by the use of simple and economic procedures.

8. A realistic estimate of the validity of a wide variety of psychological techniques as predictors of several different criteria.

9. A similarly realistic estimate of the validity of clinical inferences based on a variety of materials and an indication of some of the factors influencing the validity of such inferences.

Discussion

Implications of Findings for the Selection
of Students

The pattern of findings summarized in the preceding chapters is sufficiently clear to make
unnecessary a detailed discussion of their implications for the selection practices of departments
of psychology. It would appear that the general procedures now in use permit reasonably accurate
prediction of performance in training, especially of the kinds of performance emphasized by the
university department doing the selection.

Until more adequate objective criterion measures are developed, none of the time-consuming,
elaborate techniques used in our assessment program appear to add enough to the accuracy of
predictive judgments to justify their cost. Departments may wish to use the Miller Analogies
Test as a screen to be certain of admitting only applicants with sufficient ability to complete the
doctoral program. They may also wish to use the Strong Interest Blank to provide some indication of the probably relative motivations of applicants for the various aspects of clinical psychology. While our findings emphasize the lack of any single criterion of the good clinical psychologist, it is possible to identify persons who are most likely to acquire the kinds of competence
most valued at a given university, e.g., Academic, Diagnostic, Research, or Therapeutic (cf.
Chapter D V).

Our findings that scores on two tests show significant correlations with several criteria of
success, even for a group of students already relatively homogeneous with respect to the variables measured by the tests, suggests that local departments may find it worthwhile to compute
the "local validities" of these and any other techniques which may be used in the selection of students. Such studies will, of course, necessitate the local collection of criterion measures of
clinical competence, but this in itself will be found to be a challenging undertaking!

Validity of a Technique as Related
to Confidence of the User

Many of our findings emphasize the necessity for determining the validity of all psychological
techniques for the purpose for which they are being applied. Although tested knowledge is the
foundation of all science, the demands of practice sometimes cause the applied scientist to forget
this basic axiom. In such instances, he is strongly tempted to rely on the apparent validity of the
technique, or on his confidence in its validity. Our findings suggest that neither "face-validity"
nor "faith validity" are satisfactory bases for decision as to the value of a technique for a specific
function.

Many members of the assessment staffs had high confidence in and high hopes for the general
predictive value of a specific test, technique, or procedure used in the project. In some instances,
the findings support such expectations, in many more instances they do not. This poses the ques-
tion--are the data to be suspected--or were the expectations unreasonable ones?

Most of the techniques or procedures in which assessment staff members had particularly
high confidence were ones which require that the individual clinician function as an integral part
of the measuring instrument. Because of the difficulty and cost of follow-up studies which provide criterion measures, the actual evaluation of the validity of technique-clinician combination
is rare. The clinician without an opportunity for "reality testing" may develop unwarranted confidence in his skill with a specific technique. He may even be tempted to apply it in situations
where he and the technique have little or no validity.

This appears to have happened with respect to certain of the techniques included in the assessment battery. While there is little evidence to support the widely held belief in the value of the personal interview as a selection device, it was the general opinion of staff members that it was one of the most valuable techniques of the assessment program. At the time the research was planned there was no evidence that projective techniques would contribute to the prediction of future professional performance, yet enough people were convinced of their potential validity that considerable staff time was budgeted for their use. Similarly, we know of no evidence for the apparently widely held belief that the pooled judgments of a clinical staff are more valid than those of individual members of a staff, yet staff conferences were believed to be an essential part of any good assessment program

Improving the Accuracy of Prediction

At this point, readers are reminded of the overall findings of the project with respect to the relative accuracy of statistical and clinical predictions of future behavior; in this situation both approaches worked about equally well. Furthermore, it must be emphasized that neither approach was pushed to its limits within the project. On the basis of the findings here reported it should now be possible to train an assessment staff which could make more accurate predictions of success in clinical psychology than those made by our staffs without benefit of such knowledge. Similarly, by utilizing our new knowledge concerning the test correlates of the criterion measures, it should be possible to derive a multiple regression equation or new scoring keys for objective test items which would predict future professional performance better than any of the single test scores used in the project.

Neither of these refinements of technique have been attempted within the project; furthermore, we do not believe either to be a worthwhile undertaking at this time. There are two related reasons for this position. First, the inadequacies of currently available criterion measures of professional success impose realistic limitations on the increment in validity which might be achieved by refining either statistical or clinical procedures. Equally important is the fact that clinical psychology is a young and changing profession and any attempt to maximize the accuracy of predictions of current criteria of professional success might tend to crystallize professional functioning in a pattern which might not, in the long run, be socially defensible. Only after we have agreed on the essential functions of the clinical psychologist in society and have developed acceptable and reliable measures of these functions are refinements in the predictive techniques likely to be rewarding. And only to the degree that such criterion measures become available will it be possible to identify the essential aptitudes for professional functioning and to evaluate the contribution of specific training procedures to such functioning.

We have no illusions that we shall ever have completely objective criteria of professional success in clinical psychology. It is the essence of a profession that the activities of its members transcend simple or routine procedures which are readily measured. Professional activities include the weighing of evidence and the making of professional judgments which are often based in part on social values. To this extent, professional success will always have to be evaluated in the context of social norms. Furthermore, the opportunity to function as a professional person is likely to continue to be in large part determined by the opinion of one's professional colleagues. A man may be a good diagnostician but if his colleagues do not think so, it is not likely that his diagnostic competence will be very much utilized in the handling of patients. Another person might be a poor diagnostician by objective standards, but if he is regarded as a good diagnostician, his judgments are likely to be weighted heavily in staff conferences.

Interrelatedness of the Problems Investigated

Such considerations serve to re-emphasize the interrelatedness of the many problems investigated within this project. We started out with the disarmingly simple question: "How shall we select future clinical psychologists?" One approach would have been to determine the characteristics of persons so employed in 1947 and then to select applicants on the basis of the degree to which their characteristics approximated the typical clinical psychologist. This approach was followed in the development of the ad hoc Va Clinical Psychologist Key for the Strong Vocational Interest Blank. Such an approach assumes that the modal members of the profession represent the ideal. This assumption was not acceptable to us, especially in view of the fluid state of the field, and we began to ask "How does the good clinical psychologist differ from the one who is not so good?" This question immediately led to the next, "Good for what?" Thus we found ourselves deep in the problem of the criteria of professional functioning. We were even asking "What is it that the clinical psychologist does that makes a difference in the lives of the patients whom he serves?"

For practical reasons our assessment program was carried out without a preceding formal job analysis of the functions of the clinical psychologist. However, since the assessment staffs were composed largely of clinical psychologists, much of the time of the staff conferences was devoted to an interchange of opinion concerning the appropriate functioning of the clinical psychologist as well as consideration of the aptitudes and personality characteristics essential for such functioning. Since many of the procedures used in the assessment programs were those widely employed by clinical psychologists in current diagnostic practice, evaluation of these procedures as predictors of professional success was bound to have implication for their use in other situations. The interrelatedness of the problems of assessment and the job functions of the clinical psychologist was made even more obvious by our attempts to measure diagnostic competence.

Special Problems in Clinical Prediction

Although we find that clinical psychologists did make judgments which had some validity for the prediction of subsequent performance, these products of professional minds were admittedly not as good as many had hoped they would be. Furthermore, much of the evidence demands that we recognize the current limitations of the clinician using present theories and techniques as an instrument for evaluating personality and predicting future behavior. Our findings indicate that human judges can predict some of the variance of future behavior on the basis of remarkably diverse kinds of behavioral records or observations. But these same findings are equally indicative of the limitations of the human judge in the prediction situation. They also demand that we question the alleged superiority of any one type of behavior sample* as holding the key to the evaluation of personality and force us to doubt untested assumptions concerning the relative validity of specific techniques or procedures for a specific function. Perhaps, even more sobering are the doubts which certain of the findings raise concerning the theories underlying some of our clinical practices. For example, it is commonly assumed that the value of Rorschach interpretations depends on the clinical interpretation of the pattern of the scored determinants. However, for this prediction problem, we find that M% scores show significant correlations with most of our criterion measures whereas none of the ratings made by the clinicians on the basis of the total Rorschach pattern achieve statistical significance. By contrast, in spite of the generally significant validities of teammates' ratings, none of a number of indices based on sociometric choices was found to be significantly related to the criterion measures.

---

*Handwriting analysis was not used as a routine assessment procedure, largely because of the non-availability of staff persons with appropriate training. However, in the fall of 1949, Steven G. Vandenberg, a graduate assistant with European training in graphology, rated 62 of the 1947 cases on 42 variables on the basis of samples of handwriting selected from the autobiographies for lack of contextual cues. Correlations of these ratings with assessment ratings and criterion ratings suggest that they are about as meaningful as ratings based on other individual projective techniques.

In retrospect, we cannot help but wonder whether it is unreasonable to expect a human being to function at the extraordinary level of efficiency required by the complex process of predicting behavior. The complexity of the prediction process is suggested by reference to a relatively simple problem in multiple correlation. Let us assume that variance in the behavior to be predicted (X_1) is determined by three independent variables X_2, X_3, and X_4. This problem may be portrayed graphically as follows:

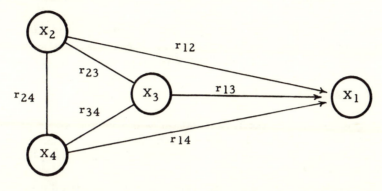

E I-1 Diagram Illustrating Relationships between Variables Involved in Multiple Prediction.

The most accurate statistical prediction of X_1 requires a knowledge not only of the correlations between the criterion and the three independent variables $(r_{12}, r_{13},$ and $r_{14})$ but also of the intercorrelations between each of the independent variables $(r_{23}, r_{24},$ and $r_{34})$. Given all of this information, it is possible to derive a multiple regression equation which permits prediction for any individual of his most probable standing on the criterion X_1. The resulting equation is, however, not a simple one and it seems unlikely that any human being, given these correlational values and the values of an individual on X_2, X_3, and X_4, could mentally compute the best X_1 value accurately without the aid of the proper equation (and perhaps a calculating machine!).

Let us contrast this relatively ideal situation with that typical of the clinician confronted with the prediction of individual behavior. For the sake of simplicity, let us still assume that the behavior X_1 is determined by only three independent variables, X_2, X_3 and X_4. Instead of accurate estimates of the values for $4r_{12}$, r_{13}, and r_{14}, the clinician tends to rely on his subjective impression of their relative magnitudes. Even more important, he is not likely to know even the approximate values for r_{23}, r_{24}, and r_{34}. Yet knowledge of these values is essential if fundamental errors in predictions are to be avoided. For example, if variables X_2 and X_3 are equally correlated with X_1, the clinician is inclined to give both variables equal weight in arriving at his prediction of X_1. This is justified only if X_2 and X_3 are not correlated. To the extent that they are measures of the same underlying variable, assigning the same weight to each tends to overweight whatever they are measuring in common and introduces error in the resulting prediction.

Any lack of information concerning the degree of correlation among the variables not only precludes the assignment of the optimum predictive weights to each of the independent variables but provides a tempting opportunity for the clinician to weight the independent variables in accordance with personal or theoretical biases. Each time he does so, he is likely to introduce more error variance into his prediction.

The situation which we have outlined above is far simpler than that involved in most clinical
The situation which we have outlined above is far simpler than that involved in most clinical work or in the assessment situation. Ordinarily, many more than three independent variables are involved--yet the addition of each new variable increases the number of intercorrelations which must be allowed for by (n - 1). Perhaps here we have the explanation of the markedly non-linear relationship between the accuracy of assessment predictions and the amount of data on which the predictions are based. If the above analysis is correct, it follows that the mere addition of new information (more variables) does not necessarily increase the accuracy of prediction although

it probably results in a feeling of increased confidence on the part of the clinician. Even though
the correlation between the criterion and the added variable is known, the new information is not
likely to increase the accuracy of prediction unless its correlation with the criterion is higher than
with any other independent variable. Viewed in this light, it is perhaps unreasonable to expect
clinical predictions to compete in accuracy with statistical prediction in situations where the
variables involved are amenable to reasonably accurate measurement.

An alternative hypothesis is that the most accurate clinical predictions of the behavior of
a specific individual results not from the application of correlational data based on groups, but
from a study of the unique pattern of the variables for that individual (cf. Horst, 1941). This alternative hypothesis is a tenable one; furthermore it is a testable one. As of the present date,
however, we know of no available evidence to support it.

It is entirely possible that extensive investigation would reveal some gifted persons who by
procedures, not presently communicable, can make clinical predictions superior to those possible
by statistical or psychometric procedures. If this should be the case, it is essential that efforts
be made to identify the methods employed by such persons so that these methods may be communicated to others in training. If their methods cannot be identified or communicated, it would
still be worthwhile to identify the essential characteristics of such persons so that others similarly gifted might be selected to function in a similar manner.

It is our own belief that there are a few relatively gifted individuals whose intuitive insights
may provide a basis not only for superior prediction in individual cases, but for the development
of new and powerful techniques for the evaluation of personality and the prediction of individual
behavior. There appears to be considerable danger, however, in assuming that such intuitive
insights can be transmitted to less gifted persons without serious loss of validity. The insight
of a genius is likely to be used effectively by lesser mortals only after instrumentation which
makes it less dependent on variations in the talents of the user.

This line of thinking is not likely to be acceptable to those who wish to see clinical psychology
remain more of an art than an applied science. Such persons are inclined to view the development of objective techniques, not requiring clinical skill in their application, as a threat to the
future role of the clinician. This we consider to be a very shortsighted view of the situation.
The development of any objective technique which can be used by a clinician (or a technician)
to do better what the clinician now does only frees the clinician for higher level professional
responsibilities. No matter how many objective techniques are developed for specific predictive
functions, nor how efficient they may be, there will always be a social need for the professionally
trained person. His judgment will be required for the decisions as to which of the available techniques are best suited for specific situations and for the process of integrating the findings of the
techniques. Furthermore, there will always be special situations for which it will be uneconom-
ical to develop specific techniques. In such future situations, as now, the trained clinician will
be expected to use his ability, his training, his experience and his wisdom in arriving at the best
possible professional decisions. The quality of such decisions should be even higher if he is able
to use techniques with tested validities.

APPENDICES

Appendix		Page
I-A	Basic Rating Scale Used in the 1947 Assessment Program	206
I-B	Sociometric Questionnaire	214
I-C	Assessment Report on Case 2	216
I-D	Sentence Completion Test	217
I-E	Biographical Inventory	220
I-F	Form for Autobiography	240
II-A	Criterion Rating Scale	244
II-B 1	Qualitative Description of VA Trainee's Performance	256
II-B 2	Qualitative Description of VA Trainee's Research Performance	259
II-C	Qualitative Description by Supervisors of Case 38	262
II-D	Training Experience Inventory	264
II-E	Predictions on Diagnostic Cases	274
II-F	Instructions to Judges for Scoring Progress Notes	277
II-G	Rejected Criterion Procedures	285
III-A	Correlations between Final Pooled Ratings (1947 Ann Arbor Assessment)	287
III-B	Oblique Factor Matrix for Final Pooled Ratings (1947 Ann Arbor Assessment)	288
III-C	Second-Order Factor Matrix (1947 Ann Arbor Assessment)	289
III-D	Correlations between Primary Vectors (1947 Ann Arbor Assessment)	290
IV	Thesis Abstracts	291

APPENDIX I-A

BASIC RATING SCALE USED IN THE 1947 ASSESSMENT PROGRAM

REFERENCE POPULATIONS FOR RATINGS

For Scales A and B the candidate is rated as he is today. The reference group is first year clinical psychology graduate students in universities accredited by the APA to offer training in clinical psychology.

For the Criterion Skills (Scale C), the candidate is rated as he will be five years from now. The reference population is VA clinical psychologists who have had four years of academic and on-the-job training. (P-4 and above.) In rating a candidate on the Criterion Skills, the assumption is made that he will have completed the training and will have been employed by the VA. A rating of 3 or below means that it is doubtful that the candidate will ever qualify for a P-4 rating with respect to the trait being rated. It is possible that some candidates will later qualify for a P-4 position even though they rate 3 or below on a few Criterion Skills.

RATING SCALE

All ratings will be made in terms of an eight point scale illustrated graphically as follows:

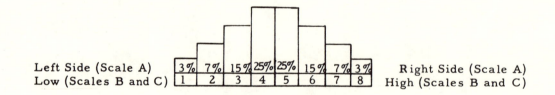

Left Side (Scale A)	3%	7%	15%	25%	25%	15%	7%	3%	Right Side (Scale A)
Low (Scales B and C)	1	2	3	4	5	6	7	8	High (Scales B and C)

RATING SCALE DEFINITIONS

SCALE A
(No. 1-22)

(For ratings on this scale, 1 = extreme on left side, 8 = extreme on right side.)

Note: The attributes in Scale A refer to behavior which can be directly observed on the surface. In using this scale, disregard any inferences about underlying dynamics or causes.

1. <u>Readiness to cooperate</u>   -v-   <u>Obstructiveness</u>
   Finds ways of cooperating despite difficulties.
          Frequently is "difficult."

2. <u>Consistent</u>   -v-   <u>Inconsistent</u>
   Behaves in the same general way from day to day.
          Shows changing and unpredictable moods and behavior.

3. <u>Assertive</u>   -v-   <u>Submissive</u>
   Attempts to dominate or influence his associates.
          Tends to let people have their way.

4. <u>Depressed</u>   -v-   <u>Cheerful</u>
   Does not smile or laugh easily or frequently.
          Generally bubbling over with good cheer. Optimistic. Enthusiastic. Prone to cheerful, witty remarks.

5. <u>Irresponsible</u>   -v-   <u>Serious</u>
   Not inclined to take responsibilities seriously. Thoughtless. Unaware of responsibilities of his age. (Do not confuse with No. 17: Conscientious vs. Not Conscientious.)
          Accepts appropriate responsibilities toward others. Shows seriousness of purpose.

6. <u>Gregarious (adient toward people)</u>   -v-   <u>Non-gregarious (abient from people)</u>
   Is attracted by and moves toward people in social situations.
          In social groupings, isolates himself.

7. <u>Easily Upset</u>   -v-   <u>Unshakable</u>
   Easily embarrassed or put off balance. Gets confused in emergency. Blushes, shows excitability, becomes incoherent. Momentary "nervousness," <u>not</u> general emotionality.
          Self possessed. Does not lose composure under emotional provocation.

8. <u>Narrow Interests</u>   -v-   <u>Broad Interests</u>
   Uninformed in many areas. Narrow, simple interests. Provincial outlook.
          Talks and acts <u>in an informed way</u> in a wide variety of areas.

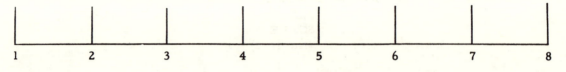

1	2	3	4	5	6	7	8

9. **Suspicious**   -v-   **Trustful**

Believes rather too quickly that he is being unfairly treated. Imagines on insufficient grounds that people strongly dislike him. Interprets things as having reference to himself when none is intended. Feels persecuted.

Accepts statements of others without suspicion (not necessarily "gullible").

10. **Generous**   -v-   **Self-centered, Selfish**

Generous and considerate in actions involving others at considerable self-sacrifice.

Irritable and resentful or withdrawing from situations requiring consideration of others. Talks and acts exclusively in terms of own interests.

11. **Silent**   -v-   **Talkative**

Says very little.

Talks a lot, to everybody. Takes the initiative in conversations. When addressed, responds quickly.

12. **Cautious**   -v-   **Adventurous**

Avoids the strange and new. Looks at all aspects of a situation overcautiously. Does the safe thing.

Seeks and readily enters into new experiences and situations.

13. **Socially Poised and Adept**   -v-   **Socially Clumsy, Awkward in Social Situations**

Polite, poised, and tactful in social situations. Deals with people gracefully and skillfully.

Tactless in social situations. Crude in speech and manners. Omits proper formalities. Does not meet people gracefully. Gauche. Note: Applies to relationships with one or more people.

14. **Rigid**   -v-   **Adaptable, Flexible**

Sticks to his own ideas and does not adapt to ways of doing things differently from his own. Does not change and broaden with experience.

Appropriately modifies his behavior to situations. Accepts compromises where needed. Is not upset, surprised, baffled, or irritable if things are different from what he expected.

15. **Dependent**   -v-   **Self-sufficent**

Asks for reassurance and support. Attaches himself to individuals and groups instead of relying on himself.

Does not lean on others in situations calling for independent action.

16. **Placid**   -v-   **Worrying, Anxious**

Outwardly calm and relaxed.

Appears to worry constantly, harried; overtly anxious. Shows agitation.

17. **Conscientious**   -v-   **Not Conscientious**

Behavior characterized by truthfulness, honesty, unselfishness.

Not too careful about right and wrong where own wishes are concerned. Not particularly just, honest, or unselfish. Inclined to somewhat shady transactions.

1	2	3	4	5	6	7	8

18. <u>Imaginative</u>   -v-   <u>Unimaginative</u>

Has a rich and vivid imagination. Thinks of unusual angles and aspects of a question. Sensitive to a multitude of emotional and other possibilities not realized by the average person.

Lack in imagination. Approaches problems in a literal matter-of-fact fashion. Unresponsive to the subtleties in a situation.

19. <u>Marked Overt Interest in Opposite Sex</u>   -v-   <u>Slight Overt Interest in Opposite Sex</u>

Dates a good deal and/or talks a lot about opposite sex. Extremely aware of women as women. (Disregard <u>inferred</u> needs or drives.)

Talks very little about women. Does not use opportunities for contacts with women.

20. <u>Frank</u>   -v-   <u>Secretive</u>

<u>C</u>omes out readily with his real feelings on various questions. Expresses his feelings, sad or gay, easily and constantly.

Keeps his thoughts and feelings to himself.

21. <u>Dependent Minded</u>   -v-   <u>Independent Minded</u>

Intellectually dependent on others. Generally accepts the opinion of a group or of authority without much thought.

Thinks things out for himself. Examines every question persistently and individualistically. Makes up his own mind.

22. <u>Limited Overt Emotional Expression</u>   -v-   <u>Marked Overt Emotional Expression</u>

<u>I</u>s apathetic, sluggish, or constricted.

Shows hyperkinetic, agitated behavioral responses; is overly excitable and over-demonstrative.

SCALE B

(Nos. 23-31)

(For ratings on this scale, 1 = left side or low, 8 = right side or high.)

1   2   3   4   5   6   7   8

Since many of the following attributes (Nos. 23-30) are broad factors, it is unlikely that any person will fit all of the phrases grouped together at one pole of a given variable. Note also that for some items, neither extreme necessarily represents a desirable attribute.

23a.* Ability to Develop and Maintain Warm Interpersonal Relationships.

23b. Social Adjustment: How well does he adjust to varied interpersonal situations? (Includes sexual adjustment only as it affects social adjustment in general.)

Acts without consideration for feelings of others; often rejected by others, often appears aloof, hostile, or irritable.	Actively considers feelings of others; readily gains acceptance in interpersonal relationships; maintains a friendly and likeable manner.

24. Appropriateness of Emotional Expression: How appropriate are his emotional responses to the situation?

Fails to adapt his emotional responses to the needs of the situation; shows disorganized or overly constricted emotional responses.	Shows emotional responses of a quality and intensity befitting the situation; reacts spontaneously but appropriately; shows well integrated and flexible patterns of emotional behavior.

25. Characteristic Intensity of Inner Emotional Tension: How intense is his inner emotional life as inferred from all available clues?

Inner emotional life characterized by a minimum of persistent internal tensions.	Has strongly repressed emotional drives resulting in inner turmoil; great inner conflict and strong pent-up emotions.

26. Sexual Adjustment: To what degree do his sexual needs and activities affect his overall adjustment?

His sexual needs and activities seriously interfere with his overall adjustment.	His sexual needs and activities definitely enhance his overall adjustment.

27. Motivation for Professional Status: How strong is his drive for the status-rewards of a professional career?

---

*This variable was added between the third and fourth classes of 1947 Ann Arbor Assessment.

1	2	3	4	5	6	7	8

28. Motivation for Scientific Understanding of People: How strong are his drives toward acquiring the facts, theories, and skills necessary for the scientific understanding of individual human beings?

29. Insight into Others: How much insight does he have into the attitudes, emotions, and motivations of others?

Interprets behavior at its face value; insensitive to any but gross differences in behavior; does not develop any integrated understanding of behavior or of people.

Has good awareness of underlying dynamics of behavior; is sensitive to subtle nuances of behavioral responses; is able to develop integrated understanding of the behavior of people.

30. Insight into Himself: How much insight does he have into the underlying dynamics of his own attitudes, emotions and motivations?

31. Quality of Intellectual Accomplishments: What is the characteristic quality of his intellectual output?

Intellectual work is characteristically of low quality.

Characteristically produces intellectual work of high quality.

SCALE C--CRITERION SKILLS
(Nos. 32-42)

(For ratings on this scale, 1 = low, 8 = high.)

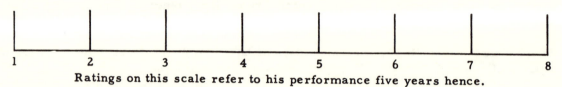

Ratings on this scale refer to his performance five years hence.

What will be his level of competence or skill in the varied aspects of:

32. Academic Performance: (during next three or four years) How well will he:

Effectively master course content, successfully complete courses in general psychology, clinical psychology, statistics, and related fields; satisfy language requirements for the doctorate; pass general examinations.

33. Clinical Diagnosis: How well will he:

Recognize dynamics underlying particular responses in both objective and projective tests, observe significant interrelationships among responses, relate findings to case history and other clinical data.

Elicit from the patient information required for mental status examinations and case histories; ascertain and evaluate attitudes and incidents of psychological significance in the patient.

Synthesize clinical findings to arrive at an integrated picture of personality development, structure, and function.

34. Individual Psychotherapy: How effectively will he:

Conduct various types of individual psychotherapy.

35. Group Psychotherapy: How effectively will he:

Conduct various types of group psychotherapy.

36. Research: How well will he:

Recognize and define important research problems in clinical psychology; critically evaluate and apply the research findings of others; think with originality and scientific rigor; employ appropriate experimental design and statistical methods; grasp practical implications of findings; present results and conclusions in clear, comprehensive and well-organized form.

37. Administration: How well will he:

Plan and develop psychological programs; make proper administrative decisions; delegate responsibility appropriately; elicit cooperation from subordinates and superiors; maintain high morale among his staff; carry out or direct an appropriate public relations program.

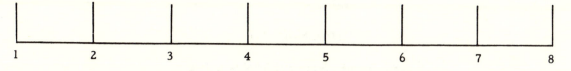

38. Supervising Clinical Psychologists: How well will he:

Carry out the professional supervision of subordinates assigned to him for duty and on-the-job instruction; assign their duties; evaluate their performance; instruct them in clinical techniques; perform other aspects of in-service training.

39. Teaching Psychology (in a College or University): How well will he:

Teach college courses in general psychology; motivate students, present concepts and procedures, stimulate critical thinking about and integration of course materials, evaluate the products of learning.

40. Professional Interpersonal Relations: How well will he:

Work cooperatively with superiors, subordinates, members of the mental hygiene team, and other professional personnel concerned with the patient's welfare; participate in the give and take of staff conferences; contribute to group decisions.

41. Integrity of Personal and Professional Behavior: How well will he:

Recognize and fulfill professional responsibilities; live up to personal commitments; show loyalty to professional obligations in the event of outside pressure or promise of personal gain; maintain discretion concerning professional matters; appropriately conform with commonly accepted standards of moral and social behavior; refrain from coloring facts, evasion, lying, etc.

42. Overall Suitability for Clinical Psychology: In view of his assets and liabilities, how well will he be able to:

Carry out the several duties, diagnosis, therapy, and research specified for the position of clinical psychologist (P-4 and above) in the VA.

APPENDIX I-B

SOCIOMETRIC QUESTIONNAIRE

Name:

1. Which persons would you prefer as your co-workers in a psychological clinic engaged in diagnosis and therapy?

2. Which persons would you least prefer as co-workers?

3. If your wife or fiancee had a serious emotional problem, to which persons would you particularly advise her to go?

4. Which persons would you steer her away from?

5. Which persons would you prefer to have as your immediate superior in a psychological clinic?

6. Which persons would you least prefer?

7. Which person would you pick as an intimate friend?

8. If you had $25,000 to be granted to a person to originate and evaluate a new clinical technique which person would you pick?

9. Which persons would you prefer to have as a companion on a two-week camping trip?

10. Which persons would you least prefer to have as a companion on a two-week camping trip?

11. Assuming that he had the necessary knowledge, which person would you prefer to take a course under in clinical psychology?

12. Which person do you think understands you best?

13. Which person do you understand best?

14. Which persons did you find the most difficult to analyze or size-up?

15. Which person would you choose as trouble-shooter to investigate and handle on-the-spot problems of professional interpersonal relations?

APPENDIX I -C

Assessment Report on Case 2

Striking infantilism and egocentricity, so marked as to interfere with objectivity in thinking and adaptability. The personality structure conforms so closely to the infantile that the oedipal complex is manifest even now, within the family.

His present teachers stress his industry and earnestness. Here he showed vagueness and poor adaptability in dealing with problems and a preoccupation with such things as "unity" and "realizing the potential of humanity" which reflected an unrealized striving for omnipotence, and which prevented him from being clear or precise. There is a frank resistance to accepting the world on its own terms.

Under pressure he is actually unable to relate to others in communication by words, assumes like the infant that the listener understands what he says obscurely because he understands it himself.

Motivation, to be understood in terms of his egocentricity and need to order the universe with himself as center. Dislikes working with individuals in a clinic, wants to reach forth and cure the "community." He may not be able to accept his training courses as they are structured. He will find it hard to fulfil his assignments as a clinical psychologist, except insofar as he can play the paternal role.

He is about average in acceptance by the group, but voted one of the most difficult to analyze. Socializes fairly well, is not openly assertive, competitive with men, works to win over women. Claims to be ascetic, is not an attention seeker, sets a premium on idealism and earnestness-- would be a high priest rather than a dictator. He cannot tolerate a world or society which demands realistic adaptations.

Chief assets are his industry in study, his drive for status, and the control of power-drive which makes him inoffensive socially.

Liabilities--mediocre intellect, extreme ego-centricity, affecting clarity and precision of thinking. Any worldly occupation will be unrewarding. Will derive some gratification from playing the paternal role, should be sympathetic toward women.

Doubt that he will respond to therapy, which may well prove disturbing. Shows some superficial insights, is eager for counseling, but would hardly face his actual problems.

If his teachers are at all critical in rating him, will he be able to complete the training course?

APPENDIX I-D

SENTENCE COMPLETION TEST

Name _____ Date _____

1. Most people who are praised

2. The nicest experience in my youth

3. I sometimes wondered whether

4. Some people would do anything in order to

5. Freedom seems

6. Most women are

7. It is wrong to make people

8. A friend can get in your hair when

9. I get angriest when

10. I need

11. I like children who are

12. The difference between Mom and Dad was

13. I get distracted when

14. The most important thing in my life was

15. I despise

16. Compared to boys, girls

17. I used to feel bad about

18. I can work best when my supervisor

19. When people make fun of me

20. My home

21. My idea of a mature adult is one who

22. As a youth my greatest trouble

23. I cannot understand what makes me

24. Most of all, I wanted to

25. Most people are

26. A man wants a woman who

27. When I think back, I am ashamed that

28. In supervising other men, I

29. I could hate a person who

30. A sister

31. When the "boss" says, "you can do it," I

32. Mother was all right but

33. I dream

34. As a youth my greatest unfilled emotional need was

35. I am

36. She disliked him when he

37. A white man who has intercourse with a black woman

38. As a child, I feared people who

39. I could not control myself if

40. God

41. I like people at parties who

42. The rest of the family felt that Mom and Dad

43. When I get down in the dumps

44. I used to daydream about

45. I hope

46. She was happiest when I

47. We tend to forget the type of experiences which

48. The kind of people who irritate me

49. I could feel like smashing things if

50. Sin

51. The thing I want most in my closest friend

52. I sometimes hated father because

53. I suffer most from

54. I couldn't get along without

55. Love

56. He often argued with her because

57. The dirtiest thing a woman can do to a man

58. When I felt that others were doing better, I

59. When he struck me in the face

60. I failed when

61. As a youth, I became attached to people who

62. Because of Mom, I

63. Some people get upset when

64. I often wished

65. I am afraid

66. He hated her when

67. One must never

68. When I am criticized for my behavior, I

69. I could murder a man who

70. Discipline

71. The kind of people I like most are

72. During my school years what mattered most was

73. It makes me nervous to

74. My personality would be much better if

75. Death

76. Although he loved her, she

77. The worst thing a man can do to a woman

78. When people are criticized, they

79. I boil up when

80. Relatives

81. When praised for my behavior, I

82. The trouble with my home

83. My greatest fault

84. I used to feel "down in the dumps" when

85. If I only

86. He felt better when she

87. Sexual pleasure

88. To get along well in a group, you have to

89. I have to watch what I say when

90. A brother

91. I feel very close to people who

92. I liked Dad when

93. I may get blue when

94. My greatest ambition is

95. I was happiest when

96. After he had been married for a few years, he

97. I am too selfish about

98. When the boss says I can't do it, I

99. When people push me around

100. Authority

APPENDIX I-E

BIOGRAPHICAL INVENTORY

On these pages, you are asked for certain information concerning your background, attitudes, and interests. These items either singly or in patterns, are believed to be related to success in the field of clinical psychology. To save your time, we are asking for the information in this form, rather than in your free-style autobiography.

For each item below, check or write in the answer which best applies to you. Check only one answer (unless special instructions are given). If none of the choices seems to fit you very well, check the one which most closely fits you. Write in any comments or qualifications that you care to make. Work rapidly. Be sure to answer every item.

Name _____ Date _____

Date of Birth: Year ___ Mo. ___ ; Place of birth: City _____ State _____

College or University last attended: _____ Location: _____

University you plan to attend (1st choice): _____

Civil Service Classification you expect to receive if you are employed by the VA next Fall:
    P-1 _____ ; P-2 _____ ; P-3 _____ .

Marital Status: Single _____ ; Married _____ ; Widowed _____ ; Divorced _____ ; Separated _____ .

Your children: No. _____ ; Ages of boys _____ ; Ages of girls _____ .

1. Father: Age (if living) _____ Age at death _____ .

        Your age at his death _____

        Cause of death _____

        Birthplace _____

        Education: Elem. School: 1 2 3 4 5 6 7 8
        (circle highest year)   High School: 1 2 3 4 5
                                       College: 1 2 3 4 5 6 7

        Occupation: _____ unskilled occupation
                    _____ semi-skilled occupation
                    _____ skilled occupation (craftsman)
                    _____ farmer
                    _____ business man
                    _____ professional man

Check only one answer (unless special instructions are given). Write in comments. Do not omit any item.

2. Mother: Age (if living) _____ Age at death _____

    Your age at her death _____

    Cause of death _____

    Birthplace _____

    Education: Elem. School: 1 2 3 4 5 6 7 8
    (circle highest year)   High School: 1 2 3 4 5
                         College: 1 2 3 4 5 6 7

    Occupation before marriage: _____

3. Religious practices of parents:

    Denominational preference of father _____

    Denominational preference of mother _____

    Church attendance of father: _____ regular; _____ occasional; _____ rarely or never

    Church attendance of mother: _____ regular; _____ occasional; _____ rarely or never

4. Marital happiness of parents:

    _____ very happy
    _____ fairly happy
    _____ fairly unhappy
    _____ unhappy

5. Amount of friction between father and mother:

    _____ none at all
    _____ very little
    _____ as much as most people
    _____ constant friction

6. Which of your parents was more to blame for the disagreements between them?

    _____ father, almost always
    _____ father, usually
    _____ mother, usually
    _____ mother, almost always

7. Parental marriage:

    _____ Divorced; _____ Your age at divorce
    _____ Separated; _____ Your age at separation
    _____ Marriage broken by death of one parent
    _____ Marriage unbroken

8. Which parent do you more closely resemble?

_____ resemble father a great deal
_____ resemble father somewhat
_____ resemble mother somewhat
_____ resemble mother a great deal

9. Brothers:

	Age	Education	Occupation	Deceased	Year
1.					
2.					
3.					
4.					

Sisters:

	Age	Education	Occupation	Deceased	Year
1.					
2.					
3.					
4.					

10. As a child, how did you feel about the number of brothers and sisters you had:

_____ certainly too few
_____ probably too few
_____ just right
_____ probably too many
_____ certainly too many

11. Age of parents at your birth: _____ Father; _____ Mother

12. Birth:

_____ full term, uneventful
_____ premature
_____ caesarian
_____ full term with complications (difficult labor, birth injury, etc.)
_____ no information

13. Infant feeding:

_____ breast fed for 6 mos. or longer
_____ breast fed for 1 to 6 mos.
_____ bottle fed from birth or 1st month
_____ no information

14. Toilet training:

_____ completed uneventfully by second birthday
_____ completed by third birthday
_____ occasional soiling or wetting after third birthday
_____ no information

15. Behavior patterns in childhood:

	Your age at occurrence (e.g. 6-12)	Severity			
		mild	moderate	marked	No inform.
Thumbsucking					
Nailbiting					
Night terrors					
Convulsions					
Fears					
Stammering					
Tantrums					
Enuresis					
Food finickiness					
Sleepwalking					

16. Childhood happiness:

_____ extremely happy
_____ more happy than average
_____ about average
_____ rather unhappy
_____ extremely unhappy

17. Type of home during most of childhood:

_____ home with both true parents present
_____ home with one true parent and one step-parent
_____ home with only one true parent
_____ foster home

18. Cultural and intellectual status of your home during your childhood:

_____ excellent
_____ superior
_____ average
_____ below average
_____ poor

19. Economic status of home during your childhood (ages 5 - 15).

_____ wealthy
_____ well-to-do
_____ comfortable
_____ meager
_____ poor

20. Chief residence in childhood

_____ city
_____ suburban area
_____ small town
_____ farm

21. How many times did your family move to a new community before you were 15 years of age?

_____

224

22. Amount of time spent with parents in childhood (5 - 16):

_____ never played or worked with parents
_____ rarely played or worked with parents
_____ sometimes played or worked with parents
_____ often played or worked with parents
_____ very often played or worked with parents

23. Playmates in childhood (check one answer in each group):

_____ few
_____ average
_____ many

_____ mostly same sex as self
_____ mostly opposite sex

_____ mostly older
_____ mostly your age (within a year)
_____ mostly younger

24. Religious training:

_____ very strict
_____ strict
_____ considerable amount
_____ little
_____ none

25. Type of childhood discipline:

_____ exceedingly strict
_____ firm, but not harsh
_____ usually allowed to have my own way
_____ had my own way about everything
_____ inconsistent (sometimes strict, sometimes lax)

26. Amount of punishment:

_____ punished severely for every little thing
_____ punished frequently
_____ punished occasionally
_____ never punished

27. Your reactions to childhood punishments (check one or more):

_____ occasionally felt rebellious, imagined revenge
_____ occasionally felt sorry for self
_____ occasionally felt shame or self-reproach
_____ never felt any of these

28. Final authority in your discipline:

_____ always father
_____ usually father
_____ usually mother
_____ always mother

29. Leadership as a child:

    _____ never a leader
    _____ rarely a leader
    _____ sometimes a leader
    _____ often a leader

30. As a child:

    _____ I never had fantasies
    _____ I rarely had fantasies
    _____ I had fantasies occasionally
    _____ I had vivid fantasies
    _____ I had fantasies as vivid as real life

31. Guilt feelings in childhood:

    _____ never experienced them
    _____ rarely experienced them
    _____ occasionally experienced them
    _____ frequently experienced them

32. Inferiority feelings in childhood:

    _____ never experienced them
    _____ rarely experienced them
    _____ occasionally experienced them
    _____ frequently experienced them

33. Amount of friction between you and your father:

    _____ none
    _____ very little
    _____ little
    _____ moderate
    _____ a good deal

    Amount of friction between you and your mother:

    _____ none
    _____ very little
    _____ little
    _____ moderate
    _____ a good deal

34. Degree of attachment to father:

    _____ none
    _____ very little
    _____ little
    _____ moderate
    _____ a good deal

Degree of attachment to mother:

_____ none
_____ very little
_____ little
_____ moderate
_____ a good deal

35. I was a favorite of:

_____ my father
_____ my mother
_____ both my parents
_____ neither parent

36. School history (before college):   Type: (check one)

School	Location	Your Age	Rural	City	Public	Parochial	Private (boys only)
Elementary							
Elementary							
Jr. High							
Jr. High							
High							
High							

37. Did you receive any special promotions in school?

_____ yes
_____ no

38. Did you have an special difficulties in grade school with:

_____ reading
_____ spelling
_____ arithmetic
_____ none of the above

39. Check one or more in each of the four columns:

In High School			In College	

I had much difficulty with:		I did my best work in:	I had much difficulty with:		I did my best work in:
_____	English Composition	_____	_____	English Composition	_____
_____	English Literature	_____	_____	English Literature	_____
_____	Foreign Languages	_____	_____	Foreign Languages	_____
_____	Mathematics	_____	_____	Mathematics	_____
_____	Social Sciences	_____	_____	Social Sciences	_____
_____	Sciences	_____	_____	Physical Sciences	_____
			_____	Biological Sciences	_____

40. How did you feel about the marks which you received in high school?

_____ very well satisfied
_____ satisfied
_____ rather dissatisfied
_____ dissatisfied

How did your parents feel about the marks you made in high school?

_____ very well satisfied
_____ satisfied
_____ rather dissatisfied
_____ dissatisfied

41. In high school I (check one or more):

_____ held a class or school office or was on the student council
_____ played on a varsity or intramural team
_____ was in band, orchestra or glee club
_____ held an office in a club or society
_____ was on the debating team

_____ was in a school play
_____ was an editor on a school publication
_____ wrote for a school publication
_____ was in other extra-curricular activities
_____ was in no extra-curricular activities

42. I feel now that the quality of my social adjustment during the period immediately before entering college was generally:

_____ unusually good
_____ good
_____ fair
_____ poor
_____ very poor

43. I feel now that the quality of my emotional adjustment during the period immediately before entering college was generally:

_____ unusually good
_____ good
_____ fair
_____ poor
_____ very poor

44. In college I (check any that apply):

_____ held a class or college office or was on the student council
_____ played on a varsity or intramural team
_____ was in the band, orchestra, or glee club
_____ held an office in a club or society
_____ was on the debating team

_____ was in a college play
_____ was an editor on a college publication
_____ wrote for a college publication
_____ was in other extra-curricular activities
_____ was in no extra-curricular activities

45. Special academic honors in college (omit if none):

_____ Phi Beta Kappa
_____ Phi Kappa Phi
_____ Sigma Xi
_____ Graduation with distinction
_____ Scholarship for academic performance

46. How often did you cut classes in college:

_____ never without a very good reason
_____ once or twice a year
_____ once or twice a month
_____ once or twice a week

47. How often did you cheat in examinations in college:

_____ never
_____ once
_____ twice
_____ occasionally
_____ whenever you had a favorable opportunity

48. How was the last four years of your schooling before the war paid for:

_____ entirely by my own earnings
_____ largely by my own earnings
_____ in small part by my own earnings
_____ entirely by parents, relatives, etc. or by some source other than my own earnings

49. What was your first part-time job? _____ How did you get it? _____
_____ ; Age _____

50. Age when you first received fairly comprehensive sex information _____

51. Major sources of sex information (check one or more):

_____ Father   _____ Older friend
_____ Mother   _____ Friend your own age
_____ Brother   _____ Books
_____ Sister   _____ Physician

52. Reactions to masturbation:

_____ marked guilt feelings
_____ some guilt feelings
_____ little guilt feelings
_____ no guilt feelings at any time

53. Age at which you had your first date:

_____ before 13
_____ 13 - 14
_____ 15 - 16
_____ 17 - 18
_____ 19 or later

54. How many times have you been engaged to be married? _____

(Omit 55 - 61 if unmarried)

55. Wife: _____ Age; _____ Age at marriage to you

Education: School   7 8 9 10 11 12
(circle highest year)   College   1 2 3 4
                           Graduate 1 2 3 4

56. Attitude of your parents toward your marriage:

_____ encouraged me to marry
_____ indifferent to my marriage
_____ discouraged my marriage

57. Wife, before marriage to you:

_____ had been married
_____ had been married and widowed
_____ had been engaged to someone else
_____ had been neither married nor engaged to anyone else

58. Wife's occupation before marriage to you: _____
     Her approximate annual income at that time: _____

59. Occupation of your father-in-law: _____
     Approximate annual income of your father-in-law: _____

60. Religious preference of your wife: (denomination) _____

     Regularity of her church attendance:

_____ regular
_____ occasional
_____ rare or never

61. Who handles the budget in your family:
_____ self
_____ both of you
_____ spouse

62. Who is your favorite contemporary author? _____
     Who is your favorite poet? _____
     Who is your favorite author? _____
     Who is your favorite classical composer? _____
     Who is your favorite popular song-writer? _____

63. List your hobbies, if any: _____
     How many hours a week do you devote to them: _____

64. What are your three favorite forms of recreation or amusement (underline your first choice):

     _____

230

65. Number of organizational memberships:

_____ Fraternal. List: _____

_____ Professional. List: _____

_____ Political. List: _____

_____ Business and Civic. List: _____

_____ Social. List: _____

_____ Other. List: _____

66. Leadership in organization. Offices held:

Fraternal _____

Professional _____

Political _____

Business and Civic _____

Social _____

Other _____

67. Your religious preference: (denomination) _____

Regularity of your church attendance:

_____ regular

_____ occasional

_____ rare or never

68. During the past year, how many times did you attend:

Art exhibits:	_____	0 or 1;	_____	2-5;	_____ 5 or more
Athletic events:	_____	0 or 1;	_____	2-5;	_____ 5 or more
Classical concerts:	_____	0 or 1;	_____	2-5;	_____ 5 or more
Popular concerts:	_____	0 or 1;	_____	2-5;	_____ 5 or more
Lectures (other than professional)	_____	0 or 1;	_____	2-5;	_____ 5 or more

69. During weekdays, about how many hours a day do you devote to:

_____ hrs. working, studying

_____ hrs. sleeping

_____ hrs. recreation or amusement

_____ hrs. family activities

70. Using the following scale, indicate how well you perform the following activities (a. exceptionally well; b. well; c. fairly well; d. poorly; e. do not engage in the activity)

_____ playing a musical instrument

_____ contact sports (football, soccer, boxing, wrestling, etc.)

_____ marksmanship (rifle, pistol, archery, etc.)

_____ singing

_____ diving, ski-jumping, or horsemanship

_____ endurance sports (crew, long-distance running, etc.)

_____ tennis, squash, handball, ping-pong, or badminton

_____ dancing

71. I read at least one book a year in the field of: (check one or more)

_____ fiction (other than current)
_____ poetry
_____ plays
_____ biography
_____ none of these fields

72. What is the lowest annual income with which you would be content to support a wife and two children, for work which you enjoyed:

_____ $2,000   _____ $7,000
_____ $3,000   _____ $8,000
_____ $4,000   _____ $9,000
_____ $5,000   _____ $10,000 or above
_____ $6,000

73. Which of the following factors do you consider most important to a successful marriage to yourself.   (Check only one):

_____ similar educational backgrounds
_____ similar intellectual interests
_____ similar religious beliefs
_____ similar preferences for recreation
_____ similar cultural backgrounds
_____ similar attitudes toward sexual matters

74. How many children do you want:

_____ no. of boys
_____ no. of girls

75. I first decided to become a psychologist (check one) (See No. 76):

_____ before my sophomore year in college
_____ during my sophomore year
_____ during my junior year
_____ during my senior year
_____ after graduating from college

76. I first decided to become a clinical psychologist (check one or more) (See No. 75):

_____ at the time I decided to become a psychologist
_____ while I was in college
_____ while I was in graduate school
_____ while I was (specify) _____
_____ I have not finally decided to become a clinical psychologist

77. If I could omit one of the following courses in my training, my first choice for omission would be:

_____ statistics
_____ research methods
_____ history of psychological theory
_____ physiological psychology

78. Among the following fields of study, my <u>strongest</u> aptitude is in:

　_____ statistics
　_____ physiological psychology
　_____ history of psychological theory
　_____ foreign languages
　_____ experimental psychology

79. Among the following fields of study, my <u>weakest</u> aptitude is in:

　_____ statistics
　_____ physiological psychology
　_____ history of psychological theory
　_____ foreign languages
　_____ experimental psychology

80. When a full-time clinical psychologist, the proportion of time which I would prefer to devote to research in clinical psychology is:

　_____ 0-20%
　_____ 25%
　_____ 35%
　_____ 45%
　_____ 55% or more

81. When a full-time clinical psychologist, I should prefer to spend the largest part of my time doing (check one):

　_____ diagnostic interviewing
　_____ therapy
　_____ research on clinical problems
　_____ tests of intellectual functions
　_____ analysis of projective tests

82. Other things being equal, I would prefer to be a clinical psychologist in a (check one):

　_____ mental hygiene clinic (adults)
　_____ mental hygiene clinic (children)
　_____ psychiatric hospital
　_____ neuropsychiatric hospital
　_____ institution for mental defectives

83. When I finish training, my first preference would be to be allowed to make decisions:

　_____ alone and with sole responsibility
　_____ under the direction of a psychologist
　_____ under the direction of a psychiatrist
　_____ in consultation with other psychologists
　_____ in consultant with psychiatrists

84. I would prefer that the proportion of women among my professional colleagues be (check one):

　_____ 0%
　_____ 20%
　_____ 30%
　_____ 40%
　_____ 50% or more

85. If I were to do counselling, I should prefer to work with cases involving (check one):

     _____ vocational problems
     _____ educational problems
     _____ marital problems
     _____ juvenile delinquency

86. Other things being equal, I would prefer to avoid working with neuropsychiatric cases who were also (check one or more):

     _____ amputees
     _____ bed-ridden cases
     _____ mentally borderline
     _____ syphilitics
     _____ tubercular patients

87. If I could choose my superior, I would (check one):

     _____ always choose a man
     _____ definitely prefer a man
     _____ have a slight preference for a man
     _____ have a slight preference for a woman
     _____ definitely prefer a woman
     _____ always choose a woman

88. I would prefer that the proportion of women among my patients be (check one):

     _____ 0-10%
     _____ 25%
     _____ 35%
     _____ 45%
     _____ 55% or more

89. I prefer to have an assignment where the basic duties are (check one):

     _____ left up to me
     _____ sketched out roughly for me
     _____ fairly fully stated to me
     _____ very fully stated to me

90. If I find I cannot meet a deadline set by my superior, I am likely to (check one):

     _____ work at my usual pace and forget the deadline
     _____ tell him I cannot meet it
     _____ ask him if the deadline is necessary
     _____ work as fast as I can, but not be concerned if I cannot meet it.
     _____ work as fast as I can, but worry and/or become greatly upset

91. When somebody sets a deadline for me, I usually feel it is (check one):

     _____ unnecessary
     _____ a necessary nuisance
     _____ a guard against procrastination
     _____ a challenge

234

92. Among the following fields, the one which has made the greatest contribution to our knowledge of human nature is:

_____ anthropology
_____ biology
_____ education
_____ literature
_____ sociology

93. Among the following fields, the one which has made the least contribution to our knowledge of human nature is:

_____ anthropology
_____ biology
_____ education
_____ literature
_____ sociology

94. The best understanding of human nature is found among:

_____ teachers
_____ ministers and priests
_____ lawyers
_____ authors
_____ advertising men or salesmen

95. At the age of 50 I would prefer to be (check first choice only):

_____ the editor of one or more psychological journals
_____ an officer of the American Psychological Association
_____ the inventor of an important personality test (e.g., Projective)
_____ the author of a psychological theory
_____ a leader in one field of psychology

96. At the age of 50 I would prefer most to be (check one):

_____ chairman of a psychology department
_____ professor in a large university
_____ professor in a small college
_____ director of a major research institute
_____ research investigator with an ample 10-year grant

97. Handedness:

In Childhood

_____ left handed
_____ ambidextrous
_____ right handed

Now

_____ left handed
_____ ambidextrous
_____ right handed

98. I have had:

_____ asthma or hayfever
_____ allergies
_____ fits or convulsions
_____ stomach ulcers

_____ hemorrhoids
_____ marked weight fluctuations
_____ nervous breakdown

99. Have you ever had any speech difficulty:

_____ yes
_____ no
Specify _____

100. I have had headaches with nausea or vomitting:

_____ never
_____ once in several months or rarely
_____ two or three times a month
_____ four or more times a month

101. I have almost fainted (I did not pass out but felt like it):

_____ never
_____ once in my life
_____ two or three times
_____ four or more times

102. I have been unconscious but not in a faint, through a blow to the head or any other reason:

_____ never
_____ once in my life
_____ two or three times
_____ four or more times

103. My sleep may be described as:

_____ very deep
_____ deep
_____ light
_____ very light

104. My eating habits:

_____ I can eat almost anything
_____ 1 or 2 things do not agree
_____ I have to be careful about a number of foods
_____ there are many things I cannot eat

105. I take a bicarbonate of soda or an alkali or some other medicine for a stomach ailment:

_____ never
_____ once in one or several months
_____ once in one or several weeks
_____ every day or two

106. My emotional state may be described as:

_____ steady
_____ somewhat moody
_____ ups and downs
_____ usually up or usually down

107. I get so discouraged that it interferes with my work:

     _____ never
     _____ once or twice a year
     _____ once in one or several months
     _____ once in one or several weeks

108. In relation to people I meet for the first time, I am:

     _____ friendly
     _____ shy until I get to know them
     _____ rather withdrawn
     _____ on guard

109. Of the people I do know, I have:

     _____ many friends, intimate and otherwise
     _____ many friends, a few intimates
     _____ some or many friends, few intimates
     _____ one or two intimates, no others

110. I have gone to a doctor:

     _____ never
     _____ only when very ill
     _____ once or twice a year
     _____ three or more times a year

111. I have gone to a doctor for "nervousness," nervous symptom, personality difficulty, or personal problem:

     _____ never
     _____ once or twice
     _____ three times
     _____ more than three times

112. My associates consider me:

     _____ unduly attentive to details
     _____ very careful about details
     _____ a little careless about details
     _____ very careless about details

113. In the face of sudden physical danger I am:

     _____ generally calm and well controlled
     _____ anxious though well controlled
     _____ frightened and poorly controlled
     _____ panicky

114. In regard to social activity and solitude:

     _____ I can't stand being alone
     _____ I prefer social activity but like to be alone sometimes
     _____ it's about fifty-fifty
     _____ I often prefer to be alone

115. I smoke:

_____ a great deal or excessively
_____ fairly often
_____ only occasionally
_____ almost never or never

116. In social situations I drink:

_____ a very great deal
_____ a considerable amount
_____ some
_____ a little
_____ almost nothing or nothing

117. I have drunk so much that I regretted it the next day:

_____ never
_____ once or twice
_____ many times
_____ more often than I like to recall

118. I find that expressing my emotions is:

_____ almost always difficult
_____ usually difficult
_____ sometimes difficult
_____ rarely difficult
_____ never difficult

119. I find that controlling my emotions is:

_____ almost impossible
_____ exceedingly difficult
_____ rather difficult
_____ rather easy
_____ very easy

120. I express my emotions:

_____ habitually
_____ often
_____ rarely
_____ never

121. During adoleseence, my overall social experience was:

_____ very extensive; I had a great many friends
_____ fairly extensive; I had quite a few friends
_____ somewhat limited; I had only a few friends
_____ limited to one or no close friends

122. During the adolescent period, I found my parent (s):

_____ extremely understanding, tolerant and permissive
_____ fairly understanding
_____ somewhat lacking in understanding and permissiveness
_____ completely or almost completely lacking in understanding and permissiveness

123. During adoleseence, I was inclined to be:

_____ extremely "bookish" and/or intellectual
_____ fairly "bookish" and/or intellectual
_____ only moderately "bookish" and/or intellectual
_____ rarely "bookish" and/or intellectual

124. My relations with the opposite sex during adolescence were:

_____ extensive and very easy and pleasant
_____ extensive but somewhat difficult and trying
_____ somewhat limited, but easy and pleasant
_____ somewhat limited, but difficult and trying
_____ very limited and very difficult and/or trying

125. During adolescence, I found the process of "weaning" myself from my parents:

_____ a very difficult and persistent problem
_____ a moderately difficult problem
_____ a moderately easy task
_____ a very simple aspect of my growth and development

126. My total sexual experience during adolescence was:

_____ negligible or almost entirely absent
_____ moderately extensive but limited to social relationships and petting
_____ moderately extensive but not limited to social relationships and petting
_____ very extensive and very varied.

127. During adoleseence, my participation in athletics consisted of:

_____ extensive individual and group experience
_____ extensive individual, but limited group experience
_____ extensive group, but limited individual experience
_____ moderate individual and group experience
_____ moderate individual, but extensive group experience
_____ moderate group, but extensive individual experience
_____ limited group and individual experience
_____ limited individual, but some group experience
_____ limited group, but some individual experience

128. During adolescence, I was chosen a leader of the group (discussion, athletic, or social):

_____ most of the time
_____ fairly often
_____ only occasionally
_____ seldom or never

129. I was a member of a well knit gang, club or group during adolescence:

_____ all or most of the period
_____ a good part of the period
_____ only a short part of the period
_____ during no part of the period

130. My parents felt that during my adolescence:

_____ I was extremely difficult to understand or manage
_____ I was fairly difficult to understand or manage
_____ I was only moderately difficult to understand or manage
_____ I was not any problem at all.

131. Attitude toward filling out this inventory:

_____ I enjoyed it
_____ I found it mildly interesting
_____ I found it rather dull or boring or distasteful
_____ I disliked it or hated it very much

APPENDIX I-F

FORM FOR AUTOBIOGRAPHY

Directions. Please glance over this outline to get a general idea of what is required; and then, without consulting it, write your life-history in chronological order. When you have finished writing, go over this outline carefully, and add, as a supplement, whatever information you omitted in your original account. You have the rest of the day for this autobiography. It is not necessary to repeat any material given in the Biographical Inventory you have just completed.

A. Family History

1. Parents
    a. Economic and social status, offices, abilities, interests, sentiments, dominant traits and state of health of each parent.
        Position of your family in the community. Were they rejected, disregarded, accepted, popular, highly respected? Rise or fall of family status in recent years. Marked successes or failures of mother or father.
    b. Father-mother relationship. Was it marked by mutual trust and affection, harmony, discord, constant quarreling, separation, divorce?
    c. Parent-self relationships, general attitude of each parent. Was he (or she) affectionate, devoted, companionable, generous, oversolicitous, nagging, demanding, anxious, possessive, stern, domineering, hateful, indifferent?
        Your attitude to each parent; was it affectionate, dependent, submissive, respectful, obliging, cooperative, independent, rebellious, hostile, distrustful? Attitude of your parents to you. Which parent is your favorite? Which has most disappointed you? Which do you most respect?
    d. Parental standards and disciplines. What virtues and vices were specially stressed at home by example or teaching? How, by whom and for what were you punished? What were your reactions to punishment? (resentment, vengeance, flight, deceit, mortification, acquiescence, submission, self-pity?)
        Moral and religious instruction.

2. Siblings
    a. Dominant traits, sentiments, interests, and abilities of each sibling.
    b. Sibling-self relationships: attachments, quarrels, rivalry, conflicts.
        To which siblings did you feel superior or inferior, and in what respects?
        Attitudes of your parents to your siblings.

3. Larger Family Circle
    Characterize briefly grandparents, relatives, or nurses who affected or influenced you.

B. Physical Environment, Neighborhoods, Homes

1. Places of Residence
    a. Give some account of where you have lived; the physical surroundings that have impressed you; the characteristics of the community.
    b. Homes: rooming and sleeping arrangements, comfort, and taste of furnishings.
        Did you have a feeling of permanence in your environment?
        How did you react to each change of place?

2. Places Visited

      Give some account of places visited, trips taken, travels.

C. Personal History

1. Childhood
   a. Feeding: Age of weaning. Was there any difficulty in feeding you? Did you cry a great deal? Were you finnicky about food then or later? Did you enjoy certain foods particularly, eat between meals, steal food out of kitchen?
   b. Preliminary learning. Were you precocious or retarded in learning to walk and talk? Were you confident on your feet, in running, jumping, climbing? Did you remain close to your parents, or stray away, adventuring into the unknown? Did you experience any serious falls?
          Describe your first memory.
   c. Toilet training. Was your mother (or nurse) particular about your having a daily bowel movement? Were you difficult to train? Did you suffer from diarrhea or constipation? Did you soil the bed or your clothes? Did you play with your faeces or use them for smearing?
   d. Common habits: duration of thumb-sucking, nail-biting, bed-wetting. Did you stammer?
   e. Temper. Did you have tantrums or explosive rages? Did you ever destroy your toys, torture animals or cruelly attack another child?
   f. Fears and Nightmares. What were you afraid of as a child? (darkness, heights, fires, solitariness, closed or open spaces, insects, animals, burglars, kidnappers, demons, ghosts, God's wrath?) Did you have many nightmares? Did you walk in your sleep?
   g. Illnesses and Accidents. Did you suffer from any long, severe or unusual illnesses? convulsions? accidents? operations? What were your reactions to your illnesses and accidents? How did your parents react?
   h. Fantasies and Dreams. Did you imagine yourself a hero (or heroine), or identify yourself with some story-book character? Recall some of your fantasies and dreams. What were your favorite books?
   i. Play: favorite pastimes and games in childhood. Did you play with dolls, mechanical toys, soldiers, animals? Did you like to build retreats and hiding places? Did you have all the companions you desired? Were you accepted by the other children? Were you a bully, or were you bullied by others? Did you spend some time each summer in the country, on a farm, in the mountains or by the sea?
   j. General Attitude. Was your general attitude adaptive (cooperative and obliging), aggressive (competitive and assertive), refractory (negative and resistant), timid (sensitive and fearful), or guileful (teasing and wily)? Were you self-confident at home? among your companions?

2. School History
   a. Describe briefly the course of your intellectual interests and abilities.
   b. Influential teachers. Characterize the teachers, if any, who have influenced you.
   c. Social relationships. Were you rejected, ignored, accepted, popular, ridiculed, bullied, respected, elected to office? Characterize some of your best friends. Were your friendships casual or deep, temporary or enduring? Did you have many quarrels? Did you have periods of moodiness and solitariness?
   d. Membership in groups. What cliques, organizations, or clubs did you belong to? Did you engage in public speaking? What interests did you share with others? Were you a leader?

    e. Athletic record. What games did you play? Did you excel at any sports, make any teams?

    f. Miscellaneous interests and amusements. How did you spend your spare time? Did you have any hobbies? Did you collect anything?

    g. Ambitions and ideals, hero-worship. What did you most want to be in later life? Was there any particular person (historical or contemporary) whom you accepted as a model to emulate? What qualities in others did you particularly admire?

    h. General attitude in school. How would you characterize your customary attitude? (genial, confident, shy, submissive, fearful, timid, forward, assertive, boisterous, show-off, aloof, indifferent, defensive?)

3. Sex History

    a. Sex knowledge. (1) Curiosity about body of other sex, about where children come from, about sexual relations. Did you ask many questions? Did you conduct investigations? play post-office, etc.? Did you exhibit yourself before others? What theories did you hold about childbirth? What information was given you, at what age, and by whom? (2) Sexual relations of parents. Did you ever overhear or oversee sexual intercourse between your parents? Were you shocked or disillusioned when you were told of it?

    b. Sexual practices. (1) Masturbation. When did you begin to masturbate? Who taught you? How frequent has it been? How much guilt have you felt about it? (2) Homosexual. Have you ever indulged in mutual masturbation or any other form of sexual activity with one of your own sex? Are you sexually excited by members of your own sex? Do you feel guilty about it? (3) Heterosexual. Did you play sex games as a child? Have you ever been in love? how often? What type of person is selected? Do you quarrel? Do you do much dating, petting, necking? Have you had sexual intercourse? How much guilt has been associated with sex? (4) Erotic fantasies. Give some account of your sexual fantasies. What kind of preliminary activity is specially pleasurable in your imagination? What kind of partner appears most exciting in fantasy? (5) Emotions. In connection with sexuality which of these feelings have you experienced most acutely: excitement, embarrassment, anxiety, affection, devotion, worshipful love, disgust, shame, remorse, loss of self-respect, What is your attitude toward marriage?

4. Work History

    How have you liked each of your jobs?

D. Present Sentiments, Aspirations and Ideals

1. Sentiments

    a. Positive. What things, people, professions, groups, institutions do you esteem most highly at the present time? What human achievements, what historical characters do you admire most? What guiding principles, or philosophy, do you accept as worth following?

    b. Negative. What things, people, professions, groups, institutions do you dislike most? Name some of your pet aversions and annoyances. Mention some of the all-too-human traits of others that go against your grain.

2. Aims

    a. Immediate. What are your chief aims for the immediate future?

    b. Distant. What, would you guess, will be your main sources of satisfaction in later life? What do you hope to accomplish? What is the limit of your ambition? What ideals, would you say, are worth striving for?

E. Estimate of Self and World

State briefly what you believe to be:

a. Your general estimate of and attitude toward the social world.
b. The world's estimate of and attitude toward you.
c. Your general estimate of yourself.

F. Expectations

Which of these harms and benefits coming from your fellowmen do you chiefly antici-pate: competition, envy, hostility, injustice, meanness, malicious criticism, goodwill, generosity, a helping-hand, sympathy, companionship, love, disloyalty, trickery, hyp-ocrisy, ridicule, slander, abuse, exclusiveness, depreciation, discrimination, recogni-tion, honor, praise, respect, neglect, indifference.

How much money do you expect to be making in ten years? To what extent will your happiness depend on the size of your income?

If you could (within reason) remodel the world to your heart's desire how would you have it and what role would you like to play in such a world?

APPENDIX II-A

VA Research Project on Selection of Clinical Psychologists

CRITERION RATING SCALE

Each of the following pages is a rating scale of the type described in the Instruction Sheet. The definition of the variable to be evaluated appears at the top of each page.

You are asked to complete each page, i. e. , arrange the identification numbers of all trainees in the column before continuing. This request is made in the hope of reducing halo to a reasonable minimum.

It is suggested that you check each page by counting the number of identification numbers in the column.

DIAGNOSTIC COMPETENCE

Diagnostic competence is defined as the ability to recognize dynamics underlying particular responses in all diagnostic tests; observe significant interrelationships among responses; relate findings to case history and other clinical data, elicit from the patient information required for mental status examinations and case histories; ascertain and evaluate attitudes and incidents of psychological significance in the patient.

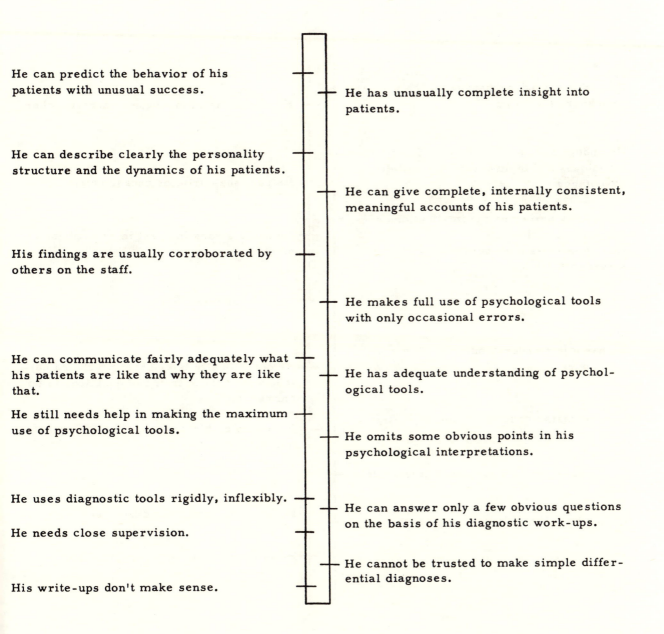

He can predict the behavior of his patients with unusual success.

He has unusually complete insight into patients.

He can describe clearly the personality structure and the dynamics of his patients.

He can give complete, internally consistent, meaningful accounts of his patients.

His findings are usually corroborated by others on the staff.

He makes full use of psychological tools with only occasional errors.

He can communicate fairly adequately what his patients are like and why they are like that.

He has adequate understanding of psychological tools.

He still needs help in making the maximum use of psychological tools.

He omits some obvious points in his psychological interpretations.

He uses diagnostic tools rigidly, inflexibly.

He can answer only a few obvious questions on the basis of his diagnostic work-ups.

He needs close supervision.

He cannot be trusted to make simple differential diagnoses.

His write-ups don't make sense.

RESEARCH COMPETENCE

Research is defined as the ability to recognize and define important research problems in clinical psychology; critically evaluate and apply the research findings of others; think with originality and scientific rigor; employ appropriate experimental design and statistical methods; grasp practical implications of findings; present results and conclusions in clear, comprehensive and well-organized form.

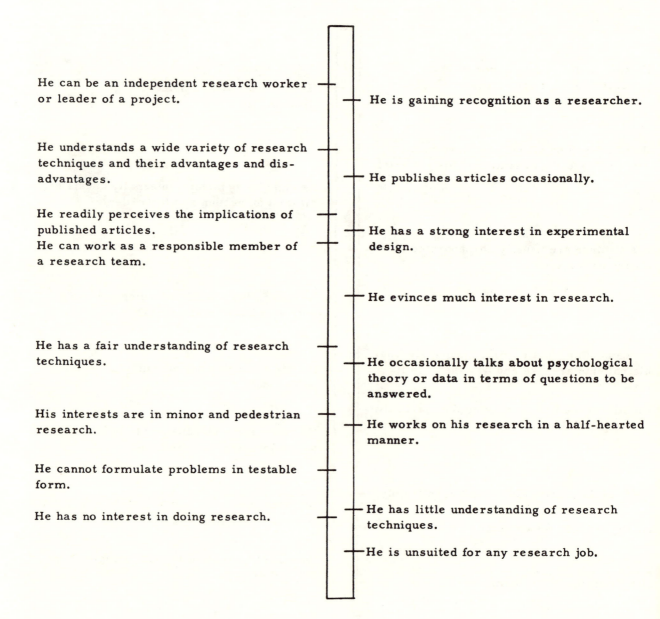

He can be an independent research worker or leader of a project.

He is gaining recognition as a researcher.

He understands a wide variety of research techniques and their advantages and dis-advantages.

He publishes articles occasionally.

He readily perceives the implications of published articles.
He can work as a responsible member of a research team.

He has a strong interest in experimental design.

He evinces much interest in research.

He has a fair understanding of research techniques.

He occasionally talks about psychological theory or data in terms of questions to be answered.

His interests are in minor and pedestrian research.

He works on his research in a half-hearted manner.

He cannot formulate problems in testable form.

He has no interest in doing research.

He has little understanding of research techniques.

He is unsuited for any research job.

INDIVIDUAL PSYCHOTHERAPY

Individual psychotherapy is used here in its broadest sense to include anything that is called psychotherapy at your institution.

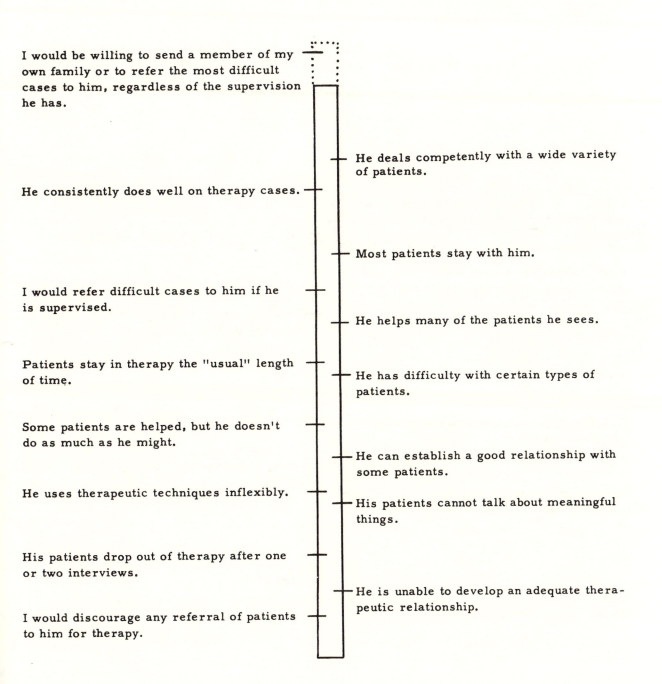

I would be willing to send a member of my own family or to refer the most difficult cases to him, regardless of the supervision he has.

He deals competently with a wide variety of patients.

He consistently does well on therapy cases.

Most patients stay with him.

I would refer difficult cases to him if he is supervised.

He helps many of the patients he sees.

Patients stay in therapy the "usual" length of time.

He has difficulty with certain types of patients.

Some patients are helped, but he doesn't do as much as he might.

He can establish a good relationship with some patients.

He uses therapeutic techniques inflexibly.

His patients cannot talk about meaningful things.

His patients drop out of therapy after one or two interviews.

He is unable to develop an adequate therapeutic relationship.

I would discourage any referral of patients to him for therapy.

GROUP PSYCHOTHERAPY

The term group psychotherapy is used here in its broadest sense to include anything that is called group psychotherapy at your institution.

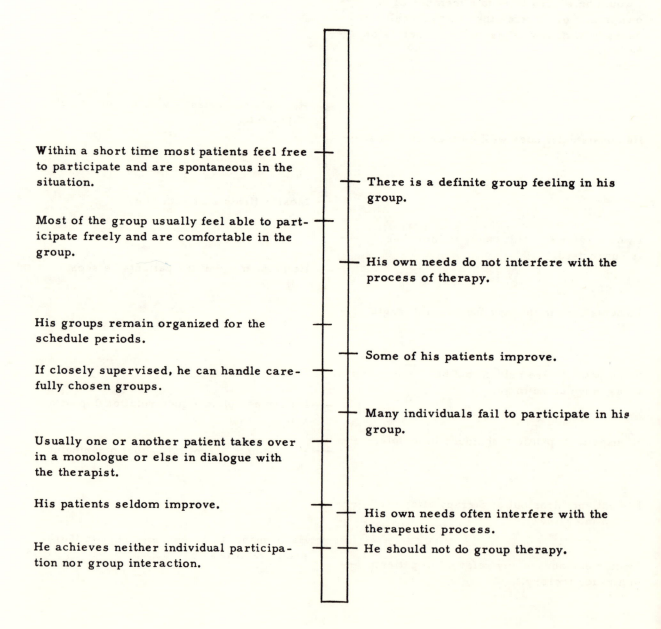

Within a short time most patients feel free to participate and are spontaneous in the situation.

There is a definite group feeling in his group.

Most of the group usually feel able to participate freely and are comfortable in the group.

His own needs do not interfere with the process of therapy.

His groups remain organized for the schedule periods.

Some of his patients improve.

If closely supervised, he can handle carefully chosen groups.

Many individuals fail to participate in his group.

Usually one or another patient takes over in a monologue or else in dialogue with the therapist.

His patients seldom improve.

His own needs often interfere with the therapeutic process.

He achieves neither individual participation nor group interaction.

He should not do group therapy.

INTEGRITY OF PERSONAL AND PROFESSIONAL BEHAVIOR

Integrity is defined as the capacity to recognize and fulfill professional responsibilities; live up to personal commitments; show loyalty to professional obligations in the event of outside pressure of promise of personal gain; maintain discretion concerning professional matters; appropriately conform with commonly accepted standards of moral and social behavior; refrain from coloring facts, evasion, lying, etc.

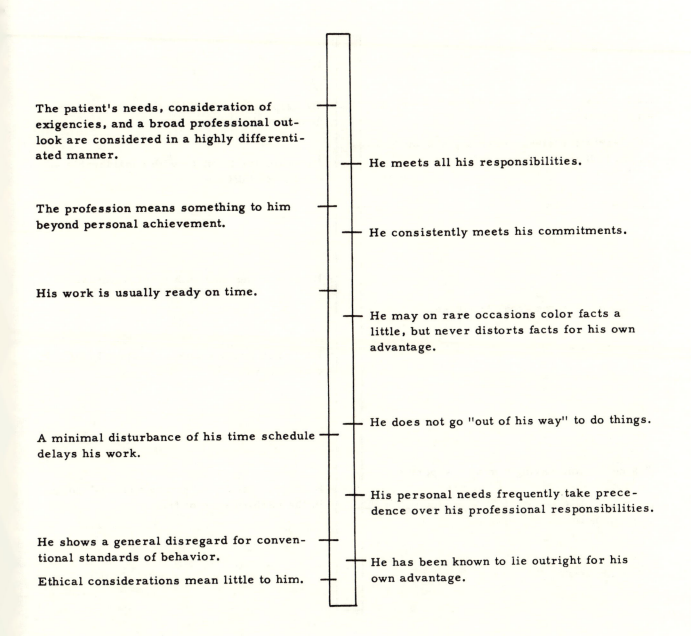

The patient's needs, consideration of exigencies, and a broad professional outlook are considered in a highly differentiated manner.

He meets all his responsibilities.

The profession means something to him beyond personal achievement.

He consistently meets his commitments.

His work is usually ready on time.

He may on rare occasions color facts a little, but never distorts facts for his own advantage.

He does not go "out of his way" to do things.

A minimal disturbance of his time schedule delays his work.

His personal needs frequently take precedence over his professional responsibilities.

He shows a general disregard for conventional standards of behavior.

He has been known to lie outright for his own advantage.

Ethical considerations mean little to him.

SUPERVISING CLINICAL PSYCHOLOGISTS

Supervising is defined as the capacity to carry out the professional supervision of subordinates assigned to him for duty and on-the-job instruction; assign their duties; evaluate their performance; instruct them in clinical techniques; perform other aspects of in-service training.

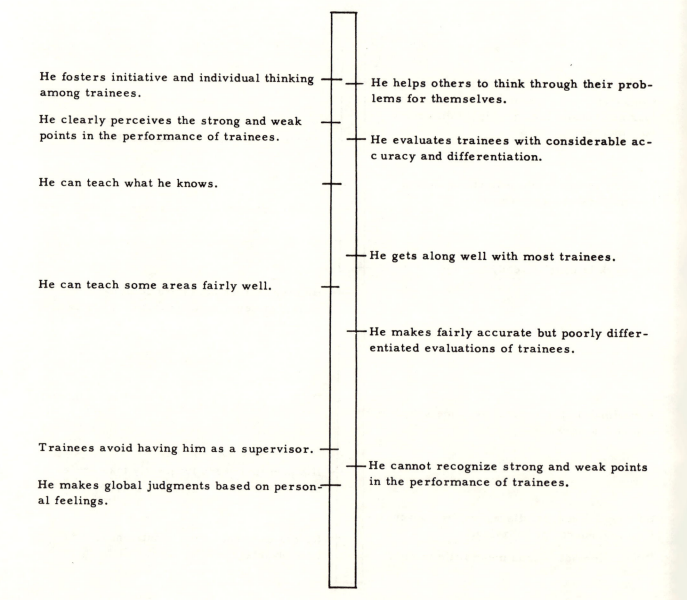

He fosters initiative and individual thinking among trainees.

He helps others to think through their problems for themselves.

He clearly perceives the strong and weak points in the performance of trainees.

He evaluates trainees with considerable accuracy and differentiation.

He can teach what he knows.

He gets along well with most trainees.

He can teach some areas fairly well.

He makes fairly accurate but poorly differentiated evaluations of trainees.

Trainees avoid having him as a supervisor.

He cannot recognize strong and weak points in the performance of trainees.

He makes global judgments based on personal feelings.

PROFESSIONAL INTERPERSONAL RELATIONS

Professional interpersonal relations are defined as the ability to work cooperatively with superiors, subordinates, members of the mental hygiene team, and other professional personnel concerned with the patient's welfare; participate in the give and take of staff conferences; contribute to group decisions.

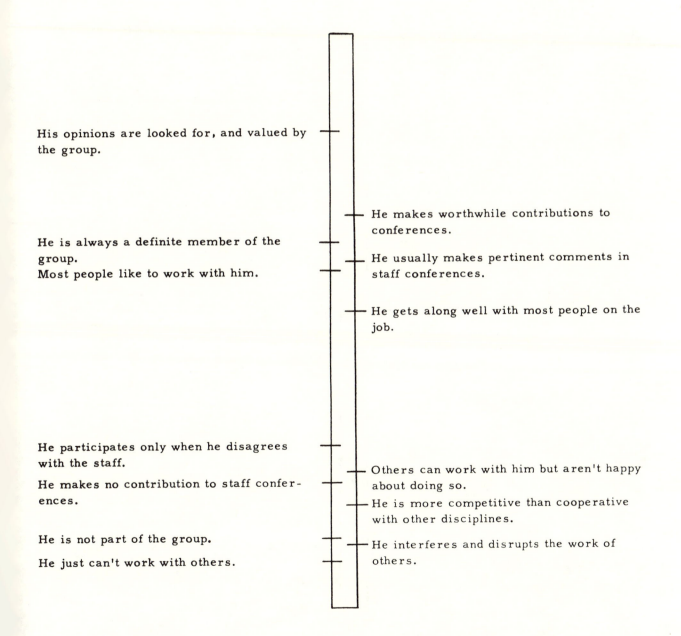

His opinions are looked for, and valued by the group.

He makes worthwhile contributions to conferences.

He is always a definite member of the group.
Most people like to work with him.

He usually makes pertinent comments in staff conferences.

He gets along well with most people on the job.

He participates only when he disagrees with the staff.

Others can work with him but aren't happy about doing so.

He makes no contribution to staff conferences.

He is more competitive than cooperative with other disciplines.

He is not part of the group.

He interferes and disrupts the work of others.

He just can't work with others.

252

OVERALL CLINICAL COMPETENCE

On the previous scales you have been asked to evaluate trainees on each of several dimensions of clinical competence. This permitted you to rate a trainee relatively high on one dimension and low on another. On the scale below we should like you to arrange the trainees in order of what you regard as their overall competence in clinical psychology. Here you may "weight" each aspect of clinical competence as you believe it should be weighted. However, try to avoid including your "liking for him as a person" in this judgment.

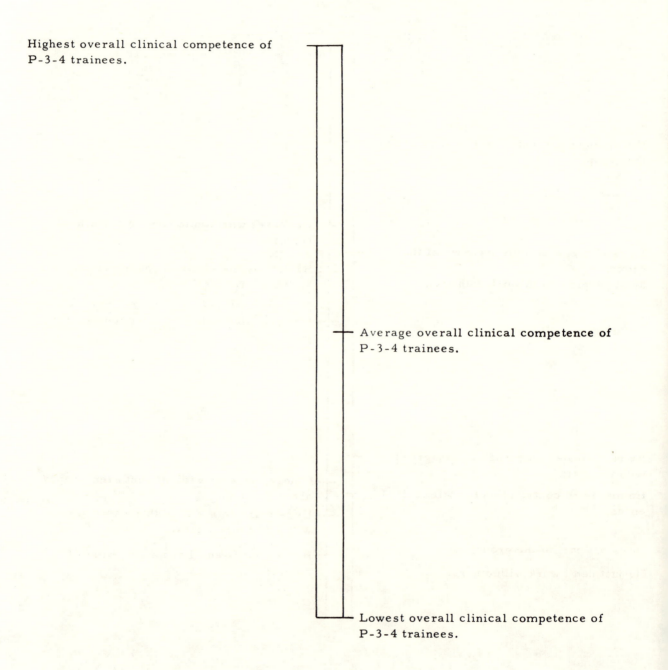

Highest overall clinical competence of P-3-4 trainees.

Average overall clinical competence of P-3-4 trainees.

Lowest overall clinical competence of P-3-4 trainees.

PREFERENCE FOR HIRING

Put yourself in the role of the chief psychologist in a VA hospital or clinic. Indicate your preference for hiring as psychologists in your installation each person whose name appears on your Instruction Sheet. In making this evaluation you will probably want to consider all of the factors involved in judging overall clinical competence, but you may wish to weight them differently. You may also wish to allow your personal liking for the trainee to influence your judgment.

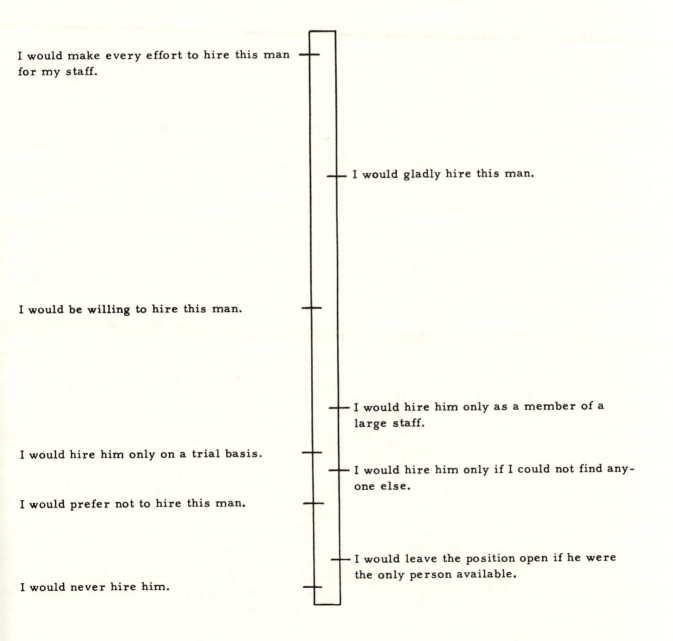

I would make every effort to hire this man for my staff.

I would gladly hire this man.

I would be willing to hire this man.

I would hire him only as a member of a large staff.

I would hire him only on a trial basis.

I would hire him only if I could not find anyone else.

I would prefer not to hire this man.

I would leave the position open if he were the only person available.

I would never hire him.

LIKING

Finally, we should like you to evaluate the trainees simply in terms of your personal liking for each as a human being. Evidence collected at the time of assessment suggests that this may be a very important variable in professional success.

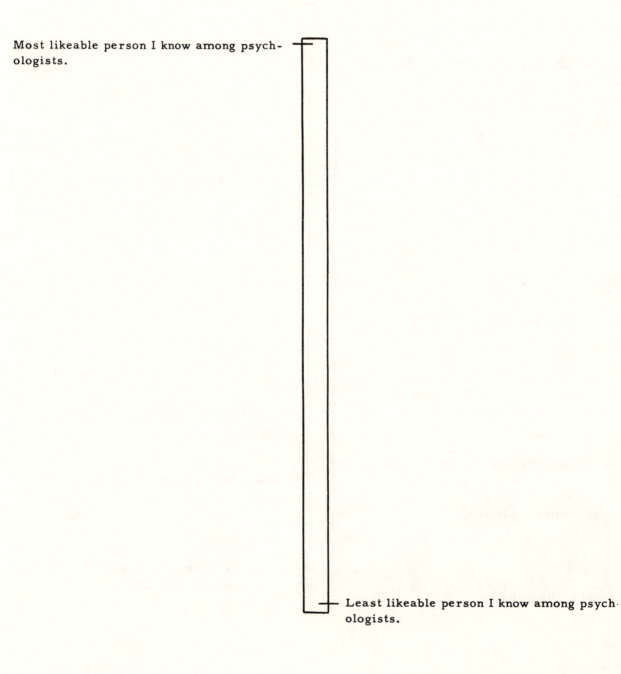

Most likeable person I know among psychologists.

Least likeable person I know among psychologists.

OVERALL ACADEMIC PERFORMANCE

Effectively master course content, successfully complete courses in general psychology, clinical psychology, statistics, and related fields; satisfy language requirements for the doctorate; pass general examinations.

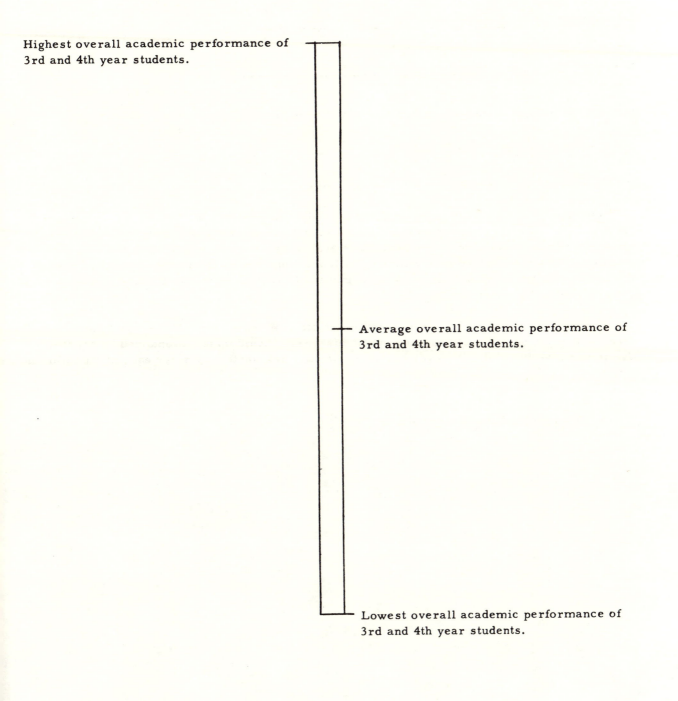

Highest overall academic performance of 3rd and 4th year students.

Average overall academic performance of 3rd and 4th year students.

Lowest overall academic performance of 3rd and 4th year students.

APPENDIX II-B 1

Qualitative Description of VA Trainee's Performance

Trainee: _____

Installation: _____

Evaluated by: _____

Indicate the periods during which you have supervised him:

(a) Diagnosis: from _____ , 19 ___ to _____ , 19 ___

(b) Therapy: from _____ , 19 ___ to _____ , 19 ___

Until now, the VA Selection Project has depended upon ratings of trainees as a principal criterion. In order to examine the predictable aspects of unquantified characteristics of graduate performance, we need to obtain qualitative evaluations for a selected group of assessed trainees. We are therefore asking field installation supervisors to provide qualitative evaluations of competence in clinical skills and a university representative to provide a similar evaluation of research competence.

Describe the above person as he functions in the clinical setting. Write about only those areas where you have direct knowledge about his work. Avoid material obtained by hearsay. Use illustrative incidents wherever possible. Write a few sentences under each of the following topics:

A. Your general impression of him.

B. His relationships with others in the group and with persons in allied professions.

C. His relationships with patients, his adeptness in dealing with them, or with special groups of them, his ability to diagnose and/or treat them.

D. His strong points and limitations in clinical work.

E. Mention any other job functions at your installation about which you can give information--
e. g. , administration, supervision, interprofessional relations, teaching, research, etc.

APPENDIX II-B 2

Qualitative Description of VA Trainee's Research Performance

Trainee's name: _____

University: _____

Evaluated by: _____

Basis for evaluation: Evaluator: is trainee's dissertation sponsor: _____
                                 is on trainee's dissertation committee: _____
                                 has taught trainee: _____

    Until now, the VA Selection Project has depended upon ratings of trainees as a principal criterion. In order to examine the predictable aspects of unquantified characteristics of graduate performance, we need to obtain qualitative evaluations for a selected group of assessed trainees. We are therefore asking field installation supervisors to provide qualitative evaluations of competence in clinical skills and a university representative to provide a similar evaluation of research competence.

    Describe the above person as a research worker by writing a few sentences under each of the topics listed below (A-E). Indicate those areas where you have direct knowledge about his work, and those areas where you have only secondhand evidence. Use illustrative incidents wherever possible.

A. The amount of research he has done, including work as an assistant to other research workers, research done for thesis or dissertation, research done for courses, and any other research, such as that which he initiated spontaneously.

B. The quality of his research: his originality, creativity, and skill in finding problems, form- ulating problems and hypotheses, designing experiments, devising methods and techniques, interpreting his research findings.

C. The degree of his technical competence: his skill in collecting and analyzing data and in drawing appropriate conclusions.

D. The help he required on the research he has done: help in finding problems, choosing methods, analyzing data, interpreting findings.

E. The assistance he has given to fellow students in their research work.

APPENDIX II-C

Qualitative Description by Supervisors of Case 38

I. Installation Supervisor

A. Your general impression of him.

He makes what might almost be called a distinguished appearance, and the first impression is that he is exceptionally polite, cooperative, controlled and poised. Later it is noted that his fingernails are pretty badly bitten and that he actually feels anxious in the clinical situation. With some trainees you know a good deal about their personal life in a short time, but not so with Mr. S. He does not feel comfortable in close personal contacts with most colleagues and patients, though he is capable of more intense relationships in certain cases. It is probably significant that he has spent much of his energy on group psychotherapy and avoided individual psychotherapy as much as possible. He feels more comfortable in the less intense relationships of the group. In spite of his tension he is able to perform at an acceptable level and to carry his share of the load, though he has never been known to volunteer for an extra assignment.

B. His relationships with others.

With colleagues he is definitely a member of the group, though rarely assumes any position of leadership except in connection with psychodramatic group therapy. His contacts with those in allied professions are at a minimum and their reaction, when they have one, is usually favorable because his manner is invariably pleasant and cooperative.

C. His relationships with patients.

His relationships with patients as with all others are pleasant, though with a tendency for them not to become very intense. In very brief individual psychotherapy and with group psychotherapy he does well. In the diagnostic situation he does an adequate job.

D. His strong points and limitations in clinical work.

His principal assets are good basic ability, considerable insight into personality dynamics, and the ability to maintain a pleasant, non-aggressive exterior even under trying circumstances. His greatest liability is his feeling of inadequacy in the intense relationships of individual psychotherapy. Another liability is an aspiration level that isn't too high.

E. Other job functions.

He is not research minded and has a good deal of difficulty formulating a research problem and getting started on it.

II. University Supervisor

A. Amount of research.

Has done none at all.

B. Quality of his research.

He comes in for a conference on some vague research plan about once a year, some suggestions and preliminary steps are arrived at, and nothing more is heard of it.

C. The degree of technical competence.

He has never carried out any research to the point where one could say anything about this.

D. The help he required on research he has done.

Even what conferences he has had about research have been largely matters of suggestions, proposals, and so on from others. So far it has ended there.

E. The assistance he has given to fellow students.

None at all I should imagine.

APPENDIX II-D

TRAINING EXPERIENCE INVENTORY

University: _____   Name: _____

Present VA Installation: _____   P-level at entry to program: _____

                                            Present P-level: _____

   We feel that because of the wide differences in the kinds of training experiences to which VA clinical students have been exposed, it is important to know something about these differences.

   Since these data, like all others on the project, are regarded as confidential, you are asked to return the completed forms to your VA Chief in a sealed envelope. However, this procedure places on you the full responsibility for checking to make sure you have answered all questions and included all materials requested.

   We are primarily interested in what has happened to you since you were assessed. However, we need a brief summary of your experience prior to your entrance into the VA training program; use the space below to indicate briefly courses studied and the nature and amount of experience you have had with various clinical techniques and with various kinds of patients.

   Please fill in all the blanks listing only experience since entering the VA training program.

A. Diagnosis

   1. Classroom instruction

	no. of semester hrs: (quarter hrs. = 2/3 semester hours)	rated quality of instruction A - excellent; B - good; C - adequate; D - inadequate (circle one)
Objective tests	_____	A B C D
Projective tests	_____	A B C D
Other (e.g. sociometrics, psychodrama, etc.) Specify:		
_____	_____	A B C D
_____	_____	A B C D

2. Testing experience

	estimated total number given	estimated number interpreted	estimated no. interpreted under super-vision*	rated quality of supervision A-excellent; B-good; C-adequate; D-inadequate (circle one)
Bender-Gestalt	_____	_____	_____	A B C D
Diagnostic Inter-viewing	_____	_____	_____	A B C D
Draw-a-Man	_____	_____	_____	A B C D
Guilford-Martin	_____	_____	_____	A B C D
MMPI	_____	_____	_____	A B C D
Rorschach	_____	_____	_____	A B C D
Sentence Completion	_____	_____	_____	A B C D
Stanford-Binet	_____	_____	_____	A B C D
TAT	_____	_____	_____	A B C D
Wechsler-Bellevue	_____	_____	_____	A B C D
Others (Specify):				
_____	_____	_____	_____	A B C D
_____	_____	_____	_____	A B C D

3. Types of subjects

Type:	estimated total number tested	estimated no. tested under super-vision	rated quality of supervision: A-excellent; B-good; C-adequate; D-inadequate (circle one)
Adult character disorder	_____	_____	A B C D
" neurotic	_____	_____	A B C D
" normal	_____	_____	A B C D
" psychotic	_____	_____	A B C D
" organic	_____	_____	A B C D
Child behavior problem	_____	_____	A B C D
" normal	_____	_____	A B C D
" organic	_____	_____	A B C D
Other (Specify)			
_____	_____	_____	A B C D
_____	_____	_____	A B C D

Approximate total number of female subjects tested: _____

4. Diagnostic conferences: Estimated number of times you presented cases to staff confer-ences _____ . Estimated number of times you sat in on staff conferences _____ .

5. Supervisory experiences: Estimated number of trainees whose diagnostic work you have supervised _____ .

---

*The phrase "under supervision" means that your supervisor checked your work prior to our final report.

266

6. Rank these tests in the order in which you prefer to use them. (Place a 1 next to the test you most prefer to use; place a 2 beside your next preference, etc.): Bender-Gestalt ____ ; Diagnostic Interview ____ ; Draw-a-Man ____ ; Guilford-Martin ____ ; MMPI ____ ; Rorschach ____ ; Sentence Completion ____ ; Stanford-Binet ____ ; Strong ____ ; TAT ____ ; Wechsler-Bellevue ____ ; Other (Specify): _____

7. Rank these subjects in the order in which you prefer to work with them: Adult character disorder ____ ; Adult neurotic ____ ; Adult normal ____ ; Adult psychotic ____ ; Adult organic ____ ; Child behavior problem ____ ; Child normal ____ ; Child organic ____ ; Other (Specify): _____

8. What is your general evaluation of the quality of your overall diagnostic training? Excellent ____ ; Good ____ ; Adequate ____ ; Inadequate ____

B. Psychotherapy (including counseling):

1. Classroom instruction

	no. of semester hrs. (quarter hrs. = 2/3 semester hours)	rated quality of instruction: A-excellent; B-good; C-adequate; D-inadequate (circle one)
Lecture	____	A B C D
Laboratory (not practicum)	____	A B C D

2. Field experience in psychotherapy

	estimated total number treated	estimated no. of those treated under super-vision	average length of contact	rated quality of instruction: A-excellent; B-good; C-adequate; D-inadequate (circle one)
Adult character				
disorder	____	____	____	A B C D
" neurotic	____	____	____	A B C D
" normal	____	____	____	A B C D
" psychotic	____	____	____	A B C D
" organic	____	____	____	A B C D
Child behavior				
problem	____	____	____	A B C D
" normal	____	____	____	A B C D
" organic	____	____	____	A B C D
Other (Specify):				
_____	____	____	____	A B C D
_____	____	____	____	A B C D

3. Rank these "schools of psychotherapy" in the order in which you prefer their theoretical orientation: Adlerian ____ ; Freudian ____ ; Learning theory ____ ; Meyerian ____ ; Neo-Freudian ____ ; Rankian ____ ; Rogerian ____ ; Washington School ____ ; Other _____

4. Rank these "schools of psychotherapy" in the order of importance placed upon them by your university: Adlerian ____ ; Freudian ____ ; Learning theory ____ ; Meyerian ____ ; Neo-Freudian ____ ; Rankian ____ ; Rogerian ____ ; Washington School ____ ; Other _____

5. Rank these "schools of psychotherapy" in the order of importance placed upon them by your installation (s): Adlerian ____ ; Freudian ____ ; Learning theory ____ ; Meyerian ____ ; Neo-Freudian ____ ; Rankian ____ ; Rogerian ____ ; Washington School ____ ; Other _____

C. Personal therapy:

1. Personal therapy status (fill in one):

   a. Have had no therapy ____ .
   b. Have had some therapy but interrupted ____ ; ____ (no.) hours, extended over ____ (no.) months.
   c. Therapy completed ____ ; ____ (no.) hours, extended over ____ (no.) months.
   d. Therapy in progress at the present time ____ ; ____ (no.) hours, extended over ____ (no.) months, to date.

2. If you checked b, c, or d above, fill out the following items. If you checked a above, skip to 3.

   a. Motivation for seeking therapy (check one):
      Primarily because of personal difficulties ____
      Primarily to improve clinical skill ____

   b. Type of therapy
      (check one)
      Adlerian ____ ; Analytically oriented therapy ____ ; Non-directive ____ ;
      Orthodox analysis ____ ; Other (Specify): _____

      (check one)
      Individual therapy ____ ; Group therapy ____

   c. Type of therapist (check one):
      Psychiatrist ____ ; Psychologist ____ ; Other (Specify): _____

   d. Depth of therapy (check one):
      Intensive ____ ; Moderately intensive ____ ; Superficial ____

   e. Effect of therapy upon your social adjustment (check one):
      Better adjustment ____ ; Poorer adjustment ____ ; No change ____

   f. Effect of therapy upon your clinical skill (check one):
      More skilful ____ ; Less skilful ____ ; No change ____

g. Effect of therapy upon your approach to clinical problems (check one):
Became more quantitatively minded _____ ; Became less quantitatively minded _____ ;
No change _____

h. Other effects of therapy (Specify):

3. Do you intend to obtain personal therapy after Ph.D.? Yes _____ ; No _____

If yes, what type of therapy:

(check one)
Adlerian _____ ; Analytically oriented therapy _____ ; Non-directive _____ ;
Orthodox analysis _____ ; Other (Specify): _____

(check one)
Individual therapy _____ ; Group therapy _____

4. Attitude of your training institution toward personal therapy (check one):
Actively helps students to obtain therapy _____ ; Encourages students to seek personal
therapy _____ ; Discourages students from seeking personal therapy _____ ; Takes no
position _____

D. Research:

1. Classroom instruction:

	no. of semester hrs. (quarter hrs. = 2/3 semester hours)	rated quality of instruction A-excellent; B-good; C-adequate; D-inadequate (circle one)
Research design	_____	A B C D
Statistics	_____	A B C D
Mathematics (other than statistics)	_____	A B C D

2. What is your general evaluation of the quality of your overall research training?
Excellent _____ ; Good _____ ; Adequate _____ ; Inadequate _____

3. Give the title of your Doctoral Dissertation. Attach your dissertation proposal or describe in 500 to 1000 words your hypotheses, experimental design, findings and interpretation of findings. Indicate how far along you are toward completing your dissertation.

Title: _____

Chairman: _____

(continue on following page)

4. List all research in which you have been engaged and describe in a paragraph the contents of each. Include minor research (e. g. exploratory studies, projects to fulfill course requirements, research done on the job; but omit papers based on library research only unless accepted for publication.

_____ Title or Problem: _____

Date: _____

_____ Title or Problem: _____

Date: _____

_____ Title or Problem: _____

Date: _____

_____ Title or Problem: _____
      Date: _____

_____ Title or Problem: _____
      Date: _____

_____ Title or Problem: _____
      Date: _____

Now go back and code each of the research projects you have mentioned by placing a symbol in front of each title as follows:

(P) - Published. If any of the above research projects have resulted in a publication, place (P) in front of the title and given reference. Append a reprint if you have one.

(SP) - Submitted for Publication. If any of the above research projects have resulted in an article submitted for publication, place (SP) in front of the title and give reference.

(S) - Psychological Societies. If any of the above research projects have been presented to a psychological society, place (S) in front of the title and give the name of the association.

(*) - Individual Research. Indicate which of the above research projects were done by you individually by placing (*) in front of the titles. For items not so marked, indicate your collaborator(s).

E. Teaching:

Give a brief summary of your teaching experience (e. g. , assistant in a projective course; instructor in elementary psychology, etc.)

_____ (no.) $\begin{array}{c} \text{semesters} \\ \overline{\text{quarters}} \end{array}$: cross out one

F. Overall:

1. What is your general evaluation of the quality of your training in Clinical Psychology (check one): Excellent _____ ; Good _____ ; Adequate _____ ; Inadequate _____

2. Rank these activities in the order in which you would prefer to engage in them: Administration _____ ; Diagnosis _____ ; Research _____ ; Teaching _____ ; Therapy _____

3. Rank these branches of psychology in the order of importance placed upon them by your university: Social _____ ; Physiological _____ ; Personnel _____ ; Personality _____ ; Measurement _____ ; Learning _____ ; Industrial _____ ; History _____ ; Genetic _____ ; Educational _____ ; Comparative _____ ; Clinical _____

4. Rank these branches of psychology in the order in which you prefer them: Social _____ ; Physiological _____ ; Personnel _____ ; Personality _____ ; Measurement _____ ; Learning _____ ; Industrial _____ ; History _____ ; Genetic _____ ; Educational _____ ; Comparative _____ ; Clinical _____

5. List the field installations (including non-VA installations) in which you have worked since entering the VA training program:

Name of Installation   Date began: Date ended:

_____

_____

_____

_____

_____

APPENDIX II-E

Predictions on Diagnostic Cases

Patient's initials _____   Trainee's name _____

Patient's probable diagnosis: Date _____

_____ neurotic   Installation _____

_____ psychotic

_____ other (specify)

     One of the promising approaches to the evaluation of diagnostic competence is the prediction of the actual behavior of patients. After considerable exploration of various types of behavioral predictions, we have settled on the prediction of the patient's response to two types of items. Part 1 of this form consists of typical statements which patients have made about themselves in therapeutic interviews. These are forced-choice items where the patient's task is to select ten out of twenty statements which best describe himself. Part 2 consists of statements which a person might say about himself and which are answered simply by a "Yes" or "No" alternative.

     After you have completed your diagnostic study, you should mark the items on Part 1 and 2 of this form as you think the patient answered them. In order that we can take into account in our analyses any differences due to diagnostic instruments, please fill in the information about the diagnostic techniques on which you based your predictions:

Prediction based on:

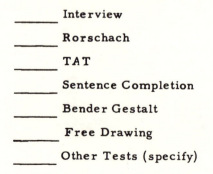

_____ Interview

_____ Rorschach

_____ TAT

_____ Sentence Completion

_____ Bender Gestalt

_____ Free Drawing

_____ Other Tests (specify)

Part 1

Below are some things that people might say about themselves. There are four sets of 20 statements. In each set of 20 statements, mark the 10 that best describe yourself. Even if you feel that the statements do not describe you very well, mark the 10 which describe you better than the others in that set.

Set A--Which 10 best describe you?

___ 1. I usually influence others more than they influence me.
___ 2. I accept suggestions readily.
___ 3. I am likely to enjoy getting a person's goat.
___ 4. I enjoy a good hot argument.
___ 5. I demand from myself more than anyone can demand from me.
___ 6. I am always ready to give or lend things to others.
___ 7. I frequently start new projects without waiting to finish what I have been doing.
___ 8. I consider a matter from every standpoint before I form an opinion.
___ 9. I finish most everything I start.
___ 10. When I wish to arrive at the truth, I make a conscious attempt to eliminate sentiment and prejudice.
___ 11. It's difficult to control my aggression.
___ 12. I am optimistic.
___ 13. I am liked by most people who know me.
___ 14. I feel helpless.
___ 15. I have the feeling I'm just not facing things.
___ 16. I have an attractive personality.
___ 17. I am confused.
___ 18. I am a failure.
___ 19. I am unreliable.
___ 20. I feel adequate.

Set B--Which 10 best describe you?

1. In matters of conduct I conform to custom . . . . ___
2. I go my own way regardless of the opinions of others . . . . ___
3. I feel nervous and anxious in the presence of superiors . . . . ___
4. I prefer the company of amusing fun-loving people . . . . ___
5. I feel that I am different from most people . . . . ___
6. I like sympathy when I am sick or depressed . . . . ___
7. I have developed a good deal of self-control . . . . ___
8. I have a strong sense of responsibility about my duties . . . . ___
9. I usually lack self-confidence when I have to compete against others . . . ___
10. I worry a lot about my ability to succeed. . . . . ___
11. Sometimes I fear that I may be injured in an accident . . . . ___
12. I have arranged my life so that it runs smoothly and without conflict . ___
13. I find it difficult to keep to any routine . . . . ___
14. When I have to act, I am usually quick to make up my mind . . . . . . ___
15. I have intense likes and dislikes . . ___
16. It takes a good deal to make me angry ___
17. My own feelings tell me what is right ___
18. I am interested in everything that is going on in the world; business, politics, social affairs . . . . ___
19. I would rather write a fine book than be an important public figure . . . . ___
20. I feel that the attempt to arrive at a deep understanding of like* is more important than practical activity . . ___

*Should be "life" but is reproduced "like" to indicate a typographical error in the forms actually used.

276

Set C--Which 10 best describe you?

___ 1. I usually like people.

___ 2. I am just sort of stubborn.

___ 3. I am a rational person.

___ 4. I try not to think about my problems.

___ 5. I am ambitious.

___ 6. I am likeable.

___ 7. I often feel humiliated.

___ 8. I doubt my sexual powers.

___ 9. I usually feel driven.

___ 10. I am sexually attractive.

___ 11. I am poised.

___ 12. I often feel resentful.

___ 13. It's important for me to know how I seem to others.
___ 14. I don't trust my emotions.

___ 15. My personality is attractive to the opposite sex.
___ 16. I am afraid of sex.

___ 17. I have a horror of failing in anything I want to accomplish.
___ 18. I feel hopeless.

___ 19. I am different from others.

___ 20. I am a good mixer.

Set D--Which 10 best describe you?

1. I put on a false front . . . . ___

2. I am a competitive person . . . .

3. I often kick myself for the things I do . . . . ___

4. I am an aloof, reserved person . ___

5. I am a responsible person . . . ___

6. I can accept most social values and standards . . . . ___

7. I express my emotions freely. . . ___

8. I can usually make up my mind and stick to it . . . .

9. I am disorganized . . . . ___

10. I have initiative . . . . ___

11. I shrink from facing a crisis or difficulty . . . .

12. I am assertive . . . . ___

13. I am afraid of disagreements with people . . . .

14. I am a hard worker . . . . ___

15. I am naturally nervous . . . . . . ___

16. I am a submissive person . . . . ___

17. I feel superior . . . . ___

18. I am self-reliant . . . . ___

19. I am inhibited . . . . ___

20. I am not accomplishing · · · · · · ___

Please check to make sure you marked 10 and only 10 statements in each set.

Part 2

Below are some questions which are to be answered by marking either "Yes" or "No." Read each question, think what your opinion or your behavior has usually been, and then put an "X" through the answer which best describes you. Mark an answer for every question even if you are uncertain which answer fits you best. There is no right answer to any of these questions except the answer that tells how you think or feel about it.

Yes   No

Y   N   1. Do you express such emotions as delight, sorrow, anger, and the like, readily?

Y   N   2. Do you find it difficult to get rid of a salesman to whom you do not care to listen or give your time?

Y   N   3. Are you afraid of deep water?

Y   N   4. Do you usually hesitate to take a seat in the front of a lecture room or church if to do so makes you appear conspicuous?

Y   N   5. Do you cry rather easily?

Y   N   6. Do you believe you have been bossed too much for your own good?

Y   N   7. Are there ever times when you feel so jumpy you could throw things at people if you did not control yourself?

Y   N   8. Do you often become irritated over little annoyances?

Y   N   9. If an acquaintance of yours has been spreading untrue and uncomplimentary stories about you, do you usually "have it out" with the person?

Y   N   10. When a parent, teacher, or boss scolds you, do you ever feel like weeping?

Y   N   11. Would you rate yourself as a tense individual?

Y   N   12. Have you often felt that you are a rather awkward person?

Y   N   13. In a group activity do you often find yourself compelled to play an unimportant part?

Y   N   14. Does it sometimes seem to you that in life's competitions you are usually left behind?

Y   N   15. Have you ever been hesitant about making application for a job in person?

Y   N   16. Do you get angry very easily?

Y   N   17. Does it bother you considerably to have your teacher or your boss call upon you unexpectedly in a group?

Y   N   18. Can you go into a dark cellar or basement alone without even the slightest trembly feeling?

Y   N   19. Do you feel tired out most of the time?

Y   N   20. Are you very good at making money as compared with others of your age and sex?

Y   N   21. Were you happier when you were younger than you are now?

Y   N   22. Do you suffer keenly from feelings of inferiority?

Y   N   23. Does it seem to you that you never do things in a way that wins the attention and approval of others?

278

Y   N   24. Do you often find yourself hurrying to get places even when there is plenty of time?

Y   N   25. Do you let others "run over you" more than you should for your own good?

Y   N   26. Do you ever wish you could have been born at a different time or place or in a different family than you were?

Y   N   27. Are you usually confident of your abilities?

Y   N   28. Do you feel that the average person has made a better adjustment to life than you have?

Y   N   29. Do you feel physically inferior to your associates?

Y   N   30. Are you able to come back to a state of calm readily after an exciting situation is past?

Y   N   31. Do you (or would you) like to go hunting with a rifle for wild game?

Y   N   32. When you become angry, do you get over it rather quickly when the cause for anger is past?

Y   N   33. Do you consider yourself a nervous person?

Y   N   34. Are you easily discouraged when things become difficult?

Y   N   35. Do your friends seem to have a better time than you do?

Y   N   36. Do you often feel reluctant to meet the most important person at a party or reception?

Y   N   37. Do you have a strong dread of fire?

Y   N   38. Do you often find that you cannot make up your mind until the time for action is past?

Y   N   39. Do you often show yourself up to your own disadvantage?

Y   N   40. Do you have any hesitation about calling down a person who does not play fair?

Items in this part were selected from the Guilford-Martin Inventory of Factors GAMIN, Copyright 1943 by the Sheridan Supply Company, Beverly Hills, California.

APPENDIX II-F

INSTRUCTIONS TO JUDGES FOR SCORING PROGRESS NOTES

You are being asked to make certain qualitative judgments about a series of "progress notes," the notations and informal records which therapists keep for their own use. These notes will therefore vary from therapist to therapist, although we have asked that they be kept reasonably short.

It will be the purpose of your judgments to evaluate the quantity and quality of abreaction per hour, that is, the number and type of feelings which the patient expresses during a particular therapy session. It will be important, therefore, to read the notes with this purpose in mind. While we do not want you to consider any remarks or evaluations by the therapist, you will need to depend to some extent on the therapist's judgment as to the depth of feeling expressed and his interpretations.

The method of rating is as follows:

1. Read through the entire interview note.

2. Reread the note and divide it into the topics of thought units which the patient is reported to have expressed. (Do not consider expressions by the therapist!) A thought unit or topic contains an expression of an attitude or feeling, a recounting of an experience. It will generally be in the form of a statement the patient is reported to have made to the therapist, and possibly elaborations of this statement by the patient. Thus, the patient might have spoken about his difficulties on the job, and then elaborated by saying that he can't get along with the worker at the same bench, that his foreman constantly assigns him dirty and unpleasant jobs, and that he is thinking of quitting. On the other hand, the patient may just have said, "I've got nothing but trouble on my job." Two topics may be found in one running sentence: "the patient attacked the therapist for not having given proper advice, then complained about his asthma." Here we find two separate topics which the therapist has reported in one sentence. The attack on the therapist, and the asthma must therefore be listed as two separate topics. On the other hand, a topic may include many expressions of feelings about the same thing. In this case it is listed as only one topic: "patient tells about difficulties in marital relations, husband is a baby, the children are extremely difficult, at times she can't stand them, her mother interferes in the marriage. She is now contemplating divorce."

Similarly, when the patient lists two or three symptoms or feelings in a manner which indicates that he considers them as belonging together, the account is listed as only one topic: " . . . he feels nervous and his stomach aches, especially after he has had a fight with his wife."

When the patient discusses and elaborates symptoms separately they should be tallied separately, e.g.; "The patient complains of (1) headaches, (2) trouble with his digestive system, and (3) inability to get along in school."

Dreams are divided into topics depending on the final acceptance of the interpretation by the patient. Thus, an uninterrupted dream is one topic, but a dream in which the patient sees one or more distinct themes is counted as one or more distinct topics.

280

After dividing the progress note into the topics expressed by the patient, classify the topics as follows:

1. INTIMATE DETAIL (ID) --weight 1--

This category includes only the following:

a. Statements by the patient which he would not ordinarily confide to other persons. By confiding these events or feelings, the patient presumably indicates that he trusts the therapist, that rapport is good, that he withholds little or nothing from his therapist.

b. Such intimate details might be facts about his sexual life, perversions, sexual (masturbatory) fantasies; anti-social feelings or acts; desire to kill his mother, wife, etc., past or present history of theft, felonies, embezzling, murder, etc.; his plans to defraud, or perjure, etc. Such a topic need not be startlingly unusual, as long as the impression is given that this would definitely not be an ordinary conversational theme for the patient.

2. FEELINGS TOWARD SIGNIFICANT OTHER PERSONS (FO)--weight 1

a. These feelings and attitudes indicate that the patient experiences some reliving of earlier traumatic events or conflicts. While the event may or may not have taken place in the past, FO is scored only if it can be reasonably assumed that the patient's statement expresses some feelings about such events during the hour. A mere intellectual recounting is obviously not subsumed under this category. The only persons to be considered in this context are persons on whom the patient is, or was, dependent for the satisfaction of his elementary affectional needs, that is, his parents, his siblings, his spouse, children, or those clearly in place of these persons, i.e., step-parents, stepbrothers or sisters, a sex partner with whom there is deep involvement. A teacher, boss, etc., although perhaps symbolically in place of the father, is not to be considered a "significant other." We are here assuming that the patient must solve his basic interpersonal relationships, and that he can do this most efficaciously by going to the source of his problems. The source of his problems is not likely to lie in current disagreements with his boss or fellow workers, and his emotional reactions about them would then not contribute to the identification and working through of the emotional experience for which the abreaction symbolically is intended. Themes containing FO are not necessarily made up of direct expressions of feeling, but may include recounting of actions which imply feelings toward significant others.

b. Examples of FO are: ". . . in so doing he contrasts himself to a brother who he infers is getting along well. Though this is framed as a positive statement regarding the brother, the undercurrent of antagonism is quite apparent." ". . . after many years the patient decided that the girl (her sister) was 'using her' and became very bitter. She feels that this girl can get along better than she always could." "And mama, too. She was scared of him (father) but I wasn't. Although I never did hit him I was mad enough. When I was about 14 I decided to run away from home. I can see mama now with tears in her eyes, telling me not to go."

3. FEELINGS TOWARD SELF (FS)--weighted 3

a. Inasmuch as the patient's feelings about himself will determine his expectations of himself and others around him, and since he will be as adjusted as his realistic perception of himself in relation to others will permit, it is clear that feelings and attitudes toward himself are very important. While the patient cannot change the personality of his deceased father or mother, nor probably of his still living parents or spouse, he can effect a change in his own personality and behavior by changing his self-concept and the perceptions and the expectations he has of others. It is therefore important to determine the extent to which the patient accepts responsibility for his own actions, and the extent to which he sees himself as out of phase with others, since this is a precondition for his desire to change. For the purpose of this rating, all self-directed feelings and attitudes, positive as well as negative, are to be scored as FS, provided they may reasonably be seen as carrying emotional convictions--a flippant statement about himself (oh, I'm a hell of a guy") may reveal feelings toward himself, but it is doubtful whether the patient is aware of these feelings. Unless this awareness exists the patient will presumably not change radically.

b. Some examples of FS are: "Most people think I am a leader, but I am really no good at this at all." " . . . I still feel guilty about this, even though it's been ten years since it happened." " . . . the patient seemed very depressed and blamed himself for the way he feels toward his child." "Patient seems elated and mentioned that he felt himself to be well qualified for the job." "Patient finally connected his stomach disorder with his anxiety." " . . . today the patient also seemed to have gotten insight into the fact that he competes with his son for his wife's affection."

4. FEELINGS TOWARD THE THERAPIST (FT)--weight 3

a. Ability to express feelings toward the therapist not only indicates considerable rapport and freedom in the interpersonal relationship, but also that the patient can test the reality of his perceptions of other people. It is only in the course of the therapy session that he can do so without penalty, but it is also extremely difficult for many patients to express their feelings directly toward their therapist. The criterion for scoring FT is that the patient must be aware of the fact that he is expressing a feeling toward the therapist, even though this feeling may be couched in a question, an exclamation, or a compliment. While the category is to be scored liberally, a polite "good morning," or "did you have a nice vacation?" does not fulfil this condition.

b. Examples of FT are: "I don't want you to get the wrong impression of me." "Are you married?" "You look angry because I didn't mention this before." "Patient then said, 'You and I ought to get acquainted better!'" "Patient expressed impatience with me for not giving him a formula for getting along."

OTHER TOPICS (OT)--weight 0

All topics of discussion which do not fall into one of the above categories are to be scored OT. They include small talk, discussion of current events, sports, purely intellectualized accounts of patient's history, talk about work, etc.

GENERAL

When two or more differently weighted subjects fall into one topic ("patient compared therapist with his father in being very generous") the higher weight is assigned to the topic (weight 3 in the preceding example).

1. If not clear whether something was actually said in the interview, assume that it was said in interview.

2. Look for themes, not topics.

282

EXAMPLES OF PROGRESS NOTES AND SCORING

Example A

Patient opens hour with following dream "Invited a woman over here. When she arrives I find that I am not sexually interested in her. The scene shifts and I am in a gambling room with a number of men, all are eating hot dogs. One man comes in--he is a political leader of some sort who looks very familiar and who objects to and prohibits the eating of hot dogs."

He goes on to describe the woman involved and how she, like so many others, interests him at first but then seems to lack something and he is disappointed. He relates the eating of hot dogs to his homosexual activity and identifies the "political leader" as the therapist. The remainder of the hour is spent in a discussion of his objections to homosexuality and to his feelings of revulsion upon completion of homosexual acts. He concludes with great pride that he has not been tempted by an old homosexual partner (in the absence of his wife).

TOPIC BREAKDOWN	SCORING
Pt. opens the hour with following dream "Invited a woman . . . eating of hot dogs"/	Since dream is associated to it is not scored.
He goes on to describe the woman involved and how she, like so many others, interests him at first but then seems to lack something and he is disappointed/	This is apparently a symptom--women disappoint him--and is scored OT.
He relates the eating of hot dogs to his homosexual activity/ and identifies the political leader as the therapist. /	Relates homosexual activity which is Intimate Detail, ID. Therapist is identified as authority figure--FT.
The remainder of the hour is spent in a discussion of his own objections to homosexuality and to his feelings of revulsion upon completion of homosexual acts. /	Pt. feels revulsion toward own acts, i.e., himself, therefore feelings toward self, FS.
He concludes with great pride that he has not been tempted by an old homosexual partner (in the absence of his wife). /	Pt. is proud of himself because he has not been tempted. A feeling toward himself, FS.

Total topics expressed	5
1 OT wt 0	0
1 ID wt 1	1
1 FT wt 3	3
2 FS wt 3	6

Total 10/5 = 2.00

Example B

Refers to being repetitious--maybe saves thinking up something new. Mentally lazy except in acting. Refers to habit of procrastinating but evades talking of feeling (or guilt) about it. Hates routine, fear of becoming part of machine. Is more tied down now but immediately describes constant changes in her baby as compensation for "schedules." Had anxiety in early weeks till he smiled, "happy he is going to be." Goal to make him carefree, independent, realizing values of life, believing in fairies.

"Mind, I'm not perfectionistic." Fable of perfect woman with mole, when removed disappeared. Pt. likes to overcome obstacles. Her chief--her family. They like a dynasty, must live by rules concerned with grandmother's standards of decency. Pt. never played Sadye Thompson or Pear (Tobacco Road). Discussion of difference between prostitutes and "modern" "so-called" girls--illustrates with long account of friend, a "week-ender," pt. not herself involved, a "spectator." Friendship based on friend not expecting too much of her. Discussion of attitudes of members of family re expectations of her. Expect her to be always gay.

Couple wanted to adopt pt. as baby, spent 1/3 of time till 7 with them. Still ties to them. Was complete "center of attention" with them.

TOPIC BREAKDOWN

Refers to being repetitious--maybe saves thinking up something new. / Mentally lazy except in acting. Refers to habit of procrastinating, but evades talking of feelings (or guilt) about it. / Hates routine, fear of becoming part of a machine. Is more tied down now/ but immediately describes constant changes in her baby as compensation for "schedules." Had anxiety in early weeks until he smiled.

"Mind, I'm not perfectionistic . . . patient likes to overcome obstacles. Her chief-- her family . . . decency.

Discussion of differences between prostitute and "weekender" . . . (Also Tobacco Road discussion)

Discussion of attitudes of family re expectations of her. Expect her always to be gay.

Couple wanted to adopt pt. as baby . . . Still ties to them . . .

SCORING

Patient talks about herself but (according to therapist) without feelings, OT.

Speaks about her baby with obvious feelings, FO.

Feeling toward herself, FS. Feelings about family, esp. grandmother (who controls her standards; FO.

Intellectualization, OT.

Patient resents family's expectations of her, thus FO.

Couple were in loco parentis to pt., therefore, scored here, FO.

Total topics		7
2 OT wt 0	0	
4 FO wt 1	4	
1 FS wt 3	3	

Total 7/7 = 1.00

284

Example C

Patient had missed previous hour; asked in hall if I had received message. I said I had not.

He described himself as having ups and downs. "I wish I could convince myself that there is nothing physically wrong with me." He went on to describe somatic complaints resembling indigestion, for which reassurance was given. He continued, saying he felt he is getting well.

We discussed his wife's plans to leave her mother's house and bring the children to an apartment of their own for him to visit and eventually be discharged to. He expressed considerable ambivalence on this score.

Discussed his attack on his oldest child the weekend before, with the therapist giving some information on the nature of hostility.

Hour changed to 10 a.m.

TOPIC BREAKDOWN

Patient had missed previous hour; asked in hall if I had received message, I said I had not. /

He described himself as having ups and downs. "I wish I could convince myself that there is nothing physically wrong with me." He went on to describe somatic complaints resembling indigestion/ for which reassurance was given. /

He continued, saying he felt he is getting well. /

We discussed his wife's plans to leave her mother's home and bring the children to an apartment of their own for him to visit and eventually be discharged to. He expressed considerable ambivalence on this score. /

Discussed his attack on his oldest child the weekend before,/ with the therapist giving some information on the nature of hostility.

Hour changed to 10 a.m.

SCORING

Not therapy proper. This is out in the hall.

Description of symptoms, therefore scored as OT. The pt's wish that he could convince himself is probably part of his symptoms. Therapist's comment, not scored.

Continuation of pt's previous comment.

Pt's account is of a plan, while it concerns his wife and children no affect seems to be connected with wife and children, ambivalence is toward bringing them. Scored OT.

Attack on child probably carried feelings, during hour, thus FO. Therapist's comment, not scored.

Not treatment proper.

Total topics	3
2 OT wt 0	0
1 FO wt 1	1

Total 1/3 = .33

APPENDIX II-G

REJECTED CRITERION PROCEDURES

In the course of our research on the development of criterion measures, we considered many possible approaches or techniques which for one reason or another were not feasible for use in this project. Some of these proposed measures were not acceptable on a priori grounds. Others were regarded as promising but could not be used within this project, either because they could not be developed within the time available or because they could not be economically administered on a nation wide basis. Such possible but rejected criterion measures are here summarized in the hope that they will be of use to other investigators concerned with the evaluation of clinical skills.

Rejected Measures of Diagnostic Competence

1. Multiple Choice Tests of Diagnostic Interpretation. The subject would be provided with projective protocols and other clinical materials and would be given a series of multiple choice items concerning the diagnostic interpretation. These items could be written at several levels of generality or at several depths of interpretation. This idea was incorporated in the Case Study Part of the Clinical Content Examination but was rejected as an independent measure of diagnostic competence primarily because the key would have to be based upon the opinion of experts.

2. Q-sorts of Diagnostic Interpretations. This test would be like that mentioned above except that the trainee would be provided with case materials and asked to sort a series of statements according to the extent to which they describe the patient. The sorts could then be scored by using the sorts of experts or the patient self-sort. The use of "canned cases" was rejected because of our inability to secure inter-case reliability with such materials. The use of card sorts was rejected because of the administration difficulties involved (cf. Diagnostic Prediction Test).

3. Matching Test. Using several categories of material from each of several patients (e. g., Rorschach, TAT, etc.) the subject would be asked to sort together these materials according to the patient which had produced them. This idea was used in an unpublished study by James A. Holsopple. This test was rejected because (a) it calls for a type of clinical activity not ordinarily assumed to be required in clinical work; (b) it involves the use of "canned" case material, (c) it requires considerable time--more than was felt trainees would be willing to devote to it. Note, however, that the scoring of such a test would be completely objective.

4. Tests of the Communication Value of Diagnostic Findings. Judges would be asked to sort self-descriptive statements for individuals on the basis of the trainee's diagnostic write-up. The accuracy of these sorts could then be compared either to the patient's own sort or to the therapist's sort for his patient (provided the patient went into therapy). This approach seemed appropriate as a measure of the adequacy of a diagnostic report, but a bit indirect as a measure of diagnostic skill. It would also be fairly expensive to employ sufficient judges to sort the items. Furthermore, our preliminary attempts to predict patient's self-descriptions on the basis of diagnostic reports led to complete failure.

5. Observations of Routine, On-the-Job, Diagnostic Work Collected with Hidden Recording Instruments, Using Standard Role Players as "Patients," without the Knowledge of the Trainee. Rejected because of cost, administrative difficulties and undesirability of trickery. We considered collecting such materials openly, but decided that the evaluations of such materials would have no more value as criterion measures than would be found for supervisor's ratings.

6. **Appraisal of Routine Diagnostic Reports, Drawn from Files.** This approach seemed to have little value in the absence of an external criterion.

7. **Presentation of a Case through Sound Movies and Typescript Data.** This procedure was regarded as too expensive; furthermore, valid scoring would require objective criteria.

8. **Development of Standard Tests for Such Activities as Rorschach Interpretation.** This approach was rejected because it overlapped with the Content Examination and because we felt that the scoring per se was unimportant as a measure of clinical skill except as it was instrumental to other diagnostic activities.

9. **Matching Tests Based on Cronbach's Procedures (1948).** Example: judges would be presented with a Rorschach protocol for a case and a series of interpretive statements including some based on the case and others from the interpretation of other cases; they would be asked to indicate which of the statements described the subject whose Rorschach protocols he had studied. A small pilot study using materials supplied by Cronbach revealed insufficient variability among the judges to warrant further exploration of this approach.

10. **Matching of Symptomatology with Minimal Protocols.** A series of thumbnail summaries of case histories would be presented to be matched with brief excerpts from projective protocols. We began an exploratory study of this as a measure of diagnostic competence, but unfortunately, the results of our pilot study were lost in the mails and time did not permit repetition.

11. **Prediction of Typical Response Patterns.** Subjects would be asked to answer a test as the modal or typical individual of a specified diagnostic category would answer it. Such a test would have little face validity but might well measure one aspect of the ability to predict the behavior of specific individuals.

Rejected Measures of Therapeutic Competence

1. **Test of the Ability to Recognize the Conscious Intentions of Therapists.** Subjects would listen to recordings of therapy or read typescripts and be asked to indicate when the therapist was trying to be supportive, when attempting to interpret, etc. (cf. Porter, 1950). This approach was rejected because it appeared too indirect.

2. **Test of Ability to Predict the Patient's Behavior in Therapy.** Subjects could be given either diagnostic test materials or a transcript of the first few therapy sessions and asked to make predictions concerning the patient's behavior in later therapy interviews. This idea was rejected primarily because there is no agreement concerning the assumption that ability to predict the patient's behavior is essential to therapeutic progress (cf. the analyses of predictions made by trainees for their therapeutic patients, Chapter C IV).

3. **Role Playing Therapeutic Situations.** Role playing could be used in several ways: the trainee could be asked to play the role of the therapist, or the role of a patient. This approach was rejected because it was too impractical and indirect.

Rejected Measures of Research Competence

1. **Multiple Choice Tests of Skill in Research Design.** Rejected because of its overlap with parts of General Section of the Content Examination.

2. **Test of the Ability to Draw Up a Research Design.** Each trainee would be asked to draw up a research design to investigate a standard problem. This plan was rejected (a) because it was felt that considerable motivation and ego-involvement are necessary for maximum creativity in research design and, (b) because of the difficulties of preparing "equivalent forms" and because of inherent difficulties in the objective evaluation of the products.

APPENDIX III-A

CORRELATIONS BETWEEN FINAL POOLED RATINGS
(1947 Ann Arbor Assessment)

	1*	2*	3*	4	5	6*	7	8	9	10*	11	12	13*	14	15	16*	17*	18*	19*	20*	21	22	23b	24	25*	26	27	28	29	30	31	32	33	34	35	36	37	38	39	40	41	42
1*		42	-33	30	44	35	23	06	57	70	-07	09	39	44	10	26	54	04	04	33	-12	-05	62	58	36	41	-30	19	28	39	11	13	34	53	56	18	45	54	26	63	58	54
2*			-18	17	37	13	29	-17	39	35	-12	-07	26	15	11	38	30	-26	-26	03	-11	-31	35	33	52	38	-02	-04	07	06	-04	04	10	19	27	-03	26	28	04	38	30	19
3*				36	-23	33	28	36	-26	-32	68	40	03	10	32	14	-35	29	41	19	48	45	-04	10	-06	01	47	25	17	14	38	33	24	03	09	24	20	08	26	-06	-26	05
4					-13	59	46	18	41	30	65	51	24	55	31	54	12	12	40	49	14	41	47	51	47	39	13	12	26	19	27	25	25	31	48	14	43	39	29	39	04	32
5						02	08	07	30	47	-32	-14	30	13	07	-11	-03	07	-35	10	08	-15	30	27	00	17	-11	38	21	33	17	17	28	37	35	23	32	38	23	46	65	39
6*							39	21	35	41	61	48	25	50	09	30	12	23	38	52	34	48	51	49	30	19	15	20	33	27	20	20	30	42	46	16	41	36	26	40	18	38
7								39	32	30	30	34	58	47	55	70	01	17	13	54	26	25	34	51	47	37	20	04	09	07	30	37	45	35	61	24	37	39	58	26	07	34
8									31	21	25	30	25	45	38	15	03	68	25	21	-14	20	62	40	-11	19	10	01	10	14	27	18	13	47	32	16	51	46	17	38	01	56
9										-04	71	05	45	52	13	37	53	-13	35	30	67	25	60	64	-01	34	31	33	25	38	36	38	17	40	49	28	45	52	71	39	16	46
10*											-04	34	23	57	11	24	02	02	36	43	49	-10	68	26	53	36	-33	07	53	54	75	66	26	61	54	65	39	48	18	58	53	54
11												50	36	34	39	18	66	26	13	49	17	66	15	47	35	03	07	23	30	14	-02	-01	20	11	63	05	49	52	22	70	66	15
12													08	08	51	24	-31	36	22	44	32	37	35	57	13	32	-06	21	28	23	30	24	25	38	19	07	21	15	25	07	-24	35
13*														49	49	61	03	31	54	14	26	41	59	38	20	41	-01	33	49	50	27	18	25	45	45	17	37	31	32	28	09	52
14															40	65	23	37	05	26	54	50	72	51	15	47	20	20	62	59	39	36	54	73	78	33	70	56	47	60	28	70
15																47	61	23	-33	08	25	20	34	41	31	42	07	04	34	32	43	42	45	32	40	41	47	44	46	72	37	37
16*																	42	05	35	21	17	33	51	38	31	-06	-03	09	27	11	31	19	29	31	45	10	42	33	22	39	-01	28
17*																		-08	02	29	-03	-06	41	51	63	42	23	33	25	36	08	05	22	47	45	14	32	42	19	54	84	48
18*																			18	23	57	20	43	30	10	-06	13	25	36	54	69	55	66	47	45	60	28	42	20	29	12	46
19*																				20	26	33	15	04	-27	18	20	04	17	14	15	19	22	19	21	33	12	12	20	14	-21	12
20*																					21	18	26	59	15	36	07	36	34	41	33	27	36	50	51	31	43	43	40	47	39	52
21																						12	09	23	08	06	20	52	40	43	66	56	61	35	32	61	37	39	58	26	07	38
22																							06	11	-13	18	15	15	08	09	22	15	13	19	07	16	06	06	17	-01	01	14
23b																								79	-15	-06	13	35	51	62	59	51	70	68	76	24	52	59	64	82	54	67
24																									54	20	20	-16	59	62	51	32	60	74	85	36	73	74	56	77	54	77
25*																										57	15	35	09	06	24	-12	07	23	37	-13	32	30	04	38	13	21
26																											-10	-14	24	29	03	10	23	42	48	07	46	45	23	47	36	38
27																												21	-04	-03	18	26	08	-06	-06	18	07	-05	13	-11	-25	-07
28																													62	64	62	63	70	63	56	67	52	58	67	54	62	62
29																														80	59	51	70	69	72	60	59	64	68	60	36	65
30																															55	51	78	73	72	62	57	70	68	65	36	71
31																																86	78	55	51	82	55	55	81	47	49	61
32																																	75	54	50	87	62	58	84	48	22	58
33																																		76	69	72	80	69	77	69	62	80
34																																			90	56	73	77	82	47	50	91
35																																				49	62	79	84	80	56	85
36																																					56	77	66	73	32	67
37																																						80	87	82	47	77
38																																							73	84	55	81
39																																								65	38	79
40																																									67	81
41																																										64
42																																										

*These variables were reflected so that the socially favored pole of these variables was on the right or high end of the rating scale, as it was for the other variables.

APPENDIX III-B

OBLIQUE FACTOR MATRIX FOR FINAL POOLED RATINGS

(1947 Ann Arbor Assessment)

	Factors									
	A	B	C	D	E	F	G	H	I	h^2
1	05	-27	30	06	32	-06	01	04	17	76
2	-05	-15	22	-04	09	-13	07	46	01	53
3	66	44	-04	-01	04	-01	-01	11	-01	87
4	41	06	01	-05	17	39	04	32	14	74
5	03	-02	64	-04	15	-26	07	05	00	80
6	59	-03	13	-02	38	20	-05	03	15	76
7	12	30	09	-07	47	-02	03	27	-02	75
8	01	23	-02	20	00	19	23	-11	02	79
9	05	-01	26	-02	04	27	-08	21	34	70
10	02	-03	32	-08	14	22	01	-06	38	80
11	62	05	-04	01	09	46	02	20	-03	89
12	25	37	-03	-02	-02	48	-07	04	30	58
13	-07	02	00	10	44	-25	10	-01	04	67
14	00	04	-05	26	01	44	-05	16	40	83
15	-02	51	03	-02	07	02	06	18	10	62
16	-04	18	-06	-05	39	06	-05	35	03	80
17	01	04	65	01	00	01	-07	00	20	93
18	-03	03	00	37	02	23	00	00	-01	75
19	13	14	-45	-03	09	19	04	-08	27	54
20	30	-01	13	03	-09	50	11	07	31	63
21	05	51	04	13	-05	00	10	05	-01	75
22	62	00	08	01	-07	45	06	-07	03	77
23	12	00	07	03	32	04	01	-03	42	89
24	09	05	08	24	07	26	-05	23	40	86
25	05	-02	-01	07	11	08	-17	49	19	73
26	07	03	01	11	-10	00	01	38	35	58
27	21	-01	-01	-02	00	00	-01	32	00	28
28	04	16	19	20	-07	12	19	-03	13	71
29	05	00	-01	56	12	00	-07	00	09	83
30	04	-03	03	49	-07	01	04	00	25	82
31	04	14	08	01	08	09	47	00	-06	94
32	04	00	00	-09	08	-07	61	-03	07	87
33	03	03	01	29	06	-03	31	-01	15	93
34	-04	00	01	19	-02	13	17	-03	53	89
35	02	02	03	19	06	16	12	08	46	88
36	-04	-01	07	04	-08	05	57	00	06	91
37	10	02	-01	-05	17	-03	35	00	43	84
38	-03	-03	05	14	-01	09	31	12	39	82
39	-03	00	-05	05	-07	10	55	-02	26	92
40	01	-02	11	05	13	00	20	02	49	92
41	-01	-02	44	04	-09	03	09	-02	37	85
42	-02	-06	04	13	-07	16	36	-03	44	90

APPENDIX III-C

SECOND-ORDER FACTOR MATRIX

(1947 Ann Arbor Assessment)

First-Order Factors	Second-Order Factors					
	AA	BB	CC	DD	EE	h^2
A	-45	03	-01	62	-02	59
B	02	58	-11	-03	-09	36
C	00	06	67	-36	-08	59
D	00	67	33	-03	14	58
E	69	07	12	-05	57	82
F	00	-04	-10	02	50	26
G	-01	80	06	-01	03	64
H	52	-01	-09	03	-09	29
I	60	-09	66	00	04	81

APPENDIX III-D

CORRELATIONS BETWEEN PRIMARY VECTORS

(1947 Ann Arbor Assessment)

	A	B	C	D	E	F	G	H	I
				First-Order					
A	1.00								
B	-05	1.00							
C	-23	-12	1.00						
D	-02	43	24	1.00					
E	-29	19	02	36	1.00				
F	-04	02	-06	16	34	1.00			
G	04	52	11	69	27	18	1.00		
H	-16	00	-22	-11	30	-04	03	1.00	
I	-16	-07	35	17	47	-06	-04	23	1.00

	AA	BB	CC	DD	EE
			Second-Order		
AA	1.00				
BB	09	1.00			
CC	-26	-05	1.00		
DD	21	04	-48	1.00	
EE	-02	34	06	-03	1.00

APPENDIX IV

THESIS ABSTRACTS

During the last five years, ten doctoral dissertations were completed which were based entirely or in part on data collected by the project. None of these dissertations was directly related to the primary objective of the project; consequently, the findings growing out of them have not been summarized in the body of this report. However, since all of the dissertations deal with problems related to procedures used in the major investigation, it is believed this series of findings will be of interest to readers of this report. Abstracts of these theses follow, the order being the same as the date of completion of the theses.

These dissertations are available in the University of Michigan Library. Microfilm copies of each may be purchased from University Microfilms, Ann Arbor, Michigan. The order numbers (e. g., Mic A48-9) are indicated.

CONSISTENCY OF THE FACTORIAL STRUCTURES IN PERSONALITY RATINGS FROM DIFFERENT SOURCES

Donald W. Fiske, Thesis (Ph. D.)
University of Michigan, 1948

During an intensive program of personality evaluation, the same 128 men were rated by three sets of people: (1) a staff team of three experienced psychologists pooled their judgments, which were based on a mass of extensive and intensive material on each subject; (2) three teammates who had spent seven days with a subject, living and working together, rated him (the median rating was used in this study); (3) the subjects rated themselves. The same 22-item scale for surface behavior, adapted from Cattell, was used throughout.

Three separate factor analyses were carried out, in each of which five factors were located. Four factors recurred in each study. One factor present in each analysis was essentially a general factor which appeared to be a form of Social Adaptability. A factor labelled Emotional Control showed a close congruence from study to study. A Conformity factor was identified in each of the three sets of ratings, although the three versions of this pattern were somewhat different. A factor of intellectual curiosity or the Searching Intellect was also found in each analysis. Two factors, one from ratings by teammates and one from self-ratings, seemed to embody a common core called Confident Self-Expression. One factor in staff ratings could not be identified and had no definite counterpart in the other sets of factors.

These findings bear certain marked resemblances to those from studies by Cattell and others, although many discrepancies are also present. It is concluded that, for ratings of relatively manifest behavior, a high degree of consistency exists between the factorial structures found in ratings from different sources. Ratings by colleagues contain fairly accurate versions of all the factors which can be identified in ratings by clinicians and in self-rating. Mic A48-145

A STUDY OF PERSONALITY RATINGS BASED ON BRIEF OBSERVATION OF BEHAVIOR IN STANDARD SITUATIONS

William F. Soskin, Thesis (Ph. D.)
University of Michigan, 1949

In the course of an intensive assessment of 128 male first-year graduate students in clinical psychology each subject participated in a series of five types of standard situations under the observation of experienced psychologists working on two types of rating teams, each of whom rated the subject on a group of thirty-one variables.

Team A first rated the subject on the basis of interviews, test scores and personal documents. Then, after observing his performance in the standard situations and studying certain other data, Team A made a set of final pooled (FinP) ratings, the criterion in this study. Team B, having had no previous familiarity with the subject, rated him solely on the basis of his performance in the situations (SitP ratings). A third type of rating (TI ratings) was made by persons who formed their judgments solely on the basis of "blind" analysis of objective and projective tests and personal documents.

In this study Team B ratings were compared with ratings by the other types of judges. It was found that:

1. The reliabilities of ratings by individuals were rather low, although the reliabilities of pooled ratings were moderately good for most variables.

2. For all variables the correlation between SitP ratings and FinP (criterion) ratings was significant at the one per cent level, although variables differed significantly with respect to the validity (i. e., agreement with criterion) with which they could be rated from behavior observed in situations.

3. For certain variables SitP ratings were found capable of accounting for a greater portion of the total variance than were either PreP or TI ratings.

4. Individuals differed significantly in ability to rate the thirty-one variables solely on the basis of behavior observed in the standard situations.

5. The distinguishing feature between "good" and "poor" raters was that the "good" raters were able to rate so-called phenotypical and genotypical variables about equally well from observations in the standard situations, whereas the "poor" judges were significantly less able to rate the genotypical variables. Mic A49-9

ABSTRACT

THE PREDICTION OF PERSONALITY ATTRIBUTES BY
MEANS OF THE RORSCHACH METHOD

Woodrow Wilbert Morris, Thesis (Ph. D.)
University of Michigan, 1949

This study is concerned with the validity of estimation of personality attributes by means of the Rorschach Method of psychodiagnosis. Two aspects of the problem are considered: (1) the validity of estimates arrived at by means of ratings based on Rorschach protocols and (2) the validity of estimates arrived at directly by means of various Rorschach scores and patterns.

The data used were secured by staff members on 120 Veterans Administration trainees in clinical psychology who underwent a week's intensive observation and assessment in the University of Michigan Project on the Selection of Clinical Psychologists. The subjects were divided into groups of 24.

The procedure involved the collection of criterion ratings on ten personality attributes, made collectively by teams of three observers, using a specially devised rating scale, at the end of each week of assessment. Ratings on the same variables, made by one or another of six Rorschach examiners and based on Rorschach records were then obtained and correlated with the criterion ratings. Analysis was also made of the ability of the individual Rorschach raters to estimate the criterion ratings. For each of the ten variables, Rorschach scores and patterns deemed to be of value were isolated. These were then taken directly from the Rorschach records and correlated with the criterion ratings.

From the results of the study, it is concluded that:

1. Clinicians, using Rorschach data, are able to make statistically significant estimates of covert personality characteristics, as represented by the sample of ten attributes here employed (correlations ranged from .23 to .43).

2. Relatively clear personality attributes and complexes are equally well estimated from certain Rorschach scores and patterns, while attributes more specifically related to clinical psychology per se, were not successfully estimated by this approach (correlations ranged from low negative to positive .52).

3. Some Rorschach examiners were adjudged "good" raters while others had to be regarded as "poor" ones, the difference seeming to lie in the differences in their backgrounds of professional training, experience, and interests.

4. While the correlations were too low to be regarded as representative of valid predictions, it is believed that this is due in large part to such errors in measurement as: (a) the relative inability of three of the judges to make statistically significant personality ratings from Rorschach data, (b) the limited range of ratings made, (c) different conceptions of the manner in which ratings should be distributed and, (d) the effect of inexperience with the rating scale upon the ratings made by the Rorschach examiners.

Suggestions are made for further investigations.

Ten figures, fourteen tables, a sample of the rating scale, and a sixty-seven item bibliography are included. Mic A49-162

AN EVALUATION OF RATINGS OF PERSONALITY TRAITS ON THE BASIS OF UNSTRUCTURED ASSESSMENT INTERVIEWS

Ernest C. Tupes, Thesis (Ph. D.)
University of Michigan, 1950

In the course of an intensive assessment program, 128 male first-year graduate students in clinical psychology were rated by trained professional persons on 31 personality variables and 11 "future performance" variables after being interviewed in two types of interview situations; the first, a one-hour Initial Interview situation with only credentials material available before the interview; and the second, a two-hour Intensive Interview situation with credentials material, objective test profiles, projective protocols, and autobiographical material available before the interview. The validity of ratings based on these two interview situations was determined by correlating these ratings with criterion ratings arrived at by a team of three psychologists who had intensively studied each subject for a period of one week.

It was found that:

1. Ratings made after both the Initial and Intensive Interview situations correlated with the criterion ratings on a better than chance basis for all variables.

2. Ratings made after the Intensive Interview situation were more valid than ratings made after the Initial Interview situation.

3. There was little difference in the contribution of the two types of interviews to the validity of ratings of personality traits, and the contribution of either was slight.

4. Significant differences were found in the validities of ratings by the different interviewers and in the validities with which the variables were rated after each interview situation.

5. There was a slight positive relationship between ability to rate after the Initial Interview situation and after the Intensive Interview situation.

It was concluded that the incremental validity of the interview as an instrument for the assessment of personality traits is slight, and that longer interviews have little, if any, more incremental validity than have shorter interviews; that there are individual differences, relatively independent of the length of interview and amount of written data available, in the ability to make ratings of personality traits; and that, at the present time, even skilled clinicians, having available a wide variety of objective test data, projective protocols, credentials material, autobiographical data, plus a face-to-face interview, do not appear to be able to make personality assessments, in the form of ratings of personality traits, which have validity as high as is needed in individual case work. Mic A50-66

ABSTRACT

AN ANALYSIS OF SOME FACTORS AFFECTING RATINGS OF PERSONALITY
TRAITS BASED ON PROJECTIVE TECHNIQUES

Henry Samuels, Thesis (Ph. D.)
University of Michigan, 1950

During an intensive assessment program, 128 male first-year graduate students in clinical psychology were rated on an eight point scale by skilled professional observers on 42 variables, of which 15 were selected for intensive study. The validity of ratings based on projective techniques was determined by correlating them with criterion ratings which represented the pooled judgment of three staff members who had studied each student intensively, and in a wide variety of ways, for a period of a week.

It was found that:

1. Ratings based on data supplied by the use of projective techniques correlated with criterion ratings more closely than would be expected by chance.

2. Correlations between ratings based on the data of projective techniques and criterion ratings were, by usual standards, low.

3. No significant differences were found in the validity of ratings which were attributable to the differences in personality traits rated.

4. There was very little intercorrelation between ratings based on different projective techniques.

5. Integrations of projective materials by a clinician did not yield more accurate predictions of criterion measures than statistical integrations of ratings based on the separate projective techniques.

6. There were significant individual differences among clinicians in ability to make valid ratings on the basis of projective techniques.

7. The largest median validity coefficient for any projective clinician on any technique was .48.

It was concluded that ratings based on projective techniques used in the assessment of specified personality characteristics of normal, superior adults, measure very little in common; that statistical and clinical integrations of data based on independent analyses of projective technique records yield equally valid assessment of personality; that there are individual differences in ability to make valid ratings of personality traits from projective techniques which appear to be independent of the technique used; that the confidence with which clinicians rate personality traits, on the basis of projective techniques, does not appear to be related to the validity of ratings; that the assessment of a subject as possessing socially desirable personality traits to varying degrees is, in part, a function of the projective technique which is used in making the assessment; that the value of projective techniques as instruments for the assessment of specified personality traits of highly educated, normal adults is apparently limited by low validities.
Mic A50-467

SOME FACTORS INFLUENCING THE ACCURACY OF UNDERSTANDING PERSONALITY

Charles Alvin Dailey, III, Thesis (Ph. D.)
University of Michigan, 1951

The general problem investigated in this thesis was the determination of conditions favorable to developing an understanding of the particular individual. The specific problem was to determine the effects of making a premature judgment of an individual upon the judge's subsequent appraisal of that individual.

The principal hypotheses were: (1) premature judgment renders the judge less able to "profit" from experience with an individual so that the judge does not improve in understanding as he is given more data about the individual; and (2) premature judgment "freezes" the judge's appraisal so that he is relatively unable to alter his judgments as he gains further information about the individual.

The following experimental designs were employed to test these hypotheses. The judges used were 41 members of classes in introductory psychology (hypothesis 1) and 91 members of classes in experimental psychology.

To test the first hypothesis, judges were allowed to read a small portion of an individual's autobiography and then required to fill out a personality inventory in the manner in which they considered the individual would respond. Filling out the inventory at this point was defined as the premature judgment.

Then they were allowed to resume reading the autobiography; when they completed a brief additional section, they were again required to fill out the inventory for the individual. The accuracy of the predictions was measured by comparing the predictions of each judge with what the individual had in fact responded to the questionnaire. The mean accuracy score (mean number of correct predictions) was compared with that of a control group which had omitted the premature judgment, substituting a pause for it, but which had read exactly the same information as had the experimental group. According to the hypothesis above (1), the control group should have earned a higher accuracy score than the experimental group.

To test the second hypothesis, judges were required to make predictions of how an individual would respond to a questionnaire at two points: (a) before they had read any of his autobiography, so that they were merely guessing; and (b) after they had read a small amount of his autobiography. (a) corresponds to the "premature judgment" described in the first experiment. The number of predictions which were identical at (a) and (b) was calculated for each judge and compared with the number of predictions which were identical at (a) and concerning some previous individual for whom the judge had previously filled out the inventory. The latter constitutes a control for "stereotypy" of the judge's predictions.

The null form of each hypothesis was rejected on the basis of the experiments described. The differences between groups in each case were in the direction theoretically expected.

The additional hypothesis was tested that, if the effect of premature judgment on understanding is linked to the freezing effect of premature decisions, there should be an inverse correlation within the experimental group used in hypothesis 1 between the judge's ability to predict the individual's inventory responses and his tendency to repeat premature judgments when making his final judgments. This correlation was found to be -.54; it differs significantly from zero.

The conclusions drawn are that premature judgment operates to "freeze" the judges' opinions of the individual at the point of premature judgment so that his ability to profit from additional data about the individual is reduced. Mic A51-138

PERSONAL INFLUENCE AND OPINION CHANGE IN CONFERENCES

Harry Levin, Thesis (Ph. D.)
University of Michigan, 1951

In a study of personal influence and opinion change in conferences, thirty four member conferences were observed. Twenty-four graduate students in clinical psychology made up these groups and were so rotated that each individual had an opportunity to work with every other at least once. The task of these groups was to arrive at group decisions on forty-two ratings concerning the prediction of success in clinical psychology of people now receiving training in graduate school. The decisions were based on test and autobiographical material available for each trainee. Each participant decided on his own ratings before the conference.

Opinion change was calculated as the difference between a participant's own rating and the group decision on that item. The amount that the other three participants changed in the direction of a participant's own rating represented his influence. In addition, the attitudes of the participants toward each other along the dimensions of liking, prestige, and value in reaching the group decision were measured by questionnaires. Also measured were the amount that each participant verbally participated and the objective quality of their own decisions. The relations between a participant's opinion change, influence, and satisfaction with the group's decisions were explored.

I. Results

   1. Participants showed no consistency in their influence and change score from item to item within a case, from case to case within a meeting, or from meeting to meeting within the program. Therefore, in these groups, influence and change are reflections of factors which are specific to each item-decision and not of factors characterizing the participants as persons.

   2. The most frequent decision making process was for the four participants to move to the mean of their own ratings.

   3. The more that a participant had to change his own rating in reaching the group decision, the less satisfied he was with that decision.

   4. The participants found those groups attractive in which the members liked, valued, and considered each other prestigeful. However, members of the attractive groups were neither more satisfied with the decisions, had no higher quality decisions, nor evidenced more sincere change of opinion than the members of the less attractive groups.

II. Conclusions

   In the groups studied, influence and opinion change in reaching a common decision are not consistent characteristics of the individual participants but are a function of the disparity in each decision between a person's initial opinion and the average opinion of the others.

   Groups which arrive at decisions in the manner of these groups are characterized as "individualistic," meaning that the participants have an attitude of low involvement with the group task and are principally concerned with their own opinions. Mic A51-155

THE RELATIONSHIP OF VARIOUS TYPES OF MOVEMENT RESPONSES
IN THE RORSCHACH TEST TO PERSONALITY TRAIT RATINGS

Robert Poindexter Barrell, Thesis (Ph. D.)
University of Michigan, 1951

This study was an experimental test of a number of current principles of interpretation of the movement responses on the Rorschach test, as reported in the literature.

The following hypotheses were investigated:

1. the number of human movement responses is significantly related to various types of intellectual functioning;

2. the various categories into which the human movement responses may be subdivided are differentially related to various categories of intellectual functioning;

3. some categories of human movement responses show significant relationships to different categories of emotional behavior;

4. the number of animal movement responses, and particularly the ratio of human to animal movement, are significantly related to various categories of emotional behavior;

5. the number of inanimate motion responses is significantly related to some personality variables.

The subjects were 121 men who had been selected for training in clinical psychology and who were studied intensively at Ann Arbor, Michigan, during the summer of 1947 in conjunction with the Veterans Administration Assessment Program for Clinical Psychologists. The Staff's pooled ratings on various intellectual and emotional traits were utilized as criterion measures. The basic hypotheses were restated in terms of traits used to test them, and the hypotheses were then tested by chi-square and correlational techniques.

Variables were eliminated which did not yield satisfactory inter-scorer reliability, except in special instances. Because of the possibility that the significant relationships of the movement variables and the criterion traits might be a function of the total number of responses, partial correlations, with total number of responses held constant, were computed. Similarly, for the subcategories of human movement, partial correlations, with number of human movements held constant, were calculated.

The following findings emerged: (1) the number of human movement responses is significantly correlated with the criteria of intellectual functioning, even when the number of responses is partialed out; (2) while the subcategories of human movement are differentially related to the intellectual variables, these relationships are not independent of the number of human movement responses; (3) the subcategories of human movement responses are not differentially related to the emotional criteria; (4) the number of animal movement responses and the ratio of human to animal movement in general yielded chance correlations with the criterion variables; (5) the number of inanimate movement responses is not related significantly to any of the criterion variables purportedly measuring "inner tension." Inter-scorer reliability on this last Rorschach variable was very low.

Our findings indicate that the clinician is justified in utilizing the number of human movement responses as a partial indicator of intellectual functioning and imagination. However, since our subcategories of human movement are not independently related either to the intellectual or emotional variables, the use of these subcategories does not appear to be justified. Neither do our data substantiate the widespread use of animal movement responses as an indicator of immaturity. The last two conclusions must be treated with caution in view of the highly selected population employed in our study, but at least justify a skeptical attitude towards these Rorschach variables pending further investigation of their possible validity. Mic A51-119

THE MEASUREMENT OF SUBJECTS' ORIENTATIONS TOWARD A SENTENCE COMPLETION TEST

Haskell R. Coplin, Thesis (Ph. D.)
University of Michigan, 1952

This study deals with the degree to which subjects modify their responses to a projective test in order to present themselves in a more favorable light, and the relationship of such behavior to aspects of personality. The study involved the development of eleven measures of various verbal orientations used by individuals in completing semi-structured sentence leads and a study of the relationships of scores on these measures to personality ratings, self-ratings, and objective test scores. Semi-objectively scored measures were developed for evasive and self-enhancing sets as well as for sets to be perceived as objective, altruistic, positive or negative toward others, as wanting to achieve, desiring independence, and as being affiliative. Estimates of test and scoring reliability were computed for all measures and found to be of acceptable magnitude. A factor analysis of the intercorrelations of subtests yielded three factors indicating general sets which were identified as "Fairmindedness," "Frankness," and "Status Drive."

The population used in this study consisted of 111 male college graduates who were subjects of intensive pre-training assessment by the VA sponsored Research Project on the Selection of Clinical Psychologists. Sentence Completion records of two matched halves of this population were scored independently by two judges for the response set variables and correlations computed for the two groups between response set scores and criterion measures. A test of the validities of ratings based on Sentence Completion subtest scores alone and in combination with the test protocol was made.

The findings are summarized as follows:

1. Of the 1320 correlates resulting from the correlation of the 11 subtest scores with 60 criterion measures for the two groups, 267 or approximately 20% were significant at the 10% level. There are 20 pairs of correlations which were significant at the 10% level in both samples and hence significant at the 1% level.

2. In spite of acceptable interscorer reliability, the pattern of relationships of some variables to criterion measures differed for the two groups scored by the different judges.

3. Ratings of half the subjects on 42 personality rating scale variables using only the Sentence Completion Subtest profile scores as the basis for the ratings, in general, showed lower validities than ratings based on the Sentence Completion subtest profile plus the content of the Sentence Completion tests.

It was concluded that the verbal behavior of an individual in a relatively unstructured test situation may be classified into a number of expressive modes which can be reliably measured. These modes are significantly related to a number of personality attributes. A profile of scores of subtests measuring these verbal orientations provides a basis for valid ratings of some personality attributes. However, a combination of these scores and the content of the Sentence Completion record permits more valid personality ratings for a larger number of variables.

Interpretation of responses to some verbal projective techniques may be influenced by the set of the interpreter even when the scoring is semi-objective. Microfilm order number not yet assigned.

A STUDY OF THE VALIDITY OF INDIVIDUAL PERSONALITY PROFILES BASED ON PROJECTIVE AND RELATED TECHNIQUES

Edward Vartan Malcom, Thesis (Ph. D.)
University of Michigan, 1952

This is a study of the validity of the personality profiles of individuals as rated solely on the basis of specific techniques of personality evaluation, including four projective tests (Rorschach) Thematic Apperception Test, Sentence Completion Test and Bender-Gestalt), a battery of situation tests and a one-hour interview plus review of credentials.

The data were collected in 1947 in a week-long assessment program of first year graduate students in clinical psychology. Subjects were evaluated by a staff of professional psychologists using an extensive array of techniques and proeedures. Personality evaluations based on specific techniques and on combinations of techniques were recorded for each subject as ratings on 31 selected personality variables. Finally the staff, using all available information about each subject, arrived at a set of "Final Pooled Ratings" on these 31 variables. Although admittedly fallible, these Final Pooled ratings are regarded as the best available criteria for evaluating the validity of personality evaluations based on specific techniques.

Previous studies have evaluated the validity of the above techniques for specific traits, i.e., the accuracy with which individual subjects were ordered on each variable. By contrast, this study is concerned with the validity with which the total personality of individual subjects was evaluated by these same techniques, i.e., the congruence of the profile of ratings based on a single technique and the profile of Final Pooled ratings. The technique employed was the Du Mas coefficient of profile similarity (r_{ps}) which was shown to yield indices comparable to those resulting from the use of more laborious statistical procedures.

Coefficients of profile similarity were computed for 61 subjects for all possible pairings of the seven profiles.

Findings

1. Using the profile based on Final Pooled ratings as a criterion the profiles of individuals based on each of the six techniques studied show an extreme range of validities; for each of the four projective techniques there were more negative validities than statistically significant positive ones.

2. The validity with which individuals are evaluated on the basis of specific techniques was not associated with the raters employing the techniques, nor in the case of the Rorschach, with any of the scoring categories.

3. The median validity of profiles based on each of the specific techniques is positive but low. For the four projective techniques the medians were: Rorschach .14, TAT .13, S-C .17, B-G .10, Somewhat higher median validities of .29 were found for profiles based on both Situation Test and the Credential-Interview procedure. Profiles based on the writer's "blind ratings" of the Rorschach protocol yielded a median validity of .13.

4. Individual profiles based on any one of the six specific techniques show but little agreement with those based on the other five techniques; the range of the 15 median inter-technique coefficients is .00 to .14 and the median of these medians is .07. For most subjects the 15 inter-technique profile comparisons tend to be low. For none of the 61 subjects were all 15 coefficients positive.

5. On the basis of all techniques, subjects were generally rated high on some variables, and low on others. Coefficients of profile similarity between profiles of mean ratings based on the four projective techniques range from .48 to .77. Consequently profiles based on raw ratings show spuriously high coefficients of similarity. It is concluded that such communality of stereotype leads to apparent validities of these techniques greater than the measured validities found in this and other rigorous validational studies. Microfilm order number not yet assigned.

BIBLIOGRAPHY

*Indicates that thesis abstract may be found in Appendix IV.

Adams, H. F.   The good judge of personality.   J. abnorm. soc. Psychol., 1927, 22, 172-181.

*Barrell, R.   The relationship of various types of movement responses in the Rorschach Test to personality trait ratings.   Unpublished doctoral thesis, Univ. of Michigan, 1950.

Bellows, R. M.   Procedures for evaluating vocational criteria.   J. appl. Psychol., 1941, 25, 499-513.

Bender, I. E. and Hastorf, A. H.   The perception of persons: forecasting another person's responses on three personality scales.   J. abnorm. soc. Psych., 1950, 45, 556-561.

Brogden, H. E. and Taylor, E. K.   The theory and classification of criterion bias.   Educ. and psychol. meas.   1950, 10, 159-186.

Bronfenbrenner, U. and Newcomb, T. M.   Improvisations--An application of psychodrama in personality diagnosis.   Sociatry, 1948, 4, 367-382.

Carr, A.   Evaluation of nine psychotherapeutic cases by the Rorschach.   J. consult. Psychol., 1947, 13, 196-205.

Cattell, R. B.   Confirmation and clarification of primary personality factors.   Psychometrika, 1947, 12, 197-220.

*Coplin, H.   The measurement of subjects' orientation toward a Sentence Completion Test.   Unpublished doctoral thesis, Univ. of Michigan, 1952.

Covner, B. J.   Studies in phonographic recording of verbal material: III the completeness and accuracy of counseling interview reports.   J. gen. Psychol., 1944, 30, 181-203.

Cronbach, L. J.   A validation design for qualitative studies of personality.   J. consult. Psychol., 1948, 12, 365-374.

*Dailey, C. A.   Some factors influencing the accuracy of understanding personality.   Unpublished doctoral thesis, Univ. of Michigan, 1950.

DuMas, F. M.   The coefficient of profile similarity.   J. clin. Psychol., 1949, 5, 123-131.

Dymond, R.   Personality and empathy.   J. consult. Psychol., 1950, 14, 343-350.

Estes, S. G.   Judging personality from expressive behavior.   J. abnorm. soc. Psychol., 1938, 33, 217-236.

Fiedler, F. E.   The concept of an ideal therapeutic relationship.   J. consult. Psychol., 1950, 14, 239-245.

Fiedler, F. E.   Factor analysis of psychoanalytic, non-directive and adlerian therapeutic relationships.   J. consult. Psychol., 1951 (a), 15, 32-38.

304

Fiedler, F. E. A method for quantification of certain counter-transference attitudes. J. clin. Psychol. , 1951 (b), 12, 101-107.

*Fiske, D. W. Consistency of the factorial structures in personality ratings from different sources. J. abnorm. soc. Psychol. , 1947, 44, 329-344.

Flanagan, J. C. Critical requirements for research personnel: a study of observed behaviors of personnel in research laboratories. Pittsburgh: American Institute for Research, 1949.

Gage, N. L. Explicit forecasting of strangers' interests from expressive behavior. Amer. Psychologist, 1951, 6, 310.

Gulliksen, H. Intrinsic validity. Amer. Psychologist, 1950, 5, 511-517.

Hart, H. et al. Verifiability ratings of articles in social science. Amer. J. Sociol. , 1947, 53, 119-124.

Hogan, R. M. Productivity in research and development. Science, 1950, 112, 613-616.

Horst, P. (Editor) The prediction of personal adjustment. Social Science Research Council. , Bull. No. 48, 1941.

Jenkins, J. G. Validity for what? J. consult. Psychol. , 1946, 10, 93-98.

Jenkins, J. G. et al. The combat criterion in naval aviation. Washington, D.C. : Division of Aviation Medicine, Bureau of Medicine and Surgery, U. S. Navy; NRC Committee on Aviation Psychology, Report No. 6, 1950.

Johnson, A. P. , Peterson, S. and Stalnaker, J. M. Panel I: Validation of professional aptitude batteries. In: Invitational conference on testing problems: Princeton: Educational Testing Service, 1951.

Kandel, I. L. Professional aptitude tests in medicine, law, and engineering. New York: Teachers College, Bureau of Publications, 1940.

Kelly, E. L. and Fiske, D. W. The prediction of success in the VA training program in clinical psychology. Amer. Psychologist, 1950, 5, 395-406.

Kendall, M. G. Rank correlation methods. London: Charles Griffin and Co. Ltd. , 1948.

Kriedt, P. H. Vocational interests of psychologists. J. appl. Psychol. , 1949, 33, 482-488.

Lepley, W. M. (Editor) Psychological research in the theatres of war. AAF Aviation Psychology Program Research Report, No. 17, Washington, D. C. : U. S. Gov't Printing Office, 1947.

*Levin, H. Personal influence and opinion change in conferences . Unpublished doctoral thesis, Univ. of Michigan, 1952.

Luft, J. Some relationships between clinical specialization and the understanding and prediction of an individual's behavior. Unpublished doctoral thesis, Univ. of California (Los Angeles), 1949.

Luft, J. Implicit hypotheses and clinical predictions. J. abnorm. soc. Psychol. , 1950, 45, 756-759.

*Malcom, E. V. A study of the validity of individual personality profiles based on projective and interview techniques. Unpublished doctoral thesis, Univ. of Michigan, 1952.

Meltzer, B. N. The productivity of social scientists. Amer. J. Sociol. , 1949, 55, 25-29.

*Morris, W. S. The prediction of personality attributes by means of the Rorschach method. Unpublished doctoral thesis, Univ. of Michigan, 1949.

Muench, G. A. An evaluation of non-directive psychotherapy by means of the Rorschach and other indices. Appl. psychol. Monog. , 1947, 13.

Murray, H. A. et al. Explorations in personality. New York: Oxford Univ. Press, 1938.

OSS Assessment Staff. The assessment of men. New York: Rinehart, 1948.

Pemberton, C. L. A study of the speed and flexibility of closure factors. Unpublished doctoral thesis, Univ. of Chicago, 1951.

Porter, E. H. , Jr. An introduction to therapeutic counseling. Boston: Houghton Mifflin, 1950.

Quinn, E. A comparative investigation of therapists' vocal expressions in psychotherapy. Unpublished doctoral thesis, Univ. of Chicago, 1950.

Reader, N. An evaluation of some aspects of non-directive therapy by means of the Rorschach Test. Unpublished doctoral thesis, Univ. of Chicago, 1948.

*Samuels, H. An analysis of some factors affecting ratings of personality traits based on projective techniques. Unpublished doctoral thesis, Univ. of Michigan, 1950. Also in Psychol. Monog. In press.

Sarbin, T. R. and Taft, R. Psychological inference. To be published.

Siegal, S. M. Prediction of psychotherapeutic improvement in psychoneurotics by means of the Rorschach Test. Unpublished doctoral thesis, Univ. of Chicago, 1951.

*Soskin, W. F. A study of personality ratings based on brief observation of behavior in standard situations. Unpublished doctoral thesis, Univ. of Michigan, 1948.

Stephenson, W. A statistical approach to typology; the study of trait universes. J. clin. Psychol. , 1950, 6, 26-38.

Strong, E. K. Jr. Permanence of interest scores over 22 years. J. appl. Psychol. , 1951, 35, 89-91.

Stuit, D. B., Dickson, G. S. , Jordan, T. F. , and Schloerb, L. Predicting success in professional schools. Washington, D. C.: Amer. Council on Education, 1949.

Taft, R. Some correlates of the ability to make accurate social judgments. Unpublished doctoral thesis, University of California (Berkeley), 1950.

306

Thorndike, R. L. Personnel selection. New York: Wiley, 1949.

*Tupes, E. C. An evaluation of personality-trait ratings obtained by unstructured assessment interviews. Psychol. Monog., 1950, 64, No. 317.

Training in clinical psychology. (Edited by Raimy, V.C.) New York: Prentice-Hall, Inc. 1950.

Vaughn, C. L. The nominating technique. In New methods in applied psychology (G. E. Kelly, Ed.) College Park, Md.: Univ. of Maryland, 1947.

Wolf, R. and Murray, H. A. Judgments of personality. Chapter IV in Murray, H. A. et al. Explorations in personality. New York: Oxford Univ. Press, 1947.

INDEX OF NAMES

Adams, H. F. , 89.
Bellows, R. M. , 11, 71.
Bender, I. E. , 98.
Blain, D. , vii.
Blum, G. S. , vii.
Bouthilet, Lorraine, vii.
Brogden, H. E. , 71.
Bronfenbrenner, U. , 44.
Butler, J. , vii.
Carlson, Rae, 192.
Carr, A. , 100.
Cattell, R. B. , 41, 60.
Covner, B. J. , 104.
Cronbach, L. J. , vii, 124.
DuMas, F. M. , 138.
Dymond, R. , 89.
Estes, S. G. , 89.
Fiedler, F. E. , vii, 102, 103, 106, 107, 111.
Fiske, D. W. , 60, 166, 174.
Flanagan, J. C. , 114.
Fletcher, F. , 11.
Freysinger, J. , vii.
Gage, N. L. , 92.
Gough, H. , 39.
Guilford, J. P. , 116.
Gulliksen, H. , 71.
Hart, H. , 114.
Hastorf, A. H. , 98.
Hawley, P. R. , vii.
Hildreth, H. M. , vii.
Hogan, R. M. , 114.
Holt, R. , vii.
Horst, P. , 202.
Hunt, H. , vii.
Hunt, W. A. , 11.
Jenkins, J. G. , 71.

Johnson, A. P. , 72.
Johnson, T. , 116.
Kandel, I. L. , 72.
Kelly, E. L. , 166, 174.
Kendall, M. G. , 139.
Lepley, W. M. , 72.
Luft, J. , 95, 98.
Luszki, W. , 69.
Mellinger; J. , 54.
Meltzer, B. N. , 114, 118.
Miller, D. , vii.
Miller, J. G. , vii.
Muench, G. A. , 100.
Murray, H. A. , 89, 93.
Newcomb, T. L. , 44.
Pemberton, Carol, 145.
Quinn, R. D. , 182.
Reader, N. , 100.
Richards, T. , 11.
Satter, G. , vii.
Schutz, W. , 116.
Shakow, D. , vii.
Siegel, S. M. , 100, 104.
Soskin, W. F. , 45, 65, 67, 93.
Stephenson, W. , 94.
Strong, E. K. , 130.
Stuit, D. B. , 11, 72.
Taft, R. , 89.
Taylor, E. K. , 71.
Thorndike, R. L. , 72, 73.
Thurstone, L. L. , 54.
Tolman, Ruth, vii.
Tupes, E. C. , 65.
Vandenberg, S. G. , 200.
Vaughn, C. L. , 71.
Wolf, R. , 89.

See also list of Contributors to Project on pp. iii and iv.

308

INDEX OF TOPICS

Underlined page references indicate a relevant table.

ABEPP, Consultants for Content Examination 11; cooperation with 9.

Ability to understand patient, 102, 103.

Academic performance, 161, 162, 163, 165, 167, 168, 169, 173, 176, 179, 189, 231.

Allport-Vernon Study of Values, 14, 15, 38, 42, 50, 70, 93, 154, 156, 191; as best predictor measure 157, 158, 159, 181.

Applications, multiple of students 10.

Assessment, definition of 6; Ann Arbor 40 ff.; Asilomar 6; FAC 6, 39; Farmingdale 6; pilot assessment 5; Wellesley 9, 49 ff., 172 ff.; assessment report 216.

Assessment staffs, iii, 49; differences between members of 66, 129.

Attitudes of trainees about their training, 26, 27.

Autobiographies, 1, 43, 50, 169, 170; outline for 240.

Bender-Gestalt Test, 42, 47, 169, 171, 172, 181, 183,

Best predictor measures, 157, 158, 179 ff.; Comparison of - for 1948 and 1947 groups 159.

Biographical Inventory, 43, 50, 169, 170, 220.

Case Study in Content Examination, 162.

Character sketches by teammates, 46, 48.

Chicago Tests of Primary Mental Abilities, 14, 15, 38, 42, 70, 145, 146; as best predictor measure 157, 158, 159, 183, 187; separate parts of PMA 145 ff.

Clinical competence, 74, 81, 160, 161, 162, 168, 169, 174, 176, 186, 187, 221, 228.

Coefficient of profile similarity, 138.

Consistency of personality over 3 years, 130 ff., 132, 133, 140; consistency of ratings 177.

Contamination, definition of 47; influence of - on validity of university predictions 143.

Content Examination, 28, 77 ff., 145 ff.; distribution of scores by universities 31; best predictors of 180.

Cooperative General Culture Test, 38, 43, 70.

Cost of assessment, 8, 48, 49.

CPA, Strong Key 184; scores of physicians, psychiatrists and psychologists 34, 35, 151, 153.

Credentials, 42, 47, 50, 167, 180, 181, 183, 187.

Criteria, composite 82; conventional 76; definition of 71; first-order vs. second-order 72; of general competence 86; of specific skills 88 ff.; selection of 73.

Criterion measures, definition of 71; rationale for 4; rejected criterion measures 75, 285; specific vs. general 74; why collected last 9; criterion rating scale 82; ratings 11, 79 ff., 244.

Criterion problem, 72, 127 ff.

"Cultural" chance, 92.

David Test, 93 ff.

Descriptive ratings: Scale A and B, 135, 230; correlations with criteria 175, 176, 188, 189.

Diagnostic competence, 161 ff.; criterion measures of 88 ff., 221; definition of 88.

Diagnostic prediction test, 92, 95, 107; correlation with other criteria 98.

Difference between 1947 and 1948 groups, 22, 23, 24, 95, 118, 119, 144, 159; on facade 173, 174.

Differences between Universities, 28; in clinical experience provided 30; influence of - on validities 128; differences between universities making predictor ratings and those who did not 141; in formal instruction 22 ff.

Draw-a-Person test, 50, 93.

Expert's opinion as criterion, 91, 102, 106.

Facade (faking good), 21, 52; Facade Key for GM 39, 52; facade in Diagnostic prediction test 99 ff.; difference between 1947 and 1948 assessees on facade 173.

Factor analysis of 1947 Final Pooled ratings, 54 ff.; of composite criterion ratings 84 ff.

Females assessed, 20.

Field experience of trainees, 23, 24, 30, 32, 33.

Frames of reference, 11, 26, 67, 79, 80, 175.

Graduate Record Examination, 39.

Graphology, 200.

Guilford-Martin Battery of Personality Inventories, 14, 16, 20, 38, 42, 50, 93, 94; as best predictor measure 157, 158, 159, 186, 187; GM Facade Key 39; correlation with ratings 69, 70; correlation with criteria 147.

Ideographic description, 3.

Implications of findings for the selection of students, 198.

Increment in prediction, after interview 63, 64; after studying objective test scores 167; based on less material 166; from additional procedures 3.

Integrity of personal and professional behavior, measure of 122, 161, 162 ff., 176, 185 ff.; criterion scale 225.

Interest patterns of physicians, psychologists, psychiatrists, 30, 34, 35.

Interview, 1, 3; increase in correlations after interview 63; initial interview 42, 46, 47, 142, 167, 168, 169; intensive interview 43, 46, 47, 48, 142, 167, 168, 169, 174.

Intuition, 89 ff., 202 ff.

Kriedt Strong Keys, see Strong.

Kuder Preference Record, 14, 38, 43, 70, 92, 154, 155; as best predictor measure 157, 158, 159, 181, 187,

Liking ratings, 230; Intercorrelations 161, 162, 164, 165; rationale for including 41, 66, 67.

Matching, comparison of qualitative and quantitative 135 ff., 137.

Menninger Foundation project on selection of VA psychiatric residents, 30; experimental Rorschach and TAT manuals of 39.

Miller Analogies Test, 8, 14, 15, 21, 22, 28, 29, 38, 42, 50, 70, 128, 145, 146, 191; as best predictor measure 157, 158, 159, 180, 187.

MMPI, 14, 17, 20, 38, 42, 70, 148, 149; as best predictor measure 157, 158; Gough Keys 39; as best predictor measure 157, 158, 159, 181, 183, 187.

Monroe Inspection technique, 39.

Motivation, 95.

Non-clinical graduate students, comparison with clinical students, 14, 15, 19, 20, 21.

Objective Tests, best predictions by the 157, 158; objective tests used 37, 38, 39, 47, 167; validities of 144 ff.

OSS Assessment, 3, 39, 71.

Overall Clinical Competence, see Clinical competence.

Pass-Fail criterion, prediction of dichotomous criterion 190.

Phenotypic variables, 138.

Pooling Conference Ann Arbor Assessment, preliminary 47; "uncontaminated" 48; Wellesley assessment 50; clinical pooling vs. arithmetical pooling 177 ff.

Postdiction, 92.

Pre-conference rater, 47, 68, 167, 168, 169, 174; definition of 47.

Prediction, based on limited material 166 ff.; by descriptive ratings 175, 176; by university departments 36, 37, 54, 55; of dichotomous criteria 190; of general competence 186; of diagnostic competence 89; of patient's behavior 93, 107, 112; of specific criteria 179 ff.

Prediction problem, 3, 72, 123 ff., 201 ff.; graphic representation of 124; psychometric analysis 127 ff.

Prediction measures, choice of 36 ff.; clinical techniques used 39, 171 ff.; objective tests used 38.

Preference for Hiring, criterion scale 121, 160, 161, 163, 164, 186, 187, 229.

Preference of trainees for diagnostic instruments, 23, 242; for various professional activities 26, 27.

Production Manager Strong Key, 184; as best predictor 159, 187; pattern for physicians, psychiatrists and psychologists 34, 35, 151, 153.

Professional Inter-personal Relations, criterion scale 227; measure of 121, <u>161</u>, 162 ff. , 186, <u>187</u>.

Progress Notes, 253 ff. ; collection of 104; relationship with other measures 111, <u>112</u>, 182, <u>185</u>; reliability of PN scoring 105 ff. ; scoring of 103, 105, 110, 277 ff.

Projective Integrator, 167, <u>168</u>, <u>169</u>, 186; definition of 47.

Projective tests, 1; reassessment of 20 cases 12.

Psychotherapy, competence in 121, <u>161</u>, 163, 164, <u>176</u>; criterion scale 223, 224; effect of - on validities of ratings 135, <u>136</u>, 165, <u>166</u>; experience of trainees in 25, 242; instruction in 22, 242; personal - of trainees 26, 243.

Ratings, criterion, reasons for using 3, 79; correlations between 81 ff. , <u>83</u>.

Rating scales, assessment 4, 206 ff. ; criterion 244; development of 40, 80 ff. ; correlation with objective test scores 69, <u>70</u>.

Reassessment, by projective methods in 1949 171, <u>172</u>; of 1947 cases in 1948 11, 12, 51; of 1947 cases in 1949 53, 173, <u>174</u>, 175.

Rejected applicants assessed, 51, <u>52</u>.

Rejected criterion measures, 283.

Reliability: agreement between 1947 and 1949 assessment 62, 63; intra-judge agreement on ratings based on different projective techniques 63; inter-judge agreement on assessment ratings 61, 129; diagnostic competence ratings 129 ff. ; diagnostic predictions test <u>96</u> ff, <u>112</u>; measures of therapeutic competence <u>112</u>; 1947 Final Pooled ratings <u>132</u>; of 1947 teammate ratings <u>132</u>; 1949 reassessment ratings 62; 1951 criterion ratings <u>83</u>, <u>112</u>, 129; Progress Notes scoring 105, 106, <u>112</u>; projective test ratings 63; of ratings based on recordings of therapy 109 ff. , <u>112</u>; research ratings 129 ff. ; university predictions 55; Wellesley ratings 62.

Reputation as criterion of competence, 91.

Research competence, prediction of <u>161</u>, 162, 163, 181; criterion scale 222; measurement of 114 ff

Research activity, 25, 161, 181, 244, 246; criteria 118; measures 119.

Rorschach, 42, 47, 50, 92, 95, <u>169</u>, 171, <u>172</u>; Menninger scoring manual 39; Monroe Inspection Technique 39; Rorschach vs. dichotomous criterion <u>191</u>.

SAS, definition of 108; relationship with other measures 110, <u>112</u>, 113.

Selection conditions, 21, 49, 52, 65, 173, 175.

Self-descriptions of David, 93; similarity of - by therapist and patient 107 ff. , <u>108</u>.

Self ratings 46, <u>169</u>, 172, 180; correlation with Final Pooled 65.

Sentence Completion Test, 42, 47, 50, 93, 169, 171, <u>172</u>, 181, <u>187</u>, 217.

Sequence of tests in 1948, 40 ff. ; of the research project 5.

Situation tests, 1, 43 ff. , 65; as best predictor 183; Block Game 45; Discussion group 43; expressive movements 45; improvisations 44; party 46; ratings based on 48, <u>68</u>, <u>169</u>, 170, 172;

Sociometric questionnaire, 46, 48, 214; scoring of 49.

Staff schedule, 46 ff.

Strong Vocational Interest profile, 8, 14, <u>18</u>, <u>19</u>, 21, <u>38</u>, <u>70</u>, <u>150</u> ff. , <u>187</u>; as best predictor measure 157, <u>158</u>, <u>159</u>; consistency over time 130; Kriedt Keys 37, <u>38</u>, 151, <u>153</u>, 180; Strong Author Journalist Key 180; Strong Lawyer Key 183; Strong Psychologist Key <u>22</u>, <u>38</u>, 144, 180; Thrown M F scores 37, <u>38</u>, 39, <u>153</u>, 154; VA Clinical Psychologist Key 21, <u>22</u>, 37, <u>38</u>, 144, <u>150</u>, 151, <u>191</u> 200.

Supervisory competence 121, 160, <u>161</u>, 163, 164, 186, <u>187</u>, 226.

TAS 110, <u>112</u>, 113; definition of 108.

TAT, 43, 47, 93, <u>169</u>, 171, <u>172</u>, 183; experimental Menninger scoring manual 39.

Tau, 139.

Teammate ratings, 46, 69, <u>169</u>, 172, 181, <u>187</u>; correlations with colleague ratings 131, <u>132-3</u>; with Final Pooled 65.

Test of ability to predict patient's self-descriptions, 90 ff.

Therapeutic competence, intercorrelations of measures 111, <u>112</u>; intercorrelations with predictor measures <u>161</u>, 162, <u>168</u>, <u>169</u>, 171, 181, 188, <u>189</u>; measurement of 99 ff. ; measures used 110; prediction of patient's responses as measure 98, 111; rationale for indirect measurement 101 ff. requirements for measure 100 ff.

Therapy, conceptions of 164; recordings 109 ff. ; ideal relationship 102.

Training Experience Inventory, 12, 21, 100, 118, 262.

University departments, 2, 7 ff. , 13, 14; as criterion raters 81; autonomy of 1, 20; battery of
    tests administered by 14; differences between 28, 29, 31, 32, 33; predictions by 36, 37, 54, 55,
    141, 142.

Validities of assessment predictions, 184 ff. ; of clinical techniques,171 ff. ; of objective tests 144;
    of university predictions 36, 54.

VA Strong Key, see Strong.

Veterans Administration, vii, 1.